P9-APS-016

Contents

ECONOMIC REFORM AND POLITICAL CHANGE IN EASTERN EUROPE

Economic Reform and Political Change in Eastern Europe

A Comparison of the Czechoslovak and Hungarian Experiences

Judy Batt

St. Martin's Press New York

Scholarly & Reference Division,
St. Martin's Press, Inc., 175 Fifth Avenue, New York, NY 10010

First published in the United States of America in 1988

Printed in Hong Kong

ISBN 0–312–01196–2

Library of Congress Cataloging in Publication Data
Batt, Judy.
Economic reform and political change in Eastern Europe: a comparison of the Czechoslovak and Hungarian experiences / Judy Batt.
p. cm.
Bibliography: p.
Includes index.
ISBN 0–312–01196–2 : $30.00 (est.)
1. Czechoslovakia—Economic policy—1945– 2. Czechoslovakia––Economic conditions—1945– 3. Czechoslovakia—Politics and government—1945– 4. Hungary—Economic policy—1945– 5. Hungary––Economic conditions—1945– 6. Hungary—Politics and government—1945– I. University of Birmingham. Centre for Russian and East European Studies. II. Title.
HC270.28.B37 1987
338.9437—dc 19 87–24065
CIP

Acknowledgements

I would like to thank in particular Professors Ron Amann and Phil Hanson of the Centre for Russian and East European Studies, University of Birmingham, for many years of illuminating, challenging and painstaking supervision of my PhD thesis, on which this book is based, and for their encouragement of my work in general. My indebtedness to them both extends back also to my years as an undergraduate in CREES. They have thus certainly had the most profound influence on my intellectual development. Naturally, they cannot be held responsible for its shortcomings. I would also like to acknowledge the help and advice given by Professor Włodzimierz Brus of the University of Oxford and Dr John Hoffman of the University of Leicester, who read and commented in considerable detail on various chapters.

I received two scholarships from the British Council in 1978 and 1982 and one from the British Academy in 1985, which enabled me to study in Prague and Budapest. I also received financial assistance from the University of Leicester Research Board towards three short research visits to Budapest. I am very much indebted to Ildikó Melis and Zsolt Krokovay, who introduced me to Hungary and its delights.

Finally, I am especially grateful to Martin Cherry, who provided the reassurance and cheering company which saw me and my thesis through some difficult patches.

JUDY BATT

List of Abbreviations

AVH	*Államvedelmi Hatóság* (Hungarian Secret Police)
CC	Central Committee
CPB	Central Planning Board
CPS	Communist Party of Slovakia
CPCS	Czechoslovak Communist Party
CPSU	Communist Party of Soviet Union
GDR	German Democratic Republic
HSWP	Hungarian Socialist Workers' Party
HWP	Hungarian Workers' Party
NCTU	National Council of Trade Unions
NEM	New Economic Mechanism
RFER	Radio Free Europe Research
SDP	Social Democratic Party
STR	Scientific and Technological Revolution
VHJ	*výrobně hospodářská jednotka* (economic production unit)

'Forward!'
Jiři Jirásek, from *Literární Listy* (Prague), 20 June 1968.

Introduction

The central assumption upon which the theory of socialism is founded is that there exists a 'social interest', and the central aim of socialism is the realisation of the 'social interest' through the organisation of the economy. The idea of a 'social interest' or 'common good' is not unique to socialism of course. It appears in classical political philosophy, Christian theology, and also in the rational liberalism of the Enlightenment. The socialist concept of the 'social interest' derives most directly from the last-mentioned tradition of thought, taking over key elements of Enlightenment philosophy and recombining them into a distinctive new synthesis.[1] The 'social interest' in socialist theory involves both rationalism and egalitarianism. Socialism in practice is to realise 'true' freedom and democracy by abolishing the material inequalities between men which arise from the private ownership of the means of production, and to use the economic resources of society rationally to meet 'social need', not individually appropriated profit, through 'conscious, planned control' of the economy. A classical statement of the aims, formulated by Marx, puts it thus:

> The national centralisation of the means of production will become the natural base for a society which will consist of an association of free and equal producers acting consciously according to a general and rational plan.[2]

Socialists traditionally have seen the market as 'anarchic' and therefore irrational, productive of cyclical economic crises and wasteful of both human and material resources; and also as the source of class division, social inequality and exploitation. The 'freedom' proclaimed by the ideologists of liberal capitalism was argued to be fundamentally vitiated by its limitation to political rights alone. Socialists take up the argument that power has an economic dimension too, and they hold that men cannot be free where they are not equal in respect of their most basic conditions of existence. Private ownership of the means of production deprives non-owners of the possibility of free self-realisation, since for their productive activity – identified as the central characteristic of human existence – they are dependent on access to the means of production which are owned and controlled by others. Furthermore, the market is argued to be a source of human 'alienation'. Productive activity is guided not consciously and directly according to 'real social need', but abstractly and indirectly through the pursuit of profit, accruing to individual capitalists as the result of productive activity which is essentially a cooperative, social effort.

On this basis, by the time of the first practical attempt to create a socialist society, in Russia after the Revolution, there was no dispute among socialists that the superiority of socialism would find expression in the abolition of private ownership of the means of production and the direction of the economy through central planning, which definitely excluded use of the market. But even before the first experiment in the practical application of socialism had had time to provide convincing evidence, non-socialist theorists had identified crucial problems of principle with the socialist argument, which led them to predict that in practice the socialist 'Utopia' would be neither rational nor democratic. Subsequently, the experience of central planning in the Soviet Union and, after the Second World War, in Eastern Europe, appeared to confirm this pessimistic conclusion. Moreover, the alternative explanation of the shortcomings of socialism in the Soviet Union, which referred to the legacy of Russian economic backwardness and autocratic traditions as the main obstacles to the realisation of socialist goals, began to look less convincing with the passage of time. For how long after the socialist revolution could 'remnants of the past' continue to provide a convincing explanation of the shortcomings of the present? Furthermore, the application of the Soviet model to at least one European country with a developed economy and democratic political culture – Czechoslovakia – produced depressingly familiar results.

The death of Stalin in 1953 provided the first condition for a reexamination by East Europeans of the systemic origins of the problems of 'real socialism', but the main impetus came from the events of 1956, when popular revolts in Poland and Hungary revealed the enormous gap between the claims of socialism – both economic and political – and the reality as experienced by the people in whose name the regimes pretended to rule. Economic failure underlay the crises, but its implications in the context of 'socialism' spread rapidly and extensively into the political sphere. The legitimacy of the system itself was at stake. Economic reform thus entered the agenda as a political necessity in the broadest sense. It is at this point that the dilemma of socialism in Eastern Europe – the subject matter of this book – emerged. The relationship between economic failure and political crisis was to a large extent direct and clear-cut, and this was appreciated by the regimes which undertook reform of the economic system after 1956. But the relationship between economic *reform* and political *stability* was to emerge as far more problematic, both in theory and practice. The book approaches this problem in the following way.

Part I provides a background to the consideration of economic reform as a goal by reviewing the main elements of the theoretical debate surrounding the questions of the feasibility of socialism in economic terms, and the compatibility of a socialist economy with the political goals of freedom and democratic government. This rather abstract approach serves to highlight fundamental questions which any attempt to introduce economic reform in practice in Eastern Europe must confront: if a workable economic model can be devised, can it nevertheless satisfy the central ideological criterion of socialism, that of serving the 'social interest'? And (a rather less elevated concern) can it continue to sustain the 'leading role of the Party', the central political pivot of socialism in the context of the Soviet bloc?

Part II of the book presents detailed historical and political analyses of two countries – Czechoslovakia and Hungary – which both attempted economic reform of a broadly similar type in the late 1960s, but which experienced very different political results. Through broad comparisons of the process of economic reform at its various stages – from partial 'tinkerings' with the system to commitment to a coherent conceptual 'alternative model', thence to its practical implementation – a set of conclusions is reached about the political conditions, consequences, and necessary adaptations involved, which have some general relevance for other countries in the bloc, including the Soviet Union.

Although in neither of the cases studied was economic reform successfully realised, the conclusions drawn are not wholly pessimistic. On the one hand, the basic model of economic reform adopted was by no means unfeasible *per se*, in either economic or ideological–political terms, and indeed had important attractions. To that extent, we can expect that model, or some variant or extension of it, to be put forward again in response to still-unresolved economic problems, and to find influential supporters in Eastern Europe, and in the Soviet Union as well. At the same time, while the practical political obstacles to reform – chiefly diehard ideological and vested bureaucratic interests, popular apathy and disaffection – can be shown to be formidable, that is not the same as proving they are inherently insurmountable. The experience of Eastern Europe and the Soviet Union up to the present day embraces not only the past failures of economic reform, but the ever-present and intensifying pressures towards reform from the accelerating pace of technological change in the world outside and the rising expectations of the populations at home. The passage of time itself opens up new opportunities for change, as generational turnover brings new leaders, and profoundly affects the outlook, expectations, moods and dispositions to change in the Parties and societies at large. This is particularly true today, not only of the Soviet Union, where such changes are clearly under way with the accession to power of Mikhail Gorbachev, but also of those countries on which this study has focused – Czechoslovakia and Hungary – where leaders formed by experiences of wartime resistance, Stalinist rule, popular revolt, aborted reforms and Soviet armed intervention, are now due for retirement, and new political and social generations are entering the arena.

Part I

Planning, Markets and Political Systems

1 Economics

A THE ANTI-SOCIALIST CASE

It was Ludwig von Mises who, in 1920, threw down the gauntlet which began the 'Great Debate' among academic economists on the rationality of the socialist economy. He argued that under socialism, with the abolition of the market, there can be no objective indicator of value, which will be supplanted by the politically-based preferences of the State administration. While the State may be able to obtain knowledge of what commodities are required by society, and may thus draw up a coherent list of priorities of 'social need', it will be unable to direct the use of the means of production rationally to the given ends, since it will have no way of calculating their relative values. Prices in this sector would of necessity be arbitrary, and could give no information on relative scarcity. Thus there would be no possibility of calculating costs of production, and therefore no possibility of producing the commodities identified as needed in an efficient, economical way:

> In place of the economy of the 'anarchic' method of production, recourse will be had to the senseless output of an absurd apparatus. The wheels will turn, but will run to no effect.[1]

For von Mises, the market mechanism is inseparable from private property in the means of production, since the motive force of the market economy is the drive to maximise profit. The pursuit of private material gain is what 'induces entrepreneurs to appropriately limit their demand for factors of production to cost-minimising proportions'.[2] The search for profit thus acts towards the efficient allocation of resources in a competitive market economy; it is at the same time the basis for individual motivation. Von Mises sees the lack of personal responsibility, and of opportunity for individual initiative, as an inherent feature of socialism, which further reduces the possibility of rational economic activity, since there can be no direct relationship between individual effort and reward: 'While the well-being of any particular individual is dependent on the diligence of others, one's own welfare is independent of one's own diligence.'[3]

The argument was later further elaborated by F.A. Hayek, for whom the central flaw in the socialist proposals was the assumption of the possibility of an omniscient centre, capable of amassing the sheer quantity of information necessary to the 'objective' definition of an unambiguous 'social interest' in every detail:

> The economic problem of society is not merely a problem of how to allocate 'given' resources – if 'given' is taken to mean given to a single mind which deliberately solves the problem set by these 'data'. It is rather a problem of how to secure the best use of resources known to any of the members of society, for ends whose relative importance only these individuals know. Or, to put it briefly, it is a problem of the utilisation of knowledge not given to anyone in its totality.[4]

The knowledge required for rational economic activity is not only or even mainly scientific knowledge – if it were, then Hayek concedes that a 'body of suitably chosen experts may be in the best position to command all the best knowledge available'.[5] But the larger part of relevant knowledge is not of this type – it is unorganised, intimate local knowledge of the particularities of time and place, which, moreover, are in a state of constant change. The sheer quantity of information which planners would have to have amassed would be quite overwhelming, unless their statistics contained some degree of aggregation, 'abstracting from minor differences between things, by lumping together, as resources of one kind, items which differ as regards location, quality, and other particulars, in a way which may be very significant for the specific decision'.[6] It is thus inescapably a less efficient system of knowledge.

It is the price mechanism which, in the market economy, can deal with specific, local information and the state of constant change, 'by attaching to each scarce resource a numerical index which cannot be derived from any property possessed by that particular thing, but which reflects, or in which is condensed, its significance in view of the whole means–end structure'.[7] Hayek's point is that it is simply not necessary for rational economic activity that all or any of the participants know everything about the whole economy – it is only necessary that each possess sufficient information to enable him to carry out his own particular individual task. The spontaneous adjustments of the price system not only provide information in an intelligible form, but also integrate individuals' activities without the intermediation of a 'superior intelligence'.

The Polish economist Oskar Lange attempted to counter these arguments in his 'Competitive solution', by which he sought to show that a rational system of efficiency pricing could be constructed, without the operation of a free market, in the context of a socialised economy.[8] The model assumes free choice of occupation and consumer goods. A Central Planning Board (CPB) is responsible for setting the prices of goods and services, including the interest rate on capital. The point is to demonstrate how this price setting can be made 'rational', rather than 'arbitrary' or purely political, without the operation of a free market.

In practice, the CPB's initial set of prices would be based on the historical experience of relative values, taken over from the free prices of the previous market economy, and so they need not be widely off the mark. Managers of enterprises are instructed to regard prices as 'parametric', that is, although they know prices have been consciously set by the CPB, they must treat them as if they were independent of any individual actions, by themselves or by others (as do participants in a perfectly competitive market). The objective function of managers is no longer the maximisation of profit, but to 'produce exactly as much of a commodity as can be sold or "accounted for" to other industries at a price which equals the marginal cost incurred by the industry in producing this amount'.[9] In doing this, the managers are to observe two rules set by the CPB: 'Use always the method of production (i.e. combination of factors) which minimises average costs and ... produce as much of each commodity as will equalise marginal cost and the price of the product'.[10]

On the basis of these rules, for each price set, a given quantity of goods will be supplied. If supply does not match demand, there will be a clear indication of this to the CPB: 'Any price different from the equilibrium price would show at the end of the accounting period a surplus or a shortage of the commodity in question'.[11] The CPB would then merely alter the price to rectify the situation. Through this 'trial-and-error' process, analogous to the prices in a competitive market, but taking place without it, short-run equilibrium is reached, thus in effect – insofar as the CPB is merely reacting passively to changes in demand and costs of production – merely simulating the operation of the free market. Why then have a CPB at all?

The answer is that by concentrating price-setting authority in the hands of the CPB, at crucial points prices which differ from free market prices can be enforced, and thus, overall, the economy can be guided in the 'social interest'. The CPB can intervene to set accounting prices to enterprises which differ from the prices paid by consumers, where such a move is felt to be justified by considerations of social welfare. Significantly, Lange observes that this opportunity must be fairly limited (although he does not specify the means by which such limits might be determined), since its widespread use would be politically unacceptable, implying that the CPB had a different scale of values and priorities from the people as a whole.[12]

Further advantage which Lange claims for this system derive from the possibility it affords of rational control over the overall rate of saving, thus offering a long-term perspective which the market is unable to provide; from the possibility of allowing for 'externalities' in prices, thus rendering prices a more accurate reflection of true social costs; and from the realisation of social justice in distribution, which requires more detailed explanation.

While households, having free choice of occupation, sell their labour to the highest bidder, or in such a way as to maximise utility (i.e. weighing up material reward against the content or location of work, or the degree of leisure time allowed), the market is not left to determine the final distribution of income. A social dividend, derived from the return on capital and land, which, under private ownership, would have accrued to individual proprietors, is also paid out by the CPB, but in such a way as not to interfere with the function of wages in obtaining optimum distribution of labour services between different occupations and industries. The social dividend may be used to compensate for economically unjustified inequality, such as that arising from variation in the number of dependents per given wage-earner. The system can thus approximate more closely than the free market to maximum social welfare – where market demand at each price will reflect the relative urgency of the needs of different individuals – since the equality of income required for that effect will only be varied to the extent to which income differentiation reflects the marginal disutility to the individual of the pursuit of any given occupation. This contrasts with capitalism, where private ownership determines to a large extent the distribution of income, and large inequalities prevail.

However, this ingenious 'solution' to the problem of economic calculation in socialism was found by Hayek to suffer from serious shortcomings:

> There is of course no *logical impossibility* of conceiving a distinct organ of the collective economy which ... would be in a position to change without delay every price by just the amount required. When, however, one proceeds to consider the actual apparatus by which this

> sort of adjustment is to be brought about, one begins to wonder whether anyone should be prepared to suggest that, within the domain of practical possibility, such a system will ever distantly approach the efficiency of a system where the required changes are brought about by the spontaneous action of the persons immediately concerned.[13]

Lange's model does not answer Hayek's point noted earlier, that the planners will be forced to deal in statistical aggregates. The feasibility of the model, no less than in the case of the non-price planning model, depends on the CPB dealing only with large, general categories of goods. Thus small but significant differences between goods will be ignored, with the result that 'a great many prices would be at most times in such a system substantially different from what they would be in a free system',[14] and to that extent it would produce inefficient, irrational results.

Nor can the model cope with Hayek's insistence on the inevitability in the real world of constant change. Lange is preoccupied with efficiency in terms of static equilibrium. It is assumed that once an equilibrium price is found, it will remain stable for long periods. But, as Hayek sees it:

> The practical problem is not whether a particular method would eventually lead to a hypothetical equilibrium, but which method will secure the more rapid and complete adjustment to the daily changing conditions in different places and different industries.[15]

If prices are set by the CPB for fixed periods, changes in conditions within those periods will mean that prices are no longer reliable as guides to rational economic activity. But the requirement for constant adjustment of prices would be a truly vast apparatus, which must be cumbersome and slow-moving in operation, thus reducing the effectiveness of the information transmitted by prices, and creating further problems of integration within the CPB itself – to say nothing of the costs of maintaining this army of non-productive bureaucratic workers.

'Bureaucratisation' as an inherent tendency of the Lange model is further promoted by the problem of motivation. How is a system of incentives to be constructed to induce managers to observe the rules set by the CPB? Lange nowhere provides a clear criterion for judging and rewarding managerial success. Unlike the situation in the capitalist market economy, managers cannot be judged simply by enterprise profits, since (a) they are not instructed to maximise enterprise profits; and (b) the size of the profit they produce, if they follow the two rules of behaviour set by the CPB, is determined by the centrally set prices. Thus what is required is some means by which the CPB can check that the rules themselves had been followed scrupulously. But this would require probing deeply into the enterprise's internal records:

> This will not be a perfunctory auditing directed to find out whether his [the manager's] costs have actually been what he says they have been. It will have to establish whether they have been the lowest ones. This means that the control will have to consider not only what he actually did, but also what he might have done and ought to have done.[16]

The requirement would be for a considerable extension of the CPB's activities, and thus of course, of its personnel, which, as Bergson notes, 'it is a cardinal concern of the Competitive Solution to limit'.[17]

How are managers to be induced to take risks? Lange provides no indication of the means which might be built into the model to overcome the 'asymmetry' of the effects of success and failure for the manager, where the penalties for failure greatly exceed the gains of success. In such circumstances, it is only rational for managers to prefer safe but unspectacular progress to the greater but less assured benefits of, for example, a policy of substantial innovation. Moreover, the fact that prices are set consciously and deliberately by an identifiable body, rather than emerging spontaneously and impersonally through the market, adds an extra dimension. Anticipation of future price changes is an important part of managerial decision-making, especially where risk is concerned. But a manager 'can hardly be held responsible for anticipating future changes correctly, if these changes depend entirely on the decision of the authority',[18] while at the same time, managers will be tempted to try to mitigate risks by direct appeal to, or pressure on, the price-setters. And what happens if the price-setters get it wrong? As Bergson notes, 'responsibility for such error might easily become controversial'.[19] Inescapably, managers will be dependent on their superiors for assessment, and so 'in consequence all the difficulties will arise in connection with freedom of initiative and the assessment of responsibility which are usually associated with bureaucracy'.[20] Lange himself conceded as much, 'It seems to us indeed, that the *real danger of socialism is that of the bureaucratisation of economic life*'.[21]

B ALTERNATIVE MODELS OF 'MARKET SOCIALISM'

It was not so much the arguments of the anti-socialist theorists as the practical experience of central planning in the Soviet Union and Eastern Europe which provoked further attempts to come to grips with the problem of the market and socialism. What Hayek and other liberals concluded on the basis of logic had become evident in practice. 'Real Socialism' was both undemocratic and economically inefficient. In contrast to Lange's 'Competitive Solution', the possibility which socialist theorists now contemplated was the use of a real, functioning market within the context of social ownership of the means of production. The theoretical task was twofold – to demonstrate the logical independence of the market from private property, and to show how a market was, furthermore, compatible with the socialist aim of production guided by the criterion of the 'social interest'.

The first attempt to tackle this task was made in Yugoslavia after 1950. After the expulsion of the Yugoslav communists from the Cominform in 1948, the leadership came to see that it was necessary to develop a full-blown alternative to the Stalinist model (hitherto equated with socialism itself) for the purposes of legitimating a regime now isolated and excommunicated from the world communist movement. The Yugoslavs took up the idea of self-management. (It should be noted that in the discussion of the model that follows, we will not be referring to the way in which the Yugoslav economy works in practice, but to the essential general principles which lie behind it.)

The basic principle of the model is maximum decentralisation, where 'decision-making is carried out on a lower level and ... only those decisions are reserved to a higher level which otherwise would lead to damage of the interests of some individuals or groups'.[22] Self-management of the enterprise is exercised by a Workers' Council, elected by all members of the enterprise collective, which has basic responsibility for determining the goals of the enterprise. Day-to-day operational management is entrusted to a managerial board, headed by the enterprise director, who is appointed by the Workers' Council, but who may, in the interests of effective coordination of the executive managerial function, nominate his own managerial subordinates, with the approval of the Workers' Council.[23]

Decision-making by autonomous self-managed enterprises is thus guided not by directive targets set 'from above' by a command plan, but by the self-interest of the members of the enterprise collective, realised on a competitive market. The 'vertical' system of coordination of central planning is thus replaced by 'horizontal' market-based relations.[24] The objective function of the self-managed enterprise, however, is not the same as that of the capitalist firm, since a collective, in pursuit of its members' self-interest, will tend to focus on maximisation of net income per employee, rather than profit. Thus labour-power is not a 'commodity', as it is in the capitalist system – reward is determined not as 'wages' according to supply and demand on the market, but as a share in the residual surplus earned from sales of the enterprise's products on the market, after deductions for depreciation, taxation, etc. The distribution of income within the enterprise – the shares to be allocated to members of the collective according to their contributions to the final output – is decided democratically by the collective. The broader social distribution, between enterprises, branches and regions, is, in principle, left to the market to determine.

This system, however, does not altogether exclude planning or the role of the State from the economy. But it is planning of a very different type from that envisaged by traditional socialists and their critics; and the role of the State is seen not as replacing the market but as complementing it:

> In this context, the state political centre emerges as the source of regulatory impulses which reflect the constant, previously anticipated rules of the market. On that basis economic decision-makers obtain reliable parameters for their decisions and, seeking to maximise their incomes, carry out the intentions of the plan by their own initiative. In that way the plan and its adequate fulfilment represent the necessary condition for the autonomy of enterprises.[25]

The type of planning involved here, in contrast to the 'command' model previously seen as the only possible form of planning, is 'indicative'. Like command planning, however, this form of planning is not specifically tied to socialist forms of economy, but can also be found in the experience of capitalist economies, such as France, where there have existed traditions of a strong central state, and of interventionism and cooperation rather than the competitive individualism assumed by Hayek.[26] The main characteristics of indicative planning have been defined by Egon Neuberger as follows:

First, the plan is not drawn up by an autonomous team of experts, but emerges from a process of consultation and bargaining among representatives of the major groups involved in economic activity. In France, this has included business, employers, labour and consumer representatives, with the government participating merely as 'first among equals'. Regional representation might also be included. The object of bargaining would be to arrive at consensus on the broad, general goals of economic policy, and the focus would tend to be long-term rather than immediate.

Second, motivation to comply with the plan derives not from compulsion but from self-interest, and also from 'solidarity' – that is, the conscious and willing subordination of self-interest to the 'good of the community'. Nobody would have the right to enforce compliance upon enterprises. The only sanction would be economic, exerted through the market on an enterprise which wrong-headedly disregarded the plan framework. The enterprise thus has the right to disregard the plan if it considers it contrary to its interests.

Third, the indicative plan produces not compulsory targets, but a centralised source of information on the current and projected future market, made available to all those engaged in economic activity. The assumption is that the provision of information alone is sufficient to influence enterprise behaviour. Given that the market provides only imperfect information on future prices, costs and demand, this may be able to overcome such negative features of the operation of the market as wasteful duplication of investment, the lack of information about the future intentions of other firms and so on, which can greatly improve the possibilities of rational planning within the firm.[27]

However, there are other aspects of the role of the State in this model which are necessary to its economic viability. A variety of state institutions is necessary in addition to the Planning Board.[28] Economic ministries would be established to carry out economic policy measures. The overall control of the money market would be maintained through a National Bank, with regulatory powers over commercial banks operating directly on the market. A Social Accounting Service would be responsible for verification of the legality of enterprise activity, without having any powers of command over enterprises. Horvat also envisages two Intervention Funds, with responsibility and the resources, for smoothing out price fluctuations in agriculture and in materials supply. A third intervention fund would also back exports. This would be necessary to counteract 'unfair competition' on the world market, which is 'under the control of mammoth multinational corporations, international cartels, and state and intergovernmental organisations'.[29] There would also be an Arbitration Board for Incomes and Prices, to combat abuse of monopoly and to check against government measures which discriminate against a particular industry (and to determine, where necessary, the level of compensation to be made). All these institutions are aimed at stabilising and equalising conditions on the market. A further essential function is the stimulation of growth, and, closely connected with it, the establishment of new enterprises.

A key set of problems of the self-managed market economy, manifesting themselves rather differently from the way they do in the capitalist economy, is the establishment and entry on to the market of new firms, the associated problem of monopoly, and the broader question of investment.

In the context of self-management, responsibility for setting up new enterprises may rest not only with the central State, but also with local public authorities, enterprises, groups of workers and individuals. In practice, the possibilities of the two last-mentioned will be restricted in the context of a socialist economy by the improbability of their having sufficient capital to set up a firm independently, or of being able to obtain a sufficiently large bank loan. Furthermore, enterprises' willingness to invest in new firms is likely to be fairly low, given that, first, where resources exist in a firm over and above its own investment needs, there will be considerable pressure to distribute this for increased consumption; and that, second, there will be an absence of incentive to invest outside the firm, where the workers of an existing enterprise are not allowed to derive an income from such investment – since the only legitimate claim to an income is from participation in work at one's one enterprise. Thus the major role in the establishment of new firms will fall to state authorities at both central and local levels, which must therefore be able to draw resources in the form of taxation from existing firms. In principle, once the State has intervened to establish a new firm, it will withdraw, handing all decision-making authority over to the Workers' Council of the newly-formed enterprise collective. The State will decide on where to invest in new firms according to information derived from the market, and it can use this form of intervention to counteract monopoly, which is likely to be a crucial problem for the self-managed economy, as for the capitalist economy; and to maintain full employment, which, while it is a vital condition of an identifiably 'socialist' economy, is also likely to be a problem area, for the reason given that the self-managed firm, maximising net income per employee, will tend to opt for more capital-intensive means of increasing output than the capitalist firm maximising profit.[30] In principle, short-run equilibrium will be reached at a lower level of employment, *ceteris paribus*, than in the capitalist economy.

It should be noted that it appears that, in principle, the State will have no direct control over the basic macroeconomic decision on the overall rate of saving and investment in the economy. This is left to the market. The primary source of investment funds will be enterprise profit, supplemented to a greater or lesser extent by commercial bank loans. The instruments available to the State to promote economic growth will thus be limited to those available to the government of a capitalist economic system – for example, taxation policy. These instruments would be supplemented, but not radically altered in character, by Horvat's proposed Interventionary Investment Fund, which has two tasks:

> (a) to participate in financing those projects that require an exceptionally large concentration of capital and/or long period of construction; and (b) to intervene in eliminating disproportions in capacity ... whenever for some reason the market does not succeed in balancing supply and demand.[31]

A further subdivison of the fund would concentrate on regional development: 'Economic growth can always be accelerated if pockets of insufficiently employed human and natural resources are eliminated, or, in other words, if the development of underdeveloped regions is accelerated'.[32]

In assessing this model, we can start from the point that it can be expected to maximise the accepted advantages of the market in terms of rationality and efficiency. Although it has been argued that a self-managed firm will operate rather differently from a capitalist firm under similar market conditions,[33] the State can be given resources to enable it to counteract dysfunctional tendencies, particularly associated with employment levels. The role of the State, supplementing not replacing the market, would appear to go no further than that identified by Hayek as compatible with a market economy.[34] But precisely for this reason, it has been noted that 'it seems odd that many socialists who recognised the problems arising from decentralised capitalism with some acuity have not considered how far such problems may be endemic to all decentralised economic systems'.[35] For example, the problem of 'externalities', and the irrationalities associated with it, will recur in the self-management model, since 'such problems as pollution are clearly not confined to capitalism'.[36] Yet more serious problems for a system purporting to be 'socialist' are income distribution, inflation and long-term development/investment.

Incomes, according to the socialist principle, are to be derived only from work – more precisely, from one's direct and immediate contribution to the work effort of a collective of which one is a member. 'Distribution according to work' means, in this model, 'distribution according to the results of work'[37] – that is, according to the judgement of the market on the results of work, rather than according to type of work, qualification and skill. Differentiation according to these latter criteria can be democratically decided within the enterprise in its decision-making about distribution of its own income among members; but the situation could well arise where an unskilled worker in a successful firm earned more than a skilled worker in an unsuccessful firm. This is likely to be controversial in the context of a socialist economy, as it will obscure the relationship between the individual worker's efforts and his or her reward, especially where the conditions for enterprises competing on the market are not equal. External factors, such as changes in the world market conditions, or the historical legacy of the past privileged conditions for a particular branch will inevitably intervene – in which case differences in incomes may be more accurately described as economic rent, rather than as reward for actual work performed.[38] This is especially likely where the predominant part of investment resources is left at the disposition of enterprises, since past success will secure future advantages for the enterprise in giving it greater opportunities to invest and modernise. Inequalities will thus tend to be cumulative, as 'success breeds success', and a concentration of capital occurs, with the result that

> The government is faced with the unpleasant choice of attempting to tax away excess profits from rich enterprises and to subsidise poor ones, thereby lessening incentives, or allowing highly inequitable income differentials to continue, with obvious political, social and economic consequences.[39]

The model also has implications for the problem of inflation. It has been argued by Jan Vanek that the self-managed economy may be less prone to inflation insofar as this is due to 'wage-push' factors in capitalist economies, since wage-labour is abolished and earnings are a residual.[40] But James Meade notes that this is a simplistic approach – wage-push is not the only cause of inflation.[41] In a self-managed economy, an increase in effective demand leads to firms raising prices. In a capitalist market, this situation increases the incentive to expand investment in capital equipment and to increase output. But in the same circumstances in the self-managed economy, there is no such incentive to invest. The incomes of workers in existing firms simply rise, without a corresponding increase in output. New demand has to be met by the State establishing new firms, but this further increases effective demand. It is not clear how the inflationary pressures generated in this way could be managed.

Criticisms of the implications of the model for long-term development and the determination of the rate of investment refer not only to the economic rationality of the model, but also to its claim to be a 'socialist' form of economy. As noted above, the State has no direct control over the long-term development and growth of the economy, while at the microeconomic level the incentive to invest is limited by the inadmissibility of non-work incomes. Workers will only be persuaded to defer present consumption for the sake of expanding capacity if this will lead to greater future incomes from economies of scale. But why should an existing enterprise collective sacrifice its present consumption, if expansion only replicates the present marginal rate of productivity of capital with a larger workforce? The macroeconomic implications of this are both unemployment and low growth rates.

It is difficult to assess the rationality of the model from a purely economic viewpoint, since the concept of 'rationality' itself implies some purpose towards which a system is directed. Unlike the capitalist market, the criterion of rationality is not maximisation of individual self-interest, but is claimed to be maximisation of the 'social interest'. Thus it is not enough for the model merely to demonstrate that it can replicate the same degree of functional rationality as the capitalist market, since the respective ends of the two economic systems are fundamentally different. Thus we must ask not only whether the model allocates resources efficiently, but whether it is also able to maximise the 'social interest'. The key problem is whether the 'social interest' is understood as comprising merely allocative efficiency, or whether it also contains substantive goals of social justice. This problem will be analysed more fully in the following chapter, but, for the purposes of the present argument, it is sufficient to note of the self-management model that it appears to reject implicitly the concept of a 'social interest' in substantive terms, insofar as it restricts the role of the State and planning to supplementing the market rather than replacing it, and to this extent it falls within the individualist tradition espoused by Hayek (although the 'individual' here is not a physical person but an artificial one – the self-managing enterprise collective). The 'social interest' is seen not in terms of a concrete and specific set of hierarchically-ranked priorities, but in a set of conditions – worker self-management, enterprise autonomy, maximum scope for the market – as ends in themselves.

But if the 'social interest' is taken to mean equality in income distribution, or at least some concept of a socially just distribution, plus macroeconomic control over the price level and the pattern and rate of long-term development, then the self-management model appears not appreciably superior to the capitalist market system in achieving these ends. Leaving discussion of the relative merits of these alternative concepts of the 'social interest' to the next chapter, let us consider a further possible model which attempts to combine the advantages of the market in terms of achieving a microeconomic efficiency with the pursuit of such substantive social goals which have normally been at the heart of socialist thinking. This is the 'regulated market' model of Włodzimierz Brus.

For Brus, an economic system can only properly be regarded as 'socialist' insofar as it fulfils two basic criteria: (i) the means of production must be employed in the interests of society, and (ii) society must have effective disposition over the means of production it owns.[42] These two criteria do not *per se* rule out the use of the market. On the contrary, the non-market *étatiste* model falls down on both counts. In the first place, the poor economic performance in practice of the *étatiste* model in the Soviet Union and Eastern Europe undermines the ideological assertion that the transfer of the means of production from private ownership into the hands of the State is enough of itself to guarantee that they will be used in the 'social interest'; and in the absence both of the market as a source of objective information, and of democratic control over the State, there is no means of verifying that the State does in fact represent the general interest of society, rather than the narrow self-interest of a self-appointed élite group monopolising the State.[43]

Thus the market plays an essential role in the socialist economy, Brus argues, not merely for guiding individual choice of profession, place of work, and expenditure of personal income (which is not excluded in the *étatiste* model either), but also as a basis for decision-making in the enterprise and industrial branch concerning the size and structure of output, sources of supplies and direction of sales, structure of personnel and the form and methods of remuneration within the enterprise or branch.[44] Brus accepts the basic arguments in favour of the market in terms of increasing efficiency, making producers more responsive to customer requirements, providing incentives and fostering the development of creative initiative at the local level. He also recognises the link between enterprise autonomy provided by the use of the market and the creation of the 'real preconditions for workers' self-management as the vital element in socialist democracy'.[45] To the extent that the market makes self-management possible, it thus enhances 'effective disposition' by members of society over the means of production. It also enhances the effectiveness of general control over the economy by the State, in supplying more accurate economic information on which the central authorities can base their decision-making. But in so doing, it only *improves* the process of planning, but it cannot *replace* it. While the market is a necessary component of the socialist economy, it too has what Brus identifies as 'objective limitations': 'a socialist society is, in the last analysis, the producer of use-values'.[46] The advocacy of the primacy of the market, as in the self-management model, implies the dominance of production for exchange, or, in Marxist terms, 'commodity fetishism', with 'the disappearance of the hierarchical structure of aims ... as well as the priority accorded to the production of use-values for which the production of exchange values can only be an effective means but which cannot be a substitute'.[47]

Thus, Brus argues, the self-management model, by depriving the State of effective control over macroeconomic decision-making, which it leaves to the spontaneous operation of the market, avoids the basic responsibility of a socialist economy for the 'social interest' by depoliticising what are 'in the nature of things political decisions since they set and assess the objectives of the economy, they establish the general criteria and the framework which give economic calculation a definite character'.[48] In the practice of the model in Yugoslavia, he notes, there is a clear tendency to attach pejorative overtones to the adjective 'political', as being synonymous with arbitrariness and irrationality. But 'political decisions can obviously be arbitrary and mistaken, but this does not mean that they should (and can) be eliminated at any price in favour of partial decisions based on free market criteria'.[49] If political decision-making is regularly arbitrary and irrational, this is a symptom of the lack of effective democracy in the political system, he argues.

Brus's model falls into the category of what have been described as 'visible hand' systems,[50] as 'an attempt to reap the benefits of central planning while avoiding some of the costs'.[51] Central authorities are required in this model to relinquish their power to intervene in microeconomic decision-making by the individual enterprise, but to retain power over key decisions in the name of assuring the 'social interest'. This is realised through the following functions of the centre:[52]

1. Basic macroeconomic decision-making, especially as concerns long-term development. This involves the division of the national income between accumulation and consumption; the determination of the main areas of investment; and the distribution of consumption income between different groups of the population. The key factor is 'to ensure central control over the basic flow of investment outlays' by giving the central authorities sufficient resources to be able 'decisively to affect the size and structure of growth of productive capacities'.[53]
2. Central determination of the 'rules of behaviour' for the enterprises. The 'natural' objective functions of enterprises, whether maximisation of profit, or of net income per employee, are not sufficient: 'It is necessary to lay down objective functions for the subsystems [i.e. enterprises] using criteria drawn from consideration of the system as a whole'.[54] This involves centrally-set rules concerning the formation of enterprise funds for investment and wages. Thus the central authorities can ensure that the wage fund is 'compatible both with market equilibrium and with the social structure of incomes'.[55]
3. Central control over prices, to ensure that they 'express the preferences of society as a whole', in order that they guide economic units toward socially rational decisions. The 'parametric' character of prices should be maintained, but direct intervention by the centre may at times be necessary. This, however, should be regarded as exceptional 'if the logic of this mechanism for the functioning of the economy is to be maintained'.[56]

The principles of 'solidarity' and 'mutual responsibility' inherent in socialism also require an active role for the State in those areas where 'social and individual preferences diverge to such an extent that to leave the provision of such services to individual choice would endanger the satisfaction of socially important needs'[57] – for example, in health, welfare, education and defence. The State also has a role in compensating for inequalities of income, where the incentive effect of income differentiation is less socially desirable than the positive effects of ensuring 'equality of opportunity'. Of course, this function is not excluded in either the Lange model, or the self-management model; nor, of course, is it absent from capitalist economies.

Enterprises in Brus's model are legally autonomous. Although they do not own their assets, they have full right of disposition over them. They draw up their own plans covering product mix, the introduction of new products, technological development and the use of their own internal investment resources, and the distribution of the wage and bonus funds. They are fully responsible for their debts up to the limit of their assets. The State is not allowed to take assets from the enterprise in order to transfer them to another at will; nor can the State issue direct orders to enterprises to produce a specific item, except in emergencies or special circumstances (e.g. for defence purposes or to meet unexpected foreign trade needs). If fulfilling such an exceptional task involves the enterprise in financial loss, the State is obliged to provide compensation. The expansion of the enterprise is not entirely a matter of its own decision, however. While enterprises will have some investment funds at their disposal, major expansion will only be possible in conformity with the objectives of the centrally-set plan. While banks will have funds to allocate on commercial terms to competing enterprise projects, there will be centrally-set investment quotas for branches, and banks will act as an arm of central policy, exercising financial supervision over the execution by enterprises of investment projects basically financed centrally according to the planned concept of development.

Although Brus sees the degree of enterprise autonomy created in the 'regulated market' model as providing the conditions for effective worker-participation in enterprise management, it should be noted that there is no necessity for this form of organisation as an inherent requirement of the model. A more traditional hierarchical system of authority within the enterprise could also be retained. But various problems are associated with this – first, who would then be responsible for managerial appointment? It would inevitably devolve upon the State. However, if this meant a continuation of the practice found in the traditional Soviet model of managerial appointment by industrial branch ministries, there would arise the danger of reproducing the relationship of personal dependence of the enterprise manager on his bureaucratic 'superiors', with serious implications both for the autonomy of the enterprise and the objectivity and impartiality of central economic policy. This would be a particular problem for reform of the 'regulated market' type in the specific context of Eastern Europe, where deeply ingrained habits and attitudes derived from long years of experience of the Soviet-type system would strengthen this tendency by provoking resistance on the part of both managers and ministerial officials to the 'cutting loose' of the enterprise from its familiar and security-enhancing network of contacts. But it is not 'merely' a problem of the subjective perceptions of the participants based on their habits of mind and assumptions inherited from former organisational patterns. The problem is to create an arm of the State institutionally separate from the economic policy-making and policy-implementing arm, with the special function of managerial appointment. What is required is a form of 'separation of powers' within the central authorities themselves, while at the same time maintaining a coherent and unified definition of the 'social interest'. Who would appoint the appointers of managers? Obviously not the policy-making and policy-implementing apparatus. The answer would appear to lie in the representative parliamentary institutions of the political system.

Such a system would appear in principle to be feasible, but it is not clear why it should be preferred on economic grounds to election of the manager by enterprise employees. The dangers of self-management pointed out above would be unlikely to recur in the very different economic context of the regulated market, where the enterprise is structurally conditioned, by the constraints exercised by the central authorities, to pursue the centrally-determined 'social interest' in pursuing its own interest. Moreover, the considerable advantages of worker self-management in terms of motivation, which Brus emphasises, would be forgone. Effective motivation 'demands not only that the whole workforce understand its target, but also that it identify itself with the aims of the organisation'.[58] This is especially true of a more sophisticated modern workforce. Self-management also has an important socialising function: 'Real self-management at the enterprise level should have enormous educational significance for the development of socialist attitudes to work and ownership at a general level'.[59] This in turn would bring economic advantage in terms of motivation and commitment, and avoid the losses associated with careless and irresponsible use of equipment and theft of common property.

Furthermore, participation in enterprise decision-making could compensate to some extent for the lower material incentives available in the model because of central wage-regulation. This feature of the model is likely to cause serious problems only to the extent that (i) the central wage policy is perceived as unjust, and (ii) material incentives are in fact the most important motivating factor. It should be noted that the model assumes a high degree of social consensus in favour of a relatively egalitarian distribution pattern (this point will be pursued in the next chapter), but also it builds in the possibility of differential reward. This in turn could be legitimised, as in the self-management model, by democratisation of decision-making within the firm on the distribution of the wage fund. Given general social consensus in favour of egalitarian principles, the model also builds in safeguards to counteract the possibility of excessive differentiation, through general control of the operation of the market, the prevention of cumulative inequality between enterprises, and state social welfare measures which both presuppose and reinforce the sense of 'social solidarity' and 'mutual responsibility'.

On point (ii), Brus argues that material incentives are likely to decline in importance for motivation once a certain level of affluence has been reached, and the workforce itself becomes more sophisticated.[60] Indeed, it could be argued that the more sophisticated the economy, the more difficult it becomes to create a really effective incentive system based on accurately rewarding each *individual's* contribution, when the end product is inextricably a result of cooperation. Under these circumstances, it would appear that the more democratic form of internal enterprise organisation is likely to prove economically more successful than the 'technocratic' or authoritarian variant.

2 Politics

Our task in this chapter is to elaborate on the political implications of the respective models of a socialist economy. Each model embodies a particular understanding of the 'social interest' in terms of their implications for freedom and democracy in the political system. The basic question is the relationship between individual and group 'private' interests and the 'social interest'.

The chapter looks at this issue in four sections. First, in Section A, we examine Hayek's critique of planning as inherently despotic; and consider the objection that Hayek's implicit alternative of the market economy based on private ownership neglects the impact that inequality can have on the realisation of freedom. Section B examines the self-management model, which is built upon a critique of central planning very similar to that of Hayek. While it is concerned to some extent with equality, this model is also based upon a form of private ownership. It shares with Hayek an ambiguous, negative definition of the 'social interest' and an incoherent theory of the State. Section C argues that Brus's model, combining plan and market, can sustain a coherent definition of the 'social interest' in democratic terms, and is thus not incompatible with freedom; on the other hand, it cannot be shown that it is necessarily accompanied by democracy. Given the high degree of social consensus it assumes, it is likely to be realised in its democratic variant only exceptionally; it is thus more likely to be realised without democracy. Finally, Section D draws out the conclusions from the preceding analysis of the internal logic of the respective models, and relates them to the question of change, of movement from one model to another, thus in turn introducing the empirical material to be covered in Part II: the comparison of reform in Czechoslovakia and Hungary.

A HAYEK, PLANNING AND FREEDOM

The first model of socialism presented in the previous chapter was that of central planning, based on the assumption of the possibility of objective determination of the 'social interest' in detail by an omniscient centre, with the role of the market limited to individual choice of occupation and pattern of personal consumer expenditure, within the range of alternatives made available by the State. Hayek's attack on socialism referred to this model, and was not limited to the question of its economic rationality, but was developed, in his work *The Road to Serfdom*, into a political argument against planning as a threat to freedom and democracy.[1]

The essence of the threat was seen to lie in the very concept of a 'social interest' itself. It was not just that the task of defining the 'social interest' in the degree of detail required for central planning was *in practice* likely to prove difficult, but that, in Hayek's view, *in principle* such a thing cannot exist: the basic flaw in the socialist programme was in the assumption of the possibility of omniscience. Hayek's central point is that knowledge is necessarily limited. It is simply not possible to know what the 'social interest' is. The range of possible interests is infinite, and the ordering of priorities can only be done by each individual for himself on the basis of his own knowledge of his circumstances and his own value system. People's perceptions of their interests, Hayek assumes, inevitably differ, and differ irreconcilably. The possibility that people might have interests other than those which they themselves determine is ruled out. Thus the only possible meaning of the 'social interest' is in the establishment of a legal framework within which individuals can maximise their self-interest, which will guarantee the security of their persons and property, enforce contracts and provide stability of expectations. The idea of the 'social interest' as a set of common *goals* can only be accepted in the case where the ends which individuals define for themselves coincidentally agree:

> What are called 'social ends' are ... merely identical ends of many individuals – or ends to the achievement of which individuals are willing to contribute in return for the assistance they receive in the satisfaction of their own desires.[2]

Moreover, the probability of agreement on common ends diminishes with the scope of collective action envisaged. Planning raises just this problem since it requires us

> to agree on a much larger number of topics than we have been used to, and ... in a planned system we cannot confine collective action to the tasks on which we can agree, but are forced to produce agreement on everything in order that any action is taken at all.[3]

The result inevitably is the resort to coercion, since 'we can rely on voluntary agreement to guide the action of the State only so long as it is confined to spheres where agreement exists'.[4]

The attempt by Lange to preserve individual freedom within the framework of central planning by allowing free choice of occupation and of personal consumption patterns is seen as wholly inadequate, since the most important decisions which ultimately determine these choices – decisions on investment and the allocation of resources between individual and collective consumption – are determined centrally by the State. Moreover, the somewhat vague reference by Lange to the State's right to interfere in the price mechanism in the interests of some conception of 'social welfare'[5] further restricts the meaning of freedom of individual choice.[6]

> We can unfortunately not indefinitely extend the sphere of common action and still leave the individual free in his own sphere. Once the communal section, in which the State controls all the means, exceeds a certain proportion of the whole, the effects of its actions dominate the whole system ... There is, then, scarcely an individual end which is not dependent for its achievement on the action of the State, and the 'social scale of values' which guides the State's action must embrace practically all individual ends.[7]

For planning to be non-coercive, it is not enough that a society should be unanimous on the necessity of central planning, since it would not follow from this that there was also agreement on the *ends* to which planning must be directed. This would be 'rather as if a group of people were to commit themselves to take a journey together without agreeing where they want to go: with the result that they may all have to make a journey which most of them do not want at all'.[8]

The idea that planning could be made non-coercive by subordinating it to the control of a democratically-elected Parliament is also rejected. Parliamentary representatives are no more likely than individuals to be able to reach agreement on the unitary goal or scale of priorities which planning requires. The result of this, where an electorate wishes to see planning introduced, would be increasing popular impatience with Parliaments as 'ineffective talking shops, unable or incompetent to carry out the tasks for which they have been chosen'.[9] The solution would then be found in removing essentially political decisions from the democratic arena and transferring them to 'experts, permanent officials or independent autonomous bodies'.[10]

Nor could Parliament approach the problem by delegating its powers to groups of experts on individual elements of the plan, while maintaining ultimate control over the final plan, since 'an economic plan, to deserve a name, must have a unitary conception ... A complex whole where all the parts must be carefully adjusted to each other, cannot be achieved by compromise between conflicting views'.[11] Thus, 'the body charged with planning has to choose between ends of whose conflict Parliament is not even aware, and ... the most that can be done is to present to it a plan which has to be accepted or rejected as a whole'.[12] The role of Parliament is thus reduced to – at best – 'a useful safety valve'. 'It may even prevent some flagrant abuses and successfully insist on particular shortcomings being remedied. But it cannot direct. It will at best be reduced to choosing the persons who are to have practically absolute power'.[13]

For Hayek, the choice is stark: either 'individualism', the market and freedom, or 'collectivism', planning and serfdom. The place of democracy, however, is rather more ambiguous. For Hayek, 'freedom' is wholly 'negative',[14] as freedom *from* arbitrary power, which is represented by the State as soon as it steps beyond its sole proper function of defining and preserving the legal framework within which individual freedom is maximised:

> it is not the source but the limitation of power which prevents it from being arbitrary. Democratic control *may* prevent power from becoming arbitrary, but it does not do so by its mere existence. If democracy resolves on a task which necessarily involves the use of power which cannot be guided by fixed rules, it must become arbitrary power.[15]

It is not democracy, but the market itself, and the minimal State, which ultimately guarantee freedom. In fact, democracies, by their very nature, being vulnerable to mass pressure to extend state power into the economy in the name of some concept of 'social justice' or equality, are potentially inimical to freedom, and 'it is at least conceivable that under the government of a very homogeneous and doctrinaire majority democratic government might be as oppressive as the worst dictatorship'.[16]

The peculiarity of Hayek's definition of freedom is in the assumption that it can be realised in the absence of equality. The only equality which Hayek sees as relevant to freedom is equality before the law. The idea that freedom might be conditional upon equality is seen as confusing 'freedom' with 'power', a confusion which Hayek maintains is 'as old as socialism itself'.[17] Freedom is seen purely 'negatively', in Isaiah Berlin's terms, as the absence of coercion; 'equality', however, requires the exercise of necessarily coercive power by the State, to redistribute resources in opposition to the results obtained on the 'free' market. However, it is neither uniquely socialist, nor necessarily a 'confusion' to point to the possibility that the market itself might have coercive aspects. Hayek's distinction between freedom and power is hard to maintain, since freedom 'from' necessarily also implies freedom 'to' do or avoid doing something. Freedom is the unobstructed realisation of some goal, 'the power of doing what one would choose without interference by other persons' action'.[18] (Indeed, it is ironic in this respect that one of Hayek's contemporary disciples entitled his book propounding a similar 'negative' concept of freedom, *Free to Choose*.[19]) To the extent that men are unequally placed on the market, they are unequal in their opportunities to realise their goals. Unless we assume (i) that resources are not limited (and therefore that one person's advantage is not necessarily realised at the expense of others'), and/or (ii) that men are fundamentally unequal also in their *goals* (in which case it is hard to see the justification even for 'equality before the law'), market inequality will also produce political inequality, and necessarily imply the limitation of freedom.

This is particularly clear where freedom leads to the concentration of ownership of the means of production. Non-owners have no choice – they are coerced – to submit themselves to the authority of those who own and control as a condition of their existence. Milton Friedman has argued that in circumstances where not all are owners of the means of production, non-owners are still free insofar as they are not obliged to contract themselves as labourers to *any particular* capitalist.[20] But, as C. B. MacPherson points out, 'The proviso that is required to make every transaction strictly voluntary is *not* freedom not to enter into any *particular* exchange, but freedom not to enter into any exchange at all'.[21]

Moreover, insofar as a capitalist economy is unable to guarantee full employment, non-owners are faced with the possibility of no choice *at all* between possible employers. In this case, the lack of opportunity to pursue their goals, their lack of 'freedom to choose', is as absolute in the context of dispersed but unequal access to the means of production of the capitalist economy as it would be where the State was the sole source of employment.

Furthermore, insofar as equality before the law requires some material resources for its realisation (e.g. for legal fees), inequality of income may also lead to unequal ability to realise legal rights, and thus to political inequality. For such reasons, liberal theorists, and not only socialists, have seen freedom and equality as mutually supportive, rather than mutually exclusive. 'Equality of estates causes equality of power, and equality of power is liberty', concluded Harrington in the seventeenth century.[22] The use of taxation to redistribute income certainly restricts the liberty of some, but also increases the liberty of others; but insofar as those deprived of part of their income are wealthy, thus enjoying superfluous income, while those who receive redistributed resources lack basic means of livelihood, liberty overall must be increased. 'To be forcibly deprived of superabundance or even of conveniences impairs liberty less than to be forcibly prevented from appropriating necessities'.[23]

In this respect, the loss of liberty involved in taxation is no different from the loss of liberty involved in subordinating ourselves to the rule of law itself since this also implies a restriction on our ability to do whatever we choose, but at the same time increases liberty in general by making such restrictions apply equally to all.

B SELF-MANAGEMENT, INEQUALITY AND THE 'SOCIAL INTEREST'

Let us now turn to an examination of the self-managed model, which is founded upon a critique of the central planning model of socialism in many ways similar to that of Hayek. However, as an economic system it is not based on individual private property, but on what is argued to be a 'socialist' form of ownership of the means of production.

The self-management model originated in a critique of both individual private and state forms of property as 'alienated', since in neither case, it was argued, were workers actually able to realise their rights to control the means of production. This would only meaningfully be realised in the self-management of enterprises, formally 'owned' by 'society as a whole', while actual disposition over the means of production was enjoyed by the members of the enterprise work collective. The market, it was appreciated, was a necessary condition of realising self-management, and to that extent was necessary to the realisation of freedom in socialism. Effective workers' control could not be realised under central planning, since all major decisions would be made by others. The self-management model thus shares with Hayek a profound suspicion of the State, as liable to develop an interest of its own, separate from that of workers, as soon as its functions are extended beyond merely guaranteeing the conditions within which autonomous enterprises exercise their decision-making rights. The proper functions of the State in this model, as explained in the previous chapter, are the provision and enforcement of a framework of rules of behaviour, and the support of the operation of the market. To this extent, the model shares Hayek's approach to the question of the 'social interest', which can be no more than a shared interest in these limited functions of the State, and/or the coincidental agreement of partial (in this case, group rather than individual) interests. Work collectives, as 'artificial individuals', can be relied upon to arrive spontaneously at the social good by pursuing their own interests; the 'social interest' cannot be identified substantively as consensus on a concrete, specific end or unified hierarchy of ends, but resides in the condition of minimum restriction on the individual's (Hayek) or group's (self-management) pursuit of his/its ends.

While democracy is essential to the self-management model at the level of the firm, as the essential means by which the interest of the work collective is defined, democracy at the level of the whole society, in the State, appears, as in Hayek's argument, to be possible, but not necessary. In practice, of course, in Yugoslavia, the self-managed model has been found compatible with the maintenance of one-party rule. This might even be argued to have been the *condition* for the continuing viability of the model in practice, since greater democracy at the level of the State, in a country such as Yugoslavia with profound regional socioeconomic inequalities, would inevitably have led to the type of mass pressure on the State which Hayek feared, leading to redistribution of resources by the State between regions, sectors and enterprises, thus undermining the market, enterprise autonomy and workers' property rights in the name of a substantive concept of the 'social interest' which is held to be incompatible with the aims of the model.

However, property rights in the self-management model are described by its advocates as 'socialist' in character, not private and individual, which would also lead to 'alienation' of the workers. What difference does this make? C. B. MacPherson defines property as 'a right in the sense of an enforceable claim to some use or benefit of something, whether it is a right to share in some common resource or an individual right in some particular/things'.[24] He identifies basically two forms of property – common and private:

> Common property is created by the guarantee to each individual that he will not be excluded from the use or benefit of something; private property is created by the guarantee that an individual can exclude others from the use or benefit of something.[25]

Is it acceptable to argue that property in the self-managed model is not 'private' but 'common' (which would appear to be necessary in order for the model to be described as 'socialist')? To the extent that workers enjoy full autonomy in their decision-making, and receive in full the fruits of their use of the means of production assembled in the enterprise, the work collective would appear to be in fact the *private* owner of it. What we have is a new form of corporate private property. Access to the means of production and the right to income from its use is not open to *any* member of the whole society, but only to the members of the work collective of a specific enterprise. This in itself must cast doubt on the definition of the model as 'socialist'.

On the other hand, a peculiar feature of this form of private property is that while it excludes non-members of a work collective from the rights to property in a specific enterprise, it also provides the possibility for *all* members of society to enjoy ownership rights in *some* enterprise. The role of the State is to guarantee that all have the opportunity to become part of a corporate private owner, by establishing new enterprises, which is not only necessary to the market in providing effective competition, but at the same time, deals with the problem of unemployment. Thus the private nature of enterprise property does not lead to fundamental inequality in the sense of division of society into owners and non-owners of the means of production. The model can in this respect provide greater equality than the capitalist market economy, and to this extent, greater freedom.

However, the model also will produce distributive inequality, insofar as the market is unrestricted and enterprise autonomy is guaranteed. The legitimacy of such distributive inequality depends on the assertion that incomes derive solely 'from work', not from property itself.[26] This in turn requires equality between competing enterprises, which their very autonomy makes impossible, since it allows successful enterprises to enhance their future advantages by retaining – within limits which can be set by the State – their profits from past performance which they may reinvest. Their future income will depend not only on future work but on past work; income thus acquires in part the character of property income, or economic rent. Not only would it contradict the economic logic of the model to tax away that element of income from enterprises – it would be an infringement of the basic property right of the work collective, and as such would not be a legitimate course for the State. The only legitimate basis of taxation would be to provide the State with the necessary resources to establish new enterprises, which is a condition of the system functioning at all, as explained in Chapter 1.[27] This need not necessarily remove all rent income from enterprises – there is no reason why the quantities should be the same. In any case, in principle taxation cannot be based on the idea of removing rent income, but can only be justified by the requirements of maintaining market equilibrium, which alone is held to constitute the 'social interest'. It is, as in Hayek, *assumed* that all have an equal interest in the maintenance of market equilibrium, but insofar as there is inequality between enterprises, this cannot be so.

The source of the problem, common to both Hayek and the self-management model, would appear to lie in their rejection of a substantive, or positive, concept of the 'social interest' as implying equality. This leads to an incoherence in their respective implicit theories of the State.

Both Hayek and self-management theorists reject central planning as inherently despotic, since it rests on a monolithic substantive concept of the 'social interest' which denies the legitimacy of individual and group interests, and can only be realised through coercion. Up to this point, their analysis is convincing. But they then proceed to suggest that *any* substantive concept of the 'social interest' must be monolithic and therefore inimical to freedom for the individual. The assumption is that individual and/or group interests are the only legitimate, meaningful interests, with the further implication that conflict is normal, necessary, and natural; consensus is sporadic, exceptional and very possibly forced. What then holds *society* together? The common framework of rules guaranteed by the minimal State. But this itself assumes a fundamental social consensus, deeper than the conflict of individual and/or group interests. There must be consensus on the rules, and shared principles of justice, in order for conflicting parties to agree to be bound by the arbitration of the State.[28]

On what basis might such consensus be achieved? It must depend on equality of individuals and groups, leading to their conviction that their interests are served equally by the framework of rules adopted.

But the market and enterprise autonomy serve to produce cumulative inequalities. Thus the role of the State cannot be impartial – its role of enforcing the rules of the game and stabilising the market serves the interests of some more than others. In the absence of equality as the basis of consensus, both Hayek and the self-management model assume consensus on the justice of the unequal distribution of resources, which implies that the disadvantaged accept that it is in their interest to be disadvantaged. Now this is only rational if the disadvantaged are so temporarily – if they have equal opportunity to become advantaged. This they cannot have insofar as the market allows the cumulation of inequalities. Equality of opportunity requires the active intervention of the State in the redistribution of resources.

In other words, where what divides men in a society is more important that what holds them together, the role of the State cannot be impartial, but will favour particular interests, and not serve the 'social interest', no matter how limited it is in scope. On the other hand, if the State is to play the role of impartial arbiter of the rules of the game, there must be a consensus, i.e. that what holds men together must be stronger than that which divides them. This in turn requires equality, or legitimation of inequality by the provision of equality of opportunity and the prevention of cumulative and self-perpetuating inequalities.

It follows from this that the concept of a 'social interest' does not necessarily have to mean unanimity, total consensus; all it implies is at least a minimal consensus. Where minimal consensus coexists with conflicting individual and group interests, it would appear also that a necessary condition of the impartiality of the State is democracy. It is therefore hard to accept Hayek's arguments against democracy, particularly his suggestion that democracy could prove more tyrannical than non-representative forms of regime. One can accept Hayek's point that majority rule may develop in a tyrannical way where society is divided into relatively permanent majority and minority factions.[29] Minority rights must also be institutionally guaranteed and protected. But this is not an argument against democracy *per se*, but only an illustration that democracy is unlikely to survive without broad social consensus. If a permanent majority persists in exercising its rights at the expense of a minority, this would lead to a violation of the fundamental consensus, leading either to civil war, the breakdown of the society and the secession of the minority, or the voluntary adjustment of the rules of the game by the majority, to rectify the position of the minority, indicating that the majority accepts the continued membership of the minority in the society as being in its *own* interests – thus reaffirming the initial consensus.

C THE 'REGULATED MARKET', CONSENSUS AND DEMOCRACY

Now, if the notion of a substantive 'social interest' is not unique to socialism, but is implied to some extent also in liberal theory (whether individualist or pluralist), then the argument against planning as inherently undemocratic and inimical to freedom must be modified.

First, it is logically possible that a society characterised by complete homogeneity and equality could in fact democratically sustain full consensus on a unified hierarchy of ends, and thus combine central planning of the detailed 'monolithic' type with full individual freedom. In such a situation, there could be no conflict between individual and group interests and the social interest.[30] Of course, in practical terms the achievement of such a situation is unimaginable without the initial application of a very high degree of coercion to ensure total equality, and a sustained programme of enforced indoctrination to produce a homogeneity of values – thus fundamentally vitiating the quality of the consensus achieved. There is, moreover, no evidence that when such an attempt has been made (for example, in Cambodia under Pol Pot) that it has come anywhere near succeeding. This possibility is thus put forward for consideration not as a practical proposition, but as an abstract logical point.

But let us consider a less extreme position. Hayek asserts that 'in a planned system we cannot confine collective action to the tasks on which we can agree, but are forced to produce agreement on everything in order that any action is taken at all'.[31] But is this in fact the case? If the 'social interest' assumes consensus, but not necessarily total unanimity, why must planning itself be all-embracing? We have seen how Brus's concept of planning does not require that everything be planned, but that it be limited to specifically political decisions at the macroeconomic level, which *can* be left to the market, but which *ought* not to be, since this would produce a result contrary to the 'social interest'. In this case, planning requires not 'agreement on everything' but merely the existence of basic social consensus on substantive goals such as the distribution of income, the long-term objectives of development, the rate of saving, etc. In principle, there is no reason why agreement on such matters should not be reached – under certain practical circumstances, to which we will return below. At this point, however, we should pause to note that while Brus defends his 'regulated market' model as the embodiment of *socialist* principles, it is not necessarily incompatible with the realisation of freedom and democracy in liberal terms. Following from the arguments presented above, in principle it might even realise these goals more fully than either the capitalist market or the self-management systems.

To return, however, to the question of consensus. It is clear that Brus's model requires not merely basic consensus, but a rather high degree of consensus in practice – otherwise its implementation does indeed raise all the problems of enforced compliance which Hayek quite rightly identifies. The question is not whether consensus is in principle possible, but whether in practice this high degree of consensus is unrealistic, therefore only sustainable through coercion. *Some* degree of consensus is essential to the existence of a democratic society; the degree of consensus achieved, and therefore the democratically acceptable limits to the role of the State, will vary according to historical circumstances and the equality and homogeneity of the society. Both historical and systemic factors affect this.

The size of a country in which the model was introduced might be highly relevant to the formation of consensus. A small country is more likely (although it is by no means guaranteed) to generate a strong sense of community through the high degree of personal interaction possible among its members. This would be enhanced by ethnic, cultural and linguistic homogeneity within the society, especially where this led to the development of a strong sense of national identity, which has often legitimised an interventionist State. Alternatively, even a deeply divided society might be united in the face of an external threat, in the form of larger neighbouring powers with suspected imperialistic designs. This fear might be real enough to induce sectional leaders to tolerate and promote a highly regulated framework of interest reconciliation, to prevent centrifugal pressures from threatening the integrity of the State.[32]

In systemic terms, the degree of consensus required by Brus's model presupposes that the pattern of property ownership should not produce irreconcilable division of socioeconomic interests. This would appear to require either equality of private ownership, or a form of communal ownership. As we have already seen, however, the rights implied in private ownership (whether the individual or group type) necessarily lead to cumulative inequality and non-work incomes, since the State cannot legitimately intervene to control and redistribute investment resources. Communal ownership entails the 'right not to be excluded from the use or benefit' of the means of production.[33] The question is whether Brus's model can satisfy the criterion of this form of ownership.

The model is similar to the self-management model insofar as it posits a right for all members of society not to be excluded from access to the means of production; but it differs from the self-management model in that workers' property rights in the enterprise in which they work are limited by correspondingly greater rights of the State, particularly in the field of investment, and in controlling the rules by which workers' personal incomes are to be formed from enterprise income. The operation of the market is limited by the State's powers of regulation in such a way as to maximise equality of opportunity. Income inequality is related to differential results of work realised on a market which is regulated by the State according to a concept of the 'social interest' embodied in economic policy covering investment, prices and incomes. The possibility that inequality may become cumulative is counteracted by the State's right to control the use of, or to remove resources from the enterprise for investment purposes; by the existence of a statutory incomes policy; and by a high degree of provision for collective consumption of goods and services necessary to maintain equality of opportunity (health, welfare and education). Incomes are thus derived from two sources – from work, and from redistribution by the State, as a share in socially-owned property.

To this extent, property in Brus's model would appear to be 'communal' in character, and as such, is likely to be supportive of social consensus.

There is thus a certain circularity in Brus's model. For the degree of State intervention which it implies to be compatible with democracy, there must be a high degree of social consensus. Such consensus requires a highly egalitarian property and distribution system – for which the model also provides. On the other hand, if the State is not subject to democratic control, the whole logical chain of connections breaks down, since the State's claim to represent the 'social interest' cannot then be legitimate. In this case, the means of production cannot be said to be 'socially owned', and the position of workers, their freedom, is as restricted as under full central planning of the *étatiste* type. The pluralism of decision-making by relatively autonomous enterprises becomes a sham – they are not 'free' in their relations with the market, but manipulated. Democracy, Brus therefore argues, is a 'necessary' element in the model. But here what is meant by 'necessary' is logical, definitional necessity – it is necessary, for the model to be described as 'socialist', that it incorporate political democracy. But Brus also wishes to argue that democracy is an 'objective' necessity. This implies something different: that in practice the model is practically unworkable without democracy.

An argument for the objective necessity of democracy in this model would have to show that without it, the behaviour of individuals, groups and the State itself would be radically different, and in particular that they would act significantly less rationally in economic terms. It would appear to be possible to demonstrate quite convincingly the economic advantages of democracy in this model; however, it cannot be shown that the economic losses incurred by a non-democratic variant of the model would be sufficient to render the model wholly unworkable.

First, we have seen in Chapter 1 that Brus argues that democracy has a significant impact on motivation, and that this may have clear economic advantages.[34] But he does not demonstrate that without democracy at either the level of the enterprise or of the State, the model would cease to function. It seems possible that the motivational advantages might be forgone without systemic collapse. The system would simply not be maximising its full potential – a fairly common state of affairs in the real world.

Further arguments put forward by Brus are similarly ultimately inconclusive. Without the check of open, competitive politics, it is certainly possible, even likely, that less competent and able people will be appointed to key positions in the State, since, if not crude favouritism, at least patronage will hold sway.[35] However, democracy itself cannot be a watertight guarantee that the most able will in fact hold power – by definition there can be no requirement of minimum IQ, or even education and qualification for holding elective office. The possibility of incompetents coming to power cannot be ruled out. Their tenure on office, however, may be less secure.

It follows from this that the problem of democratic control over the process of planning remains. As Hayek pointed out, planning necessarily requires the use of experts, who, by virtue of their own expertise and the amateur status of politicians in a democracy, are in a position to exercise great influence over the entire process of defining the 'social interest'.

There is an assumption in Brus's argument that the broad objectives of policy will be accessible to the non-expert but educated and informed politician; and that a democratic framework will bring forth coherent variants of plan and policy for discussion.[36] This does not seem an unreasonable argument. It does assume that the electorate will tend to favour the educated and informed candidate over a populistic demagogue. It also assumes that there will be more than one centre of planning – possibly universities might be commissioned to put forward rival plans to those produced by the State Planning Board. Neither of these assumptions would appear to be infeasible.

It is furthermore worth noting that Hayek's depiction of planning as 'rule by experts' is not accurate when applied, for example, to Soviet practice itself. The undisputed centres of power are the General Secretary, the Central Committee Secretariat and the Politburo of the Party. The majority of men who have occupied these posts have not been 'experts' themselves, but have evolved a highly effective set of means of maintaining political control over the experts, chiefly through the system of *nomenklatura*. Thus the Planning Commission, while itself a very powerful institution, is nevertheless subordinate to the Party. This would appear to demonstrate, in contradiction to Hayek, that experts and planners *can* be brought under political control. However, on the other hand, one may have justifiable doubts as to whether a democratic political system could evolve a similarly effective means of supervising its planners.

A third line of argument in favour of democracy in the model points to the danger of suppression of valid criticism where there are no guaranteed rights to free expression, publication and discussion. Democratic debate, discussion and criticism of the State can provide an effective check on 'voluntarism' or wishful thinking in the plan and economic policy.[37] It is not only that without free discussion and the observance of democratic procedure in policy-making, the legitimacy of the State's claim to represent the 'social interest' is undermined, but that this may lead it to produce *bad policies*. The example of Poland under the Gierek regime springs readily to mind.[38] However, at the same time, it cannot be completely ruled out in principle that a regime of 'enlightened absolutism' could construct a rational and coherent plan and economic policy. This could not legitimately be described as being in the 'social interest' in the absence of democracy, but this need not in itself affect the economic rationality of the model. All one can argue is that, on balance, a democratic regime is less likely to produce an economic catastrophe than is a self-appointed élite.

A further argument which is relevant to the case concerns the impartiality of the State and the role of sectional interests. It can be argued that, without democracy, the ability of the State to act impartially must be impaired, and that this is likely to reduce economic rationality substantially.

The model concentrates control over substantial economic resources in the hands of the State. This must make the State the focus of very strong sectional pressures for the allocation of resources in a particular way – in the interests of particular sectional groups, which inevitably will present their claims in terms of the 'social interest'. If the State is not sufficiently strong or independent to resist certain sectional pressures, or if political leaders are in fact merely representatives of some (the most powerful) interests in society, then the result in the plan and economic policy might be the sacrifice of overall economic rationality in social terms to the protection of partial vested interests.

Hayek fears that precisely this would be the case – any definition of the 'social interest' in substantive terms will be a mere façade concealing sectional self-interest. Moreover, in his opinion democracy is more likely than non-democratic regimes to lead to such irrational bias. But Hayek assumes that his own 'Leviathan' could be impartial without democracy, merely by virtue of its being limited in scope – which, as we have already argued, is a highly problematic position. On the other hand, it can be argued that it is precisely democracy which can provide the way out. The ability of the State to resist sectional pressures must be enhanced by the relative openness of group activity in a democratic context. Open debate and public criticism, on the one hand, serve to expose spurious claims by sectional interests to represent the 'social interest'. On the other hand, the state's authority, its ability to override sectional pressures in the interests of overall rationality, of the pursuit of the 'social interest', would be strengthened by its democratic credentials, which enable it to claim legitimately that its definition of the 'social interest' must prevail.

Of course, democracy is not fail-safe – under certain conditions a democratic political framework might produce irrationality. Democratic theory does not necessarily assume that politicians are motivated by the disinterested pursuit of the common good; but it does assume that electoral politics leads politicians to play a role of aggregating and harmonising diverse interests.[39] This in turn assumes what we have already argued to be necessary conditions for democracy to work – that political resources are dispersed, and dispersed fairly equally through society; and that the diverse interests in society are predisposed, by an underlying social consensus, to bargain, accommodate and compromise. However, where interest conflicts are irreconcilable, where there is cumulation rather than dispersal of political resources and inequality, politicians may well turn to the exploitation of differences, and the pursuit of a sectional line in policy-making.[40]

Again, our conclusion on this point cannot be clear-cut. There is no reason to hold, as Hayek does, that democracy will be *more* vulnerable than non-democratic regimes to sectional bias; democracy provides significant checks against this; but under certain adverse circumstances, even a democratic regime cannot guarantee that a plan and economic policy will be rational in terms of the 'social interest'. The biggest problem for empirically-based argument on this question is that most democracies in practice are, for most of the time, operating under less than ideal circumstances.

Moreover, ultimately Brus's model cannot guarantee the ideal circumstances required for it to work both rationally and democratically. It does indeed provide the possibility of assuring a high degree of socioeconomic equality which will promote consensus, but it does not on the other hand guarantee it: there are, after all, other sources of conflict than socioeconomic inequality – for example, value conflict on religious or national grounds. While the origins of such conflicts can usually be traced back historically to socioeconomic inequality and exploitation, they do not necessarily melt away with the equalisation of society. Value conflict cannot ultimately be reduced to conflicts of material interest. Where a society is deeply divided along religious or national lines, Brus's model might only be workable *in the absence of* democracy in the State. While the model is in principle certainly not incompatible with democracy, it is not necessarily democratic. While the assumption of a high degree of consensus which it embodies is not in principle wholly unrealistic, in practice, the circumstances in which the model might be realised, as both rational *and* democratic, are likely to be exceptional.

D THE DYNAMIC PERSPECTIVE – MARKETISATION, PLURALISATION AND DEMOCRACY

In the preceding three sections we have examined in a theoretical way the political implications of the respective models of socialism from what might be described as a 'static' perspective, by identifying the internal logic of the given model. In this final section of the chapter, we will relate the conclusions derived from this approach to a 'dynamic' context – of change from one model to another – specifically, in the context of the introduction of market-type reform into a centrally planned economy.

We have seen how the monolithic definition of the 'social interest' inherent in the centrally planned model necessarily produces a political system which is totalitarian, in the sense of denying the legitimacy of group and individual autonomy, or relegating them to a position of secondary, residual importance, permitted to exist only within a framework which is controlled and dominated by the superior 'social interest'. An economic system based on these assumptions is only compatible with freedom and democracy where the society is characterised by absolute consensus. Since such consensus is practically unobtainable, the model has always been accompanied politically by a high degree of coercion exercised by a single Party. The legitimation of the model as based on the 'social interest' rather than the interests of the self-appointed party is derived from the Party's assertion that it possesses 'objectively correct' knowledge. Democracy as a means of defining the 'social interest' on the basis of individual and group participation is ruled out as superfluous, or even possibly counter-productive, since individual and group perceptions are necessarily of a lower order and subject to 'bias'. Coercion is redefined as 'freedom', since coercion is held to be necessary to the realisation of the 'true' interests of groups and individuals.[41]

The introduction of market-type economic reform, whether of the self-management or regulated market variety, necessarily challenges the totalitarian political framework of the centrally planned system in a fundamental way, since it requires recognition of group and individual interests as both 'objectively necessary' and legitimate. Market-type reform thus requires a fundamental revision of the Party's legitimation doctrine, since it is not compatible with the requirements of market models that the 'social interest' be understood as all-embracing and monolithic, standing above individual and group interests and enjoying a *a priori* superiority over them. It thus requires the definition of the limits of the role of the State, and the acceptance of a degree of pluralism.[42] But does it imply the necessity of democracy in the State itself? The answer is clearly no – we have already seen that neither the self-management nor the regulated market model requires democracy at the level of the State. Both are logically compatible with either a democratic, or a non-democratic (single party) regime.

The central point is to avoid the confusion of 'pluralisation' with 'democratisation'. 'Pluralisation' should be regarded as a quantitative measure, rather than as a qualitative, systemic characteristic of a political system. 'Democracy' is such a qualitative characteristic, referring not to the existence of separate group and individual interests, but to the context in which they emerge and the manner of their reconciliation. 'Democratisation' as a process can only refer to improvement in the operation of already existing political guarantees embedded in democratic institutions. The transition from a non-democratic to a democratic regime cannot be achieved simply by moving along the quantitative axis of pluralisation, but requires a leap, a 'transformation of quantity into quality', in the form of a political revolution, establishing institutional guarantees of basic rights and freedoms for individuals and groups. The lists of such guarantees is familiar: freedom of association, of alternative sources of information, and of expression; the right to vote in free and fair elections; the right to stand for election, to compete for political support; and the periodic repetition of elections.[43]

'Pluralism' and 'democracy' are thus logically separate. A democratic regime may be more or less pluralistic: it may even, as in Rousseau's individualistic–participatory model, be non-pluralistic, in the sense that Rousseau rejects the legitimacy of organised groups as participants in the process of defining the 'General Will'. On the other hand, non-democratic regimes need not necessarily be totalitarian. Indeed, the pure model of totalitarianism has long been recognised as inadequate to the understanding of the realities of politics in communist one-party states. As an ideal type, it has never existed except as an aspiration – as indeed, neither has pure pluralism. Communist regimes have been categorised along a continuum of pluralisation by H. G. Skilling, who identifies 'quasi-totalitarian', 'consultative authoritarian', and 'democratising and pluralistic authoritarian' variants of single party rule,[44] none of which can properly be regarded as democratic. The latter stage, however, is inherently unstable, and describes a revolutionary situation, being the point at which the quantitative degree of pluralisation provokes systemic crisis by putting the establishment of democratic institutions on the agenda.

In identifying the political implications of market-type reform of centrally planned socialism of the Soviet type, we need to distinguish between political change as spontaneous, evolutionary and incremental adaptation, and conscious and active remodelling of a system such as takes place in revolution. Whether marketisation leads to revolution will depend not on the 'objective requirements' of the reform model itself so much as the 'subjective' element in the particular historical context, including the willingness of the Party leadership to undertake reform and the adaptation which it requires. This is not to suggest that marketisation will not be a politically-fraught process; nor that marketisation without democraticisation can be introduced without some costs in terms of efficiency. But it is implied here that marketisation is possible without the collapse of one-party rule and democratic revolution; and that the costs of avoiding democratic political transformation need not be intolerably high.

The aim of Part I of this book has been to elaborate in abstract theoretical terms the nature of the underlying problems of socialism, economic rationality, freedom and democracy. Part II involves a comparative study of two cases of market-type reform, in Czechoslovakia and Hungary. These two countries have been selected for the similarity of their starting-point as socialist systems based on the centrally-planned model; for the similarity of their initial choice of reform model, of a regulated market type; and for the contrasting political developments they experienced – Czechoslovakia undergoing an 'interrupted revolution' in 1968, Hungary developing through the 1970s, not without conflict, but without systemic political crisis of the revolutionary kind. The aim of the comparative empirical study is to demonstrate how these cases illustrate the theoretical points presented in Part I.

First, in Chapter 3, we will look at the political starting-points of reform – the respective contexts into which economic reform was introduced. This background material will highlight the extent to which the differing patterns of political change which took place alongside economic reform were products of a particular, unique historical context, rather than of the functional requirements of the economic reform itself. Chapter 4 focuses on the immediate political circumstances in which the decision to undertake reform was made in the respective countries. The major contrast to emerge is between the unity of the Kádár leadership, and its positive commitment to a coherent model of economic reform, and the political disarray of the Czechoslovak leadership, divided on many issues including the real meaning of reform. In Chapter 5, we return to the theoretical issues raised in Part I. The chapter traces the development of reform thought in Hungary and Czechoslovakia. In both countries, intellectuals were aware of the political implications of the economic reform as a reconceptualisation of the 'social interest', but in Hungary public discussion of political reform as a necessary concomitant of economic reform was stifled, while in Czechoslovakia the blossoming of sociology and political science promoted a much more far-reaching examination of the economic reform's social and political ramifications. In Chapter 6, we describe the political circumstances in Czechoslovakia which allowed economic reform to become a component part of a political movement of the intelligentsia driving towards 'democratisation' – the legitimation of pluralism and its incorporation, via political reform, into the institutions of the political system. The 'politicisation' of the economic reform in Czechoslovakia, the chapter argues, was not a product of the 'objective' requirements of economic reform in practice, since very little of it was ever implemented. It was rather a product of the peculiar nature of the Novotný regime, which alienated a large part of the intelligentsia and thus focused attention on the need for systemic political change not merely as a functional prerequisite of economic reform, but as an absolute good in itself. When we turn to Hungary in Chapter 7, we see a contrasting picture of economic reform introduced without either radical reform of the political system or political crisis as occurred in Czechoslovakia. The question raised by the Hungarian experience is, however, whether this 'depoliticised' reform, avoiding political change as far as possible, did not require compromises in the consistency of its implementation which eventually were to threaten the effectiveness of the whole endeavour.

Part II

The Politics of Reform in Czechoslovakia and Hungary

Part II

The Politics of Reform in Czechoslovakia and Hungary

3 The Political Preconditions of Reform

A THE ORIGINS OF THE COMMUNIST REGIME

The social, economic and political histories of Czechoslovakia and Hungary prior to the Second World War show striking long-term contrasts which were to have significant formative impact on their respective Communist Parties. These contrasts persisted under the surface of the enforced uniformity of their political and economic organisational patterns, which followed the establishment of communist single-party regimes in 1948. Both countries inherited strong nationalist traditions from their experiences under the Habsburg empire, but the Czechs, the dominant nation in the new Czechoslovak Republic which came into existence in 1918 after the collapse of the empire, combined their nationalism with a commitment to democracy and also, on the part of the majority, to socialistic ideologies. In Hungary, however, the development of democratic institutions took second place to the achievement of Magyar autonomy; in the wake of the 1919 communist revolution socialism, which never won majority support, was rejected as an alien creed, hostile to the national cause.

Behind this divergence lay contrasting social structures and levels of economic development. The Czechs and Slovaks were nations whose aristocracies had been wiped out in the course of establishing Habsburg and Magyar domination over their respective territories. Furthermore, the Czech provinces were the most highly developed industrial areas of the empire: a substantial proportion of the Czech nation consisted of the industrial workforce of largely German-owned factories. Class and national conflicts to a considerable degree overlapped.[1] The roots of social democracy in the nation were to be found in this established working class which already in 1848 was a major political actor, and later in the nineteenth century gained significant trade union experience. The Social Democratic party (SDP), founded in 1878, was the oldest organised political force of the Czech nation, and after 1896 gained experience of electoral and parliamentary politics. With the achievement of the universal franchise in 1907, the SDP won twenty-four seats in the Austrian Parliament, and, with a mass membership of 130 000, it had become the largest and strongest Czech party, closely associated with the national cause.[2] A non-Marxist socialist party existed, the National Socialists, drawing support mainly from middle-class professionals and bureaucrats, which was weaker in numerical terms but disproportionately influential in national life by virtue of the support of Tomáš Masaryk, founder-President of the First Republic, and the Party's joint leader, Edvard Beneš, Foreign Minister in the Republic and later President, succeeding Masaryk in 1935.

When the First Republic was established, it took with it two-thirds of the old empire's industry, but only one-quarter of its population and one-fifth of its land area.[3] Socially relatively egalitarian and economically advanced (with the exception of Slovakia which had been preserved in a state of rural stagnation under Magyar rule), the politics of the Republic were democratic in form and progressive, social-reformist in policy orientation.[4] In the first elections to the National Assembly in 1920, the SDP emerged as by far the strongest party, winning seventy-four of the 281 seats on the basis of 25.6 per cent of the popular vote.[5] From 1919 to 1920 a Social Democrat Prime Minister led the multi-party coalition government, and the party remained a member of the government coalitions throughout the duration of the Republic.

The foundation of the Czechoslovak Communist Party (CPCS) was not, as elsewhere in the region, a direct result of Soviet/Comintern initiative, but to a large extent reflected internal developments. Frustration of a large part of the mass party with the limitations on the scope and pace of social reform within the framework of SDP participation in the government, combined with admiration for Soviet Russia, was exploited by the leftist group of deputies, led by Bohumír Šmeral, and produced a split in the SDP. The Communist Party, officially founded as an affiliate of the Comintern in October 1921,[6] took a majority of the SDP support. At the 1925 general election, the Communist Party won forty-one seats as against the SDP's twenty-nine.

Despite commitment to the Comintern, in the period 1921–9 under Šmeral's leadership, the CPCS continued a somewhat independent course, resisting Comintern directives where these were seen as inappropriate to Czechoslovak conditions.[7] It remained a mass movement rather than following the Leninist pattern; and Šmeral opposed the 1924 Comintern line on national self-determination, which he saw as implying the dismemberment of the Czechoslovak state by the secession of Slovak, German and Hungarian minorities. This line alienated a certain amount of Czech working-class support, while increasing the Party's appeal to the national minorities.

Division within the Party over these issues led in 1929 to the replacement of the old leadership, tainted by their social democratic origins, by Klement Gottwald, Moscow's preferred candidate. A purge followed in an attempt to bring the Party more into line with the Leninist concept, which reduced the membership from 100 000 to 24 000 by April 1929, recovering somewhat to 39 000 by the end of that year.[8] It also lost electoral support, winning only thirty seats in the 1929 general election.[9]

The combined impact of economic crisis, the rise of Hitler, and the new Comintern 'Popular Front' strategy benefited the Party's popular support. Communists were able once again to identify themselves with the Republic, and in 1935 offered support to President Beneš. The Nazi–Soviet pact, however, was a catastrophic blow to the Party's image, since it required communists to defend the Munich agreement. But the pact was short-lived, and the situation was retrieved after 1941 when the communists participated in the resistance and again turned to defend the Republic in its 1918 borders.

Hungarian experience contrasts with that of Czechoslovakia in almost all respects. The social structure of Hungary, preserved virtually intact until the Second World War, was that of a markedly backward agrarian society on the European 'periphery',[10] with strong feudalistic elements surviving. According to the Hungarian census of 1941, only 25 per cent of the labour force was employed in industry or mining. Moreover, in 1938, almost half those employed in industry were in handicrafts. The largest proportion of the population – 48 per cent in 1941 – was employed in agriculture; the vast bulk of these were peasants farming very small holdings and ruthlessly exploited by the surviving Magyar aristocratic landowners.[11] The 1935 Agricultural Census reveals that 0.8 per cent of landholders owned 46.4 per cent of agricultural land, while 76.1 per cent owned 12 per cent.[12]

Such a social structure provided a far narrower base than did Czechoslovakia for socialist, let alone communist, ideology, and this was further eroded by the impact of the 1919 'Soviet' revolution, led by Béla Kun, which provoked a strong negative reaction. The succeeding Horthy regime repressed the communists vigorously, and in this, it seems likely that it was in large measure supported by the majority of the population. The Kun regime, while drawing some support from the small Hungarian urban proletariat, 'was deeply pessimistic about the ability of the masses to see their own enlightened self-interest and to take a "correct" position at every turn of history',[13] and thus took the form of an élite minority dictatorship, exercising power in a highly repressive, even terroristic fashion. Its leaders and followers exhibited a profound contempt for the peasantry – the vast majority of the people – and earned the peasants' enduring mistrust through their commitment to the socialisation of the land. Furthermore, the regime's followers, 'as revolutionary purists ... remained not only true to their internationalist persuasion, but went out of their way to offend national sentiment'.[14] The result of this was to produce a widespread popular perception of socialism as alien and hostile to national identity.

In both the Habsburg and inter-war periods, we see in Hungary a pattern of politics characterised as '*étatiste* authoritarian regimes with a constitutional facade'.[15] Inter-war politics was marked by 'a good deal of violence and arbitrary action',[16] on the part of both the Kun and the Horthy regimes. The latter was not so much a dictatorship, however, as 'a semi-democracy or diluted dictatorship'.[17] There was an elected Parliament, albeit of limited effectiveness, dominated by a 'government party' and based on a highly restrictive franchise and with open balloting in rural areas.[18] Trade unions existed but their actions were tightly circumscribed. There was, on the other hand, a relatively free press, and a general commitment to legality on the part of the élite, despite the inefficiency, arbitrariness, and corruption of the bureaucracy.

The combination of popular and governmental reaction against the 1919 'Soviet' experience, and the characteristics of the basic social structure, naturally had a profound impact on the development of Hungarian communism. Isolated and fragmented in the underground, its leading members imprisoned or forced to live abroad, mainly in the Soviet Union, it rapidly lost touch with the day-to-day reality of the life of the country. Radical and progressive thought turned rather into populist channels, reflecting the plight of the peasants as the central social problem, rather than finding much sense in the Marxist-inspired analyses.[19] The conditions in which it worked in its early years made Hungarian communism into a movement characterised by conspiratorial methods and a tendency to extremism in ideology. It has been argued that this tendency, inherent in the external conditions within which it operated, was enhanced by the internal composition of the leadership itself, many of whom were of Jewish origin. The larger

Jewish population provided the bulk not only of industrial entrepreneurs, but also of intellectuals from the late nineteenth century onwards. Ferenc Fejtő attributes the 'sectarian, mystical and inquisitorial character' of Hungarian communism to its Jewish component,[20] which includes Mátyás Rákosi, the Party leader appointed by Moscow in 1940 after Kun's execution in the Stalinist purges in 1939; Révai, a brilliant intellectual, later to dominate cultural affairs in the Stalinist period; Tibor Szamuely, Béla Kun's 'Cheka' head, and Gábor Péter, the police chief in the Stalinist period in Hungary. Jews were also later to play a leading role in the violent reaction to Stalinism in the 1950s. Whatever weight one attributes to the ethnic factor as compared with the historical and social factors shaping the movement, there can be no doubt that the 'flavour' of Hungarian communism was distinctively different from the Czechoslovak variant, based on a legal, mass party, operating in the inter-war period, within the framework of a liberal democratic regime. Soviet-type communism was the creed of a tiny minority in Hungary and was perceived by the society as 'alien'.

From the end of the Second World War, we see a trend towards ever-closer convergence of the historical experiences of these two very different countries, as their Communist Parties moved into the centre of the political stage. It appears that at the end of the war Czechoslovakia and Hungary shared a common position in Stalin's strategic security objectives, which sets them apart from Poland, Romania and Bulgaria, where politics was quite quickly brought under direct Soviet control.[21] Possibly desiring to deflect mounting Western alarm at Soviet actions in these countries (particularly in Poland), Stalin appeared content to allow free elections in Hungary in November 1945 and in Czechoslovakia in May 1946. Communists were to be held back, and a longer time-scale for establishing a power monopoly – fifteen to twenty years – was envisaged in these countries.[22] In the meantime, they were to participate in relatively open and democratic coalition governments, winning power through the ballot-box, and sharing it with Social Democratic, reformed middle-class, Catholic and peasant parties.

In Czechoslovakia, the immediate post-war years saw an astonishing resurgence of support for the Communist Party, whose membership rose to over one million by 1946. In the May election, the Party emerged as by far the strongest political force, winning 38 per cent of the popular vote – 'a stunning electoral victory that remains a record for a communist party in twentieth-century Europe'.[23] Party membership continued to expand rapidly, to more than two million by the end of 1948, thus including about one-third of the economically active population.[24] The reasons for this are many – the underlying socialistic political culture was reinforced by pro-Soviet sentiment, enhanced by gratitude for liberation. In addition, there was, at the end of the war, a widespread, genuine desire for radical reform. There was profound disappointment at the failure of the First Republic, which tainted the reputation of the other parties. The espousal of a 'national road to socialism' by the CPCS once again linked socialism to Czechoslovak democratic and nationalist traditions. The Party launched a vigorous recruitment drive to expand its basis of support, and successfully drew upon opportunist motives on the part of many new recruits, anxious for career promotion in the new Republic.[25]

By contrast, in Hungary, the coalition strategy proved less successful in bringing about immediate political gains for the communists. Party membership indeed grew rapidly, from 3000 in November 1944 to 500 000 (5.7 per cent of the population) in October 1945.[26] However, much of their support came not from genuine converts to the cause, but from opportunists, including defectors from the fascist Arrow Cross rank-and-file. Working-class support went rather to the Social Democrats, especially in Budapest. But the vast bulk of popular support went to the Smallholders Party, a 'catch-all' party attracting support from both rural and urban areas, from middle peasants to urban professionals and the rump of the conservative gentry. Poor peasant interests were represented by the National Peasant Party. The November 1945 elections, generally regarded as having been freely conducted, produced the following result:[27]

Smallholders Party	57.03%
Social Democrats	17.41%
Communist Party	16.95%
National Peasants	6.87%
Others	1.74%

The Smallholders came first in every electoral district in the country, and won an absolute majority in thirteen out of the sixteen electoral districts.[28] Communism was clearly not going to be offered power through the ballot-box, which was no surprise in view of Hungary's past, but the failure of this approach gave strength to a militantly radical Party faction, including some 'home' communists of the wartime resistance, who had always entertained doubts about the wisdom of the 'Muscovite' leadership's strategy of gradualism.[29]

1947 was a turning-point for Czechoslovakia and Hungary, a year in which the illusion of a possible 'third way' of relative independence, sustained through an East–West balancing act, gradually evaporated. As the Cold War began, the 'gradualist' strategy broke down, and the real hold which the Soviet Union had over Czechoslovakia and Hungary emerged clearly. The Czechoslovak government, with Gottwald as its Prime Minister, unanimously agreed to accept Marshall Aid – but then, summoned to Moscow, it was forced to retract.[30] The last basically free election in Hungary took place in August 1947. Despite two years of communist effort to improve their support, and intense, only partly concealed pressure on voters, the communists still only polled 22 per cent of the vote. Meanwhile, Czechoslovak communists were beginning to entertain doubts about their ability to sustain their electoral support at the general election due in 1948, as the economic situation deteriorated, and a poor harvest in 1947 made food shortages likely.

The signal for a change of course came from outside, however, with the foundation of the Cominform in September. At the first meeting, Czechoslovakia came under attack, as the only East European country which had not achieved 'complete victory over the bourgeoisie'; and the exclusion of the French and Italian Communist Parties from power in their respective governments was seen as a product of 'parliamentary cretinism', a handicap from which, by implication, the Czechoslovak party also suffered.[31] The message which the parties took home with them from Sklarska Poreba was clear.

Increasing tensions were provoked within the Czechoslovak coalition in late 1947 by communist tactics in Slovakia, in the ministries, and especially in the police. A government crisis was fomented by the Party leadership, and the non-communist politicians unwittingly played into Gottwald's hands. In February 1948, representatives of the non-communist parties in the government resigned *en masse*, unaware that Gottwald had already prepared an alternative government team, including suborned crypto-communist members of the non-communist parties themselves. Mass pressure was mobilised by extra-constitutional bodies dominated by the Communists (the trade unions and the People's Militia), and President Beneš felt unable to refuse his approval of the new Gottwald government, now effectively wholly controlled by the communists. Thus a veneer of legality was spread over what amounted to a bloodless *coup d'état*, an 'elegant takeover' indeed, as it has been described.[32] The elections of May 1948 were conducted on the basis of a single list, as an enforced vote of mass approbation of the *fait accompli*. The Social Democratic Party disappeared through its manipulated merger with the Communist Party.

In Hungary, such elegance could not be repeated. Rakosi stepped up his notorious 'salami tactics', slicing away his opposition, undermining and fragmenting the Smallholders, and, through a process of electoral fraud, covert coercion, bribery, blackmail and threat, his tactics eventually subverted the National Peasant Party and forced the Social Democrats to merge with the Communists in a 'new' Hungarian Workers' Party in 1948. 'Elections' in May 1949 gave a spurious constitutional seal to the communist monopoly of power.[33] The Soviet Union – in contrast to Czechoslovakia – played a large part in the process, through the presence of the Red Army, the Soviet domination of the Allied Control Commission, and the Soviet Ambassador in Budapest.[34]

B STALINISATION

(i) Economics

The state of the Hungarian economy at the end of the war presents a stark contrast with Czechoslovakia. As noted above, the overall level of development of Hungary was far below that of Czechoslovakia in the inter-war period. In both countries, however, intensive development of the economy to meet war needs took place. The Czechoslovak engineering industry became a major source of armaments production for the Nazi war-machine. Unlike Czechoslovakia, Hungarian industry suffered extensive war damage, as the final battles of the war in Europe were fought out over Hungarian soil. Of the 4863 factories in existence in 1944, 651 were completely destroyed, and 3864 were damaged. The loss of industrial capacity is estimated at around one-third.[35]

After 1947, post-war recovery and reconstruction in Czechoslovakia and Hungary[35] were organised by two- and three-year plans respectively, which did not envisage major structural changes in the economy, but which greatly increased the share of the national income going to investment. As part of its recovery programme, the Czechoslovak government had initially agreed to accept Marshall Aid. Economic policy here was based on the assumption of continued and expanded participation in the world economy, trading with East and West in roughly equal proportions.[36] Planning in both countries was flexible, based on enterprise decision-making autonomy, rather than the breakdown of detailed compulsory directives by the Planning Office. In Czechoslovakia, enterprise management was 'democratised' through the elected workers' councils. Direct state control over the economy was also limited by continuing private ownership.[37] In Hungary after 1945, only 40 per cent of the industrial labour force was employed in state-owned factories, while in Czechoslovakia, the 1945 nationalisation law brought nearly 60 per cent of industrial workers into the state sector.[38] Nationalisation affected mainly those factories already owned by the state before 1945 (a large proportion in both countries), with the addition of enterprises expropriated from collaborationists. In Czechoslovakia, private banking was virtually eliminated immediately after liberation.[39]

By the end of the period, with the onset of the Cold War, nationalisation began to accelerate. In Czechoslovakia, even before the 1948 coup, nationalisation continued, but after the coup it expanded to bring virtually all workers into the state sector, leaving the private sector with only 3.6 per cent of total industrial employment. In Hungary, in the spring of 1948, a new nationalised banking system was set up, and firms with over 100 employees were nationalised, bringing 84 per cent of workers in manufacturing, mining and transport into state employment. In December 1949, nationalisation was extended to firms of over ten employees, and the corresponding proportion of workers in state employment rose to 99 per cent.

In agriculture, the policy of the immediate post-war coalitions in both countries was land reform, which all parties agreed was necessary. In Hungary, the communists controlled the process of reallocation of expropriated estates, with the political aim of winning the support of small peasants. The consequence was a proliferation of very small plots of land, many hardly adequate even for self-sufficiency. The problem of land hunger was thus not solved, and clearly this first phase of land reform would have to be supplemented by further measures. At this stage, collectivisation was not on the agenda. Neither was it in Czechoslovakia, where the expropriation of German and Hungarian estates released 3.1 million hectares of agricultural land – 36.5 per cent of agricultural land in Bohemia and Moravia, 11.4 per cent in Slovakia. Large Czech and Slovak landholdings were not expropriated at this stage.[40]

However, after the communist monopoly of power was established, a radical change in economic organisation took place, with the imposition of new five-year 'development plans' of a command type as the main instrument of management of industry, which was by now almost totally nationalised. The balanced emphasis of the recovery plans was abandoned in favour of an accelerated programme of industrialisation, based on the priority of heavy industry, closely following the Soviet pattern. Collectivisation of agriculture was now in first place on the agenda for agriculture. The main features of the programme will be familiar to any student of Stalinist economics. The share of industry in investment rose dramatically, and the bulk of investment funds went to heavy industry. As a Czechoslovak government memorandum on the development plan explained:

> The centre of the whole plan is the *metal-working industry* ... and again the entire plan is focused on the *heavy engineering sector* within the metal-working industry ... Stalin's reference to the 'chief link' of the economic plan applies in this context: 'In order to carry out such a plan it is necessary to find its main link; for only after this main link has been found and grasped, can all the other links in the plan be pulled up.'[41]

In Hungary at the same time, Ernő Gerő proclaimed that Hungary was to be 'transformed into a country of steel and iron'.

Table 3.1 Planned increase in gross value of output of key industrial branches under the first Five Year Plans*

	Total industry	*Producers' goods*	*Metal-working*	*Machine-building*	*Consumers' goods*
Czechoslovakia	198	233	231	352	173
Hungary	310	380	490	n.a.	245

*Pre-plan year = 100 (Czechoslovakia – 1948; Hungary – 1949)
Source: N. Spulber, *The Economics of Communist Eastern Europe*, p. 288.

The already ambitious targets of the five-year plans (see Table 3.1) embarked upon in 1949 (Czechoslovakia) and 1950 (Hungary) were substantially raised to extraordinary levels in 1951 in connection with the Korean war and the expectation of a Third World War:

> The revisions of 1950–51 sometimes made all the difference between an ambitious, difficult but not entirely unbalanced plan and a super-taut program relentlessly concentrated on some high priority

targets without a chance to attain overall equilibrium and, particularly, to meet the (formally kept) objectives with regard to the standard of living of the population.[42]

Although the underlying rationale of this programme of forced industrialisation was undoubtedly political, the choice of the Soviet model can be argued to have made some sense in the context of the economic backwardness of Hungary. This point is maintained by Hungarian authors even today, including O. Gadó (Vice-chairman of the National Planning Office),[43] and the reformist economic historian, Iván Berend, who notes that, at the time, the Soviet model was the only available 'proven' system for rapid development of a backward economy and that, in its application in Hungary, it 'made possible the realisation of development projects that could not have been realised in any other way'.[44] It served purposes which, he argues, were important at the time – the accumulation of capital, the concentration of material resources, reducing the effect of the materials and energy shortage caused by Western embargoes. The lack of trained and competent managerial personnel has also been argued to be a factor in favour of the highly centralised, directive model adopted.

In Czechoslovakia, already an industrialised economy, the model was wholly inappropriate, and represented 'a great leap backward'. What it entailed was an irrational restructuring of the economy, skewing it in favour of heavy engineering to meet immediate Soviet demands, and cutting it off from Western markets, from which Czechoslovakia might have continued to acquire the technology to maintain its place as a leading industrial producer. Furthermore, Czechoslovakia did not lack managerial talent – this was available in abundance, but was destroyed in the course of imposition of the Soviet model by the purging of former technocrats and their replacement by 350 000 'workers' cadres':

> The Communist Party of Czechoslovakia leadership quite deliberately forfeited the economic potential of the middle classes; instead of making them a part of the new system, it virtually eliminated them.[45]

The emphasis on metallurgy was quite inappropriate in a small country lacking the necessary raw materials base. In the short term, however, Czechoslovakia's preeminent position as a supplier of engineering goods to the less developed economies of the USSR and the rest of the bloc secured the country a certain advantage. The long-term problems associated with the economic structure would not become obvious until the 1960s, when the rest of the bloc caught up with Czechoslovakia, and the ready markets for its products began to dry up.[46]

Thus Czechoslovakia was able to survive on its former economic strength, which allowed it to prevent real earnings of workers in industry from falling more than 3 per cent below the 1948 level by 1953.[47] But popular discontent was by no means absent, as demonstrated soon after the deaths of Stalin and Gottwald in the spring of 1953 by a two-day riot in Pilsen on 1–2 June. The authorities lost control of the city as workers stormed the City Hall and the Palace of Justice. A considerable amount of violence took place, and the riot was only put down by troops of the Ministry of the Interior and Workers' Militia detachments sent from Prague. The local forces of order proved both unable and unwilling to take action against the workers. 2000 arrests were made, but the central authorities managed to keep information about the revolt tightly restricted. It was the first working-class revolt of the post-Stalin era, and it provided an early warning to the regime of the precariousness of its position.[48]

By 1953, Hungary had become an industrial country – but at enormous cost. While the basic system of centralised directive planning may have had some advantages in the given circumstances, the extreme tensions generated by the vastly over-ambitious economic policy of forced-pace growth created serious imbalances, to which the relatively less-developed Hungarian economy was far more vulnerable than the stronger Czechoslovak economy. The industrial policy was especially intolerable for a country as poor in natural resources as Hungary – hence the folly of aspiring to become 'a country of steel and iron' where 80 per cent of iron ore and 90 per cent of coking coal had to be imported.[49] Thus, while, on the one hand, some form of centralised directive model might have suited Hungarian conditions, the manner in which it was implemented in practice was even more intolerable in Hungary than in the more highly developed Czechoslovakia.

The tensions generated by the over-ambitious economic policy quickly made themselves manifest (see Table 3.2). In June 1951, Gerő criticised the 'intolerable' decline in quality of output, as numbers of rejects escalated rapidly. The accumulation of stocks amounted to one-fifth of the growth of national income by 1953. The government attempted to respond to growing supply difficulties by increasing regulations, data collection, paperwork. Eventually, enterprises were even required to submit reports daily to the central authorities. Correspondingly, a huge expansion in the white:blue-col-

Table 3.2 Actual and planned rates of growth of output in Hungary

	Plan: average annual rate of growth (%)	*Actual rate of growth (previous year = 100)*			
		1950	*1951*	*1951*	*1953*
Producer Goods	56	38	41	33	18
Consumer Goods	29	39	25	16	4

Per capita crop output (tons)	*1934–8*	*1948*	*1953*
Bread grain	318	256	285
Coarse grain	349	336	349
Potatoes	232	293	209

Source: N. Spulber, *The Economics of Communist Eastern Europe*, pp. 377–9.

lar ratio occurred – while in 1941 there had been nine blue-collar workers to every one white-collar, by 1953 this had shrunk to 4:1.[50] Another means tried by the government to control the threatening chaos was, of course, moral exhortation, and political pressure on workers and managers alike. An economist who was to produce the first really substantial critique of the whole system in 1954, György Péter,[51] later reflected on the atmosphere of the time:

> It seems it was not a simple mistake or a fault made by chance, but a deliberate political attitude ... It was a period of 'keying up' political and economic public opinion – of keeping sentiments always at boiling point by artificial overheating ... The slogans of those times called for constant and increased vigilance, for watchfulness and mistrust of practically everybody ... The then prevailing attitude seemed to suggest, though it was never publicly expounded, that fundamentally everybody is indifferent and lazy without exception and willing to work only if compelled to and thus can be given only such tasks as can be easily checked.[52]

If the communists had started out with little popular support, the policies they pursued hardly served to ingratiate them with any section of society. In agriculture, forced collectivisation was deeply resented, and insult was heaped on injury by the system of forced deliveries at state-fixed low prices. Agricultural production declined to below the pre-war level, and food shortages resulted. The conditions of life in the villages were especially hard-hit by the politically-inspired repression of handicrafts. The Party economic weekly in 1956 referred to this as the 'deliberate corruption of the world-famous Hungarian small-scale industry in 1949–53'. This left nearly two-thirds of villages without cartwrights, blacksmiths, shoemakers, barbers and tailors.[53] Instead of the 50 per cent rise in living standards envisaged by the plan, real wages fell by more than 20 per cent by 1953.[54] The workers developed an intense and seething hatred of the regime, which ultimately was to find expression in the almost elemental fury of the crowd which in 1956 hung communists from the lampposts. As one worker from the giant Csepel engineering works in Budapest recalled:

> The communists nationalised all the factories and similar enterprises, proclaiming the slogan, 'The factory is yours – you work for yourself'. Exactly the opposite of this was true. They promised us everything, at the same time subjugating us and pulling us down to the greatest misery conceivable.[55]

Working-class resistance was sporadic and unorganised until 1953, when a strike broke out in Csepel. But evidence of the growing resentment is given by Imre Nagy, who revealed that of the burgeoning prison population:

> the majority of those convicted have come from the ranks of the working class, the industrial workers. This, more than anything else, is evidence of the degeneration of power and economic and social conditions under which the working class is carrying on its task of socialist construction, and of the moral and ethical crisis that was brought about by these conditions.[56]

Thus the regime had allowed itself to become drawn into an escalating spiral. Isolated and mistrustful of the population, it embarked on a programme which enhanced the mistrust in which it was held by that population, which in turn confirmed its own disdain for them, and led it to resort to ever-increasing centralisation and coercion, which in turn simply exacerbated the crisis. The logic of this process was later described by József Bognár:

> a powerful bureaucracy builds up which often identifies the movements and rules of economic life with the internal norms of the state apparatus, and which looks upon itself as the most consistent representative and exponent of transformation. This layer – sometimes unintentionally – endeavours to consolidate and strengthen itself... It is therefore evident that the directive system must be made totalitarian.[57]

In fact, by 1952, well before Stalin's death, resistance to this course was building up, both within the Hungarian apparatus, and in Moscow itself. Nagy, who had been removed from a central political position in 1949 as a result of his opposition to collectivisation, was brought back into the Politburo in 1951. Nagy quickly began to criticise Rákosi's economic policy, with some encouragement probably from Malenkov, and also, Fejtő suggests, finding substantial support in the HWP (Hungarian Workers Party) Central Committee itself, and among leading party managerial cadres, support which by 1952 'had become too strong to be eliminated by police methods alone'.[58] When Stalin died in 1953, the economic situation was one of open and profound crisis. Conditions were ripe for a change of course.

(ii) Politics

The main political feature of Stalinisation was the elevation of terror to the central pivot of rule. It was the transfer of Stalin's personal paranoia on to the practice of politics. While the impetus for the purge trials which racked Eastern Europe came from Moscow via Soviet 'advisers' sent into each country to set the process in motion, in Hungary there was also, in the Party leader Mátyás Rákosi, a 'personality' of a degeneracy and ruthlessness to embrace willingly and to thrive on Stalin's own politics of paranoia. The Czechoslovak Party 'did not produce any individuals with Stalin's skill for intrigue and desire for uncontrolled power ... [N]either Gottwald nor Slánský could measure up to Stalin'.[59] But once the trials got under way in Czechoslovakia, the comrades made up for lost time: 'The Stalinist terror assumed the most appalling aspects precisely in that Central European country where it had been the least anticipated.'[60] The Czechoslovak trials were the most extensive in the bloc, in terms both of numbers prosecuted, and of death penalties carried out.[61]

A major stimulant to the East European trials was undoubtedly the bugbear of 'Titoism' after the 1948 Comintern split. In Hungary, László Rajk, a leader of the 'home' communist faction, was seized upon as a 'Titoist spy'. It was not wholly inappropriate to label Rajk as a 'Titoist', since he shared certain of Tito's radical and nationalist political postures,[62] although all the other attributes lumped together with this 'crime' by Rákosi and Stalin (i.e. 'spy', 'imperialist agent', etc.) were of course quite fanciful. This attack on Rajk enabled Rákosi to dispose conveniently of a popular leader who might have gathered an independent following within the Party. The purges subsequently extended to other 'home' communists. Rajk, Pálffy (Chief of Staff of the Army; Deputy Minister of Defence; head of Army Party Organisation; Central Committee member), Szőnyi (CC Secretary; member of the Central Control Commission) and Szalai (Szőnyi's deputy) were tried and hanged in October 1949. In the early 1950s, the purge turned to former Social Democrats who had collaborated in the merger of their party with the Communists in 1948, but who still remained suspect. The Army was purged in late 1950. In spring 1951, more 'home' communists of the pre-war generation, including János Kádár, Kállai, Donáth and Losonczy were purged – all of whom were later to play prominent roles in the post-1953 and post-1956 political life. As the reformist journalist Tamás Aczél later remarked, 'Never had an executioner hanged so many Communists, not even in the days of the bloodiest "White Terror" of the Horthy era. The regime had hanged its best party workers, its most talented public servants.'[63]

Gottwald appears to have been slower to appreciate the 'necessity' of show trials, possibly arguing that the massive support for the communists in Czechoslovakia was a sufficient indicator of strength against 'class enemies'. The Party membership peaked at over 2.3 million (17 per cent of the total population in Czechoslovakia) in May 1949,[64] and by 1950 a thorough purge of the membership to weed out opportunists had reduced the Party by one-third to 1.7 million.[65] But it was still a mass party, and for Stalin that in itself appears to have spelt danger. The initiation of the purge of the Party leadership came not only from Moscow, however, but also from Mátyás Rákosi. 'Evidence' produced in the investigation of the Rajk case was pointing to 'links' within the Czechoslovak Party.[66] The search for a 'Czechoslovak Rajk' began. The Party's General Secretary, Rudolf Slánský, was implicated. Gottwald's initial resistance to this conclusion appears to be demonstrated by his ordering a stop to all investigation of Slánský in July 1951, after consultation with Stalin.[67] But he was ultimately unable to protect him. Slánský was arrested in November 1951.

Meanwhile, Soviet 'advisers', aided by the Czechoslovak Ministry of National Security (established in 1950), were casting a wide net to catch any and every possible source of deviation – including veteran 'Interbrigadists' of the Spanish Civil War; former Social Democrats; anyone who had spent the war years in the West; economic experts; and, in particular, Jews, and 'bourgeois nationalists' in the Slovak Party. Representatives of all these groups were linked in an alleged

'Anti-State Conspiratorial Centre' formed by Slánský. Eleven of them were hanged in December 1952 shortly after their trial. Eight further major trials took place, extending even into 1954, that is, *after* the death of Stalin, and also after the execution of Beria. The number of death sentences carried out between 1948 and 1952 has been estimated at 178.[68] The total of political prisoners created by the trials of this period has been put at 80 000.[69]

The sheer scale of repression led to the development of a massive apparatus of terror, which the Soviet advisers sent by Beria set in motion but which was manned faithfully by Czechs and Slovaks. Individual members of the Party leadership became directly responsible for the operation of the machine, which thus ground on relentlessly even when the external impetus from Moscow had been withdrawn. This had a peculiar effect on the complexion of the post-Stalin and post-Gottwald leadership, since there was not one of them who was not personally involved in the trials, by virtue of membership in the Party's Political Secretariat, as was explained by the 1968 commission of enquiry set up by the Dubček government:

> The responsibility of this Political Secretariat is chiefly that in contravention of the Constitution and the law it took power into its own hands and, in the last resort, approved the preparation, conduct and findings of the political trials ... The members of this select group, whom no-one had elected, were the men who had usurped the function of decision-making and the authority of the elected bodies (the Presidium and the Central Committee) and they bear the heaviest responsibility for all that happened in those days.[70]

The former members of the Political Secretariat numbered the top seven ranking members of the Politburo confirmed in office at the X Congress of the CPCS in 1954 – Zápotocký, Široký, Dolanský, Balícek, Čepička, Kopecký and Novotný. The 1968 report's section on 'personal responsibility' documents in detail the extent of each individual's involvement.[71] The two remaining Politburo members, Fierlinger and Barák, were also implicated – Fierlinger somewhat less directly, but Barák, rising to the Politburo only in 1954, was nevertheless directly involved not only through his participation in the denunciation of Otto Šling, and persecution of Party members alleged to have been 'connected' with him, but also in the later trials of 1953–4. A further Czech source from 1968 confirms the guilt of each man:

Kopecký, Široký, Balícek, Zápotocký and Novotný were directly involved in the trial of the so-called anti-state conspiratorial centre of R. Slánský; Široký and Bacílek, especially prominently in the trial of the so-called bourgeois nationalists in the KSS, [Communist Party of Slovakia], Husák, Novomeský and others; A. Novotný and R. Barák (from 14.9.1953 Minister of the Interior) bear undeniable political responsibility for the later trials, which went on from 1953 (M. Švermová, the economists, the Supreme Council etc.).[72]

The effect of the trials was not only to produce a paralysis among those at the top on account of their guilt, but, because of the very extensiveness of the trials within the ruling élite, to ensure the survival and promotion of men of a particular kind:

> They were not for the most part dogmatists of the old ideologically dedicated type (though there were some of these as well), but rather, relatively unqualified men whose careers had been made by devotion to the line and observance of discipline. These men either feared or were incapable of the independent thought needed for liberalisation.[73]

The purges had wiped out possible independent-minded individuals like Gomułka or Nagy, who had survived the onslaught of Stalinism in prison. The nearest thing the CPCS had had to such a type – the solid Party man redeemed by a streak of humanity, possessing an elementary, if not highly evolved, conscience and a certain practical common sense – had been Vlado Clementis, a Slovak executed with Slánský and others in 1952. What remained would later be described by L. Vaculík as the triumph of mediocrity:

> At every stage of the selection, the average man came out on top. And the complicated characters disappeared from the stage – those with personal charm, and particularly those who, because of their qualities and accomplishments... were a measure of the public conscience.[74]

This 'rump' of uninspiring men was highly conservative, but it was a specific sort of conservatism, which, as Taborsky rather acutely points out 'might at first glance be mistaken for loyalty to the doctrine, but in reality, it is a symptom of Czechoslovak communism's sterility and ideological stagnation'.[75] Thus, where no one takes the doctrine itself seriously, no one will be motivated to risk 'rocking the boat' to 'revive' the ideology by going back to its roots as a source of alternatives.

The political situation in terms of the Party leaderships in Czechoslovakia and Hungary at the time of Stalin's death were thus very different. Gottwald died from a cold caught at Stalin's funeral, exacerbated by his advanced syphilitic condition and chronic alcoholism. Thus was removed the dominant Czechoslovak political leader, who, if and when necessary, could then be blamed with impunity for the outrages of the era of the 'cult of personality'. The Czechoslovak Party Politburo was not factionalised, but was rather a collection of individuals who found it in their interests to slip naturally into the new Soviet mode of 'collective leadership'. By contrast, Hungary possessed in Rákosi a 'personality' of a distinctly 'cultish' stamp, who could with justice be blamed for many personal grievances and general policy 'mistakes' – but he was very much alive and clinging fast to power. What is more, he had failed to eliminate physically his leading potential opponents, of whom Imre Nagy was the most prominent, while Kádár and the other 'home' communists were to become another source of opposition. The Party was thus riven by basic divisions, representing different groups with different power bases, and potentially differing perceptions about the requirements of 'building socialism'.

C FROM THE 'NEW COURSE' TO PARTIAL REFORMS

(i) Czechoslovakia

After Gottwald's death, the top Party and state posts were shared out amongst his survivors. Following the example of Moscow after Stalin, the highest-ranking Party leaders took on state posts, with Antonín Zápotocký replacing Gottwald as President of the Republic. He probably carried most authority by virtue of his long service and his popularity in the Party, and to some extent outside it. He had played a particularly crucial part in the establishment of the regime in the years 1945–8 as leader of the trade union movement.[76] The Presidency was regarded as the highest political post, partly because of the origins of the Czechoslovak constitution in the French inter-war model, and partly because of the immense personal authority of its former occupants, Masaryk, Beneš and Gottwald. The second-ranking Party man, Vilem Široký, moved from his position as First Secretary of the Slovak Communist Party into Zápotocký's former post as Prime Minister. As with Khrushchev's appointment in the USSR, the post of Party First Secretary went to a lesser-ranking communist, little known outside the party apparatus, Antonín Novotný. Roy and Zhores

Medvedev's account of Khrushchev's promotion probably also applies to Novotný:

> Almost all of Khrushchev's colleagues considered him to be hardworking but uninspired, therefore hardly a political figure of national stature. They believed he was weak in political theory, a rather ordinary, sometimes crude man who would never aspire to excessive power and who would always pay dutiful attention to the opinions of 'his betters' – the more experienced Party leaders.[77]

All sources seem to concur in an assessment of Novotný as rather grey and obscure, a not particularly highly respected figure of the Party apparatus. A member of the pre-war 'old guard' as a regional party functionary, he was promoted in 1945 to leading secretary of the Prague regional apparatus, where he was not noted for any outstanding intellectual or organisational qualities. In fact, as Zdeněk Mlynář remarks, 'There were many minor everyday incidents indicating that Novotný was not a man of penetrating intelligence.'[78] As mentioned above, his rise in the party seems to have been clearly related to his assiduous preparation of evidence for use in the political trials of 1951–2, on which Mlynář comments, 'Novotný may well have been born without some basic human qualities.'[79] But this lack of personal presence, intellect, or even basic morality, was precisely in tune with the times. Novotný was chosen to be General Secretary Slánský's deputy in charge of the central secretariat, and:

> It is possible that at that time, in 1951, the decisive factor was the fact that A. Novotný was a man without a very marked personal programme and apparently without political ambition. That is a type, as it were, 'uncommitted' and 'harmless'.[80]

Novotný was, in fact, the personification of what the party had become:

> Novotný's major source of strength was the new type of Party man who, as a result of the purges, formed more than the backbone of the Party: the middle level functionary, the *apparatchik* who owed his position, whether it be as factory manager or state bureaucrat, to unimaginative obedience to the Party line ... While such a regime may in some respects be less dangerous than the former brand of Stalinism, it is basically less secure both because it is more vulnerable from within and because it is rarely capable of producing original solutions to the

increasingly complicated problems facing twentieth-century societies.[81]

But there was an important chink in the armour of this faceless bureaucrat – a deep sense of his own inadequacy. Mlynář relates a story told him by Novotný's niece, who had been present when Novotný, visiting his brother soon after his appointment to First Secretary in 1954, broke down and wept, acknowledging that 'I'm not up to this job, I can't do it, I haven't got what it takes.'[82] While he certainly gained confidence over the years, this recognition of his personal inadequacy helps to explain his rather complicated relationship with intellectuals of all disciplines in the 1960s.

By the last years of Stalin's rule, the Party, and in particular the Central Committee, had effectively ceased to play any significant part in the political process. While Stalin was General Secretary of the Party, he was also head of the state apparatus, and it was the latter he used as the main instrument of his personal dictatorship in the final years of his rule. It was presumably on these grounds that the top Soviet communists, Malenkov and Molotov, and the top Czechoslovak communists, Zápotocký and Široký, took over state posts, leaving the Party posts to lesser ranking colleagues. But, as Khrushchev became a major contender in the power struggle in Moscow, so the relative institutional weights of the state and the Party changed, in favour of the latter. This undoubtedly also contributed to Novotný's own rapid emergence as a top-ranking leader, a process which was further accelerated by Zápotocký's age and failing health.

The new line on 'collective leadership' in Moscow represented a temporary and highly unstable truce, a breathing-space before intense factional conflict broke out. In Czechoslovakia, however, it was an accurate reflection of a fairly stable balance of forces, with little factional activity. As Taborsky, Beneš's former private secretary and a man with intimate knowledge of Czechoslovak politics, observed:

> Unlike his counterparts in Russia, none of the present Politburo members owes his promotion to any particular colleague. Hence, there are no protégés who would feel the necessity of staying in the good graces of their protectors and of constituting a coterie around him.[83]

The impact of the purges, and the collective responsibility of the party leadership for them, meant that there was little scope for differences in policy orientation between the leaders, and strong collective interest in limiting criticism of the 'mistakes of the past' to the absolute minimum. Thus the issue surrounding the 'New Course' and the criticism of the 'cult of personality', which were the key weapons in the Soviet power struggle, and which the satellite Parties were also expected to take up, failed to become a source of conflict and found only a muffled echo in Czechoslovakia. Zápotocký and Široký are reported in a 1968 Czech source as having been more open to the 'New Course' and to wider discussion of the proceedings of the Soviet XX Party Congress,[84] but to have been effectively resisted by Novotný, whom they describe as a 'type of politician–administrator, secretary and manipulator of political apparatuses'.[85] He is alleged to have accused Zápotocký of 'infringement of the principle of collective leadership and with creating a cult of the personality around Zápotocký'.[86] Even so, as Skilling concludes, 'the contrasts in personal character and background between Novotný and Zápotocký were not serious enough to produce an open conflict between advocates of a "hard" and "soft" line such as occurred in the USSR and in other block countries'.[87]

On the issue of the trials, there was an especially clear common interest in letting sleeping dogs lie. A review of the trials was initiated as a gesture to the Moscow line in January 1955, under the chairmanship of Rudolf Barák. But the brief of the commission of enquiry was restricted to the period 1949–52, thus leaving out the important later trials. Although Barák himself was not implicated in these particular trials, he was implicated in the later trials, and other members of the commission had personally taken part in the earlier trials as well.[88] Barák may have tried later to use the information acquired here for his own personal career ambitions,[89] but he was effectively silenced by dismissal from his post as Minister of the Interior in 1962 on formal charges of embezzlement – but with pungent hints from Novotný at the time of Barák's 'political adventurism'.[90] The impact of the 1955 trials commission was negligible, as one would expect given its composition, and given the fact that its findings, and even its very existence, were kept secret from the Central Committee:

> The Commission was not concerned with rehabilitation, or with endeavouring objectively and truthfully to probe the violations of the law and their causes; its chief consideration was to salve the conscience of the Politburo by putting a political full-stop to the matter.[91]

In fact, the Commission neatly turned the exercise on its head by identifying the main victim, Slánský, as the 'Czech Beria' who had held most responsibility for the terror to which he himself had then fallen victim. There is probably a certain rough justice in this conclusion, whose main purpose was, however, to suit the current convenience of Novotný and his colleagues, by allowing them to present themselves as fortunate escapees of Slánský's terror, rather than as perpetrators of it themselves.[92] At the same time, the leadership's commitment to the past was dramatically demonstrated by the unveiling of a huge statue of Stalin, dominating the Vltava river in Prague, on 1 May 1955.

But the XX Congress of the Communist Party of the Soviet Union could not be ignored completely. There is some evidence of mounting restiveness on the part of students and the creative intelligentsia at this time. The II Congress of Writers in April 1956 saw the poet Jaroslav Siefert advocate a role for artists as 'conscience of the nation',[93] while the Party pronouncements throughout the early post-Stalin years continually griped at 'liberal' tendencies on the cultural front.[94] Lower-level party organisations apparently voiced demands for an Extraordinary Congress in 1956, but such 'completely wrong demands' were firmly squashed. An ordinary Party Conference was convened in June, at which Novotný led a vigorous offensive against 'revisionism', the heresy currently sweeping Hungary and Poland, but the session appears to have received this docilely.

Skilling brings in Czechoslovak political culture to explain this calm in 1956:

> Among intellectuals the task of reassessing the system was hindered not only by severe restrictions on the freedom of expression, but by a continuing belief in socialism and its merits, persisting faith in the Soviet Union, as well as a fear of Western 'imperialism'. The absence of a revolutionary tradition, or of a deep hostility to the Russians and the memories of French and British betrayal in 1938 and Western inaction in 1948, contributed to the failure of the Czechs and Slovaks to join the Hungarians and Poles in resistance. In fact, the democratic tradition proved to be as impotent in 1956 as it had been in 1948, and may even have been a hindrance to militant action against dictatorial repression.[95]

The impact of the Hungarian revolution only served to reinforce intellectual inertia, and to bolster up Novotný by the impact it had on any would-be reformer in the Party, as Mlynář recalls:

> [T]he pacification of critical tendencies inside the CPC [Communist Party] was not simply a consequence of the

> repressions ... we communists were quite simply afraid ... [T]here was the quite concrete image of a lynch mob hanging Communists from lampposts. And from conversations I had at the time with various Communists of different generations, I recall that they were all preoccupied with the same thought as well. This was an important assistance to Novotný in subduing the wave of criticism precipitated in the CPC by Khrushchev's critique.[96]

Immediately after the Hungarian events, the Party Central Committee congratulated itself in the name of the people:

> The firm unity of the working people did not allow even the smallest attempt by enemies from the remnants of the defeated exploiting classes to damage our people's democratic regime. Our Party, our working class and the entire working people honourably stood the test of the past few days.[97]

The ultimately crucial factor in assuring political stability throughout 1956 was the quiescence of the working class, which had already demonstrated its ability to translate the Czechoslovak democratic tradition into a revolutionary idiom in Pilsen in 1953. This had been a clear early-warning signal to the regime of the dangers of ignoring material welfare as a source of political stability. Although for the reasons described above, it was not prepared to countenance a radical change of economic policy, it did nevertheless subscribe to the 'New Course', and it was able to make up for its half-heartedness in this by drawing upon Czechoslovakia's underlying economic resources to effect a reversal of the impact of the May 1953 currency reform on the standard of living. The period 1954–7 saw an economic 'thaw', as investments in production were held back, and greater emphasis was placed on consumer goods production.[98] As elsewhere in the bloc, concessions to agriculture were made, in terms of taxation on private farming, improved state purchase prices and reduced compulsory quotas.[99] Although in 1953–4 it was also permitted for peasants to leave collective farms, a mass exodus did not take place, as it did in Hungary and Poland, and the regime was able, in 1955, to renew the collectivisation drive.[100]

The most telling data are the cost of living and real-earnings tables compiled by Jan Michal (see Table 3.3), which demonstrate the steady and improving situation for workers in manufacturing industry.

Wage rises were directed specifically at strategically important groups, such as miners and industrial workers.[101] Workers' earnings

Table 3.3 Index of trends in cost of living and real earnings in manufacturing (1948 = 100)

	1948	*1952*	*1953*	*1954*	*1955*	*1956*	*1957*
Cost of living	100	150	164	160	152	147	148
Real earnings	100	97	97	108	115	122	122

Source: J. Michal, *Central Planning in Czechoslovakia*, p. 198.

rose twice as fast as average *per capita* personal incomes of the population (by 22 per cent and 10 per cent respectively).[102] Politically weaker groups, such as pensioners, suffered – old-age benefits in real terms declined each year until 1956, and, even after that, remained below the 1948 level.[103] Although probably seen through the rose-tinted spectacles of a young and enthusiastic communist with a bright career ahead, Mlynář's memories of the time confirm a general impression of adequate, if not entirely satisfactory, welfare:

> Some of the essential ideas of our communist faith had been realised, and society had, by all appearances, accepted them- ... Poverty as a social phenomenon had disappeared. People going about in rags, beggars in the streets, slums in urban peripheries – things I could still remember from childhood (and what I had seen in Moscow) – had disappeared for good and were known by the younger generation only from movies. The fear of sickness or old age that comes from material insecurity also vanished from everyday life. It was taken for granted that the spectre of economic depression and unemployment was no longer a threat ... In everyday life, the exhausting rat-race of competition, common in capitalist society, disappeared from the lives of working people. Of course there were other, negative features in everyday life: inadequate public services, an utter lack of labor-saving household appliances, and a shortage of consumer goods ... But the more relaxed pace of working and living on the whole made many of these negative features more palatable.[104]

Even the most serious problem, the lack of housing, reaching crisis proportions,[105] 'seemed to be soluble in time'. The effect of all this led to a quite widespread, if not enthusiastic, acceptance of the regime: 'Criticism and opposition continued, of course, but they were directed toward change on the basis of the new economic, social and political conditions and not of turning back the clock to the capitalist past.'[106]

The stability of Czechoslovakia throughout 1956 earned the heartfelt gratitude of Moscow. Voroshilov greeted a visiting Czechoslovak delegation in January 1957 with a declaration that the Czechoslovaks were 'the best, closest and dearest friends of the CPSU';[107] and Khrushchev, on a return visit in July, acknowledged his own gratitude to Czechoslovakia:

> When the counter-revolution broke out in Hungary, our enemies asked themselves more than once: what about the Czechs and Slovaks? Whom will they support? We all know our enemies did not count on having their hopes dashed ... Their hopes burst like soap bubbles ... The Communist Party of Czechoslovakia fully supported the decisions of the Communist Party of the Soviet Union. This testifies to the deep friendship between our parties.[108]

At the end of his visit, he told workers at a Prague factory, 'We are leaving you with the conviction that the cause of Leninism in Czechoslovakia is in good hands.'[109]

The period 1957–60 in Czechoslovakia saw two new developments, tending in rather contradictory directions. In November 1957, Zápotocký died, and his position as President of the Republic was filled by Novotný, who also retained his Party post. He was now in a position to consolidate his personal power, breaking up the old 'collective leadership' of the preceding years. Široký had obviously lost ground in the political ranking order, and, in proposing Novotný for the Presidency in Zápotocký's place, acknowledged that 'the primary need is for people to draw even more closely together under the leadership of the Communist Party'.[110] This departure from the 'collective leadership' approach was sanctioned by a similar concentration of personal power in the Soviet Union at that time, with Khrushchev's defeat of the 'anti-Party Group' in June 1957, and his subsequent assumption of the Chairmanship of the Council of Ministers, in addition to his Party post, in 1958.

As in Moscow, this concentration of personal power was accompanied by a series of administrative reforms, which, while they signalled a certain decentralisation of the state economic apparatus, with a view to improving the management of the economy, were also part of power politics, providing an opportunity to break up possible sources of resistance to the new leader, assuring the dominance of the Party – which was now the key power base – over the State.[111]

The first mention of organisational change was not made by either Zápotocký or Široký, but by Novotný himself, at the June 1956 Party Conference, when he alluded to 'a decision to decentralise and simplify the state apparatus'.[112] In fact, the changes mirrored quite closely those being introduced at the same time by Khrushchev. State officials were to be transferred to Slovakia, and to the regional National Committees, which were given greater resources. At the same time, a purge of state officials was undertaken. It has been suggested that both Gottwald and Zápotocký had shown an understanding of the need for qualified and experienced administrators in the state apparatus, and had therefore prevented too much disruption of state personnel after the 1948 coup.[113] Indeed, substantial sections of it had already supported the communists. But by the end of 1957, the protection of potentially 'unreliable elements' under the patronage of influential Party personalities came under threat as Zápotocký weakened. In October 1957, only days before Zápotocký died, *Rudé Právo* announced a drive against 'bourgeois cadres': 'Party authorities, seeking the easiest way out, often overlooked the requirement of working-class origin for cadres and looked mainly for specialised cadres.'[114]

A more important aspect of the administrative reforms than territorial decentralisation in smaller East European countries was vertical devolution of economic management. In the GDR, most of the industrial ministries were abolished, following the Soviet example, and large conglomerations of enterprises were formed. Czechoslovakia did not abolish the ministries outright, but it did establish large concentrated industrial associations (the VHJ – *výrobně hospodářská jednotka*), and in fact for a time went further than anywhere in the bloc in devolving decision-making authority to them. By 1959, Czechoslovak industry was more concentrated than anywhere else in Eastern Europe. The 1417 firms which had existed in 1948 had been reduced by merger to 929, of which 487 were grouped into sixty-seven associations.[115] The aim, as explained in the February 1958 resolution of the Central Committee, was to bring 'concrete economic management as close as possible to actual production through substantially increasing the authority of the individual enterprises, while at the same time strengthening central direction in all fundamental questions'.[116]

The new associations were given greater freedom than before in their sources of supply, output and sales. The number of centrally-fixed plan targets was reduced and the incentive system shifted from emphasis on gross output to profit and labour productivity. A set of norms was established defining the firm's share in profits, depreciation allowances, and the wage and bonus funds. Managers were given greater decision-making authority in the area of product mix, technical innovation and organisation, and, to a certain extent, also in the expansion of capacity, in new capital formation as well as simple replacement.[117] However, the crucial element of the market was missing:

> neither the resolutions nor the reorganisation could assure the necessary technical development and a shift over to intensive production, because they did not essentially eliminate the old way of planning or stimulate the material interest of enterprises.[118]

The central plan still contained detailed directives, and, even if the attempt was made to diminish the purely quantitative approach of the plan, this nevertheless crept back in by the back door, in the absence of a system of value parameters.[119] Wholesale price reforms in 1958 reduced subsidies somewhat, but did not entirely eliminate them, and the new prices were based on the traditional price-setting formulae.[120] When the leadership announced at the XI Party Congress in 1958 that the pace of economic growth was to be accelerated, all the potentially useful aspects of the reform were undermined, even torpedoed, by the return to extensive patterns of growth and the corresponding centralisation of the economic mechanism.

Not only was command planning not abandoned, but at the same time (as in Khrushchev's reforms)[121] direct Party supervision of the economy was stepped up, further eroding managerial authority. Measures were taken which effectively gave the Party the right of veto over managerial decisions – 'the right to enquire into and suspend wrong and socially harmful decisions by management' and to prevent 'misunderstandings of the new and not yet well-defined managerial powers'.[122] 'Class origins', 'political maturity', and 'devotion to the Party and the working class' were emphasised more strongly than ever in the field of managerial appointments.

The leadership itself appears to have held highly ambiguous views on the purposes of the reforms, becoming increasingly suspicious of their own political vulnerability in the face of their dependence on complex technical expertise in the whole project, and fearing above all to relinquish any power. At the first hint of economic problems, the partial reforms were reversed. The economic difficulties which began to emerge in 1959 and 1960 were in fact seen as a result of the reforms, rather than of the basically unaltered centralised system. A Central Committee plenum in 1962, which deliberated upon what had by then become a major economic crisis, condemned the reforms for neglecting the principle of 'democratic centralism', with the result, as the resolution put it, that 'in practice, a one-sided "decentralisation" took place, i.e., mainly a decentralisation of central direction'.[123]

But this is already to run ahead, for it was that crisis of the early 1960s that finally brought home to the Czechoslovak leadership the meaning of the legacy of Stalinism for the economy, and set off, at last, consideration of reform in its broadest ramifications. At the turn of the decade, however, Czechoslovak communism still exuded unquestioning self-confidence, and Novotný personally was at the height of his power. Czechoslovakia was proclaimed to have reached the stage of 'socialism' – the only country beside the Soviet Union to have attained that pinnacle of human progress. A new constitution was duly introduced in 1960.

(ii) Hungary

Nagy described the situation in Hungary in the summer of 1953 as follows:

> In the economic field we were faced with a completely hopeless situation ... Industry began to show a steady shortage of materials. The quality of products was deteriorating rapidly. Export difficulties became everyday phenomena, and foreign debts were rising steeply. Development of agricultural production had come to a standstill, and there was a danger of it going downhill altogether. The area of uncultivated land increased. The standard of living was deteriorating, and a further decrease became a certainty ... Increasing dissatisfaction could be observed in the ranks of the workers' class. The keeping and consolidation of power as the principal task facing the Party showed up in its full extent.[124]

In this context, Hungary was clearly as ripe for the 'New Course' as the Soviet Union itself, but, on the other hand, lacked the crucial political requirement – Rákosi, the 'little Stalin' was still alive, and in control of the essential levers of power. But the very gravity of the economic situation forced changed upon him. He and a group of his associates, along with Imre Nagy, were summoned to Moscow in June 1953, and instructed, in the best traditions of comradely and fraternal relations, to set matters right, or else, as Khrushchev put it, they would be 'booted out'. Malenkov, reportedly, was 'staggered' by Rákosi's intransigence,[125] but, nevertheless, the Soviet leadership prevailed, and Nagy was instructed to take over the Premiership from Rákosi, who was, however, left in control of the Party. On their return to Budapest, a Central Committee meeting heard a speech by Nagy (which became available only in 1985)[126] in which he roundly criticised past practices and outlined the 'New Course' for Hungarian conditions. Rákosi was forced into self-criticism, but in fact, in the following months, did everything possible to obstruct and subvert Nagy's efforts, as the latter outlines in great detail in his *Defence of the New Course*, written after he was finally manoeuvred out of his position in April 1955. Hungary's economic and political situation in 1953 left it open to external pressure from Moscow in a way which Czechoslovakia was not, because of the latter's more stable economy, and 'natural' transition to collective leadership after Gottwald's death. In Hungary this openness worked in two ways, both for, and ultimately, against change: the economic situation rendered the 'New Course' essential in 1953, but change had to come from outside pressure, since Rákosi dominated the core of the political system – the Party machinery. Although there does seem to have been a growing realisation of the wrongheadedness of Rákosi's line within the Hungarian Party, the Central Committee which unanimously approved the 'New Course' in June 1953 was clearly doing so primarily out of obedience to the authority of Moscow, rather than out of majority conviction – an interpretation borne out by the equally unanimous condemnation of Nagy by the same Committee less than two years later, in March 1955. Thus it was basically a pliant, malleable instrument of the prevailing authority, and in the authority structure of the movement, Rákosi was subordinate only to Moscow. But the Moscow leadership itself was, in those crucial years, highly unstable. The weakness of Nagy's domestic power-base – first, that he owed his appointment to Moscow, and, second, that he headed the State apparatus – served to render the Hungarian system vulnerable once again to developments beyond its frontiers. The years 1953–6 were years of power struggle in Moscow, in the course of which Khrushchev, as party leader, effectively defeated Malenkov, who appears to have acted in this period as Nagy's protector. The trend towards party ascendancy over the state apparatus, and with it, Malenkov's personal demise, gave Rákosi the opportunity to bend the central Committee of the Hungarian Party round, against the policy of the 'New Course' (which was undergoing modification in

Moscow, as Khrushchev turned to defend heavy industry as a tactic against Malenkov), and against his personal rival, Nagy.

But, just as Rákosi might have thought he had consolidated his position in early 1955, a new Moscow line, this time the rapprochement with Tito and the acknowledgement of the 'socialist' validity of the Yugoslav course, once again cut the ground from under his feet. For Rákosi, foremost opponent of the Titoist heresy in Eastern Europe, this again presented a profound personal threat. For the growing number of Nagy's supporters, it was a faint glimmer of hope on what had seemed, in mid-1955, an irretrievably bleak prospect of continued rule by Rákosi. At first, Rákosi seemed able to cling on to power, despite everything. But after the Twentieth Party Congress in February 1956, the basis of his position collapsed, as did the entire Party itself by the end of 1956. For our purposes, it is not necessary to go through the details of the historical development of the 1956 revolution (this has anyway been adequately covered elsewhere).[127] However, it is of interest, from the point of view of tracing the origins and history of economic reform in Hungary, to consider briefly whether the 'New Course' can be regarded as a first step towards economic reform. The impact of 1956 is relevant too for the origins and course of the reform, and will be considered later.

To what extent can the origins of the economic reform be attributed to Nagy and the experience of his period of rule from summer 1953 to spring 1955? In Fetjő's opinion, Nagy's speech to the Hungarian Parliament in June 1953 revealed his indebtedness to Bukharin,[128] whose ideas, in turn, have been examined in depth as a major influence on the post-Stalin reformist theorists.[129] There are indeed clear parallels with 'Bukharinist' ideas in Nagy's policies – in particular, his emphasis on the adaptation of Marxism to the actual conditions, rather than forcing reality to conform with a dogmatised ideology. For Bukharin, in the context of the Soviet Union in the 1920s, this meant coming to terms with the overwhelmingly peasant nature of the economy, a far cry from the conditions in which Marx had envisaged communists coming to power. In Bukharin's view, the peasants could not be forced into collective farms – this was unthinkable both in *political* terms, since it implied massive reliance on coercive forms of rule which would lead to a degeneration of the socialist state, and also in *economic* terms, since anyway industry was not yet at a level to provide adequate means of mechanisation, the essential precondition for large-scale farming. Bukharin was *not* opposed to industrialisation *per se* (although his opponents accused him of this), but rather was concerned with a development policy based on *balance* between economic sectors – that agriculture and industry and, within industry, light and heavy branches, should develop alongside each other. Thus he diverged from the radical leftist plan of forced-pace industrialisation through priority to heavy industry and subordination of all other sectors and branches, and of popular consumption, to the goal of maximum increase of output of heavy industry.[130]

Nagy clearly followed a similar pattern of thought, although there is no evidence of conscious or overt indebtedness to Bukharin. It was a pragmatic response to the situation in Hungary, which, in the early post-war years, had certain rough parallels with the Soviet economic conditions of the 1920s, in its underdeveloped agrarian structure. Nagy, like Bukharin, believed firmly in adapting Marxism to fit national conditions – which, in the Hungarian context, involved not only paying attention to the surrounding reality, but also rejecting the Soviet experience as a universally valid 'model' for all 'builders of socialism' to follow. While Bukharin foresaw the political and moral implications of the leftist path of forced industrialisation, Nagy based his policies on the actual consequences of its practical implementation. He shared with Bukharin an indelible streak of basic decency and humanism which aroused in the latter apprehension for the future, and, in Nagy, horror at the past. Both men's thought is marked by an emphasis on gradualism, flexibility, patience, tolerance and a preference for persuasion over coercion as the normal instrument of government.

In concrete policy terms, Nagy followed a line parallel to that advocated by Bukharin in the Soviet Union. First, he stressed the need to develop and expand agriculture, but also conceded that this could not be done through the collective farms, which, based on forced membership, repression of the most successful, *kulak* farmers, and inadequately supplied with machinery and equipment, had led to near disaster by 1953. Correspondingly, he announced in his July speech to the Parliament,[131] that membership of the collectives would no longer be obligatory, that government support and guarantees of security would henceforth go to private producers, and that investments in agriculture would rise (by over 20 per cent in the year 1953–4).[132] The permitted size of household plots was raised from between half and three-quarters of an acre to between one and one-and-a-half acres. Compulsory delivery quotas from the collectives were ended, and the state prices for deliveries under contract were raised. The concomitant of this policy was an equally rapid turnabout in industrial policy. Investment in heavy industry was cut by 41.1 per cent in 1953–4. 'The development of socialist heavy industry cannot constitute an end in itself', he declared in 1953.[133] But, as he repeatedly emphasised in his 1955 self-justification, he was *not* opposed to industrialisation itself, but to 'ultra-industrialisation', the disproportionate way in which the Rákosi policy had enforced it. Thus he saw the 'New Course' *not* as a reversal of the basic 'strategy' – the 'construction of socialism' – but as a revision of the *tactics*. The disproportionate development of the Rákosi period required, he argued, a temporary halt in the pace of industrial development, to allow agriculture to catch up, and, within industry, to allow light and consumer goods industry to gain ground. The 'basic law' of socialism, he argued, was *not* the primacy of production of the means of production, but the 'constant raising of living standards of the population'.[134]

To what extent can Nagy's 'New Course' be seen as the forerunner of reform? In two respects, it clearly is – first, in the general philosophical approach of pragmatism, as opposed to abstract, overtheorised dogmatism; and second, in the reassertion of consumption as the primary goal of the economy, as opposed to 'production for production's sake'. This attitude and this basic policy assumption appear to be the essential *preconditions* for reform, but it is not clear that they are sufficient. In fact, Nagy's 'New Course' seems to have been less developed as a coherent, systemic critique of Stalinism than Bukharin's concept of the NEP as presented by his biographer, Stephen Cohen. Lomax, in a healthily sceptical appraisal of Nagy as a thinker, refers to the 'enshrouding verbiage of self-righteousness, common-sense moralising and third-rate Marxist–Leninist theorising' with characterises his main work, *In Defence of the New Course*.[135] Lomax also points to the unsystematic nature of his critique of Stalinism – Nagy, like Khrushchev, saw it as a question of the abuse of power by an evil man, rather than as due to a structural defect of the political system established after the Bolshevik revolution.[136] In the economic sphere, too, Berend argues that the introduction of the 'New Course' in 1953 'brought no new insights into the real nature of the economic mechanism … the system of planning was thoroughly identified with the socialist system itself. All they thought that could be done was to use the given system more rationally'.[137] In a sense, of course, this was perfectly natural – the very excesses of Rákosi's economic policy were so obvious that they would tend to overshadow or camouflage the underlying systemic defects.[138] Thus Nagy's 'New Course' was rather a *reculer pour mieux sauter*, in the manner of Lenin's original conception of the NEP, than a developed blueprint, which 'Bukharinism' became. Nagy, while emphasising the 'fundamental' nature of the break which the 'New Course' represented from Rákosi's policy, also emphasised that the basis task of 'building socialism' remained. An essential element of later developed economic reformism was *market competition*. Competition, as advocated by Nagy, meant mainly competition between the private and public sectors. While it was acknowledged that this would require some change in the manner in which the state sector was organised, this was not developed at the time. The coexistence of private and public sectors was, moreover, seen as a temporary necessity – in time, as the economy developed, the division would be superceded as production became more fully 'social' in character. The concept of the *future* system of more developed socialism did not undergo revision – particularly with regard to the directive concept of the plan – while one of the later, central arguments of the reformers was to be that it was precisely the *developed*, advanced nature of the economy which necessitated change in the basis concept of socialism to incorporate the use of competition, the market, enterprise autonomy, and flexible, 'indicative' planning. Thus, owing to the lack of understanding of the *systemic* nature of the problem, measures taken to put things right misfired, as Berend explained:

> The system ... made no use of economic incentives; the material incentives to fulfilling the plan were reinforced by administrative regulations aimed at guaranteeing the realisation of the central goal. The last resort in this system of incentives was thus, disciplinary, and, what is more, legal action. After 1953, however, when one-sided administrative measures were criticised and discarded, these kinds of incentives quickly disappeared from the economy. However, this happened without any change in the system of planning. In this way, the last compulsion to comply with the centrally set objectives was done away with, without anything being put in its place ... Thus, despite the efforts made to rationalise the system of central planning, in practice it was worse after 1953 than before.[139]

There were two possible conclusions which could be, and were, drawn from this experience. First, the conservative 'common sense' of the *apparat* concluded that this proved the folly of such tinkerings with the machine, and indeed, after Nagy's removal in 1955, a return to the old patterns occurred.[140] The second, more sophisticated, conclusion was that the system itself had to change. While Nagy himself may not have grasped fully the systemic aspect of the economic problem, a few economists began very soon to focus on precisely this, and, in the more liberal and self-critical atmosphere of the period of Nagy's premiership, research proceeded in this direction.[141]

The 1956 revolution was an event of cataclysmic significance for Hungary, for all sections of society, for the population and for its rulers alike. The essential lessons drawn by the new Party leadership from the experience provided the seeds of change in economic approach: first, it was henceforth axiomatic that the one unquestionable purpose of economic policy must be to maintain and constantly improve the standard of living of the population; and second, following on from this, it was recognised that commitment to Marxist–Leninist ideology must always be tempered by pragmatic considerations. These two lessons created the propensity in the new Kádár leadership to follow a reformist course after 1956, instead of merely reasserting the *status quo* in the economic field.

There is strong evidence, in the December 1956 programme put forward by Kádár, that he seriously hoped it would be possible to introduce radical economic reform from the very beginning. A committee of 200 experts was set up in early 1957 under the chairmanship of the economist (and former member of the Smallholders' Party) Dr István Varga, with instructions to investigate the existing economic system in full, and to make proposals 'for the revision of the economic mechanism'. As Robinson notes, 'In contrast to the pre-1956 period ... official attention now began to focus on the economic mechanism and not merely on policy and planning targets'.[142] The explanation of this shift of focus would appear to lie, as suggested above, in the experience of the Nagy period. The dire state of the economy too – an estimated 20 per cent of GNP was lost as a result of the 1956 upheaval – would have acted as a further catalyst for urgent thought about a solution. Moreover, there was also that irreversible shift in the basic economic policy assumption 'that the primary object of the distribution of national income and the preparation of economic investment plans should be a gradual rise in the living standard of the workers'.[143]

The Varga Committee debated long and hard with itself. 'In the course of the preparatory work, extremely divergent views were advanced, including the proposal of a return to a decentralised market economy.'[144] The Yugoslav self-management model was clearly an attraction for the most radical economists, who also hoped that in this way the revolutionary Workers' Councils set up in 1956 to resist the Soviet invasion could be preserved, and thus some of what people had hoped for in 1956 might be attained. The Yugoslav model was apparently especially influential in the Budapest party – in fact, of course, Kádár's own original power base.[145] But the Yugoslav option was quite quickly ruled out politically, by the suppression of the Workers' Councils in 1957. What the Varga Committee produced, in late 1957, was a three-part study, consisting of: (i) an analysis of the economic situation, which provided a systemic critique of the economic mechanism of Stalinism; (ii) an assessment of the prerequisites for economic development, which outlined basic economic policy measures for balanced growth, recommended energy and employment projects, and an agricultural policy based on cooperation of the private and collective sectors; and (iii) a rather general outline of the new concept of 'economic guidance', which was advocated in place of administrative direction of the economy. This involved the use of the price system and credit policy, to allow enterprises greater autonomy – with the attendant risk of closure for unprofitable producers – and thus, to allow central planning to focus on the long term, leaving annual and operational planning to the enterprises themselves.[146] Thus, the Varga Committee's report can be seen, with hindsight, to have been the 'first step' on the road to reform.[147] However – it was not to be implemented straight away.

The political situation both internally and externally made the introduction of such a reform, marking a significant break with Soviet practice, impossible at that time. As we shall see in Chapter 4, until the early 1960s hardline views were preponderant in the internal policy-making bodies, reflecting general trends in the international communist movement and the particular twists and turns of leadership politics in Moscow. The main task put in front of the Kádár regime was the restoration of order, which involved repression of autonomous social and political forces and the consolidation of strong central power. There is an obvious, inherent contradiction in introducing measures to promote decentralisation of control and autonomy in economic life, while carrying out a thoroughgoing programme of coercive recentralisation in the political sphere. Even had the main Party bodies been fully in support of Kádár on the question of economic reform, in the immediate aftermath of 1956, the country was *not* effectively autonomously governed. The Soviet army, the Soviet embassy, and Soviet 'advisors' installed in all key points of the apparatus, effectively ran the country. Thus, until the Soviet leadership was confident that political power had been fully consolidated, and furthermore, until they themselves began to recognise the need for fundamental change in the economic system, reform in Hungary along the lines of the Varga commission's proposals was ruled out.

The goal of securing the standard of living of the people had therefore to be achieved without fundamental reform, insofar as it could be achieved at all. A wage rise of 10 per cent was granted in January 1957, but had to be rescinded in August because of economic pressures on the government,[148] and this in turn reinforced the immediate political trend towards the use of force rather than persuasion in dealing with society. But the provision of some $300 million of Soviet goods and credit aid,[149] cuts in the rate of investment, the virtual abolition of defence spending (as the Army had been disbanded), and three years' good harvests, all contributed to a steady rise in the population's consumption, by 3.1 per cent in 1958, 6.4 per cent in 1959, and 6.2 per cent in 1960.[150]

Further evidence of the hard-line trend in economic policy was the decision to recollectivise agriculture. As noted above, the breakdown of the cooperatives was intolerable for the Soviet Union and other neighbouring bloc countries, and for the prevailing Central Committee majority. In fact, the number of private farms increased by 15 per cent between mid-1956 and mid-1957, reaching their 1949 level of 1 662 700.[151] In July 1957, the Central Committee reasserted the principle of collectivisation, but little happened until December 1958, when the Central Committee passed a resolution of 'accelerating' the pace of collectivisation; in March 1959, the decision was made to go ahead, after Kádár returned from a visit to Moscow in January. But it was a measure which divided the Party bitterly. Three schools of thought have been identified by Robinson:

1. those who were keen to drive peasants into the cooperatives by deliberate impoverishment of non-joiners, with no regard to the losses this would involve;
2. those who opposed collectivisation at that time, fearing precisely what the first group wanted, and seeing the overriding policy aim as maintaining agricultural output;
3. those who acquiesced in the policy of collectivisation, but also advocated the use of persuasion and voluntary recruitment; and who maintained, or rather hoped, that agricultural production

could be kept at a constant level by the use of incentives and subsidies. Kádár appears to have adhered to this group, as Robinson argues, 'in an attempt to maintain control over a movement he was unable to prevent in the first place'.[152]

But in practice, some coercion was inevitable. The appeal for 'voluntary' subscription to the cooperatives simply could not have been met with a genuine popular response in the context of the recent history of the agricultural sector. But excesses did not go unpunished. In the winter of 1959, 100 Party activists were disciplined, and twenty-three prosecuted for the unjustified use of force.[153] This allowed Kádár to dismiss Dögei, the hard-line Minister of Agriculture, in January 1960, and replace him with a competent collective farm manager, Pál Losonczi. By 1961, the process was declared complete – while only 10 per cent of arable lands had been in the cooperatives in 1956, by 1961, only 10 per cent remained in private hands.[154] Thus, the Central Committee was able to declare in February 1961, 'socialist conditions of production have become dominant in agriculture'.[155]

What was achieved by this? Undoubtedly, the gains were all political. Total agricultural production in 1961 was stagnant, at its 1934–8 average level, exacerbated by a drought. But Kádár had appeased the hard-liners at home and elsewhere in the bloc and had brought the pattern of ownership relations into line with the rest of the bloc. Thus on the one hand, he had covered himself against further anti-reformist ideological attacks upon himself as a 'defender of the petty-bourgeoisie', while, at the same time, the negative economic consequences would ultimately serve to strengthen the case of reformers, advocating systemic change as the only means of securing the primary aim – a guaranteed continual rise in the standard of living.

Thus, despite the prevailing hard-line trends, changes in the methods of management of the economy were not entirely ruled out. Compulsory agricultural deliveries were abolished; a new incentive system to promote technical innovation and an enterprise profit-sharing scheme were introduced; a reform in the method of calculating producer prices was carried out. Later, in the early 1960s, as in other CMEA states including Czechoslovakia, a merger programme was implemented in the organisational structure of industry. Thus, throughout the period 1957 to 1961, a series of partial changes was introduced. While the political context favoured the choice of what the Deputy Chairman of the Planning Office described (rather optimistically) as 'purposeful, quick and efficient'[156] central measures to put right the immediate effects of the 'mistakes' of the past economic practice, on the other hand, a 'change in social atmosphere', a 'clear break with arbitrariness'[157] was noted in the economic apparatus. Despite the rejection of the Varga report, it was made clear that the use of experts and specialists in economic policy-making would continue and expand.[158] Economics as a science was to be promoted, and by the end of the period under consideration, the President of the Hungarian Economic Association was able to report:

> After a somewhat difficult task, when its advocates were but few, this widening and intensifying movement [of devising the reform] begins now to embrace every branch of economic science, compelling them to evaluate their experience and theorems. Under its influence, a bustling intellectual activity has been started, even in such fields where a few years ago inclination towards innovations was but moderate.[159]

The role of the economist as a *partner* to decision-makers in socialism began in these years, as later expressed by Kornai – 'He has ceased to be in "opposition" and belongs now to "government". It is his duty to think of the ways to render his own system more efficient.'[160]

The change of attitude towards economists and specialists reflected the basic change in the nature of the regime – its pragmatism: '*The sound recognition of realities* gained preference in economic policy', as Berend puts it.[161] These were years, he argues, more important possibly for their intellectual and educative impact, than for their practical achievements, when there began a process of 'rethinking on a number of basic questions, which had formerly been regarded almost as taboos'.[162] The pragmatism at the heart of the regime thus kept it open to a process of learning by the experience – none too successful – of partial change:

> Economic leadership approached the economy in the practical realisation of its economic policy not on grounds of preconceived ideas, or doctrines, but on the grounds of reality, flexibility in responding to facts, sensibly perceiving the social effects of economic policy and seeking creative answers to the emerging practical problems. This practice of leadership explains why the correction phase (1957–61) underwent a continuous development and carried in itself the possibility of progress.[163]

In the course of the 1950s, in both Czechoslovakia and Hungary, the question of economic reform had begun to enter the political agenda. In fact, a varied experience of different types of planning had been amassed – from the immediate post-war recovery programmes, through the period of Stalinist centralism to the partial adjustments of the 'New Course', and the limited changes of the later 1950s. All this provided food for thought for economic specialists. This was particularly true of Hungary, where the more open atmosphere of the Nagy period had permitted some far-reaching questioning and analysis, bearing fruit in the work of the Varga Commission. But in Czechoslovakia too, the experience of limited reform at the end of the 1950s stimulated rethinking among traditional 'political economists' such as Ota Šik, suggesting the usefulness of reexamining alternative forms of planned economy, such as that of 1945–8. Among the economic intelligentsia, a coherent concept of a fundamentally different socialist economy was emerging. But the key to this concept's adoption as official economic strategy was of course politics, both internal and external. A move as significant as the introduction of economic reform required the conviction of Party leaderships – in Moscow as well as in Prague or Budapest – of the necessity of further change, beyond the partial and inconsistent adjustments being tried; and it required the consolidation of support below the top Party leadership for such a move.

In Czechoslovakia, the Novotný leadership, consolidated at the end of the 1950s, was profoundly and inherently hostile to change of any sort, and extraordinarily complacent about the economic situation. A decision to change, to bring about fundamental reform, would come only in response to deep economic crisis – but an effective response to the economic crisis would not itself be possible without far-reaching changes of the entrenched and conservative personnel who dominated the political apparatus. In those circumstances, economic reform would be placed at the centre of what was to become a protracted period of political conflict and instability, when ultimately, in 1968, 'democratisation' of the political system was advocated as an essential concomitant of successful economic reform.

The political context in Hungary was shaped by the trauma of 1956, and contained a degree of ambiguity in the later 1950s. On the one hand, the task of restoring firm Party control to the satisfaction of the Soviet leadership tended to support a fairly hard-line political atmosphere. On the other hand, the experience of popular revolt had given birth to an appreciation of the need to temper ideological commitment by pragmatic considerations, at least as far as the management of the economy was concerned. This pragmatism was behind an underlying propensity of the Kádár regime to contemplate economic reform; but the introduction of a coherent reform programme was not possible until the early 1960s, when the political situation in Hungary had become 'stabilised', and Kádár himself had consolidated his control over the Party and political apparatus. Until the early 1960s, Kádár's leadership rested on an apparatus almost as hostile to reform as the Novotný team. Thus turnover of political personnel would be an important precondition of reform in Hungary, no less than in Czechoslovakia. But in contrast to the latter country, when élite turnover took place, it would serve to consolidate a reformist leadership, rather than provoke a crisis in the regime. This opened up the opportunity of economic reform being introduced as a means of political stabilisation of the Kádár regime, as the basis of legitimation, through mass material welfare, of an essentially undemocratic political system.

4 The Decision to Reform

Why did the Hungarian and Czechoslovak regimes decide to undertake economic reform in the early 1960s? The obvious answer would refer to the inexorable pressure of economic failure produced by the recession which affected the whole of the Soviet bloc in the early 1960s, confronting the regimes with the 'objective necessity' of change. But as Robert Tucker has argued in another context, 'circumstances do not carry their own self-evident meaning ... what people and political leaders *act upon* is always the circumstances *as perceived and defined by them*'.[1]

The decision to reform thus reflects not only economic circumstances of the time, but the political perceptions of the regimes. It would in fact have been open to a regime not only to deal with the economic problems by partial adjustments (which the Hungarian regime continued to do up until 1964), but also to reject any change whatsoever, and to seek a solution in an even more rigorous assertion of the centralistic principles of the old system (as the Czechoslovak regime did until 1963).[2] Ultimately, however, both regimes gave approval to reforms which involved systemic change in the management of the economy, which indicates that more or less far-reaching political changes had in the meanwhile taken place.

An examination of the circumstances in which the decision to reform was taken is an essential component of the explanation of the differing experiences of the practice of reform in Czechoslovakia and Hungary. The decision to reform embodies the key factors on which the later success of the reform depends – the coherence and consistency of the concept of reform itself, and the political will and authority of the political leadership in the whole venture. As we shall see in the comparative analysis that follows, while both countries underwent political change in terms of leadership personnel and style of rule, in Czechoslovakia this was not sufficient for the production of an authoritative leadership with a commitment to a coherent reform programme, and, as we shall see in Chapter 6, continuing political controversy surrounding the issue of economic reform throughout the 1960s contributed significantly to a broadening political crisis, in which political change of a systemic type – i.e. democratisation – came to be seen as a necessary component of economic reform. In Hungary, however, we have a contrasting situation, where political change of a limited sort (élite personnel turnover and a pragmatic political style) was adequate for the initial requirement of reform – the emergence of an authoritative leadership committed to a coherent and consistent reform concept. In this context, economic reform could have quite different political implications, as the basis for political stabilisation of a still essentially undemocratic regime, legitimised in the eyes of its population by enhanced economic effectiveness. The question of whether the reform in practice would ultimately prove successful without systemic political change will be taken up in Chapter 7.

A ECONOMIC DIFFICULTIES

(i) Czechoslovakia

Czechoslovakia entered the 1960s on a wave of self-confidence, buoyed up by the political 'success' of the regime in surviving the 1956 upheaval, and also by the apparently strong performance of the economy. The final years of the second five-year plan had seen national income rising by 7–8 per cent a year, industrial output by 11 per cent, and labour productivity by 7 per cent.[3] Agriculture, however, lagged behind, rising by 2–4 per cent a year, which might have given rise (though it apparently did not) to some longer-term anxieties on the part of the government. A further early warning of the dangers ahead, not sufficiently understood at the time, was the failure of certain key investment projects to be completed on time. Otakar Šimůnek, the chairman of the State Planning Commission, made optimistic and ambitious predictions at the Party Conference in July 1960 that Czechoslovakia would 'outproduce capitalism' in the course of the next five-year plan (1961–5)[4], which envisaged a continued acceleration of growth fuelled by a massive investment programme. National income was to rise by 8.4 per cent a year, industrial output by 11.2 per cent, and labour productivity by 7.2 per cent a year. Agriculture was set a lower target of 4.4 per cent average annual growth.[5]

In 1961, however, it quickly became clear that the economy was overstrained, and key objectives of the plan came under threat, as all industrial branches registered a slower pace of growth than in previous years, while only the chemical and consumer goods industries fulfilled their plans.[6] At the same time, the performance of agriculture, particularly crop production, proved to be well below the planned level. Total output was stagnant, while crop output fell 3 per cent.[7] Labour shortages held back coal production, revealing the precariousness of the Czechoslovak energy base, and also began to affect seriously the ambitious investment programme, additionally burdened by the backlog of uncompleted investment projects carried over from the previous five-year plan. The investment field in fact highlighted growing problems throughout the economy. The underfulfilment of the industrial output plan was most notable in the metallurgical branch, planned to grow by 10.3 per cent and in fact only achieving 7.5 per cent.[8] This in turn held back output of the engineering branches, causing failure to deliver investment equipment to priority projects. In addition, the building materials and construction industries proved quite unable to meet the demands of the investment programme. Decentralisation of investment – a component of the 1958–9 reforms – in fact exacerbated the problems, leading to competition for resources (without adequate economic checks) and drawing resources away from the priority centralised projects, which were underfulfilled by 8 per cent in 1961. Again, important projects remained unfinished, while the investment front expanded, and the volume of unfinished work rose inexorably.[9]

A major element of the mounting crisis was the foreign trade factor. The ambitious industrial growth rates envisaged in the plan would, in themselves, have been enough to generate tensions in the balance of payments, but the situation became acute in 1961 with the shortfall in the planned output of engineering – the major export branch – and the poor performance of agriculture, necessitating increased food imports. The situation was compounded by the impact of the Sino–Soviet rift on Czechoslovak trade. Exports to China, most of which consisted of machinery and equipment specifically designed for Chinese local requirements and thus not readily disposable elsewhere, fell from Kčs 787 m in 1960 to only Kčs 86 m in 1961. Imports from China, on the other hand, consisted mainly of food items – precisely what Czechoslovakia needed in 1961 – but these fell from Kčs 672 m to Kčs 184 m.[10] The importance of China as a source of foodstuffs is illustrated by the fact that in 1960 China had provided 38 per cent of total red meat imports (9 per cent of meat sold) and 22 per cent of poultry imports (10 per cent of marketed supplies).[11] Given the unavailability of food for import from other socialist countries, Czechoslovakia was forced to turn to hard currency sources of supply, which in turn posed a severe strain on the hard-currency balance of payments. Between 1960 and 1962, the trade deficit with developed capitalist countries rose by 30 per cent.[12] An additional strain was created by large credits, amounting to possibly $330 m or even more, granted to Third World countries in the period 1953–61, some of which appear not to have been repaid on time.[13]

1962 saw a further deepening of the crisis, as the growth of national income slowed from 6.8 per cent in 1961 to 1.4 per cent. A central assumption of the plan had been that output growth targets would be achieved by substantial annual rises in labour productivity, but the 5.2 per cent and 3.2 per cent increases recorded in 1961 and 1962 had fallen well short of the plan.[14] Growth of output had in fact been achieved in the past by increased employment, which resulted in increasing labour shortages. Unfinished construction in 1962 amounted to the value of Kčs 40 bn in total, equivalent to the entire amount allocated to investment in that year.[15] Only 106 out of 161 centralised investment projects scheduled for completion in 1962 were in fact finished, while the average gestation period had become twice as long as that envisaged in the plan. Shortages of raw materials, resulting from import cuts to restore the balance of payments, led to an estimated quarter of capacity in the engineering industry standing idle in 1962,[16] while the pressure to increase exports starved the domestic market both of producer and consumer goods. Bad weather in 1962 was the final blow to the staggering economy, leading to a disastrous harvest. Crop production fell 11.4 per cent below the poor 1961 level, while animal production fell 3.0 per cent.[17]

Half-way through 1962 it was already clear that the five-year plan was simply unrealisable. In August, it was announced that it had been abandoned. Otakar Šimůnek was replaced as planning chief by a trusted hard-liner, Alois Indra. A one-year plan was to be drawn up for 1963, with the purpose of stabilising the economy; it was intended to carry out urgent readjustments on the basis of a standstill in the growth rate. This would be followed by a seven-year plan for 1964–70, in which it was hoped that growth could be resumed along a revised course.

But 1963, intended to be a year of 'consolidation' and readjustment, turned out to be worse than ever. The one-year plan was found to have been ill-prepared, was subjected to constant revisions, and the economy quickly dissolved into chaos. A large part of the problem was the bad winter, which thoroughly disorganised transport and industry. National income in 1963 fell by 2.2 per cent, industrial output fell by 0.6 per cent, while agriculture – reviving by 7.3 per cent – still remained below the 1960 level (and below that of 1936).[18] Major problems of industrial reorganisation were not tackled, and stocks rose by a further Kčs 7 bn.[19] Investment goods piled up in warehouses; the projects for which they had been destined were cancelled as investment fell by 12 per cent. The energy situation, despite improved coal output, remained tense throughout the year, as indicated by the introduction of rationing of electricity in August.

An analytical account of the economic crisis by M. Bernášek concludes that the causes were rooted in the basic political objectives of the regime, and in the economic system itself.[20] The political objective of maximum quantitative growth of industrial output inherited from Stalin was reinforced in the late 1950s by Khrushchev's slogan of 'catching up and overtaking' advanced capitalist countries in industrial production, particularly in the output of coal, steel, cement, heavy engineering and electricity. The Czechoslovak leadership had accepted this task, disregarding the real constraints imposed by the relatively poor domestic raw-materials base for such a pattern of growth and such a high rate of growth. This had led to a long-term misallocation of investment resources, and to the growing balance-of-payments difficulties. The imposition of the command planning model had eliminated warning signals which might have been provided by a functioning price mechanism. The prevailing atmosphere of political terror had made rational economic debate impossible, and the arrest and imprisonment of leading economists had deprived economic policy-makers of expert advice. But the government's response to the crisis avoided confronting these issues.

The measures taken by the government to deal with the immediate situation led to a complete reversal of the decentralising measures of the 1958–9 reforms. The Planning Commission began to intervene directly, first in 1961, placing severe restrictions on enterprise decentralised investment; and, subsequently, it resumed control over balancing and allocation of certain goods which the reform had placed in the hands of enterprises. More and more items came under direct control by the Planning Commission and the Ministries, and centrally-set norms of material consumption were reintroduced.[21] In September 1963, the government issued a decree on 'Measures to strengthen the central direction of material and technical supplies', to come into effect in 1964, which formalised the re-centralisation of control.[22] The distinction between 'centralised' and 'decentralised' investments, in practice whittled away since 1961, was abolished.

Recentralisation was probably unavoidable in the circumstances, as an immediate response to the crisis, but the government and Party leadership made a virtue out of necessity, and clearly did not see it as a temporary measure. The initial response of the leadership was to attach the major part of the blame for the crisis not only on the exogenous factors (bad weather, the Chinese factor), but also, and most emphatically, on the decentralisation of the late 1950s. Thus, far from deducing from the crisis the inevitability of systemic reform, it took the opportunity to reassert the principle of 'democratic centralism'. A Central Committee document produced in August 1962 saw the solution in the following terms:

> In the first place, there is an urgent need to strengthen central management, that is, to perfect planning, the organisational and supervisory activity of the State and economic organs ... It is necessary at the same time to put an end to any uncontrolled elements, infringements of all-social interests, the underestimation of the law of planned, proportional development of the economy.[23]

The prevalence of the centralist approach was marked by Novotný's speech at the XII Party Congress in December 1962, in which he argued that 'Central management must be strengthened, and responsibility and state discipline must be improved at all stages.'[24]

If a reformist conclusion was to be drawn from the experience of the economic crisis, it would only emerge after political change had taken place. The economic experience was clearly not enough of itself to produce the necessary change of approach, so the possibility of reform came as a result of a political crisis which erupted in 1963 around a rather different issue – the legacy of the political trials of the 1950s.

(ii) Hungary

In many ways, the basic economic predicament which Hungary faced in the early 1960s was similar to that of Czechoslovakia, as a small country, poor in natural resources, and heavily dependent on foreign trade. But while Hungary was by no means immune to the effects of the bloc-wide recession of the early 1960s, in general terms it weathered it better than Czechoslovakia, and in some respects managed quite well. The explanation for this must lie not in any natural advantages the country possessed in comparison with Czechoslovakia, but in already existing differences in the political climate, reflected in the greater imagination, flexibility and sophistication of its approach to the management of the economy. A large part of the relatively stable economic development at this time can be attributed to the continuation of piecemeal reforms in response to economic problems, which enabled the government to steer the economy through the reefs on which Czechoslovakia foundered. Nevertheless, underlying the development of the economy were serious problems of which the government became fully aware by 1964.

Despite high growth rates in the late 1950s and in 1960–1, the Hungarian government did not submit to the temptation to accelerate the pace still further in the plan for 1961–5. National income was set to rise by 6.3 per cent a year on average, industrial output by 8 per cent.[25] This reflected an appreciation that the Hungarian economy had reached a new and more complex phase of development. The rapid growth trend, characteristic of an economy at the earlier stage of industrialisation, could not realistically be expected to continue. In contrast to the Czechoslovak regime's 'predilection for taut, pace-forcing plans',[26] the Hungarian government was aware of the dangers of overstraining the economy by disregarding the balance-of-payments implications of excessively high industrial-growth targets. In fact, the regime now placed foreign trade above quantitative growth as the priority of its long-term economic strategy, reversing the former tendencies towards autarky. Furthermore, it is significant of the overall political perspective of the regime that, unlike anywhere else in the bloc at this time, it aimed at increasing trade as much with Western markets as with the Council for Mutual Economic Assistance (CMEA).[27] Correspondingly, the plan for 1961–5 incorporated as its central objectives balanced growth, structural change towards products with high skilled-labour processing and low raw-material inputs, and emphasised quality, and matching production to demand, over quantitative growth.

In 1961, Hungarian industry returned the most successful results in the Soviet-bloc, with global output expanding by 11 per cent. Particularly rapid growth was recorded in chemicals (20 per cent, mainly accounted for by pharmaceuticals), electrical engineering (21 per cent), and precision engineering (18 per cent), all of which was in line with the planned structural development and the aim to increase exports from precisely these branches.[28] But the government's response to this was cautious, rather than euphoric, and, in 1962, measures were taken to discourage over-plan production, unless the enterprise could demonstrate that the raw material inputs were available without detriment to plan-fulfilment elsewhere, and further, that firm orders for the extra output had been placed.[29] From 1961, moreover, managerial bonuses were linked to the volume of sales or orders on the books, rather than to gross output, which induced managers to pay greater attention to meeting demand.[30]

A major, continuing problem which Hungary suffered, as did the other Soviet-bloc economies, was control over investments. The period of the plan for 1958–60 had seen a resumption of the trend for excessive growth in investments, which rose by 27 per cent in 1958, 34 per cent in 1959, and 11 per cent in 1960.[31] By 1960, investment accounted for 21 per cent of GNP.[32] This was seen as excessive, and a drastic 20 per cent cut was enforced in 1961, and careful control was maintained thereafter. A Hungarian Investment Bank survey revealed the massive escalation of costs which had occurred in past years. Only 57 per cent of the 262 major projects completed in 1961 had been within 10 per cent of their budgeted costs, while 6 per cent of projects had overrun cost plans by 50–100 per cent, and a further 5 per cent had more than doubled their budgeted costs. The planned average gestation period of 30 months had risen in practice to 38 months; less than one-third of the projects had been finished on schedule.[33]

A similar line was taken to the situation in stocks. As the Economic Commission for Europe reported in 1962, 'The Hungarian economy has not escaped the problems of misuse of inputs and accumulation of unusable output ... but such problems have been much less acute than in some other countries.'[34] In particular, a reversal of the trend in industry of growing useless production ('immobile stocks') was secured by 1963, when they were cut by 13 per cent. However, hoarding of stocks continued to be excessive, rising faster than global industrial output, and indicating the failure of partial reform measures to effect real change in efficiency. From January 1964, a further measure to this end was introduced, in the form of a 5 per cent charge on capital, calculated on the gross book value of fixed and working capital.[35] But, in the absence of any change in the wholesale price system, companies' net receipts remained guaranteed irrespective of the efficiency with which they used their capital, and thus the effectiveness of the measure was neutralised.[36]

A major problem area for Hungary, as for Czechoslovakia, was agriculture. The investment cuts of 1961 adversely affected the development of this sector, which, moreover, increasingly suffered from labour shortages, especially after 1963.[37] A major factor was the 'flight from the land' provoked by recollectivisation, completed in

1961. The labour shortage and peasant demoralisation resulting from recollectivisation, and the lack of the technological preconditions for large-scale farming, had to be made good by a massive injection of resources. 'The social problems involved had to be surmounted, and the economic sacrifices entailed by the organisation of large-scale farms had to be shouldered.'[38]

The plans for agriculture proved over-ambitious in the early 1960s. Agricultural output fell in 1960 and in 1961, and only reached its 1959 level in 1963.[39] From 1963, large-scale investment in agriculture took place. In that year, investment rose by 21 per cent. Supplies of machinery rose rapidly – 30 per cent more tractors and 50 per cent more combine-harvesters were provided. A further 14 per cent rise in investment was planned for 1964.[40] A sharp increase in the application of chemical fertilisers took place in the early 1960s.[41]

Of equal importance to the investments made available to agriculture, however, was the political flexibility of the regime, demonstrated in its approach to the internal organisation of the new cooperatives, which showed concern for peasant morale.[42] A key element of policy was also the relaxation of restrictions on private plots. In both respects, Hungary can be contrasted with Czechoslovakia, where agriculture remained a low priority, collectivisation was accompanied by maximum restriction of private plot cultivation, and no measures were taken to counteract the increasing remoteness of collective-farm management resulting from the mergers of farms into larger units.[43] In Hungary, recollectivisation was accompanied by the right of cooperative members to elect their management; successful *kulaks* were not excluded from membership, and in fact were often promoted to become 'key personalities' in the cooperatives.[44] A new share-cropping scheme was permitted, satisfying a demand raised by peasants in the 1950s.[45] Most important as an incentive was the greater toleration now shown towards the private plot. Membership of the cooperative and participation in the share-cropping schemes secured the peasants' right to retain their livestock and to obtain fodder. About 40 per cent of livestock remained in private hands.[46] In 1962, the Prime Minister declared that the household plots still had a great role to play in the supply of agricultural produce.[47] The 'organic unity' of cooperative and private production became an official slogan in agriculture. From 1962, cooperatives were encouraged to set up private-plot committees to administer land allocation, agree on the division of labour between cooperative and private cultivation, and organise the marketing of produce and the provision of other services, such as agronomic and veterinary advice.[48]

Flexible government attitudes and piecemeal reforms, while staving off the worst of the 1962–3 recession, were not enough, however, to bring about a fundamental change in the way the economy operated. The planned 6.3 per cent growth rate was never achieved – growth rates of 6.1 per cent, 4.7 per cent, 5.7 per cent, and 4.7 per cent were attained in 1961–4;[49] growth fell to 1 per cent in 1965.[50] In themselves, these rates in comparative terms (especially with neighbouring Czechoslovakia) need not have been regarded as disastrous, or as warranting radical, systemic change. But the Hungarian regime, as has already been noted, was not concerned purely with quantitative growth, but was even more concerned with efficiency, related to the centrality it had accorded foreign trade in its economic strategy – and it was in the area of foreign trade that, from 1963, the government became aware of mounting problems, which cast a wholly different light on the real performance of the economy.

In 1959 and 1960, imports had begun to rise rapidly, in terms of value (by 25.7 per cent and 23.1 per cent), and to outstrip exports (rising by 12.6 per cent and 13.6 per cent).[51] This led to a trade deficit of Ft 273.8 m in 1959, deteriorating to Ft 1195.6 m in 1960.[52] In 1961, Hungary appears to have been obliged to repay credits amounting to Ft 1.5 bn.[53] In 1961, the rate of growth of imports was held back to 4.7 per cent, while exports were stepped up, rising to 17.7 per cent,[54] with the result that a Ft 40 m trade surplus was achieved. But this could not be sustained. In 1962, export growth in all main commodity groups slowed, and total exports rose by only 6.9 per cent. Imports could not be held back without damage to material supplies and, more importantly, to the population's consumption. Imports thus rose by 11.9 per cent, and the trade balance was once more negative, to the amount of Ft 576.7 m.[55] The deficits were financed for the most part by short-term loans, causing a particularly tense situation in the first half of 1962, when monthly repayments were twice as high as export incomes.[56] Trade deficits continued to rise in the following years, reaching Ft 1171.2 m in 1963, and Ft 1676.2 m in 1964.[57] As Hungary's eminent economic historian, Iván Berend, has noted:

> The accumulating deficit did not arise from world market difficulties. The 1960s represented a unique decade of improving terms of trade for Hungary. The tension was a clear expression of restructuring exports and production, due to market needs and up-to-date technological requirements ... The recognition of the increasing role of exports logically led to the rediscovery of the harmful side-effects of the command economy.[58]

While the Hungarian regime in 1964 (the year in which systemic reform entered the political agenda) had avoided economic crisis and breakdown, it nevertheless confronted a 'hard budget constraint' in the form of the foreign trade problem. The necessity of change was a product of the contradiction between the objectives the regime had set itself – improved quality and efficiency with a view to gaining the benefits of foreign trade – and the possibilities of achieving those objectives within the framework of an only partially reformed economic system. A certain predisposition to reform on the part of the Kádár leadership was already apparent in 1957, but this had been diverted into what now appeared to be the blind alley of partial reform. Althought the Hungarian regime was politically more adept, and had chosen more appropriate economic policies than the Czechoslovak, it too confronted the systemic block of a basically unreformed economy. But Hungary, no less than Czechoslovakia, required not only conclusive 'objective' proof of the untenability of the old system, but also political change to secure 'subjective' recognition of systemic reform as the solution, and to consolidate a political leadership committed to carrying it out.

B POLITICAL CHANGE

The impetus for the political changes which took place in Czechoslovakia and Hungary in the early 1960s came not directly from the economic difficulties, but from outside, from the impact of the XXII Congress of the Soviet Communist Party, at which Khrushchev relaunched his 'destalinisation' strategy, interrupted after 1956 by the challenge to his power from his opponents in the 'Anti-Party' group.[59] The impact of the Congress in Czechoslovakia was quite different from that in Hungary. Developments in the former country took on the character of a political crisis, resulting in substantial change in leadership personnel, and providing the conditions in which change in the party's style of rule might have begun to take place. Novotný's personal power position was strengthened as a result of the personnel changes, but the overall result of the crisis was in fact a weakening of political leadership and authority. Although the changes which occurred forced a modification of approach on Novotný, his commitment to broader change remained highly ambiguous, based on the motive of personal survival rather than conviction, and his basic understanding of politics would remain narrowly tactical, lacking strategic conception, and increasingly out of line with the needs of the time.

In Hungary too, substantial turnover of leadership personnel took place, but the process did not take on the character of a political crisis, but rather brought about political stabilisation, since it served the purposes of consolidation of the Kádár leadership. 1962 saw the creation of the political conditions in which the lessons of 1956, as Kádár had consistently striven to define them, could be used towards the legitimation of change, both in politics itself, and in the economy.

(i) Czechoslovakia

Despite the firm line sustained by the Party leadership throughout the 1950s, revisionist, liberalising and change-oriented forces were not completely absent, but rather isolated and repressed.[60] The first sign of the re-emergence of anti-Novotný forces in the early 1960s can be traced to the still somewhat obscure events surrounding the demise of Rudolf Barák, Minister of the Interior since 1953. Evidence of a power struggle between Novotný and Barák first came to light in late 1961, with Barák's demotion to head a newly-created 'Commission for the direction of the National Committees'. This proved to be only a prelude to his dismissal in February 1962 on charges on embezzlement of state property and misuse of Party funds. In April, he was condemned to fifteen years imprisonment. However, strong political undertones were apparent in the case. Barák appears to have had a talent for self-publicity, and to have associated himself with liberalising measures in the public eye as Minister of the Interior. He appears to have enjoyed considerable popularity in the Party, and to have been regarded by some as an alternative to Novotný at a time of deepening economic crisis.[61] It has been suggested that Barák tried to make use of knowledge he had gained as Chairman of the first trials review commission of 1955 to discredit Novotný.[62] He is also reported to have cultivated connections in Moscow, notably with Andropov,[63] and to have complained to Khrushchev about Novotný's leadership of the Party.[64] Novotný himself declared in a speech broadcast over Prague radio that Barák had 'tried to seize power in the government'.[65] This much more serious charge than the one actually brought implied 'anti-state conspiracy', punishable by the death penalty. It has been suggested that the fact that this accusation was removed from the transcript of the speech published the following day in *Rudé Právo* indicated dissension at the top levels of the leadership over the appropriate method of dealing with Barák, and the existence of restraining hands on Novotný.[66]

While Barák was dealt with swiftly, the XXII Congress of the Soviet Party was to have unavoidable political repercussions. Khrushchev's relaunching of the attack on Stalin, more openly and vigorously than ever, appears to have taken the Czechoslovak leadership by surprise, and forced an embarrassing, if rather petty, series of reversals upon them. Elaborate preparations for the celebration of the 65th anniversary of Gottwald's birth, which had been going ahead in the late summer, had to be called off.[67] Gottwald's embalmed body was now to be removed from its mausoleum on Vitkov Hill, following the treatment meted out to Stalin's corpse in the course of the Soviet Party Contress. At the November Central Committee plenum, it was also announced that the giant Stalin monument, erected only in 1955, was to be demolished. But Novotný was at this time still in a position to refuse further reconsideration of the past. Slánský, the major victim of the trials, continued to be blamed for them. But the example set by Khrushchev opened the way for Czechoslovak critics – demands began to be raised, here and there, for a more systematic appraisal of the past: 'We must do something not only about the appearance, but the substance', it was said.[68] Moreover, against the background of the XXII Congress, the arrest and trial of Barák highlighted the divergence of Novotný's leadership from Khrushchev's. Novotný himself admitted that the Barák affair had caused some 'disarray' in the Party.[69] It must have aroused doubts in the minds of many loyal Party members, as well as provoking a more active alarm among progressive elements at the prospect of Novotný's reversion to the old, terroristic methods of dealing with political opponents.

In the course of 1962, the pressures on Novotný to undertake a more thoroughgoing review of the trials built up from various sources, which he was ultimately unable to resist. The example not only of Moscow, but also of neighbouring Hungary, where, as we shall see, destalinisation was being openly and effectively carried out, strengthened demands for a similar reckoning in Czechoslovakia. It is also likely that Khrushchev was exerting direct pressure on Novotný.[70] A major source of weakness of the opposition to Novotný had always been its fragmentation and isolation, but at the turn of the 1960s there emerged in the Slovak Communist Party a cohesive and sizeable political force against him. A long-standing nationalist resentment against Prague centralism had been inherited from the First Republic but was greatly exacerbated by the betrayal of Slovak post-war hopes for greater autonomy by the imposition of Stalinist centralism after 1948. Slovaks were by no means the only group to suffer from the purge trials, but they were the largest, and their grievances had been entirely neglected so far, being left out of the previous trials review, which extended only to 1952, thus excluding consideration of the later 'bourgeois nationalist' trials which affected the Slovaks. The quiet release from prison in the late 1950s of survivors of the trials, and the amnesty of 1960, were wholly inadequate to satisfy the Slovaks' thirst for revenge against Novotný himself, who had been personally responsible for the trials in which Vlado Clementis, the Slovak Party leader and Foreign Minister, had been executed, and leading Slovak intellectuals such as the poet Laco Novomeský and his close friend Gustáv Husák had been imprisoned. In addition, the 1960 Constitution itself had added insult to injury by finally eliminating what little autonomy Slovak national institutions had enjoyed.[71] The marked toning-down of celebrations of the August 1944 Slovak Uprising after 1960 further fuelled Slovak anger against Novotný, and his insulting and arrogant behaviour towards them on several occasions had earned him their enduring contempt.[72]

Against this background, in August 1962, a new trials review commission was set up under Drahomír Kolder, known at the time to be a Novotný protégé. It was revealed later in the year, at the XII Congress of the Czechoslovak Communist Party, that the commission's remit now extended through to 1954, and that its work would be complete by April 1963. The Commission proceeded in great secrecy, but its impact soon became apparent in the course of 1963.[73] In March, it became known that Josef Urválek, Chief Prosecutor in the period of the trials, had resigned. The April Central Committee plena of the Czechoslovak and Slovak Parties saw the dismissal of key targets of the mounting Slovak campaign. Karol Bacílek, a former Minister of National Security and, since 1953, First Secretary of the Slovak Party and a member of the CPCS Presidium, was dismissed, as was Pavol David, his deputy. Bruno Köhler, a founding member of the CPCS and a Central Committee secretary, was also dropped.[74] Much secrecy surrounded the meetings, but rumours began to circulate that Široký, the Prime Minister, was under threat.

While rumours were rife surrounding the issues of the April plena, by coincidence, in late April and May, a series of conferences and congresses of writers and journalists were held, which were to serve as an arena for the expression of the rising mood of defiance in certain sections of the intelligentsia, chiefly among the Slovaks. At the conference of Slovak writers on 22 April, Laco Novomeský appeared in person to announce that he had been rehabilitated, but also to declare that his case was 'only a minor part of something much bigger, much more monstrous and much more horrible'.[75] He called for further rehabilitations of repressed Slovaks, especially of Vlado Clementis. The Third Congress of Czechoslovak Writers, held in Prague in late May, was more muted, but again a Slovak voice, that of Zora Jesenská, was raised, this time against Široký himself.[76] The Congress of Slovak Journalists, occurring only a few days later in Bratislava, rounded off the heady season with a speech by Mieroslav Hysko, who made uncompromising demands for justice for victims of the 'personality cult', again pinpointing Široký in person as the next target of Slovak hostility.[77] A further contribution came from Roman Kaliský, a journalist from the leading liberalising newspaper in Czechoslovakia, the Slovak *Kultúrny Život*, who advocated political decentralisation and greater economic autonomy for Slovakia.[78] The publication of these speeches in the Slovak press illustrated the growing trend towards liberalisation in that part of the country.

In August 1963, the Kolder commission's recommendations for rehabilitations were published, but individual cases were not referred to, the question of compensation was not mentioned, and public attribution of responsibility for the injustices to individuals was not made.[79] But, at the September Central Committee plenum, Široký was removed from his posts as Prime Minister and Party Presidium member. Further dismissals of old-time Stalinists followed, including that of candidate Presidium member, Ludmila Jankovcová.[80]

The fact that Novotný himself survived the onslaught probably had much to do with its close association with the Slovak national issue. By ditching those of his closest colleagues who had held posts in Slovakia during the Stalinist period, he personally was able to survive. At the same time, he does not appear to have encountered effective opposition from a Czech destalinising lobby. As Galia Golan has perceptively suggested:

> The Slovaks decidedly were in the vanguard of the intellectuals' campaign, partially perhaps because they were temperamentally bolder than their Czech counterparts, partially because that nationalist aspect of their grievances gave them the appeal and unity of a 'wronged minority'. Thus they had relatively popular albeit

communist heroes such as Vladimir Clementis, Gustáv Husák and Laco Novomeský to avenge, while the Czechs could hardly rally much excitement over the hated Rudolf Slánský.[81]

It was not that Czechs as a nation were committed to Stalinism –Czech intellectuals also played an important part in the explosion of critical views in 1963, especially economists, as we shall see later. But the Czech intelligentsia was politically 'marginal', both in the general climate of a somewhat anti-intellectual, 'workerist' culture,[82] and in terms of their representation in the leading organs of power, especially the Central Committee. As intellectuals, moreover, their approach was to be that of a systemic critique, which is more complex to bring to fruition than the more straightforward demand for rectification of personal wrongs.

With the turnover of personnel at the top in the course of 1963, the political complexion of the regime changed. First, the underlying certainty and self-confidence of the regime had gone, as two astute observers of events noted:

> In fact, there was a gradual realisation that very little actual power resided anywhere in the supposedly supreme organs of Party and state. Demoralisation, disorganisation and diffusion of authority were felt in all spheres of national life. The collapse of authority remains the decisive factor in Czechoslovakia today.[83]

Although Novotný had survived, his position for the rest of his period of rule was to be one of weakness.[84] By temperament, ability and experience, he was a natural Stalinist,[85] but he now came to be surrounded by new men, younger than himself by as much as twenty years, untainted by the past, better educated, and somewhat more prepared for change. This can be illustrated by a few brief biographies.

The new Prime Minister, Josef Lenárt, had risen through the Slovak Party apparatus, having joined the Party when it was underground in 1943. His formal education, by comparison with others in the leadership, was quite extensive, including, in addition to the period of training in Moscow, the acquisition of a graduate degree in chemistry. He had had experience as Deputy Minister for Light Industry (1951–3), had held Party posts in Slovakia, and, from 1962, had been Chairman of the Slovak National Council ('Prime Minister' of Slovakia – although much reduced in significance since 1960). Zdeněk Mlynář describes Lenárt as 'a rational man', who 'sought out more highly-qualified people than Novotný had done for the various Party functions'.[86] Eliáš and Netík place him, along with Šik at the time, in the category of 'pragmatists' within the leadership,[87] a description soon borne out by his vigorous attack on 'low standards of management and planning' and 'inadequate efficiency' in the economy, in his maiden speech to the national assembly.[88]

The new head of the State Planning Commission, replacing Alois Indra, was Oldřich Černík, a well-qualified technocrat, with a background in heavy industry, described by Mlynář as a 'rational, pragmatic politician, a managerial type rather than an ideologue or agitator', and 'an intelligent and able organiser'[89] – qualities he was later to bring to bear on the political scene as Prime Minister in 1968. The new Minister of the Interior, who had replaced Barák, was Lubomír Štrougal, also a technocratic type, described by Mlynář as 'competent'[90] (and since 1970, Prime Minister of Czechoslovakia).

The style and methods of work of the Party apparatus also began to adjust in response to the new conditions. The Central Committee plenum of September 1963, which had carried out the major personnel changes, also introduced a new set of specialist commissions concerned with the economy, agriculture, ideology and the standard of living, headed respectively by Kolder, Jiří Hendrych, Vladimír Koucký and Jaromír Dolanský.[91] Later, in 1964, a Legal Commission was also established, under Koucký, into which Zdeněk Mlynář was drawn as secretary. Each of these commissions set up 'working groups' to cover various problems within their field, composed of experts drawn from a wide range of backgrounds. Examples of such groups were Radovan Richta's team working on the 'scientific and technological revolution',[92] and Pavel Machonin's group investigating changes in the structure of socialist society.[93] Later, in 1966, Mlynář headed a group set up to consider changes in the political system (whose unpublished report was used as the basis of the 1968 Action Programme); and, perhaps the most important of these earlier groups, Ota Šik's working-party on economic reform, to whose activities we shall return below. As Mlynář remarks on this aspect of change in the apparatus:

> The importance of these groups varied, but on the whole, the practice gradually led to a strengthening both of the party intelligentsia outside the apparatus and of reform communism. Officially speaking, the working groups were the expression of a trend in the party that demanded a higher degree of scientific

management in society; in actuality, they often reflected the inability of the apparatus to carry out any form of analysis or generalisation whatsoever.[94]

In addition, an effort was being made to improve the education of the Party apparatus at all levels. Mlynář reports on his own exhausting programme of lectures to Party and state officials at all levels, which began at about this time. He was also publishing numerous pamphlets and brochures aimed at this audience, which presented new ideas to people who had served the old regime for years. As he admits, 'I had no illusions about these being particularly scientific ideas, not even when I was propagating them inside the Communist party.'[95] But this was not the point. Mlynář was clearly optimistic about the possibilities of gradual change from within, while adopting a very pragmatic approach in his tactics. With hindsight, he is still convinced of the rightness of this approach in its time, and claims that 'thousands of party and state functionaries knew, and sympathised with' his opinions.[96]

Seminars and 'round-table' discussions involving Party, government and academic representatives were another method, increasingly used from late 1963, by which the Party leadership could draw upon a wider range of expertise. The editorial boards of various journals often took the initiative in organising discussions which they then published at some length – for example, the debates among economists in *Hospodářské Noviny*, the economic weekly, in November 1963, and in *Politická Ekonomie* in March 1964; and the questionnaire on attitudes to economic reform among legal specialists, drawn up by the editor of *Právník*, the monthly publication of the Institute of State and Law, and published in June and July 1964.[97]

Another significant indication of the greater receptiveness of the leadership to more sophisticated sources of information is the approval given, after much delay, for the establishment of sociology as an academic discipline in its own right. 'We are perhaps the only one of the developed countries where up to now there is no sociology society', one of the main proponents indignantly declared.[98] Arguments in favour of sociology emphasised its usefulness to the regime in dealing with the more complex problems of an advanced capitalist society, as 'an essential instrument in the cognitive activity of the directing organisms of socialist society and of the Communist Party itself'.[99] By late 1963, the Academy of Sciences and the Central Committee Ideological Commission had been won over to this view, and, early in

1964, the latter body announced its resolution to 'increase the share of the social sciences in solving the urgent problems of the scientific direction of society'.[100] As the first step, the Czechoslovak Sociological Society was formed in April 1964, with J. Klofáč as chairman.

Surrounded by a new breed of technocrats, Novotný began to project himself publicly as a 'reformer'. According to Mlynář, who has the benefit of an insider's experience, Novotný, now freed from the conservative influence of the old guard of the Gottwald leadership, and surrounded by men who owed their promotion to him personally, became 'genuinely committed' to a Khrushchevite approach.[101] Outside observers also noted the change in Novotný, who was seen as 'travelling on a magic carpet from Stalinist conservatism to anti-Stalinist reform',[102] 'acting no longer as a repressive, dogmatic leader, but as a middle-of-the-roader, guiding and directing the forces of reform'.[103] However, when it came to the issue of economic reform, Novotný's commitment in practice turned out to be more ambiguous. In dealing with the broader aspects of change–notably, in his dealings with those intellectuals who were less interested than Mlynář in cooperating with the political apparatus – Novotný's leadership (as, indeed, Khrushchev's) was characterised by a traditionally confrontational and repressive approach. That uninvited criticism would not be tolerated was demonstrated by Novotný in a speech at Košice directly following the writers' and journalists' conferences, where he openly attacked the publication of critical material in the Slovak press.[104]

In terms of personnel, the cultural and ideological fields remained dominated by familiar faces from the Stalinist era, chief among them Hendrych and Koucký. Both had earned themselves reputations for doctrinaire rigidity among well-informed Western analysts.[105] The promotion of Čestmír Císař, the vaguely liberal editor of the Party's theoretical journal, *Nová Mysl*, to a position in the Party Secretariat in April 1963 at first seemed to herald change in this area too. But his position was short-lived, mainly as a result of the rebelliousness at the cultural conferences in April and May, and by September he was demoted to the position of Minister of Education.[106]

Like Novotný, however, Hendrych and Koucký managed to adapt their approach. By the early 1960s, when Mlynář came to know them well, he reports that they were playing a not insubstantial part in fostering change within the apparatus (while continuing to resist its development outside), fostering the activities of the specialist groups and acting as patrons and protectors of rising young intellectuals.[107] Despite their Stalinist past, these men were similar to Novotný in typifying the classical Czechoslovak *aparátník*, whose ideological commitment was always subordinated to pragmatic and opportunistic considerations of the needs of the time. There was thus a strong element of flexibility throughout the upper reaches of the apparatus by the mid-1960s, which now, no doubt with the additional impetus of the lead given by Moscow, swung round to a new recognition of the need for change. As Mlynář recalls:

> Most frequently, the main effort went into assembling arguments to demonstrate the impracticality of certain reforms, either at a given moment or in the form proposed. But neither the leadership of the party nor its apparatus really doubted the inevitability of reforms, even in the political system itself.[108]

(ii) Hungary

An element of flexibility in the Kádár regime was present from its inception in December 1956, and is evident mainly in its approach to the economy, as we have already seen. The basic lesson which 1956 brought home to the party leadership was the absolute necessity of assuring economic stability, translated into a secure and steadily rising standard of living for the population. This correspondingly meant that commitment to Marxist–Leninist ideology had to be tempered by pragmatic considerations, as the minimum concession necessary to retaining political control. But the period of the late 1950s was characterised by considerable inconsistency[109] – on the one hand, useful and rational reform measures were introduced, while, on the other, strong elements of a dogmatic approach persisted, most clearly in evidence in the conduct of recollectivisation, and also in the half-way and partial character of the reform measures themselves. As in Czechoslovakia, change in the complexion of the political regime would be a necessary condition of the further advance of reform.

The first task for Kádár after 1956 was to rebuild the Party. The weakness of the Hungarian Workers' Party before 1956 was twofold: first, it was riven by intense factional conflict; and second, the majority of its members had probably not been committed to any faction so much as to their own personal interests in terms of the status and privilege which, until 1956, party membership conferred. The commitment of party members seems to have consisted mainly in unthinking obedience to authority rather than in intellectual conviction as to the main tenets of the ideology. Thus, in the years 1953–6, when authority relations within the Party became unclear, they looked to Moscow for guidance. But at that time the messages from Moscow were themselves unclear, inconsistent and self-contradictory. In the year of upheaval therefore, the party membership simply melted away. Of the 900 000 former members of the HWP, Kádár could muster only 37 818 at the beginning of December 1956.[110]

In rebuilding the new, renamed Hungarian Socialist Workers' Party (HSWP), Kádár intended that this should not merely be a resurrection of the hard core of Rákosi's party. The first condition for membership had to be evidence of the applicant's ability to learn the lessons of the past, as Kádár defined them. He adopted a 'two-front' approach – the 'excesses' of the revolution were to be blamed on both dogmatic, fanatical Rákosiites, and on 'right-wing' revisionists who had ignored the 'realities' of the Hungarian situation. Thus intransigent Stalinists and unrepentant revisionists alike were to be rejected, as were also opportunistic time-servers, who had equally failed the Party in 1956. Clearly, the pool of possible recruits was going to be quite restricted, and, in practice, things were not as easy as Kádár may have anticipated.

The vast majority of the pre-1956 Party members were at first hostile to his appeal. The majority of principled supporters of Nagy saw the attempt to rebuild the Party as a betrayal of the nation, and would have nothing to do with it. The opportunistic mass had tended, in 1956, to support Nagy, reflecting general popular attitudes. Now, of course, party membership had little to offer in the way of prestige and a comfortable life. As Tibor Meray put it, 'Party members are today even more a "sect" and live at even greater distance from the people than the looser and broader party membership before the Revolution. There was no glory then in being a party member, but neither was there shame.'[111]

The numbers who could be persuaded to join Kádár, simply to prevent the new Party from being dominated by former Rákosi supporters, were few indeed. Thus, by the time of the first conference of the HSWP in June 1957, Kádár had gathered 350 000 members (little over one-third of the former HWP's strength) and the overwhelming majority of these were hard-liners, or opportunists prepared to go along with the hard line.[112]

Kádár's original intention, as outlined in his December 1956 manifesto, to continue under a modified, somewhat toned-down version of Nagy's programme, was impracticable from the start. The Party's isolation from society was reflected in its own composition. The working-class membership declined to less than 30 per cent of the total, and, among these, dogmatic elements were dominant. Possibly half the total membership consisted of party functionaries, and state and security personnel.[113] At the end of 1957, 67 per cent of full-time party functionaries were members of the former HWP apparat, a large proportion of whom may safely be assumed to have been ideologically hard-line, if not Rákosi supporters. Their toleration of Kádár was almost wholly dependent on Moscow's support for him, and, at the mid-1957 conference, opinions concerning the transitory character of Kádár's leadership were openly expressed.[114] Kádár continually exercised the limits of hard-liners' toleration by his attempt to win some popular support for the regime by his conciliatory line. Particularly offensive to hard-liners was the toleration of private producers in agriculture, and licensed artisans, whose numbers had grown rapidly since 1953 with the collapse of the collectives and the more liberal licensing policy of Nagy's 'New Course'. The pressures for recollectivisation from both domestic and external sources were thus ultimately irresistible. The suppression of the revolutionary Workers' Councils was also inevitable.

In the eleven-man Politburo, on the other hand, Kádár could count on the backing of six firm supporters – Biszku, Fehér, Fock, Kállai and Szomogyi. Of the rest, Münnich, Marosán, and Rónai were, for most of the time, cooperative; the most dogmatic members, Apró and Kiss, were thus outnumbered. Moreover, the conference in mid-1957 also demonstrated the existence of some sources of internal support for Kádár. The Central Committee conceded the demand that delegates be elected from below by regional organisations, rather than be appointed. The debate on the conference 'theses' had to be held in closed session, as division still raged within the new Party as in the old. The leading old Stalinist cultural dictator, József Révai, who had been readmitted, apparently mainly on his personal anti-Rákosi credentials, met a frosty reception when he argued that 'revisionism' was the main enemy of the Party. Kádár's 'two-front' approach was accepted by the majority, and two further elements of his later 'alliance' policy first saw the light – that the Party should try to forge a cooperative relationship with non-party members, and that appointment to senior state and other posts should no longer be dependent on party membership. Thus, Kádár argued, people would no longer need to join the Party for purely careerist motives.[115]

In the early years of consolidating his leadership, Kádár was not helped by developments in the international communist movement. Although Khrushchev appeared at various times in Budapest and heaped praise upon Kádár, his own position in the immediate aftermath of 1956 was far from secure, as demonstrated by the emergence in Moscow of the 'Anti-Party' group. This in fact was interpreted by hard-liners in the Hungarian Party, notably József Révai, as an indication that Kádár's authority need not be taken seriously, but the defeat of the 'Anti-Party' group in June 1957 put an end to Révai's ambitions at least.[116] On the other hand, the degeneration of bloc relations with Yugoslavia also adversely affected Kádár's position. Tito had some part in recommending Kádár's elevation to Party Leader in November 1956,[117] a role which was deeply resented in some quarters in Moscow. The execution of Nagy in 1958 was almost certainly part of the resurgent anti-Tito campaign, and was a blow to Kádár, further isolating him from the moderate and progressive opinion in Hungary which he was anxious to court, as a counterweight to the hard-line faction. As Fejtő puts it, this created 'a new guilt complex toward the nation';[118] and, further, demonstrated to Kádár, to his hard-line opponents, and to the Hungarian public at large, that his government was indeed a mere 'puppet' of Moscow's machinations.[119]

A further source of hard-line pressure came from a pro-Chinese faction within the Party. In the late 1950s, increasing tension between the Chinese Party and Khrushchev led to the Chinese increasingly presenting themselves as a neo-Stalinist alternative to the Moscow leadership.[120] The Hungarian Minister of Agriculture, Imre Dögei, seems to have been linked with the existence of a pro-Chinese faction in the Party. This emerged at the time of his dismissal in January 1960 as a result of his excessive use of force in the conduct of the recollectivisation,[121] as will be shown later in this section.

With the consolidation of Khrushchev's position in Moscow, the Kádár regime began to take shape. Since 1956, party membership had risen steadily at the rate of 5–6 per cent a year to reach 402 456 (with a further 35 000 candidates) by the time of the VII Congress in late 1959. Khrushchev appeared at the Congress giving full support to Kádár, and endorsing a centrist approach in condemning Rákosi's leadership as a major cause of the 1956 revolution.[122] Following this, in January 1960, a reorganisation of the government took place, as Kádár took over from Ferenc Münnich the post of Prime Minister, combining it with his post as Party leader. In addition to the dismissal of Dögei, György Marosán, a 'crude and ambitious' politician,[123] was also removed from the government. Gyula Kállai, a loyal centrist supporter of Kádár, was brought in as deputy Prime Minister. The post of Minister of Agriculture was filled by Pál Losonczi, a competent former collective-farm manager.

In the meanwhile, party membership continued to rise, reaching a combined total of members and candidates of 498 644 by the end of December 1961, and 511 965 by August 1962.[124] The majority of these newer members were now Kádár supporters, drawn in by the more conciliatory approach of the leadership since 1959, younger people who had not directly participated in the 1956 events, and former HWP revisionists who began to accept the situation after the lapse of time, and for whom the argument that they should rejoin in order to act as a counterweight to the dogmatists now appeared persuasive.[125] By 1962 approximately 38 per cent of the party membership consisted of people who had joined after 1956.[126] Correspondingly, a substantial turnover of party personnel at the grass-roots began to take place after 1959. For example, in 1961, one-fifth of local secretaries and one-third of local committee members were replaced, affecting 35 000 Party functionaries.[127]

The Central Committee of the Party also underwent a considerable turnover. The 73-man Central Committee elected in December 1959 included only twelve members of the 1951 Central Committee in its membership.[128] The rest were new faces, promoted from county party organisations, the middle levels of the mass organisations, and from party cells in the ministries.[129] But further and more far-reaching change in the leadership was to occur as a result of the XXII Congress of the CPSU, which came as an enormous boost to Kádár, enabling him finally to dispose of troublesome remaining hard-liners at the top of the Party.

At the end of 1961, a Central Committee commission set up to examine the record of the Rákosi era concluded that Rákosi himself should not be allowed to return from the Soviet Union, where he had taken refuge in 1956. Members of the commission had visited him, and found that 'He refuses to weigh his responsibility, shows no contriteness, opposes the party line and pursues factional activities.'[130] In April 1962, Dögei, the dismissed Minister of Agriculture, was expelled from the Party for continuing factionalist agitation.[131] A former Minister of the Food Industry of the Rákosi era was expelled for corruption. The final reckoning came at the August 1962 Central Committee plenum, when Rákosi, Gerő,

István Kovács, Gyula Alapi, Vilmos Olti and fourteen former Államvédelmi Hatóság (AVH) (security police) officers were expelled for their abuses of power prior to 1956. Károly Kiss was removed from the Politburo for being 'still unable to see clearly the wrong practice of 1956' and unable to recognise his responsibility in it.[132] The occasion was also used to get rid of more recent hard-line opponents. Six party members were expelled for recent 'factional activities', and György Marosán was relieved of all his Party offices for attempting to rally dogmatic opposition to Kádár.[133]

The VIII HSWP Congress in November 1962 marks the consolidation of Kádár's leadership, with the confirmation in office of loyal supporters: Sándor Gáspár, Zoltán Komócsin and István Szirmai joined the Politburo. The Secretariat consisted of Kádár, Béla Biszku, Desző Nemes, Rezső Nyers, Szirmai and Károly Németh, all committed to the pragmatic centrist line. The tone of the Congress speeches emphasised 'dogmatism' rather than 'revisionism' as the main danger in political life.[134]

By 1962, Kádár had succeeded in imposing a significantly modified conception of the 'leading role' of the Party on official policy. In a major speech at the end of 1961, following his return from the XXII Congress in Moscow, he outlined the essential elements of his approach. The strength of the Party could not be measured in the size of its membership alone, but in the effectiveness of its policies. This in turn required greater emphasis on competence and expertise as criteria for admission to the Party. But this was not to play down the importance of political commitment – this was still essential for party membership – but, as he asked, 'What earthly reason is there for dragging people who are not convinced communists into the Party?'[135] While party membership was to be restricted to the actively politically committed, its need for expertise correspondingly meant that its attitude to non-party specialists would have to change. On this, Kádár was unambiguously committed. Hence the slogan characteristic of the entire Kádár approach was coined: 'He who is not against us is with us'. The basis of the Party's power would henceforth be the mutual trust of Party and people.

The VIII Congress saw the ratification of policies furthering this line. Alongside the dismissal of incompetent party members from leading positions, and the emphasis on competence and expertise in party recruitment, it was also made clear that appointment to all leading public positions was now open to non-party members. Furthermore, from 1962, political and class considerations were no longer to be taken into account in university admissions – perhaps the most immediate demonstration of Kádár's sincerity.

By the end of 1962, the Party had acquired a coherent and unified leadership, characterised by a pragmatic approach, willing to embrace change. It had sloughed off the legacy of the past by substantial personnel turnover, and by a relatively thorough and final disposal of the issue of Stalinism. Coming to terms with Stalinism had consolidated a pre-existing tendency in the leadership, rather than forcing a crisis-ridden reversal, as in Czechoslovakia. Although Kádár was no more likely than Novotný to tolerate unbridled opposition from the intelligentsia, he proved more successful in preventing its re-emergence at this time. This was due not only to the impact of 1956 on the intelligentsia and their growing mood of resignation to the new *status quo*, but also to the leadership's active encouragement of support from critical intellectuals by the clear and authoritative rejection of Stalinist dogmatism given the lead by Kádár himself; by the vigorous and genuine reassertion of the importance of intellectual expertise; and by the offer of attractive rewards for intellectuals who were prepared to cooperate, without demanding humiliating political or ideological concessions from them.[136] While in Czechoslovakia reformist forces were growing in importance at the middle levels of the *apparat*, they nevertheless remained excluded from the topmost decision-making bodies. Novotný's dominant position at the top symbolised an important element of continuity with the past, with the result that the scope of debate on the whole question of change, insofar as this required a thorough re-examination of the past, had to be more limited in Czechoslovakia than in Hungary. This had the further effect that a significant element of reformist opinion, in the cultural intelligentsia especially, remained alienated from Party-inspired reforms. The politically unacceptable oppositional activities of these groups outside the apparatus in the course of the 1960s served to complicate the position of reformers within, by increasing Novotný's mistrust of all forms of change.

Hungary, however, was by no means devoid of conservative forces after 1962 – the fact that they had been excluded from the centre of policy-making did not mean they ceased to exist. While they were not in a position to prevent the elaboration and official approval of a coherent reform programme, they would nevertheless continue to present a political challenge and, at a later stage in the reform process, they would be crucially placed in executive middle-level positions to distort and obstruct the reform in its implementation. Thus while

Hungary had the initial advantage of a leadership more unambiguously committed to reform, the progress of the reform would in the end suffer, no less than in Czechoslovakia, from the failure to effect more far-reaching change in the political system itself.

C THE DECISION TO REFORM

(i) Czechoslovakia

The publication in September 1962 in the Moscow *Pravda* of Liberman's seminal article, 'Plan, profit, premium',[137] brought the issue of economic reform onto the political agenda in Czechoslovakia too, giving encouragement to those economists who remained convinced of the basic correctness of the 1958–9 measures, and who, in opposition to the then-prevailing centralistic approach of the government, now saw the need to develop them more systematically. But the economic experts in 1962 were in a politically weak position – indeed some of their best and most experienced colleagues, such as Evžen Löbl and Josef Goldmann, had been in prison until 1960 and were still under a political cloud. The economists' only effective representative in the central organs of power was Ota Šik, head of the Academy of Sciences Institute of Economics and a Central Committee member only from 1962. The XII Congress in December 1962 had in fact quietly passed a resolution in favour of setting up a committee to investigate ways of improving the functioning of the economy,[138] but at first discussions were held behind closed doors within the Party and state apparatus, itself not over-endowed with specialist economic talent.[139] Little is known of the early stages of work on the economic question. The possibility of a policy of systemic reform being adopted was thus at first quite slight, and would have remained so, had it not been for the political crisis of 1963.

The rehabilitation of trials victims brought back leading economic experts into public life, and the political disorientation at the top brought a sudden relaxation of control over debate in the press, which provided economists with the opportunity to present more radical approaches to the solution of the economic problem. Radoslav Selucký, an economist at the Prague Technical College with a remarkable journalistic gift for clarifying and dramatising basic issues, brought the economic question right into the heart of the controversy already beginning to emerge openly around the issue of Stalinism:

> In my opinion, we have up to now overlooked the fact that along with the cult of the personality, there arose too a *cult of the plan*. It consisted in the fact that the measure of the worth of peoples' work stopped being concrete, useful and socially beneficial activity; it was replaced by another, administrative viewpoint: the fulfilment of prescribed indicators.[140]

The plan, he argued, had become an end in itself, unable to define the needs and capacities of society because it had become cut off from reality.

Selucký's bold and colourful metaphor immediately pointed to the systemic nature of the economic problem. The implications were thus radical, and his article correspondingly drew swift and sharp rebuke from *Rudé Právo*.[141] The official view was given in a reply to Selucký in *Kulturní Tvorba* by Josef Toman, who protested that:

> to regard the honest effort by people to fulfil plans as a nonsensical pursuit of indicators does not amount to anything else but deprecating their work and denigrating the authority of the state plan as the expression of all-social interests.[142]

This kind of irresponsible writing would not be tolerated, Toman indicated, concluding with the minatory rhetorical question, 'are we to witness the birth of the cult of the independent economist?' Selucký himself was apparently blacklisted after this,[143] and was personally attacked in a speech by Novotný.[144] Nevertheless, the phrase, 'cult of the plan' was extraordinarily successful, and the article provoked widespread debate, not only among economists, but within factories too.[145]

At this point, Ota Šik came forward to defend the position of the critically-thinking economist in an important article in *Nová Mysl*, entitled 'The remnants of dogmatism in political economy must be overcome'. He asked:

> Of what use are economic scientists, if they cannot draw attention in time, for whatever reason, to certain chains of events which call for momentous changes in economic policy, and if they can only repeat back and defend what the leadership of communist parties themselves think up?[146]

Šik had become a central figure in the economic question. The Economic Commission, set up under Kolder in September 1963, supervised the working group of economic experts headed by Šik which had the task of drawing up a proposal for reform. But it was clear already by the end of 1963 that the working group was encountering political obstacles to its activities, as Šik explained:

> We still encounter opinions which refuse to see our present difficulties as a consequence of shortcomings occurring over a longer period in the methods of planned management, and which point to these difficulties by contrast as a manifestation of the abandonment of 'tried-and-tested' methods of planning and management from the initial years of our socialist development.[147]

There was a deep-rooted tendency within the apparatus to cling to the original interpretation of the economic crisis, as a result of the 1958–9 decentralisation. The basic problem, as Šik saw it, was the persistence of dogmatic views, 'of oversimplified, yes, even in part, speculative Stalinist theoretical concepts', and of the traditions of 'bureaucratic, formalised red-tape'.[148] The task of the working group, as he saw it, was to produce a comprehensive and fundamental solution 'going right to the heart of the present shortcomings', but the work was provoking 'nervous flusterings' and 'panic-mongering' among some comrades.[149] At first, Šik attributed the problem merely to the low level of education and competence of the apparatus personnel, and called for an intensive educational effort. But it soon became clear that not only 'cognitive difficulties' were involved.[150]

At the Central Committee plenum in December 1963 Šik noted that within the plethora of views on the economic issue, two basic tendencies had begun to crystallise into mutually exclusive, opposing camps. Although everyone was now mouthing 'anti-dogmatic' slogans, 'in fact, dogmatism in economic opinions is terribly deep-rooted'.[151] 'Dogmatists' could still be recognised by a style of argument which, Šik admitted, he himself had propagated in the past among Party functionaries:

> Never substantiating certain theoretical assumptions by reference to reality, never concretely refuting the arguments of their opponents by showing their divergence from reality. But substantiating or refuting certain opinions by abstract theoretical notions which they brandish as a magic formula on every occasion.[152]

Following this approach, Šik argued, production in the 'social interest' is equated with maximum centralisation of control over the economy: 'In harmony with all such opinions, of course, their advocates propose as the solution to the present difficulties even further extension of the number of directives, indicators, norms and controls.'[153] Indeed, 'many comrades' were aware from their own experience that fundamental change was necessary, but were easily put off when it was suggested that the changes proposed were against 'socialism' and meant a return to capitalism.

The tenacity of dogmatic views could be explained, Šik now maintained, by 'various interests and petty concerns, ambitions, considerations of prestige etc.'. The most vehement defenders of the existing system usually proved to be those:

> who fear that they may lose their present position and comfortable life as a result of the new methods and proposals. This involves people who for years broadcast certain theoretical opinions, wrote about them, based their reputations on them, and now, for reasons of prestige, they cannot back down.[154]

As the first draft of the working party's report took shape – in the form of the 'Pink Book', submitted to the Party Presidium in January 1964[155] – Šik's tone sharpened, as he was clearly under pressure to compromise. In an article in February 1964, entitled 'No stopping half-way in the utilisation of socialist commodity relations', he struck out at:

> those bureaucrats whose own personal power positions and decision-making in every detail – irrespective of whether it is reasonable or whether it benefits society or not – are more important to them than the socially necessary development of production.[156]

Diehard opposition to reform and uncritical defence of the old system were mainly the province of 'less intelligent people and administrative organs lacking sufficient creative capacities', the economist Vladimír Kadlec declared,[157] but, in the political climate of 1963 and 1964, they were driven into retreat. 'Dogmatism' was clearly out of fashion at this time, but this did not mean that resistance to reform had also evaporated – instead it took on more subtle forms, which posed rather more difficult and elusive obstacles to reform. There remained considerable ambiguity over the whole question within the higher reaches of the Party–State establishment. The prevailing attitude was more one of grudging or fatalistic resignation, than of positive commitment. As an important critique of the

Novotný regime, published in Czechoslovakia after the 1968 invasion, confirms (from a quite different political standpoint):

> It was characteristic of the then leadership of the Party that it would make up its mind to resolve all pressing problems always at that moment when this could be understood only as a forced retreat under the pressure of ineluctable necessity, and not when that solution might have contributed to strengthening the political authority of the Party.[158]

Although the political position of economists had strengthened in general terms as a result of the increased prominence given to economic issues in 1963, and the opportunity to conduct a public debate, raising radical alternative solutions to the crisis, reformist economists still lacked direct access to decision-making at the topmost levels of the institutional hierarchy. In contrast to the situation in Hungary, the leading exponent of reform was not in a senior party position. In fact, throughout the whole period of reform in Czechoslovakia, Ota Šik was kept at arm's length by the political leadership and by those most closely involved with the economy – Lenárt, Kolder and Černík.[159] While Lenárt and Kolder, who were in the Presidium, appear to have become convinced of the necessity of reform, their commitment was limited by their narrow, technocratic approach and their subordination to Novotný.[160] They failed to grasp its significance as a component part of a much broader change in the whole system of government. They remained essentially *aparátnici*, viewing reform from within the perspective of the existing political and administrative structures. Thus they lacked the essential political will to mobilise the apparatus behind reform in an authoritative manner, and were more willing to seek compromise solutions and to take a cautious, piecemeal approach in the interest of the paramount objective of preserving political stability (which at the time appeared under threat). Political stability was equated with maintaining as far as possible intact the political–administrative system through which they had risen to power and which had shaped their whole political approach.

Novotný's public pronouncements in the course of 1964 make it clear that he recognised there was a serious problem in the economy which had to be dealt with, and that fairly drastic measures would be necessary. In his speeches, he put forward no *a priori* ideological objections to reform, and went along with the economists' arguments to the extent of acknowledging that planning had to be made more 'scientific', and that 'economic instruments' would have to be used to improve quality and to bring production in line with social need.[161] He conceded now that the resolutions of the XII Congress (which initially he had used to justify recentralisation of the economy) had implied the need for 'qualitative changes' in the economy, including 'structural and organisational changes'.[162] He acknowledged the usefulness of 'sharp criticism' and welcomed the 'practical proposals' which had been made, and the 'broad and creative participation of scholars, specialists, economic and political officials from all sectors in the solution of economic problems'.[163] But, at the same time, he was clearly equally anxious to reassert control over the general drift of the debate, denouncing the 'arrogance' of certain intellectuals, who 'simply dream things up and then present their subjective opinions and judgements in the pages of newspapers, journals, and over the microphone with pontifical arrogance',[164] or who 'put themselves above the Party in the role of some sort of saviour and redeemer, in which they attain their unsatisfied personal ambitions'.[165]

It was made clear, right from the start, that the leadership was only prepared to contemplate reform as some sort of concession to necessity, within a tightly circumscribed framework, excluding the broader questions of political change, which Novotný saw, after 1963, as personally threatening. This was first signalled by the rejection of the first reform draft, the 'Pink Book', submitted by Šik's group in early 1964. In April, Novotný indicated that the Presidium had been very dissatisfied with the proposal:

> The proposal was subjected to detailed examination and returned for fundamental revision. Our concern is that the principle of democratic centralism and responsibility should be consistently enforced in the whole of our system of management and planning.[166]

Undaunted apparently, in the second draft of the reform, the 'Yellow Book', Šik's group also included far-reaching proposals for institutional reform, aimed in particular at decentralising administration to break up the monopolistic general directorates, and for changing 'cadre policy' – presumably meaning the downgrading of political criteria in managerial appointments.[167] But, as Šik later revealed, these parts were struck out of the 'Basic principles for the improvement of the planned management of the economy', presented to the Central Committee and approved in September 1964.[168] It was not until 1968 that these issues could again be raised for serious consideration as essential components of reform.

But the reformers' case itself was weakened not only by their lack of direct access to power (which also meant they were denied access to vital sources of economic information),[169] but their own shortcomings as economists. On the one hand, their great strength was in the breadth of their vision, which, in contrast to that of the technocrats, encompassed new general philosophical and political assumptions (to be discussed in Chapter 5). But they lacked at certain points the essential grasp of detail especially in practical questions, since most of them had not had direct experience of economic management. They were, as a group, overwhelmingly academic economists by origin, not officials of the planning or ministerial apparatuses. This is especially evident in Šik's career. His knowledge of economics consisted almost entirely of Marxist 'political economy', and his work, as the Western economist John M. Montias pointed out, remained at the level of 'exegesis' rather than analysis:

> Indeed, Šik has little practical knowledge of the economy, and his quantitative understanding of its structural relations is especially deficient. While his enthusiasm for reform is real enough, he has not the facts at his command to confute the conservatives.[170]

Czechoslovak economics had been almost completely cut off from Western economics up to this time, with the result that there appears to have been little real understanding of the operation of market economies. At times Western economists found strong elements of *naiveté*[171] and a disconcerting 'messianic' enthusiasm for neoclassical concepts in reformist arguments.[172] Equally significantly, they were also practically unaware of the works of fellow-economists closer to home – for example, of the Soviet economists of the 1920s, and of Lange and Kalecki.[173] The reason for this is, of course, the impact of Stalinism on Czechoslovak economics, the arrest and imprisonment of leading figures of the older generation, and the failure of revisionist ideas to penetrate until this time.[174]

The reformers themselves were not unaware of these problems. Šik on numerous occasions drew attention to the deficiencies of Czechoslovak economics, and urged that these be made up rapidly,[175] as did speaker after speaker at a conference devoted to this at the end of 1963.[176] The immediate effect of this lack of sophistication was to force the reformists to remain at a very general level of argument, leaving key problems rather sketchily glossed over,[177] which in turn left them open to the criticism that they were 'moving in very abstract spheres', as Novotný put it.[178] Those with much greater practical experience in the economic apparatus could convincingly point to the difficulties and questions of detail which Šik's working group had neglected. While such leading economic officials were themselves not necessarily overtly anti-reform, their caveats were quickly taken up by others who had misgivings about the whole enterprise of reform, which were politically rather than technically founded. This is reflected in Novotný's position. Having recognised the inevitability of reform, he also emphasised its dangers, 'We must proceed very carefully and with the utmost circumspection. Rather let us examine matters twice or three times than take a step which we might regret.'[179] This is precisely what happened, to Šik's growing exasperation, with the reform proposals. Right to the last days before the outlines of the reform programme were to be put to the Central Committee in January 1965, the party Presidium was criticising the 'insufficient depth' of the proposals in key areas, such as prices, levies, credit and investment – the central planks of reform.[180]

M. Sokol, a senior official of the Planning Commission, pointed to the dangers involved in over-hasty implementation of economic reform in current Czechoslovak conditions, which, he argued, the reformers had overlooked in their assumption of the existence of an 'abstract equilibrium'.[181] While accepting that the basic reformist principles were satisfactory, he pointed to the prevailing massive disequilibrium as a reason for delay, with demand exceeding supply in virtually all branches of the economy, and a basic economic structure which perpetuated this situation. Reform in this context could well lead to massive inflation and unemployment, which could only be avoided by retaining a degree of central control which would undermine the aims of the reform. The question of monopoly, he also argued, was not susceptible to solution by organisational measures alone, since, on the one hand, it was a product of the sellers' market situation, and, on the other, as he claimed, it reflected an 'objective tendency', observable in capitalist economies too, towards greater efficiency through concentration and specialisation.[182]

These types of qualified objections to reform were vigorously rejected by reformist economists. Komenda replied that the fact that the new system would generate its own problems was not sufficient reason for retaining the existing system. Indeed, the problem of inflation should not be seen exclusively as a problem of the new economic system, since the existing state of disequilibrium had been produced by the unreformed system.[183] The argument for delay, pending adjustment of the economic structure, was refuted by Karel Kouba and Josef Goldmann, who argued that what was needed was not a one-off change, but the creation of an effective economic system which would force constant adaptation of the economic structure to changing needs.[184] Behind apparently technical and well-founded arguments for caution, in other words, lay a basic difference in political will. Nearly everyone claimed to be in favour of reform, but what this actually meant was not always clear. Not all were 'reformists', in the sense not necessarily of Utopian or over-enthusiastic conversion to the market, but at least of having the basic predisposition to tackle reform with its acknowledged problems, in preference to the spurious advantages of centralism. As we shall see below, this minimal political will was present in the Hungarian leadership, but – superficial appearances to the contrary – was lacking in the Czechoslovak regime.

Thus the problem for the reformists was not merely that of confronting clear-cut 'dogmatic' opposition to reform, but of overcoming the ambiguity of the leadership's commitment to it. It was not just a question of maintaining the momentum of reform (difficult enough from a position at best at the side of, rather than within, the decision-making bodies), but also involved overcoming leading officials' attempts to manipulate and fudge the meanings of fundamental concepts of the reform, which could undermine the overall coherence of the programme and thus reduce its chances of ever really being put into practice.

Examples of this game of words can be found, for instance, in obliquely expressed conflicts over the status of the reform as merely an 'improvement' of the existing system, or its 'further perfection' (itself a logical impossibility), as compared with the view that it was a fundamentally new system, or 'model'. This in turn implied certain differences in the interpretation of the old system and its relative merits. Clearly, any discussion of reform at all presupposed that the old system was inadequate at the present stage, but the way in which its deficiencies were defined had broad policy implications. Representatives of the official leadership line resolutely denied that the past practice of the regime had been in any way at fault.[185] Indeed Šik himself, whether out of political expediency or conviction, appears at this time to have maintained that the old system had been appropriate in its time but was now outdated.[186] However, Šik also recognised that a thorough re-examination of the past was an essential precondition for the development of a successful reform.[187] Novotný, clearly, was interested in keeping as much of the past under wraps as possible. The official leadership view was that the reform should not be seen as 'a negation of the system we have had up to now',[188] and that the decision to reform only illustrated once again the wisdom of the leadership, entailing 'improvement' of the existing system. As Lenárt told the Central Committee in January 1965:

> The change of system does not ... mean the supplanting of one system by another. We are mainly concerned to abolish elements that, in the old system, led to a dogmatic approach, and created the ground for uncritical judgement of management, that is, we want to work by the method of constant improvement in the forms of management.[189]

Šik, on the other hand, took the view that the reform was fundamentally new, corresponding to radically changed economic conditions, and thus had a logic of its own, different from that of the old system.[190] It could not work, therefore, if it represented a half-way compromise – this, in Šik's view, had been the main cause of the failure of the 1958 reform.[191] However, Novotný at times appeared to continue to blame the failure of the reforms of 1958–9 on the fact that they 'seized upon so-called decentralisation'[192] for the solution to economic problems. The basic changes, as he saw them, were aimed at producing 'all-sided fulfilment of the tasks of the state plan'.[193]

The definition of the role of the plan in the reformed economy could also be used to subvert the intentions of committed reformers. As we shall see in the following chapter, none of the reformists proposed the abandonment of all planning (although there were significant differences among them on the precise scope of the plan). But this was taken by some as meaning that the main goal of reform was to make the plan 'more scientific', while trying to play down the importance of the market as a necessary condition of that.[194] State Planning Commission officials appear to have been convinced of the continued 'priority of the plan' as the essential guarantee of socialism,[195] and were attacked by reformist economists as 'downgrading' the market elements of the reform 'to mere methodological components of the plan, which we may, but are not obliged to, use'.[196] On the other hand, the very weakness of the mathematical base of economics in Czechoslovakia meant there was very little interest in 'computopian' or 'push-button' economics.[197] In fact, the most prominent advocate of mathematical and cybernetic approaches, Oldřich Kýn, was a committed reformer.[198]

(ii) Hungary

The process of arriving at a decision to undertake reform in Hungary differed from that in Czechoslovakia in three main ways. First, the locus of initiative was in the heart of the party apparatus itself, centring on the person of Rezső Nyers, elected as Central Committee Secretary and put in charge of economic affairs in 1962. Second, Nyers's intention from the start was that reform should be comprehensive and consistent, and his intention was effectively translated into official policy. Key words in the presentation of official documents on the reform were the adjective 'comprehensive' (*átfogó*), invariably describing the nature of the reform; and the use of the term 'mechanism' to conceptualise the economic alternatives – unreformed or reformed – as organic wholes, comprising closely interdependent functional elements. This signified the explicit recognition that partial reforms were doomed to failure. Reform, to be successful, had to set up an entirely new operating logic. Third, Kádár's role in the reform preparation was to provide the essential political defence of it. He provided political leadership, defending the reform through continued attacks on dogmatism, and emphasis on expertise. His contribution was not so much in direct participation in the elaboration of the reform model, but in providing the political space within which economic experts were left relatively free to debate and thrash out the technical details, the relative merits of different solutions to various aspects of reform, without political interference. The process of taking the decision was thus less tortuous and protracted than in Czechoslovakia, and resulted in consensus on a more carefully-thought-through reform concept.

The first moves towards economic reform were underway behind the scenes already in 1963, as Nyers set up his own personal informal advisory body, consisting of twelve members, as a 'brains-trust' on economic questions.[199] This brought together experts from a variety of backgrounds, including both theoretical and practical economists, Party and state officials. There was apparently from the start a consensus within this body on the need for 'radical' reform.[200] At the Central Committee plenum in May 1963, Nyers outlined the four key problem areas in the economy – to accelerate the rate of growth, improve the balance of payments, raise the standard of living, and improve enterprise management. The basic approach which he saw as the solution to these problems lay in industrial reorganisation, increased enterprise autonomy, improved central planning, and changes in the incentive system.[201]

Nyers instructed the Central Committee's Economic Department to prepare a proposal for a programme of work on the question of 'the further development of economic management', which was to be ready by July 1964. On 21 July the Central Committee's Economic Committee resolved correspondingly to 'launch a comprehensive re-examination of economic management, to embrace our production, price-formation, incentive, monetary, financial and agricultural systems, and the economic structure'.[202] The research was specifically directed to result in proposals for increasing enterprise independence and responsibility. A thorough critical appraisal of the existing economic mechanism itself was to be carried out, as the essential basis upon which a 'comprehensive concept' of economic modernisation could be constructed.[203]

In the meanwhile, during 1964, Nyers undertook a campaign of publicising and defending the reform in principle, as part of a general effort to create a favourable climate of opinion. In an important article in the Party's theoretical journal, *Társadalmi szemle*, in February, he argued:

> The methods of economic management and material incentive must always be in accord with the priority objectives of economic policy at the time ... In no way would it be proper to equate the essence of socialist planned economy with a particular planning or management method. In the Marxist–Leninist conception of socialism, the method of management is a broad concept, indeed, it includes a change of methods and mechanisms from time to time and, furthermore, this is an inherent part of it.[204]

In a lecture to the Party Political Academy in March, he highlighted the issue of technological change in Hungary, by telling comparisons with advanced capitalist countries. This, he concluded, pointed to the need not only for reforms in the domestic economy, but also in the organisation of intra-CMEA cooperation, to permit direct relations across frontiers between enterprises and research institutes, bypassing the interstate level of contacts.[205]

A further contribution towards maintaining the reform impetus in public was made by the publication of some notable books criticising the Stalinist economic system in uncompromising terms. The economic historians, György Ránki and Iván Berend, both produced excellent works at this time, bringing out the systemic nature of the economic crisis which lay behind the 1956 events, and relating the economic crisis to the broader, political aspects of Rákosi's rule.[206]

At the same time, a 'Hungarian Solzhenitsyn' was discovered, in the person of the writer, József Lengyel, undoubtedly less artistically gifted than Solzhenitsyn, but nevertheless producing a shocking account of his own prison-camp experiences in the Soviet Union.[207] This flow of critical literature was managed in a rather sophisticated way by the Kádár regime to its own advantage (which was in contrast with the crude repression exercised in Czechoslovakia, which so irritated the Czech intelligentsia). The limits of the tolerable were left rather unclear, and the regime proved able to prevent criticism getting out of hand without resorting to heavy-handed measures. Rather than fretting at censorship, intellectuals seemed quite surprised at what was in fact permitted, and, mindful of the 1956 experience, were careful themselves not to overstep the mark, wherever it might lie.[208]

Kádár himself continued to press home his line on the necessity of expertise, as, for example, in his speech to the Third Congress of the Patriotic People's Front in March 1964:

> If a person does not have sufficient gumption to acquire knowledge of the somewhat more strenuous and longer method of persuasion, and if his leadership skill stops at the recipe of 'expel-jail', he cannot get on in public life today, and still less in the future. We shall fight against such people.[209]

The Party daily, *Népszabadság*, had become an effective mouthpiece of Kádár's line, as demonstrated by a vigorously expressed editorial comment in July 1964:

> No policy, and no working-class policy, is worth a damn if we do not give priority to streamlining and modernising our plants and seeing to it that they are managed expertly ... Fidelity to socialism will not make up for lack of knowledge, although knowledge itself will not replace fidelity to socialism ... The workers' power is no longer represented by commissars educated by the old regime to keep an eye on the experts.[210]

The source of resistance to the official line, against which so much effort was expended, came from the local party apparatus, and found expression in county newspapers, which published complaints from local party members, expressing doubts about the new line, about the wisdom of airing so many problems in public to the supposed benefit of 'our enemies'. The Party was felt to be 'weakening', and the virtues of loyal party workers neglected, in the new priority given to expertise in appointments.[211] But the Hungarian leadership was not alone in its striving for reform – the example of the Soviet Union could be referred to at this time as a source of authority to legitimate the new course. The Soviet press was full of debate about reform, which could not go unnoticed in Hungary. Liberman's article was published in translation at the end of 1964 in *Társadalmi szemle*, timed nicely to coincide with the crucial December plenum, at which the basic concept of the reform was to come onto the agenda.[212] '[B]y the turn of the years 1964–5, favourable conditions had been produced for putting the Hungarian economic reform into full gear', Iván Berend recalls.[213]

The December plenum approved the basic concept of reform, and instructed Nyers to set up a series of expert committees to produce the basic guidelines. Eleven work groups were set up, drawing in 130 economists, engineers, jurists, industrial and commercial experts. The groups set to work on the following areas:

- economic planning and the role of the plan in the system of economic administration;
- the methods of enterprise management in each of the main economic sectors, including questions of more effective economic integration, the relations of enterprises with each other and with the state bodies;
- the coordination of agriculture in the planned economy, and the internal democracy of agricultural cooperatives;
- improvement of the planning and financial arrangements for foreign trade, and increasing the influence of foreign trade on production;
- the development of domestic trade and problems in the supply of consumer goods and services;
- the price system;
- wages, incentive systems and labour relations;
- the preparation and execution of investment and the management of fixed capital;
- technological change;
- the economic role and functions of local councils;
- increasing worker participation in economic administration.[214]

Although the first hurdle had been surmounted, with reform now official Party policy, 1965 was to prove a difficult year for its further development. The Central Committee had approved the reform after October 1964, when Khrushchev's removal from power seemed at first to give hope to those in Hungary who continued to oppose reform. Kádár's immediate response to the change in Moscow was to assert that 'the essential, decisive fact is that the political attitude of the HSWP and the government of the Hungarian People's Republic has not changed one iota, nor will it change'.[215]

Nevertheless, political stability was further shaken in 1965, as economic difficulties became more acute, and the holding operation of the previous years, by which the worst effects of the recession had been held at bay, finally threatened to come adrift. After the unexpectedly large rise in the trade deficit in 1964, imports had had to be held back, and exports stepped up. Import cuts affected not only machinery and equipment, but also raw materials and semi-processed inputs.[216] The situation was compounded by poor performance in agriculture, with total output falling by 5.5 per cent.[217] The previous three years' steady improvement in living standards came to a halt. Measures were introduced to check the growth of real incomes through a revision of the work norms and income tax, and price rises were announced on petrol and alcoholic drinks. Real wages were stagnant or even fell slightly.[218] In some places, norms were revised upwards by as much as 14 per cent, with the inescapable result of quite large cuts in wages, and corresponding ill-effects on worker morale were noted.[219] At the end of the year, further price rises were announced, with meat prices rising by 30–50 per cent, dairy products by 13–19 per cent.[220]

Popular resentment appears to have grown in the course of the year, and to have provoked significant concern on the part of the leadership. There was a danger that this would be mobilised by political opponents of Kádár and the reformist line.[221] Indeed, the late 1965 price rises were reported as having provoked demonstrations,[222] and the Hungarian press admitted that a number of arrests had been made over the New Year period for 'anti-state incitement'.[223] Throughout 1965, there was considerable coverage in the press of the questions of 'apathy' and 'indifference', poor labour discipline, corruption and economic crime.[224] At the same time, it was also acknowledged that the press could help to combat the social evils of 'indifference' and dissatisfaction with the current economic situation by being more informative and open, providing a 'frank, authentic, objective and just familiarisation and understanding of public affairs', as Péter Veres, the former chairman of the Peasant Party, wrote in *Kortárs*.[225] The need for improvement in the press was recognised by the Politburo, which noted that 'if we do not speak of something on time, the enemy will. As a result, reticence amounts to political defeat'. The media, therefore, should not shrink from 'unfavourable facts'.[226]

The main official approach to the difficulties was thus to be a combination of swift and efficient clampdown on overt opposition in the form of protests and demonstrations, along with openness in discussion not only in the press, but in the leading political bodies. The February 1965 session of the National Assembly 'put the nation's real economic situation on the public record with unprecedented thoroughness'.[227] Kádár gave a remarkable speech, in which he twice lost his temper (the speech was broadcast live), and departed from the prepared text to attack those who wanted to restore a 'militant, strong-arm policy', and to reassert the correctness of the economic policies adopted, while railing against the incompetence of those at lower levels who were obstructing its implementation.[228]

In fact, the crowds which spontaneously gathered at the Budapest railway station to greet Kádár on his sudden return from Poland immediately after the news of Khrushchev's removal, were a testimony to the gathering genuine popular regard for Kádár, which helps to explain why the deterioration in living standards during the year was not mobilised by his opponents. At the same time, Kádár made frequent visits to Moscow in the year following Khrushchev's removal, further securing his authority.[229] Thus in November 1965, when the Central Committee again discussed the economic reform, it was clear that no back-tracking had occurred. The plenum approved the basic guidelines presented by Nyers's expert groups, and further detailed research was set into motion, in preparation for the start of implementation of preliminary measures in 1966. The essential coherence of the official line was preserved, and it strongly recalled the original reform proposals of 1957.[230] As the plenum declared:

> From the critical analysis, we have unambiguously and unanimously ascertained that fundamental change is necessary. The main shortcomings that have been established are closely interconnected, they cannot for the most part be eliminated in piecemeal fashion, but only by measures which are interconnected and comprehensive[231]

While their partial measures were still justified as having been 'appropriate in their time', the resolution noted that 'in today's situation ... something more than that is required', and concluded that 'the organic interconnection of socialist planning and the active role of commodity–money relations is historically inescapable'.[232] In Berend's view, a unique insight, occurring for the first time in the history of socialist planning, was incorporated into the November 1965 resolution, in the identification of the 'breaking down of the plan' from the centre, via the ministries, to enterprises in the form of directive targets as the key source of the problem.[233] The Central Committee presented an alternative view of the role of the plan:

> The basic task of national and economic planning is the planning of the main objectives of development and of the main proportions ... the autonomy of state enterprises should be significantly enlarged ... This can be done in such a way that ... the realisation of the plan is guided not by the breakdown of various plan indices, and thus not by prescribing administratively individual plan index numbers, but mainly by economic instruments.[234]

The magnitude and significance of the change was not played down, but on the contrary was emphasised, for example, by József Bognár, Professor of Economics at the Karl Marx University of Economics, 'The development and introduction of the new economic mechanism is beyond doubt the most important stage in the history of socialist economy since the creation of socialist relations of ownership.'[235]

Further elaboration of the main directives of the reform took place over the winter, and, in May 1966, the Central Committee gave its formal approval to the reform proposal and the programme for its implementation. Although various preparatory measures could be introduced in stages, the essential interdependence of the basic aspects of the reform meant that it would really only come into effect from 1 January 1968, with the introduction of the new price system. This meant that in the meanwhile, an enormous and complex preparatory exercise would take place:

> Everything must be prepared circumspectly and carefully, revising all details again and again, anticipating unpredictable difficulties. It would be desirable to carry out the reform step-by-step, gradually, precisely in order to avoid major shocks. But exactly the most important changes can hardly be implemented gradually. There must be a point at which a quantitative leap must be undertaken.[236]

So explained the economist György Péter, the man who had first raised the systemic question, in his path-breaking analysis published in 1954.[237] Thus the reform in Hungary could at the same time be proclaimed as a radically new and exciting stage of development, serving to legitimate the Kádár regime as fundamentally different from the Rákosi past, while drawing on equally important legitimating connections with the past in the Nagy era, and the 1957 aborted reform proposal.

5 The Logic of Reform Thought – from Economics to Politics

In practice, from the very beginning, economic reform had been closely bound up with a process of political change. At first, the extent of that political change was quite limited. As we saw in Chapter 4, the essential precondition of the acceptance of economic reform as official policy in Czechoslovakia and Hungary had been a profound disturbance of the political self-confidence of the Party leaderships. Mounting economic difficulties reaching crisis proportions had challenged the assumptions of Party omniscience and of hierarchical discipline as the guarantee of order and progress. In the interests of their own self-preservation, of political stability, the political leaders came to recognise the need for expert advice from specialists. As a result, the status and political influence of intellectuals were considerably enhanced. But the political implications of economic reform did not end there, for it was not only a question of conceding greater autonomy to experts, but of implementing their advice. The content of their advice had wide-ranging general implications, which will be discussed in this chapter.

There are two parallel themes running through the presentation of reform thought in the following pages. On the one hand, we look at the internal logic of the ideas produced by social scientists. The arguments of the economists in favour of a more rational model of economic management, incorporating elements of the market, contained an implicit revision of the central legitimating tenet of the communist system – that it operated in the 'social interest'. In Hungary, the shared memory of 1956 effectively restrained the intelligentsia from publicly teasing out the precise implications of this for the operation of the political system. In Czechoslovakia, however, a wave of new ideas gathered pace, spilling over from economics into sociology and thence to debate on the political system, which in turn washed back into economics. In the course of the 1960s, reformist ideas in each branch of the social sciences began to coalesce and mutually reinforce each other, emerging in 1968 as a new model of 'socialism' itself. While in Hungary the elaboration of the economic reform proceeded with a studious avoidance of the political question, in Czechoslovakia, political reform came to be seen as an integral part of economic reform. By the end of 1967, as we shall see in Chapter 6, as a result of the specific conditions of implementing the economic reform, political reform was eventually also seen as a necessary precondition of economic reform.

The second theme of the chapter takes up a subsidiary issue which recurs in the intellectual debate especially in Czechoslovakia – the role of 'science' and, by implication, of intellectuals in socialist society. The preoccupation with this issue reflects not only the changed position of intellectuals in general, but also the particularly acute situation in Czechoslovakia in the 1960s, where regime–intellectual relations were notably turbulent and conflict-ridden. As will be argued in Chapter 6, this was the major reason for the politicisation of economic reform in practice in that country. But it is included here as being of general theoretical significance, transcending the particularities of the Czechoslovak case, and intimately linked with the basic problem of reform. At root, the issue of 'scientific', or intellectual, autonomy is the same as that of enterprise autonomy, or social group autonomy, within the framework of a communist regime. In each case, the problem for the regime was the containment and manipulation of autonomous forces in the interests of enhancing, not undermining, effective Party control. On the one hand, intellectuals had to be allowed a measure of autonomy to think up new solutions to the problems the regime recognised as having arisen. But then this small oasis of conditional freedom which the intellectuals occupied proved hard to contain, as the ideas they produced threatened to go well beyond the limits envisaged by the Party leadership, and to challenge the power structure itself.

A THE PLAN, THE MARKET AND THE 'SOCIAL INTEREST'

A recent review by a Hungarian economist of the development of economic reform thought usefully puts forward a three-stage process of recognition of the origins and nature of the problems of the centralised system.[1] The first stage is to blame economic difficulties on extraneous factors – the impact of war, a hostile outside world, criminal sabotage. (One might also include here harvest failure caused by weather conditions.) The second stage is to put the blame on bad organisation, lack of discipline, or the low standards of management.

The corresponding solutions will then be sought in reorganisations, personnel changes, increased central supervision, more detailed central instructions. Only at the third stage does attention become focused on the economic mechanism itself, but even here, a more limited approach is first tried out (which here we will call 'stage 3a'), when the problem of the economic mechanism is seen merely in terms of faults in its incentive system. In this case, it is still not the directive nature of the plan that is seen to be at fault, but the inadequacies of the plan indices. Attention is thus directed at improving the indices in such a way as to stimulate greater interest in quality, efficiency and innovation. This approach represents a qualitative change in the understanding of the economic problem, but, the author argues, 'it stays strictly within the limits of the existing directive planning system, wants to rationalise its functioning'.[2] A final cognitive stage (to which we will refer here as '3b') is reached with the conclusion that:

> it is insufficient to modify the scope or contents of the central instructions issued to the economic agents, but the situation of the agents themselves must be changed, their relation to each other and also their economic environment. In other words, the entire system of planning, decision-making, stimulation, price, credit, wages, investment, supply, distribution, foreign and domestic trade must be revised, the economic mechanism itself must be changed.[3]

As we have seen in Chapter 4, in Czechoslovakia, the Party and government leadership's responses ran successively through stages 1 and 2, finally coming grudgingly to rest at stage 3a. In Hungary, where developments fluctuated violently, by 1956 the official perception could be described as having almost reached stage 3b, but, after mid-1957, when reform was politically ruled out, reverted to stage 2, with some elements of 3a. But by 1964, it had advanced to stage 3b, in accepting the need for comprehensive reform. However, many leading economists in both countries had, by the early 1960s, arrived firmly at point 3b, although certainly by a variety of routes. Some had indeed followed the gradual path of recognition of the need for reform by successive elimination of possible alternative explanations of economic failure. Among these could be numbered leading Party economic specialists, such as István Friss in Hungary, Ota Šik in Czechoslovakia, and Włodzimierz Brus in Poland. But other economists, more distanced from power, either arrived at the same point by 'skipping stages' in the process, or indeed, had never been under any illusions as to the economic viability of the centralised model.

It is important to note that in Hungary the establishment of economics as a 'science' occurred very early, almost immediately after the death of Stalin, as a result of the rapidly-maturing economic crisis and the pressures from the new Moscow leadership for a change in the economic course. The need for 'scientific' study of the economy was first formally recognised in the Central Committee resolution of June 1953, and found formal expression in the establishment of a new Institute of Economics in early 1955. In fact, as a result, Hungarian economists were the first in the Soviet bloc after Stalin's death to publish a systematic critique of the centralised model – seminal works were published in late 1954, which first pointed to the source of the economic problem in the system's most characteristic feature: the centralised prescription of enterprise output targets. Sándor Balazsy suggested that this practice should be abolished outright, leaving enterprises guided only by the index of net value of output and the total value of deductions to the state budget.[4] In place of centrally-set assortment plans, enterprises should be guided by delivery contracts negotiated with their customers. The article was well ahead of its time, and correspondingly drew some harsh criticism from more orthodox spokesmen, fearing 'anarchy' and the neglect of production of unprofitable articles if central directives were abolished.[5] György Péter's article appeared the following month.[6] It took a macroeconomic approach and prefigured the 'regulated market' model in its implicit recommendations. Starting from empirical observation of the ineffectiveness of plan directives in achieving the given end – the most economical use of the productive resources to meet social needs – he arrived at the conclusion that really effective control could only be realised by buyers and consumers, not by central authorities at all. The condition for effective control of this sort would be the creation of a buyer's market (although he did not use this term), and the introduction of some form of cost-based price system which would also reflect supply and demand. This latter, crucial, element was not, however, given more than sketchy treatment in his article.

The work of János Kornai *Overcentralisation in Economic Administration*[7] (researched in 1955–6 and published in Hungary in 1957) was of outstanding significance intellectually:

> Kornai's book was the first economic sociography in the post-liberation Hungarian literature. It was at the same time the first work in the entire international literature on the socialist economy which did not explain what the mechanism of the economy under central plan

directives *ought to be*, but how it did operate in reality, and why it did not ensure the expected planned development and efficiency of the socialist economy.[8]

The strength of the book lay in the comprehensiveness of the analysis – 'nobody before Kornai had carried out their factual analysis point by point, the complex description of the chain of interconnections'.[9] The book showed it was impossible to solve the basic economic problems by improving or altering the plan indices. Even the replacement of quantitative indices by profit would be ineffective, if it were not accompanied by far-reaching and integrated changes in the price system, to reflect supply and demand; by the creation of a buyer's market and competition between enterprises; by a managerial incentive system tying earnings directly to success; and by the development of indirect instruments by which the centre might guide enterprise behaviour.

Kornai's work was also significant in explicitly addressing itself to the 'sociopolitical' aspects of over-centralisation. In fact, his chapter on this issue raised the basic questions to which later reform theorists would return in the late 1960s (and which continue to exercise them today).

The major political consequence of over-centralisation which Kornai identified was *bureaucratisation*, by which he meant the stifling of initiative, increasing passivity, and the corresponding tendency to an authoritarian style of administration, the use of dictatorial command, rather than persuasion. It was no coincidence, Kornai suggested, that the height of economic centralisation in Hungary also saw the 'spread of arbitrary bullying'.[10] He pointed to the paradoxical effect of issuing every more and more detailed instructions, in an attempt to eliminate all spontaneity in the economy. This had resulted in less rather than more effective control, the 'proliferation of harmful, uncontrolled processes'[11] which he had identified in his empirical analysis (for example, the distortion and manipulation of plan targets, contrary to the centre's objectives). As the number of instructions proliferated, while, at the same time, central intentions failed to be realised, the system had come to depend ever more on coercion: '[T]he more instructions there are, the more frequent their infringement, and so the frequency of punishments goes up'.[12] He also linked to over-centralisation the endemic attitude of mistrust, particularly of the intelligentsia and of technical experts and managers, which was a natural concomitant of the system's operation.

Kornai argued that the formation of a self-aggrandising administrative machine was a necessary result of over-centralisation. This inflated machine had taken over from enterprises tasks which they should, and could, more effectively carry out for themselves. But the constantly expanding machine could not be checked merely by periodic reductions in its personnel, since, given the lack of incentives in the system for enterprises to carry out these tasks effectively, the machine was necessary to the functioning of the system itself. It was, furthermore, self-reproducing: while the constant expansion of the administrative apparatus was a necessary *effect* of the system, it had also, over time, become a *cause* of its persistence, 'for when once an inflated administrative establishment has come into existence, this will itself almost automatically produce ever-recurring attempts to promote centralisation".[13] A final sociopolitical consequence of over-centralisation which he identified was the lack of real worker participation in the economy:

> In these circumstances the main body of workers in enterprises have regarded their own part in the direction and control of production as being of no more than formal significance: they have not been able to feel that they really owned their enterprises. And the fact that the central authorities have not relied on the workers in these connexions has contributed to the need of the former to depend on an ever-expanding administrative machine.[14]

Implicit in Kornai's enumeration of the economic shortcomings and negative political aspects of over-centralisation is a coherent critique of the system as an interdependent whole. Thus not only are all the economic phenomena interlinked, but the economic system itself is intimately connected with the pattern of politics. This perception is central to what we have called 'stage 3b' in understanding. Inescapably, the systemic critique of the centralised model touched upon the most fundamental legitimating concept of the political system – that the economy was run in the 'social interest'. The old system of planning and management of productive units by directives was recognised as having displayed a long-term inability to use resources efficiently, and to produce goods which actually met users' or consumers' needs. Paradoxically, the attempt to guarantee the 'social interest' through maximum central control deprived the centre both of the ability to define the 'social interest' in accurate, realistic terms, and of the power to assert it in practice. The striving for power and maximum control had led to the opposite result.

Although open debate and publication of explicitly reformist economic literature in Hungary was virtually halted after the summer of 1957, the increasingly repressive ideological atmosphere of the late 1950s did not disrupt the continuity of development of economics as a 'scientific' discipline. The community of specialist economists was united in a consensus against returning to dogmatic concepts, and was not wracked internally by the mounting ideological offensive against 'revisionism'. Attacks on reformist concepts in economics came from outside the discipline, from non-expert workers in the ideological and political field, rather than from fellow-economists. Moreover, despite the hard line in ideology, the government itself in practice continued to recognise the importance of sound expert advice from economists, and often adopted the advice proffered in particular policy areas. Most importantly, the political attacks from the ideological apparatus did not lead to the total obliteration of economists known to persist in reformist convictions. Although some suffered career reversals, they were not prevented from working, and were even able to continue publishing:

> It is a factor not to be underestimated that in the past 30 years in Hungary – in a way which is singular in Eastern Europe – there has been full continuity in economic research ... the new starts, rediscoveries, and lapses accompanied by great intellectual losses and drops in standards could be avoided in the evolution of the discipline.[15]

By the early 1960s in Hungary, as a result of the political developments outlined in Chapter 4, the discipline was finally freed from the more crass forms of direct ideological interference. A watershed was a conference of economic experts convened by their ideological watchdogs in December 1963, with the original intention of reasserting ideological discipline in the field, berating economists for their 'lack of partisanship'. But it was to prove 'the last serious and public attempt at obstructing the economic reform demanded by the Hungarian economy and society on ideological and political grounds instead of discussing the subject on its merits'.[16] Economics as a 'science' had meanwhile found a forceful and politically powerful patron in the Central Committee Secretary, Rezső Nyers, who, when opening the conference, emphasised the urgent need for accelerated progress in the discipline, and for a broader diffusion of economic understanding throughout society. He reported that, in the opinion of the Party Central Committee, scientific knowledge could not be founded on any sort of 'revelation'. Every economist moreover, should be aware of, and learn from, developments in bourgeois economics. The struggle for a Marxist approach, he argued, should be conducted by reasoned argument: 'Let us debate constructively, that is to say, without beating about the bush, not recognising so-called 'sensitive questions', but all the same not in an undisciplined way.'[17]

As will already be clear from the previous chapter, the conditions in which economics developed in Czechoslovakia were far less favourable. Leading economists, such as Löbl and Goldmann, had been in prison for years. The relative economic stability of the 1950s, and the consistent ideological rigidity of the regime both militated against professional development of the discipline. Until the early 1960s, the field was dominated by specialists in 'political economy', who lacked the training, and often also the intellectual ability and interest required for independent, critical, and sophisticated analysis. Czech and Slovak economists were, moreover, intellectually isolated, cut off not only from developments in the discipline in the West, but even from Polish and Hungarian economic thinking.[18] The attitude of the regime to the discipline was to remain profoundly ambiguous throughout the 1960s, tending to continue to view it as more of a threat than an aid in tackling complex economic problems. Thus changing ideas among economists met with no encouragement from the authorities, a state of affairs that was symptomatic of the whole political crisis which unfolded in the course of the decade, and will be discussed in Chapter 6. Czech and Slovak economists had no such powerful patron as Nyers. Ota Šik was their leading public defender, as we have seen in Chapter 4, but was not in a position to secure their protection from repeated political assaults. The result of all these factors was the rapid and marked overt politicisation of economics, economists and the economic reform which is so characteristic of Czechoslovakia in the 1960s, in contrast to Hungary. Czechoslovak economics lacked the firmly-established professional–intellectual base which it enjoyed in Hungary, and had to fight continually for its existence. But it also lacked the broad technical competence in matters of detail which had accumulated in Hungary. Both by circumstances and by training, Czechoslovak economists were far more predisposed to enter into political questions. What Czechoslovak economics lacked in technique, it made up for in the rapidity with which it grasped the systemic aspect of the problem. While this perception was of course not absent among Hungarian economists – as is clear from the start in Kornai's early work – in the conditions of the early 1960s, they were not readily drawn into the question of political reform in their public writings. On the one hand, the trauma of 1956, still less than a decade before, had instilled in the vast majority a profound scepticism about the possibility of political reform. It seemed not only dangerous, but futile, and even counter-productive, to link economic reform with the question of political change. On the other hand, the increasingly encouraging signs of political flexibility on the part of the regime after 1962 allowed many economists to entertain the hope that adequate and positive political development might even evolve 'naturally' or spontaneously as a direct, necessary product of the pluralisation of the economy through reform.

Perhaps the single most important article at the start of the reform debate on economics in Czechoslovakia was written in 1963, and published, with some delay, in 1964 by Bohumil Komenda and Čestmír Kožušník.[19] The article went straight to the heart of the economic problem – the flawed conception of the 'social interest' embodied in the centralised model. In its hitherto accepted form, the conception of the 'social interest' was, they argued, based on two unrealistic assumptions – first, that the centre had the practical capacity to dispose of adequate information to fulfil its role of detailed, all-comprehending definition of the 'social interest' in the form of a directive plan; and, second, that there were no conflicting interests within the economic system.

Since the centre could not give detailed instructions to cover all possible circumstances, enterprises in fact had to make decisions for themselves, but they had no other guide than the plan in determining what was socially rational, and, furthermore, they had no interest in choosing a socially rational course of action. Where enterprises are interested solely in fulfilling plan indicators, they will obviously try to get the lowest possible targets set, and claim the highest possible allocation of material so as to make their task easier. But this in turn stretches resources, leaving insufficient 'slackness' in the economy, which leads to shortages, bottlenecks and so on, which in turn require central intervention to overcome them. Thus we arrive at the paradoxical situation where:

> directive management appears as the only acceptable solution to the discrepancy which it has caused, as the only guarantee which safeguards the planned nature of social production and the satisfaction of social needs against the narrow interests of the enterprise.[20]

But as this process goes on, it becomes increasingly difficult to say whether the centre really does know what 'social need' is in any specific instance. The price system gives no guidance in this, as prices are fixed by the centre and remain the same for long periods. Their use is restricted to accounting purposes, although they are a major indicator of enterprise activity. All this results in a lack of incentive for enterprises to innovate, or even to produce goods of a satisfactory quality, and also leads to a concentration on a limited assortment of goods whose production is most advantageous to the producer, irrespective of the users' requirements.

It was not a question merely of improvement within the present framework, argued Komenda and Kožušník; nor would the introduction of mathematical methods and the use of computers in planning solve the problem, as long as the role of enterprise interest was ignored, since the system would still rely on distorted information provided by the enterprise.[21] The system assumed that enterprise interest was always in accordance with the plan, in which case, planning would be a purely formal exercise, since enterprises would presumably act in the way they did regardless of the existence or non-existence of a plan; from another point of view, it regarded enterprises as mere automata, without a will of their own, which was plainly not the case. Economic activity is a purposeful, rational reaction of people to objective conditions which cannot be altered simply by directing them to act otherwise. What was required was a different sort of planning altogether, not a 'partial modification', but a 'fundamental reappraisal of the first principles and main methods and instruments of planning'.[22] The kernel of the problem is the use of the market:

> Only by using market relations is it possible to form a system of planned management of the social reproduction process, in which every step need not be prescribed from the centre for individual units of the total social cooperation, but it would be possible to use the fact that in each of these units, thinking people are working, who are capable of orienting themselves independently and taking purposeful decisions.[23]

The controversial conclusion of Komenda's and Kožušník's article was that the concept of the 'social interest' needed to be revised. It could not, they suggested, be understood in the monolithic *a priori* sense of official ideology, but could only usefully be identified in broad and general terms. Correspondingly, their proposals for reform involved a change in the definition of the role of the plan itself, which had to take on the form of a long-term, general statement of basic economic objectives, and was to be both a guide to, and guided by, the market. Differing interests within the economic system would thus no longer be suppressed but would be overtly recognised, and would be harmonised through the market, guided in the 'social interest' by the centre.

The basic point had in the meantime become fully recognised in Hungary, as illustrated by István Friss, whose ideas had developed from a traditional Stalinist standpoint towards a reformist position in economics. The plan, he wrote, which was supposed to represent a coherent expression of the 'social interest', had in fact become an '*ad hoc* jumble without a conception',[24] an incoherent aggregation of partial plans submitted by sectoral ministries on the basis of their own objectives and their own perceptions of the needs of the economy, inevitably clouded by the limited perspective of their own, sectoral priorities. The centre's role had been undermined by the inaccessibility to it of alternative, objective information apart from that provided by the administrative hierarchy which it headed. In fact, it was difficult to speak of a 'centre' at all, since central decision-making took place not through a process of detached, rational analysis, but through the playing-off of sectoral interests in a Hobbesian process of unregulated competitive bargaining, where the outcome was decided by the strongest and most skilful bargainer. This process was economically dysfunctional, in terms of assuring an outcome which could be described as in the 'social interest', as Friss explained:

> The greatest shortcoming of the procedure criticised is precisely that, by trying to give something to everyone, nobody is given enough, none of the objectives obtains as much as would be needed for its most rational realisation. The means which, had they been used in a concentrated manner, could have brought about substantial progress, are used inefficiently because of their fragmentation.[25]

The point was a recurring one in the burgeoning critical literature:

> The question of power cannot be separated from the results attained in carrying out the main objectives of a system. If the central administrative organs hold great power of decision in their hands, and yet economic growth is unsatisfactory, then – in an economic sense – we can speak only of bureaucratic but not of actual power.[26]

The broad lines of the reform models proposed in both countries were essentially the same.[27] Enterprises would no longer receive detailed instructions from the centre on what to produce, in what quantities, whether and in what direction to expand, but would be responsible for drawing up their own annual and multi-annual plans. Their basic goal would be the pursuit of profit (or gross income), earned through the realisation of their output on the market. The role of the centre, on the other hand, would not disappear, but would be adjusted to fulfil its basic function – assuring the 'social interest' – in a broader, more sophisticated, indirect way.

First, the state would not cease to plan, but would shift the emphasis in planning away from the previous fixation on detailed annual plans towards the longer term, to the five-year and also fifteen- or twenty-year plans. At the same time the plan objectives would become more general and 'strategic'.[28] As the Czechoslovak Prime Minister explained in an interview in *The Times*:

> What should be centrally planned are the major investments, the capital investments; secondly, the relationship between the various branches of industry – light and heavy, for example – and thirdly, the balance between the various regions. In these fields central planning is useful. For the rest, the door is open for local initiative.[29]

Planning would remain an essentially political activity, as the expression of conscious choice of priorities, policies and paths of development; but this choice would be made more meaningful, both by being based upon better informational 'feedback' from the market, thus a more accurate estimate of real possibilities, and also by the presentation of plan variants for open discussion, in place of the former practice of the central planning authority only submitting one plan for formal approval by the Party and the legislature. As Friss explained:

> a 'single' plan does not betray its inherent *contradictions, difficulties and problems*, while the plan variants must necessarily disclose them. A single plan inadvertently [*sic*] makes the impression that things will develop as prescribed in it, and there are no other ways and trends than them. The plan-variants, however, emphasise that society has a certain *freedom of choice*.[30]

The connection between the central plan objectives and enterprises would be made through various powers in the hands of the central authorities to condition or manipulate the market, thus indirectly influencing, rather than directly controlling, enterprise behaviour. While in principle it was recognised that unless prices reflected supply and demand the whole edifice of the new model would not work, nevertheless, as a transitional measure, it was widely accepted that price controls would be necessary, since the reform was equally likely to be undermined by the galloping inflation which would result from the sudden full introduction of the market into an economy characterised by massive excess demand and a basic structure largely unrelated to market criteria. The transitional controls would be exercised through a 'three-tier' system of categorisation of products whose prices would be centrally fixed, or would fluctuate between centrally-set upper and lower limits, or would be set freely according to the market. It was expected that gradually products would be shifted from the fixed to the limited, and from the limited to the free categories.

While enterprises would henceforth use retained profits to finance their own investments, they would also have recourse to bank credits, the allocation of which would be guided not only by pure profitability criteria (although these would play a far larger role than before), but also by central credit policy and the use of centrally-determined sectoral quotas to promote structural development in accordance with the long-term plan projections. And while in principle wages were to be dependent on the economic success of the enterprise, and much greater differentiation of reward was expected as a result, central wage controls would be used both to contain pressures in the direction of immediate, inflationary wage payments, and to guarantee a socially acceptable minimum for workers. By a complex system of rules and fiscal measures, the formation of enterprise investment, wage and other funds would be controlled, as part of the means of central regulation of the overall development of the proportions of accumulation and consumption in the distribution of national economic resources.

In addition, the right of the centre to intervene directly remained 'in exceptional cases'. It was implied that this provision was to be used only very rarely. (It was, of course, a major loophole which could be, and in the event was, abused to the detriment of the reformers' intentions.) The exercise of this right by the centre would also involve compensation to the enterprise, should compliance with central instructions prove unprofitable.

Both Czechoslovak and Hungarian advocates of reform emphasised the consistency of the proposal with basic socialist principles, in that it would *enhance* planning, and therefore realise more effectively the 'social interest'. As Friss put it, the market 'does not contradict the basic principle of central planning and control; on the contrary, it enhances the efficiency of the latter'.[31] Similarly, the Czech economist Otakar Tůrek noted, 'Relieving the plan of tasks which it cannot effectively carry out must mean an immeasurable strengthening of its role.'[32]

However, in both Czechoslovakia and Hungary, there were also economists who implicitly or explicitly rejected this conciliatory rhetoric, pointing to the inherent ambiguity of the argument that reform would lead to 'strengthening the role of the plan', by combining it with the market. The market was not only to be guided by, but a *guide to*, the formulation and/or modification of the contents of the plan itself. But it was not clear from the official reform documents and projects themselves how far this was to go, what was to be the precise division of plan and market. At least in the first phase of reform implementation, the role of the state would clearly remain uppermost. Was this merely a temporary expedient to bridge the initial phase? Or was it desirable in itself? Certain economists challenged not only the assumptions of the traditional centralist model, but also those of the 'regulated market' model, and, in so doing, suggested a radical pluralisation of the concept of the 'social interest'.

In Hungary, Tibor Liska's work, published in *Közgazdasági szemle* in 1963 under the title 'Critique and conception', provoked a furore. While in some respects appearing to follow closely the arguments in favour of a regulated market type of economic reform, in other respects his ideas went well beyond it. He baldly asserted that 'the socialist economy is not an economy producing directly for needs, but one producing for the market'.[33] Of central significance were his arguments on the price system. In contrast to the general focus of the debate going on in specialist circles at the time, he rejected all possibility of rational price-setting by a central authority, and advocated that prices be formed purely on the basis of supply and demand. His proposals included an unprecedented insistence that domestic prices should be linked directly to world market prices, and, as a concomitant, that the currency should be made convertible. This implied a massive constraint on a national state's ability to enforce its political objectives in the economy – hitherto seen as a key feature of 'socialism'.[34]

In Czechoslovakia, Evžen Löbl challenged the ambiguity of the terms in which the plan-market discussion was being conducted. Much of the debate, he felt, was marked by the 'old method of thinking':

The centre guides the socialist economy by the plan, and that the centre must guide the socialist economy is accepted as axiomatic. The question whether it is possible at all to manage the economy effectively from the centre is obviously too heretical to become a subject of serious consideration.[35]

He asked:

> What does it mean, that the plan must correct the market? In practice that must mean interventions into the market mechanism, or interventions which disrupt the market.[36]

On the other hand, there was considerable vagueness around the question of how the market was to correct the plan. It is, after all, not the abstract market, but concrete individuals, planners, who correct the plan, and they can do so only on the basis of their observation of the market, and their *subjective* assessment of it: 'The market which we have thus acquired would be such by definition, but obviously would not fulfill the function of a market, in other words, it would *de facto* not be a market.'[37]

Radoslav Selucký was one proponent of a concept of economic reform which gave clear priority to the market. The basic assumption of his 'commodity model' of a socialist economy was not the unity of social, group and individual interests, but the constant emergence of conflicts between them, their resolution, and then renewed conflicts.[38] Commodity relations were universal, embracing every sphere of the economy. The plan was thus limited to the function of 'scientific modelling of all basic future connections and processes, in the form of complex information on the anticipated and desirable changes in the development of the social economy'.[39] The plan could not, and should not, be detailed; it should be corrected on the basis of market information, and should be realised solely through the market. Central authorities could influence development only through general economic policy (covering credit, prices, wages and taxation policies), and by the provision of centralised information on the current state and expected future course of the economy. Enterprises were to be fully autonomous, entrusted with the actual execution of 'state ownership' through full disposition of their productive means, limited only by the framework of legal rules governing their use. It was a more radical model than any yet in existence, including that in Yugoslavia, Selucký admitted.[40]

Despite some important differences in emphasis,[41] by the mid-1960s the economists had carried out a fundamental reappraisal of the role of the market in the socialist economy. They had been impelled towards this common point first and foremost by the results of empirical analysis of the failures of the centralised system, which were found in all countries. The reform model was thus largely the product of experience, rather than of an abstract theoretical revolution. But a major theoretical breakthrough did occur with the work of Włodzimierz Brus. The Czech translation of Brus's work appeared in 1964 as *Modely socialistického hospodářství*, and had a tremendous impact, as Tůrek acknowledged:

> After Brus's study, the changes appeared, as it were, in a different light, their deeper significance became apparent. Each separate proposal began to be assessed as a component part of an integrated change in the model of a socialist economy.[42]

In Hungary too, where the level of development of economic thought was much higher, Brus's work is also reported as having had a profound impact on economists.[43]

The significance of Brus's thought, as with most theoretical 'breakthroughs', lay not so much in the fundamental originality of its observations, as in the unprecedented lucidity with which it incorporated already existing, but partial and fragmented knowledge into a coherent, systematic framework (see Chapters 1 and 2). It thus helped to clarify for economists where their own research should be directed; but it also pointed out the broader social and political implications of the reform, and provided a stimulating framework within which sociologists and political theorists could begin to tackle the increasingly obvious problem – the need for a reconceptualisation of the 'social interest' in a socialist society.

B SOCIOLOGY, SOCIAL INEQUALITY AND POWER

The political recognition of the necessity of economics as a 'science' was quite rapidly followed by a similar recognition of the need for empirical study of society, which had undergone profound change since the Second World War, and was now clearly far more complex than allowed for by the traditional Marxist–Leninist model of socialist social structure, which comprised only three social categories – 'working class', 'peasants' and 'working intelligentsia'. Moreover, the frequent allusions made by economists to the existence of conflicting interests required more systematic empirical elaboration, if society was to be governed effectively in future. Thus sociology, when it became formally established as a 'scientific' discipline, was, like economics, primarily justified as an aid to the government, as a source of practical knowledge.[44] The same tensions were to arise around this issue as were already emerging in economics. Could the requirements of 'scientific' empirical study be reconciled with the basically supportive political role envisaged for it by the regime?

A new concept, taken up and developed with particular vigour in Czechoslovakia, was that of the 'Scientific and Technological Revolution' (STR), whose main function was to incorporate into official ideology the notions currently floating about concerning the nature of change in socialist societies and the sense of transition to a 'new phase' of historical development.

In 1965, the Czechoslovak Academy of Sciences' Institute of Philosophy set up a working group to investigate the 'social and human implications' of the STR, headed by Radovan Richta. An interim report of findings was presented in the journal *Sociologický Časopis* in 1966, and the final product was published later that year.[45]

The concept of the STR picks up the idea first used by economists about the transition from 'extensive' to 'intensive' growth – the idea that, in the earlier stages of economic development, growth is based on quantitative factors (increased inputs of capital and labour), while at a later stage qualitative factors (innovation, new technology, more efficient combination of factors) come to the fore.[46] As Richta puts it, science becomes 'the central productive force of society'.[47] Scientific knowledge applied to production makes possible the automation and computerisation of production, and thus science 'displaces the mass of workers in general from the direct course of production to the pre-production state – towards research, science, preparation of technology etc',[48] or, more simply, 'Man now stands alongside production, whereas up to now, he was its chief agent'.[49]

The argument was developed independently by the economist Evžen Löbl, who produced a new version of the *Wealth of Nations* for modern times:[50]

> with the help of natural science we become able to transform such natural forces and in such quantities, that we are witnesses of the process in which, with declining effort and quantity of physical labour, the wealth of peoples increases.[51]

For Richta, the STR seemed to herald the beginning of the transition to communism, and was thus unambiguously a good thing. But he passed rather too quickly over some important social and political implications of the concept, to which others were more sensitive. As one contribution to the Richta team's research pointed out, science, to be effective, requires freedom from direct political interference. While accepting that the development of science could not be completely independent of the needs of society, the writers nevertheless pointed out that science would be unable to fulfil its role in promoting social progress if it were merely an 'obedient servant'. It was essential rather that it be able 'to pronounce thoughts which are not always pleasant. It is completely harmful to think that science should only give such answers as are favourable to those who commissioned the answers'.[52] The free development of man's creative faculties was clearly an 'objective necessity' for the STR, and appropriate quotes from Marx's early writings were used to demonstrate the desirability of this.

The concept of the STR and its revaluation of the role of 'science' also raised substantive sociological issues. As Löbl put it:

> the wealth of the nation in this developmental stage of humanity is not due exclusively to the quantity of labour expended in the direct process of production. In an ever-growing degree, the material wealth of the nation depends on the level of intellectual work in the sphere of the natural sciences, on the level and application of management science and political economy.[53]

But if science is to replace human labour as the 'leading variable in the national economy and the vital dimension of the growth of civilisation',[54] then the 'leading role of the working class', in particular, its material position *vis-à-vis* the intelligentsia, is brought into question. The clear implication of both Richta's and Löbl's arguments is that intellectual work must be valued more highly than manual work, and that this must find reflection in greater differentiation in material reward, privilege and social status in favour of the intelligentsia. A revision of the traditional Marxist thesis on the increasing 'homogenisation' of society as it approached communism was called for. What was required was a more elaborate and convincing explanation and justification of social inequality, to reconcile inequality with the central legitimating concept of the 'unity' of interests in socialist society.

This task was allotted to another working group, set up under Pavel Machonin to prepare a report for the XIII Party Congress in 1966. The findings of the group were later published in 1967.[55]

Machonin adopted the concept of 'non-antagonistic contradition', already available in Stalinist ideology, as his starting-point. In principle, he argued, with the achievement of socialism, the social ownership of the means of production, planning on a society-wide basis, and distribution 'according to work', a basic harmony of the long-term interests of individuals, groups, and society as a whole was attained, and a basic ideological unity of the population in favour of socialism. Class antagonism had thus ceased to be the main 'motive force' of society. In practice, however, as he pointed out, society was characterised by certain 'limitations' which gave rise to 'specific non-antagonistic contradictions' between groups and individuals within society, the overcoming of which would lead on to the future, non-contradictory communist society. These 'limitations' were conditioned by the still-inadequate level of development of the productive forces, as manifested in the 'physico–psychological–technological character of work', the inadequate amount of free time, and the low level of satisfaction of people's needs. Thus occupation, or 'character of work', had become the decisive differentiating factor, and Machonin conceptualised society as a finely-graded hierarchy, vertically differentiated according to various aspects of work – its complexity, creative and satisfying nature, level of qualification and education required, all of which were differentiated in terms of material reward and social status.

Thus, rather than a simplified two-class-and-one-stratum structure, he portrayed a structure where 'All the various types of social differentiation are mutually cross-cutting and interpenetrating, creating even more groups and subgroups'. Vertical differentiation, he argued, was both necessary and progressive in socialism, as the condition for the development of the STR, in which, because of its ultimate end – communism – all members of society had an interest. The inequalities in this system (always preceded by the qualification 'socialist') should not therefore be confused with those generated by capitalism, for 'in contrast with capitalism, these types of vertical differentiation are qualitatively less, not entrenched, non-antagonistic (in no way polarised), and they allow fairly intensive (albeit not unlimited) vertical mobility'.[56]

In fact, he argued, the extent of vertical differentiation had by no means yet attained a level adequate for the 'progressive long-term prospects of the development of society'.[57] Under the impact of a misguided ideological commitment to egalitarianism, there had been in the past 'a certain practical overvaluation of the role of physical labour', and a wholly inadequate degree of differentiation in material reward and social prestige attached to specialised, highly qualified intellectual work:

> The tendency to equalisation in the workers' incomes and in the standard of living must be an objective long-term tendency in socialism. Of course, this process must be a result, a reflection in the first place of basic changes in the character of work and the resolution of contradictions between production and consumption, of the gradual creation of a surplus of goods. In this sense, for the time being, it is not on the agenda for us.[58]

The parallels between Machonin's interpretation of the social structure of socialist society, and certain American interpretations of capitalist society, in terms of a stratified, but openly mobile hierarchy, are ironic, but by no means fortuitous. When sociology was resurrected in Czechoslovakia in the early 1960s, it inevitably looked to American sources for the sophisticated concepts which Marxist–Leninist orthodoxy had so conspicuously failed to provide. In the process, much of the structural–functionalist framework of American sociology was adopted wholesale and quite uncritically.[59]

Machonin indeed made ritual reference to the 'ideological' nature of the functionalist school in the context of the bourgeois capitalist society of the USA where, he argued, the application of the stratification model served to conceal the basic antagonism of social classes based on unequal relations of property ownership. But, given the context of socialist society where the means of production were no longer privately owned, his assumption was that the model could indeed provide an accurate empirical description of reality.

Other sociologists were not convinced. Indeed, as early as 1963, the central ideological concept underpinning Machonin's approach, that of the 'non-antagonistic' nature of 'contradictions' in socialist society, came under attack. For example, the Czech sociologist Miroslav Jodl posed the highly-charged question: what is the practical, concrete significance of the concept, if, as Machonin himself admitted, such 'contradictions' as he identifies are nevertheless 'deep'? In this case, the fact that they are 'non-antagonistic' has little meaning; and, as a result, the 'scientific' status of Machonin's work was called into question:

> In practice, this approach leads the authors abruptly to divide ordinary, everyday aspects of concrete life as it is lived by people from some 'correct reality', which, in contrast to that phenomenal aspect, is always in order.[60]

Machonin's version of 'empirical' sociological research was thus accused of being divorced from reality, and although he aimed, in Jodl's view rightly, to produce useful knowledge to aid rational social decision-making, his persisting commitment to elements of the 'old deductive method' turned his 'party-mindedness' and 'commitment' into 'sweet-sounding verbosity, ideological self-indulgence'.[61]

In his selection of occupation as the decisive stratifying factor, and his corresponding portrayal of socialist society as a mobile, meritocratic pyramid, Machonin had avoided the question of class as self-perpetuating inequality. His notion of class remained firmly in the formalistic tradition of Marxism–Leninism, which defined class solely in terms of legal relations of ownership or non-ownership of the means of production. In socialist society, the existence of class conflict was thus by definition impossible; and the possibility of the consolidation of meritocratic privilege and its transmission over generations to form a technocratic 'new class' was ruled out by Machonin on *a priori* ideological grounds:

> Numerous variants of the theory of the 'new class', proclaimed from the right with a revisionist line of argument, or from the left with a dogmatic-sectarian line of argument, we do not consider as Marxist. They have already been refuted by theoretical and historical practice.[62]

But Machonin had, furthermore, excluded from his analysis the crucial question of the inequality of *power*, which could not ultimately be ignored in the context of a system where the economy was centrally controlled by a self-selecting, monopolistic Party, and where, as a result, the distribution of all the stratifying factors Machonin identified – material reward, privilege, education, status – was not a product of spontaneous processes, but was necessarily a reflection of centrally-defined political priorities. The problem of power in socialist society was gradually, but with increasing self-confidence, being raised by social scientists in Czechoslovakia.

A critical review of William Kornhauser's classic of American political sociology, *The Politics of Mass Society*, provided food for thought for one sociologist:

> I think that the significance of his [Kornhauser's] work consists in the fact that, within the framework of his basic construction, he has raised problems which, despite the solutions with which we disagree, demand our attention ... For we surely cannot pretend any more that there does not exist in our country the problem of

relations between those who administer, represent power, and those who are in principle the source of that power, the ruling people etc. ... The problem of local and group interests, the defence of partial and group interests, the problem of control over the holders of power, their replenishment and removal, are not for us either something obvious, resolved, or insignificant.[63]

The Slovak legal specialist, Michal Lakatoš, formulated the problem with unprecedented frankness:

There exists in every society the clash between the rulers and the ruled, between those who rule and those who are the object of their rule ... The installation of the government of the people ... does not solve the problem of the manipulation of man. In socialist society, we regard such a government as meaning that the interests of those who rule are not antagonistic to the interests of those who are ruled.[64]

But without effective means of social control over the rulers themselves, there is no guarantee against the definition of the 'social interest' formulated by the rulers degenerating into an ideological smokescreen behind which a particular group preserves its own position and serves its own self-interest.[65] Lakatoš's line of argument suggested a radical break with the traditional Marxist concept of power itself. Official Marxist–Leninist ideology saw power purely as a function of property-ownership, and therefore as a 'problem' only for capitalist class societies, not for socialism. But Lakatoš identified the socialist state as an autonomous source of power and of self-perpetuating inequality – and as such the state was a problem for socialism too, a threat not only to the original socialist goal of rational economic management, but also to the legitimation of the entire system as 'socialist'.

A basically similar argument was developed in an interesting way in Hungary by András Hegedüs. The main theme of Hegedüs's writings was what he identified as the central dilemma of socialism – to find a satisfactory resolution of the often contradictory objectives of 'optimisation' and 'humanisation'.[66] He argued that the state, as an administrative apparatus separate from society, was a necessary feature of socialism, even more necessary than in capitalism since its function was the management of the socialised means of production. Direct self-management by society of the means of production was, at present, an 'illusion', and could only be realised in limited cases.[67] Society's property rights had to be exercised on its behalf by a separate professional administration, in the interests of rational use of the means of production ('optimisation'). But this raised the problem of 'bureaucracy' – that is, that this group would not manage the means of production 'optimally', in the 'social interest', but in its own particular interest. 'Optimal' decision-making by the state required that all the partial interests which 'objectively' exist in socialist society (given the persistence of the division of labour and commodity production) be taken into account. This required the development of some institutional means for the expression of these partial interests, and the prevention of any particularistic interest enjoying a privileged position.[68] At one point, he even suggested that the 'social interest' itself should be regarded less as a positive, substantive goal than as a *result of the process of group conflict*:

> the requirement that the management system should result in optimal decisions complying with the all-social interests might not always be interpreted as a direct objective, but often as a final outcome only, resulting from conflicts between decisions complying with particularist interests, under the influence of contrasted forces.[69]

The second 'imperative' of socialism for Hegedüs was 'humanisation', which included both the development of the individual's personality and abilities through, especially, the provision of extensive educational opportunities; and also, the right to participation in decision-making. While Hegedüs put forward the arguments for 'optimisation' in terms of 'objective', functional necessity, the imperative of 'humanisation' was elaborated mainly in implicitly moral terms. 'Humanisation' requires not just the provision of the means of a decent life and mass education, but also 'democratisation' of public life as the means to the elimination of alienation. This involves better information, to make participation also conform with the imperative of 'optimisation', that is, 'objective' rational decision-making. Participation should be introduced into the selection of managers, as a form of social control preferable to direct self-management in terms of the rational use of enterprise resources. Participation should also extend to the development of institutional checks on the central administrative apparatus. Hegedüs suggests that such control should be effected through the Party, Trade Unions and workers' committees. But he recognised further that in order for this function to be carried out effectively, that is, to reassert *real* 'social interests' against the interest of the bureaucracy, these bodies' present internal organisation must change, so that they become more closely in touch with the real opinions of their memberships and of society; and their present close integration with the bureaucracy itself as 'transmission belts' must end. They must cease to be merely subservient appendages of the central apparatus.[70]

For Hegedüs, 'optimisation' and 'humanisation', while often difficult to reconcile, were not mutually exclusive, and the problem was to find a balance between them. On the one hand, 'optimisation' without regard to 'humanisation' leads to 'bureaucracy', which threatens socialism itself, because it in turn can lead to sub-optimal decisions disregarding group and individual interests. It also challenges the very meaning of 'socialist ownership', which for Hegedüs (as for Brus) is not merely a legal concept but implies the effective control by society over the use of the means of production.[71] On the other hand, the pursuit of 'humanisation', without regard to optimisation, will lead to impractical decisions, anarchy, and the uncontrolled assertion of particularist interests.

The promotion of sociological research led to an increased self-consciousness on the part of sociologists, and revived a traditional sense of the role and responsibility of intellectuals.[72] There was a general acceptance that they were not in the business of knowledge 'for its own sake', and thus they were to some extent in agreement with the political authorities that they were to produce 'socially useful' knowledge, which could have practical application in improving the general management of the economy and society. But as their research progressed, the meaning of this task became more ambiguous. Their research was pointing to the diversity and complexity of society, and, further, to the possibility that the State might only inadequately represent it. What then did it mean, to 'serve society'? For some committed Party intellectuals, such as Machonin, this meant still supporting the political leadership, albeit in a more qualified and critical way. If, as Machonin's research had found, diverse and conflicting interests are present in socialism, then, as he admitted, 'it is necessary to draw conclusions from this and to allow a sufficiently free field for the manifestation of these interests. The time was ripe for 'an essential extension of socialist democracy'.[73]

Other sociologists were more actively concerned about the possible conflict between the objectives of the State and the interests of the people, which had implications for the use to which the results of their research might be put. A contribution to debate at the First Conference of Czechoslovak Sociologists in 1966 raised:

> the danger that humanising measures might get pushed to the back. The leading organs demand of sociology primarily the assurance of social conditions for higher output, [while] ordinary workers [demand] the revelation of paths to better working and other conditions.[74]

The speaker was clearly advocating political reform, not merely as a functional necessity of effective management of a complex society, but also as a moral imperative, a condition for the integrity of the sociologist: 'Only increasing self-management affords a guarantee to the sociologist that his work will not be an instrument of one-sided manipulation of people'.[75]

The problem was seen particularly acutely in Czechoslovakia, where the political leadership was morally compromised by its Stalinist past, and where the Party itself was becoming increasingly openly divided over the issues of thoroughgoing destalinisation, economic reform, and the Slovak nationality question. In this context, the 'political commitment' which was demanded – and which most intellectuals were concerned to offer – could not be unambiguously focused on a clear centre of loyalty. Intellectuals were forced to take sides, and their work correspondingly became politicised. In Hungary, by contrast, the Kádár regime, by the early 1960s, was more adept at preventing sociopolitical issues penetrating discussion of the economic reform. As noted above, economists were prepared to go along with this as the price of gaining official acceptance of their economic reform proposals. Thus András Hegedüs was an almost entirely isolated voice, kept at arm's length by the economists. In turn, Hegedüs became increasingly critical of the cooptation of intellectuals in the course of the 1960s, as part of his growing misgivings about the 'technocratic' character of the reform. In 1969, he produced a highly controversial definition of the role of sociology as the vehicle for the 'self-criticism' of socialist society.[76] This went so far as to suggest a role for intellectuals which was inherently oppositional, as the source of an alternative definition of the 'social interest' to that propounded by the 'political administration'. It was clearly politically unacceptable, as was indicated by a sharp rebuff from Béla Biszku, at the time second only to Kádár in the Party ranking order:

> We support ideological and scientific research aimed at achieving a deeper, truer, knowledge of reality, and thus helping to promote the construction of socialism and the further development of its achievements. But we most resolutely oppose attempts, disguised as

'ideological' or 'scientific' that aim by organisational means to become political forces and ultimately to make the power of the working class, the people's power, open to question.[77]

Hegedüs's small group of research workers was under attack, and Hegedüs himself was removed from his position as its head shortly afterwards.[78]

C POLITICAL REFORM OR POLITICAL CONTAINMENT?

New theorising about politics in socialism was not at first directly linked with the question of economic reform, but originated from Khrushchev's critique of the 'cult of personality' at the XX CPSU Congress in 1956. The introduction of the concept of the 'All-People's State' into Soviet ideology, and Khrushchev's experiments in transferring certain state functions to 'social organisations', such as trade unions, opened the way to reconsideration of the introduction of more meaningful popular participation in politics.[79] The Kádár regime in Hungary, once it had consolidated its power, was by no means hostile to the idea of 'expanding socialist democracy', but the development of theorising about politics was severely constrained by the legacy of 1956. While in the theoretical field, discussion was limited, in practice in the course of the 1960s some piecemeal modifications were introduced in the electoral system, the role of trade unions, and in inner-Party life, which will be covered in Chapter 7. But the idea of a general and comprehensive 'political reform' as a functional concomitant of the economic reform was suppressed.

In Czechoslovakia in the same period, the coincidence of economic crisis in the early 1960s with the political crisis of 1963, as outlined in Chapter 4, ensured that the question of political change would be closely associated with discussion of the economic reform, and the new theorising about the 'scientific and technological revolution' and the structure of socialist society reinforced the tendency to look at the problems of the day in a broad way, including politics. The collapse of authority, and division within the Party which resulted from the political crisis, opened up an opportunity for Czechoslovak intellectuals to take the discussion of the implictions of reform into politics and the basic principles on which the exercise of power was based. Kusin rightly emphasises that the demand for the establishment of a new intellectual discipline of 'political science' which arose at this time was 'yet another example of a further factor of reform emerging outside the Party-state sphere without the leadership's sanction and largely against its will'.[80]

The demand for a 'scientific' study of politics was raised in the pages of the Party's theoretical monthly, *Nová mysl*, in May 1965,[81] which provoked an extended debate in the journal over the next year. The January 1965 Central Committee resolution was used as a point of reference, since, it was argued, it had opened up a whole new range of issues, and had led to a growing agreement on the need to develop Marxism to meet modern conditions.[82] There was an 'objective need' for a 'scientific politics' in the period of the STR – but 'scientific communism', the discipline which had hitherto covered political questions, was described as inadequate for the purpose, being insufficiently empirical.[83] Traditional Marxist–Leninist studies were limited and ineffective as a means of understanding politics, confined to generalising about class relations, the history of the Party, and abstract Marxist theory. 'The time is ripe,' one contributor argued, 'to translate such general questions into much more concrete terms.'[84] The new 'science' of politics had to go beyond research into the past and the elaboration of general laws. It had to demonstrate direct, practical usefulness to society in producing a model for the future of an 'optimally functioning political system', which would act as 'a catalyst for the transformation of the present critical atmosphere in social consciousness into a motor of the internal dynamics of socialism'.[85] The need for political scientists as empirical analysts and designers of political reform was, it was said, as obvious as the need for economists:

> The contribution of economists to the solution of the problems of our national economy is unquestionable. It would indeed be useful if political science too could systematically aid the development of our political socialist model of administration and management.[86]

Official recognition of the need for empirical research on the political system came in 1966, after the XIII CPCS Congress, when, under the patronage of Hendrych and Koucký, a 'working group' was set up, based at the Institute of State and Law, under the chairmanship of Mlynář.

In the *Nová mysl* debate, many contributors linked the need for political science and political reform directly with the requirements of the new economic system. A clearer definition of the 'political sphere', that is, of the limits to the power of the State, was necessary, if the economy was to be allowed a degree of autonomy from direct political administrative interference in order to function according to its own specific laws of commodity production. The competence and jurisdiction of the component elements of the political system also required precise definition.[87] It was already clear to legal scholars such as Mlynář and Lakatoš that their work on 'socialist legality', prompted initially by the critique of the 'cult of personality' and the abuse of law in the show trials, had application also to the functioning of a reformed economy.[88] Mlynář found himself defending the role of law against economists, who, he argued, misunderstood this as a reassertion of the need for detailed administrative intervention in the economy.[89] He attacked Vyshinsky's 'faulty dogmatic concept of Law' as an instrument of class struggle: 'law degenerated in this conception into a heap of administrative decrees of arbitrary content'.[90] Mlynář's conception of law was that of a framework for resolving conflict according to established 'rules of the game'. As such, law was an essential component of the new economic system: 'Law here acts mainly not as an instrument of power resolving a particular economic problem directively, but as a binding framework for such a resolution'.[91] Its role was to be a 'relatively independent instrument of planned management of the socialist economy',[92] stabilising economic conditions and providing an authoritative definition of the spheres of competence of individual elements of the management system.

Meanwhile, economists were beginning to become more directly concerned with the political implications of economic reform, and to make connections between their ideas and the new thinking in politics. Selucký recalled (in a paper written *after* 1968) that in 1963 economists had expected a 'smooth shift to the new system within the old political structure'.[93] As in Hungary at the same time, they tended to believe that the introduction of the new economic system and the accompanying changes in the institutional structure of the economy which they envisaged as a necessary part of the economic reform would 'logically enforce the adequate political reforms'.[94] By 1966, they had become fully aware, from practical experience (see Chapter 6), that a more active concern with politics was necessary. Selucký himself at the time forcefully argued for the connection between economic reform and the realisation of freedom and democracy:

> For a long time it has been unthinkable that democracy in the political field could be combined with directive and command-based centralised management of the economy, that man as a citizen could enjoy democratic rights while as a producer was a subaltern manipulated person ... Whenever the sphere of commodity–money relations expanded, so too expanded the sphere of democracy, whether it be in the republics of antiquity, in the medieval towns or in capitalist agriculture ... From this point of view too, the commodity model [of a socialist economy] is far more humanistic than the non-commodity model, since it draws man into the decision-making process as a producer, gives him the possibility of choice as a consumer who influences production by his demand, and gives him the possibility also of choice in his free time, when he can freely assert his individual preferences.[95]

The central point of contact between economic, sociological and political thought was the question of interests. The analyses of economists and sociologists had pointed to the need for a new approach to the 'social interest': it was not static, automatically guaranteed once and for all by the abolition of private ownership of the means of production, and thereafter assured simply by the assertion of the Party's will through a hierarchical state apparatus directing all aspects of the economy. The 'social interest' was both complex and dynamic. This perception had in turn profound implications for the concept of 'democracy', which was not a 'given' characteristic of the socialist system *per se*, but had to be considered as a *process* by which the partial interests 'objectively' existing in socialism were coordinated in the formation of the 'social interest'. A more 'dialectical' concept was emerging in place of the static monolithism of the old ideological formulations. The 'social interest' could not simply be asserted *a priori* from the top of the political hierarchy; nor could it be a simple aggregate of group and individual interests, since these were conflicting. It was rather a product of institutionalised group and individual conflict. Conflict, once accepted as a normal feature of society, had to find a means of reconciliation and integration as the condition for the existence of society itself. The 'social interest' would then appear as the successful outcome of the means developed to effect reconciliation and integration, as a form of common denominator, a unified and coherent centre within the diversity of society.

This perception was of course by no means new or original, but could be argued to be the very stuff of 'politics' itself, and, as such, is at the heart of both the theory and practice of liberal democracy.[96] However, while the problem of liberal democratic theory is to find a legitimate role for the State, as the vehicle for the expression and defence of a 'common interest', given the assumed primacy of individual and group rights, the problem for East European social and political theorists was how to reconcile the acknowledged individual and group interests with the assumed primacy of the 'social interest'. In more concrete terms, the task was to explain how the process of institutionalised group conflict could be introduced in the context of a 'socialism' in which the necessity of the 'leading role of the Party', as the ultimate source of 'scientific knowledge' of the 'social interest' remained axiomatic. This was the major preoccupation of Mlynář's work:

> Political direction can no longer create unity of society around the old alternatives: capitalism or socialism (for that has been decided), but must create unity around *concrete all-social interests* in a great many diverse spheres of the activity of people, which brings to the fore the differing interests of the workers themselves, of their diverse strata and groups, in the conflict of which unity in diverse specialised spheres of human activity must be achieved in a democratic way.[97]

In an important article in *World Marxist Review* in 1965, dealing with the political aspects of the new economic system, Mlynář rehabilitated partial interests, against those 'erroneous opinions' which had 'led to a subconscious equation of individual, specific interests ... with anti-social behaviour,[98] and asserted that, according to the logic of the new economic system, the recognition of these interests would be an integral part of the definition of the social interest itself:

> We assume that the correctly defined interests of society as a whole are *at the same time* an expression of specific group interests and must be realised through, and in harmony with, these specific interests. The function of leadership is to coordinate these interests. Consequently, possible contradiction between specific group interests and the general, predefined aim of society can be regarded as a signal to leading bodies to search for the best ways of harmonising pressures.[99]

Now, the formulation of the role of 'leadership' in this way was as ambiguous as the formulation of the relative roles of plan and market had been in the economic debate. In both cases, the problem was the precise definition of the relative weights of the centre and the decentralised (market, social group, and individual) forces. Ultimately the 'leading role of the Party' was at stake, as Hendrych recognised very quickly:

> [T]here have emerged in connection with the new economic system notions which underestimate the role of the plan, notions implying that the rules and instruments of the new system might themselves automatically regulate the development of the economy. Such theories come very close to negating the role of the directing force of society and the state, which the Party represents.[100]

In other words, once the 'social interest' begins to be seen as some sort of spontaneous, self-regulating synthesis of group interests, not separate from them or 'over and above' them, then it is not at all clear that there can be any legitimate priority for the interests of the 'working class', still less that of its 'vanguard', the Party. Mlynář backed down from the problem, retreating into standard ideological assertion:

> The interests of society as a whole, which the state is called upon to guarantee, coincide with the historically-conditioned interests of the working class, which is destined to remain the leading force in socialist society, until the achievement of the classless society of the higher phase of communism.[101]

In Hungary, Rezső Nyers attempted to solve the conundrum of interests in socialism by putting forward a three-tier model. First, there was the 'social interest', which expressed the 'convergence and basic oneness of interests'[102], which was asserted to be the chief characteristic of a socialist society; then came intermediate group and regional interests; and, finally, individual and personal interests. The concrete expression of these interests was to take place through the institutions of the Party and State (representing the 'social interest'); collective units (enterprises, cooperatives, counties, trade unions, the youth movement, etc.) representing the partial and group interests of their members; and individuals, as participants on the labour and consumer goods markets, as 'citizens' in the political sphere, as persons with differing tastes and preferences. The image thus presented is that of a vertical, hierarchical structure of interests. There would continue to be limits on the exercise of group interests, as Nyers indicated with respect to the role of the trade unions as an interest-articulating organisation. The problem was the possible overlap of the unions' role as defenders of the interests of workers with the role of the Party, which saw this as its own main function. Nyers rejected the idea that the unions might develop as a movement of the workers *as a class*, since, he argued, the basis of the unity of the labour movement in capitalism – the general class confrontation of labour and capital in production – had been superseded in socialism, and the diversity of branch, craft and professional interests within the working class was now uppermost. In socialism:

> the workers as a class also have political interests in the development of the entire state, in the further progress of society, and these cannot always be represented by the Trade Unions with sufficient weight, since they can never completely abandon their craft interests. Therefore the Communist Party will always, in the future too, represent the political interests of the workers best and most effectively.[103]

The arguments of leading Party reformists in both countries thus ran up against the impossibility of abandoning central ideological tenets: first, that the conflicts of partial interests could not be 'fundamental' or irresoluble, because, in 'socialism', the conflicting parties also shared (and, presumably, shared equally) in the 'social interest'; and, following on from this, conflict between a partial interest and the 'social interest' could not occur, since, by definition, the 'social interest' always had priority. Despite the undoubted progress in conceptual thought, ultimately, Party reformers were still working within the limits of a framework inherited from Stalinism, which itself had included the notion of a 'non-antagonistic contradiction'. 'Democracy' could be advocated insofar as it was functional to 'socialism', as a source of flexibility and creativity, but this did not do away with the need, as Nyers put it, for a 'creative force which guides and leads the community', and which had the capacity to 'evaluate perspectives scientifically'.[104] Thus were preserved the essential remnants of the ideological justification for the continued dominance of the Party. But the overall coherence of the ideology was lost. As Mlynář has since candidly admitted:

> I had no illusions about these being particularly scientific ideas, not even when I was propagating them inside the Communist Party. This collection of ideological and political theses is wide open to attack from any consistently democratic position as well as from the standpoint of Marx's own theory.[105]

In fact, by 1968 Mlynář came to the conclusion that the 'leading role of the Party' was not a necessary condition of socialism. In an unpublished paper in 1967, he recognised that 'there is no scientific argument against a two-party political system in socialism. On the contrary, in principle such a solution would appear to be optimal for a pluralistic socialist society'.[106]

Ultimately, consistent following-through of the logic of reform thought undermined the position of the Party. It was not so much self-interest as genuine commitment to the practical realisation of reform which dictated compromise on this. The best that could be hoped for, in the given specific circumstances as Mlynář perceived them, was a modification of the Party's 'leading role'. Mlynář's working group provided the material for the sections of the Action Programme of 1968 which were addressed to this issue.[107]

The Action Programme reasserted the Party's 'leading role' as the 'guarantee of socialist progress'.[108] But it was not, as before, to act as a 'universal caretaker', issuing binding directives for all political activity in society. It was not to 'rule', but 'devotedly serve' society. The Party was to achieve 'informal, natural authority' not by compulsion but by persuasion, by the example of the 'moral qualities' of its functionaries, by the efficiency of its practical participation in management, and by the production of policies which responded to the interests, and met the aspirations, of the people as a whole. Internally, it was to sustain 'ideological and action unity' through free debate and discussion within its membership, guaranteed rights of its rank-and-file to participate and criticise, and an enhanced role for its elective bodies.

The Action Programme envisaged broad changes in the political system to complement the modified conception of the Party's 'leading role'.[109] The National Front and the National Assembly were to play a more active role in policy formation; 'constitutional freedoms of assembly and association', more open access to information and a wider diversity of viewpoints in the media were promised as part of a package of constitutional reforms guaranteeing 'a wide democratic concept of *personal and political rights of citizens*'.[110] But the 'Marxist–Leninist concept of socialism' was to be preserved as the 'leading principle' governing political development and setting the limits to political debate. There was an acute and obvious inconsistency in the programme, which contained neither cast-iron guarantees, nor institutionalised 'checks and balances'. The viability of this 'contained pluralism' rested entirely on the goodwill and voluntary self-restraint of both Party and people.

As is well known, by the time the Action Programme was adopted in April 1968, the grounds for hoping that such self-restraint would be exercised were disappearing. In the situation of escalating political crisis, the basis of the 'realistic' calculations of the sophisticated intellectuals who had produced the programme had disintegrated. The limits of the possible were no longer clear, and pragmatic compromise gave way to the force of consistent democratic demands appearing in the uncensored media. For Czechoslovakia, the invasion spelt the complete extirpation of reformism from public life. Repression started with the media and radical intelligentsia, whose activities were the immediate reason for the armed intervention, according to the Moscow protocol drawn up between the Soviet and Czechoslovak parties.[111] Thereafter, however, the process of 'normalisation' ground inexorably back to the roots of the pluralistic heresy in intellectual life, finally reaching the economic reform.

The invasion of Czechoslovakia had rather less impact on the development of reformist thinking in Hungary than one might have expected. In the first place, it had been tightly controlled. But it quickly became clear that, despite the increasingly hostile attacks on Ota Šik and the economic reform from both Soviet and internal Czechoslovak sources,[112] Hungary was not expected to abandon its own economic reform. The condition was the containment of its political effects, which in general terms meant that the role of the Party had to be left unchallenged – a point on which Soviet and Hungarian leaders were fully in agreement. However, Hungarian politicians and Party theorists nevertheless found room for a considerable degree of flexibility in their understanding of these general terms. While in Czechoslovakia the Action Programme was denounced as a symbol of heresy, Hungarian official pronouncements echoed, to a significant degree, the basic tenor of its approach.

In a major speech in June 1969, György Aczél, the HWSP Secretary for ideology, attacked the trend which was present in Hungarian intellectual life as well as in the neighbouring state, towards 'Marxist pluralism'. Marxism was a 'science', Aczél asserted in quite orthodox, not to say Stalinist, terms:

> The notion of Marxist pluralism is sheer nonsense, we might just as well talk about a variety of laws of gravity. Just as there is only one scientific truth valid for each question, there can only be one truly scientific world outlook.[113]

However, Aczél's position was far more complex than this

suggested, and was certainly very far from Stalinist. He was not reasserting the absolute primacy of the Party's definition of the 'truth' for all forms of knowledge. Marxism in Hungary, he explained, had a 'leading role' but not a monopoly position.[114] In fact, he reaffirmed the existing commitment of the Party to the independence of the 'other sciences', and recognised that there could be useful ideas even in works 'based on false ideological principles'.[115] The *facts* which scientists were engaged in revealing, he argued, could and should be kept separate from evaluative *conclusions*: 'Of course, facts and phenomena described by science could lead one to draw anti-Marxist conclusions but this does not nullify the objective value of the research done.'[116]

The rejection of 'Marxist pluralism' did not mean the end of discussion and debate, which was recognised as vital to the production of 'vigorous theories', which would win the interest and conviction of young people and avert the danger of a 'dogmatic revival', both key political objectives from Aczél's point of view.[117]

On the particularly sensitive case of sociology, Aczél was less tolerant. It was an exceptional subject, since its 'content is of an expressly class character'.[118] Although he did not say outright that non-Marxists would be excluded from sociology, in practice a purge was carried out.[119] The Party, Aczél announced, would see to it that its most trusted cadres, 'wholehearted and unequivocal supporters of socialism', would be directed toward sociology as a priority posting.[120] 'Scientific freedom', he explained, was conditional upon the 'consolidation of socialist society'. Once this was assured, however, 'the temporarily necessary limits which must be set to the formulation and communication of scientific thought will become fewer'.[121]

The conclusion was thus not that non-Marxist views should be suppressed, merely that they should cease to describe themselves as 'Marxist'. While party authority would not be used to dictate the results of scientific research, the Party would remain the sole authority in the question of defining what was 'Marxism'.

The Czechoslovak crisis did not stifle debate on the role of the Party in Hungary, but rather was used by reformist intellectuals to bring it to the fore. As Nyers wrote:

> The Party must be able to fulfil its central function and to express the public interest effectively. If the Party fails to do this, it is not impossible in socialism either that the party should be overtaken by events and become rigid, that it should act as a brake on development instead of furthering it.[122]

In the years immediately after the 1968 invasion, which were also the years of Hungary's first practical experience with economic reform, Imre Pozsgay published an important series of articles on the role of the Party and the necessity of developing 'democracy'. The Party exercised its 'leading role', Pozsgay asserted, with the 'consenting assistance' of the people.[123] To sustain this relationship, the Party had to take the initiative in the development of democracy, and should start by developing democracy within itself. It could not allow theoretical stagnation, nor the reassertion of 'those retrograde forces, which, referring to the interests of security, hold society back from every justified step forward and, in so doing, undermine security'.[124]

Turning to the political implications of the economic reform, Pozsgay noted that it provided great new opportunities for democracy – enterprise independence provided a basis for the realisation of 'the right to participate', a claim which Pozsgay described as 'wholly just'.[125] The economic reform had brought conflict out into the open – it had not created it, as some argued, but had shattered the 'illusory unity' enforced by the centralist system.[126] 'Participation' and the expansion of 'socialist democracy' were not only means of clarifying conflicts, stimulating initiative from below, and institutionalising criticism; they also had a vital educative function, fostering 'a growth in social consciousness, the development of a responsible type of person and socialist personality'.[127] At the level of the factory, increased participation would secure commitment to the reform, bringing workers closer to 'socialist property' by giving them responsibility for its use, and in turn, 'forcing back expectations which conflict with the interests of the community and society'.[128]

But the Party's role was essential: 'without a conscious integrating force, the parts [of society] themselves are unable to realise how to become integrated with the all-social interest'.[129]

Pozsgay had no illusions about the difficulty of the task the Party had taken upon itself as ultimate arbiter of the 'social interest'. The Party itself contained conflicting interests, reflecting the social environment within which it operated. Conflict in the process of defining the social interest was not merely a question of bad intent or mistaken judgement, but reflected the genuine conviction of various bodies that they knew best what the 'social interest' was. Partial interests tended to become put forward as general interests.[130] This could be profoundly disorientating – in order to see through the thicket, the Party had to take a step back (rather in the manner of Plato's Philosopher–King): 'It is possible to discover [the social interest] only by abstraction, thus in the first place only people with a high level of consciousness can reach its recognition.'[131] It was conceivable too that complete agreement might not be possible at all in some circumstances, in which case the Party would have to override some groups temporarily, forfeiting their support. Implicitly, the use for force would be the ultimate weapon in the Party's political arsenal.

CONCLUSION

The revision of the concept of the 'social interest' implicit in economic reform thought set in train, at the level of ideas, a logical momentum which, if allowed to run its own course, ultimately challenged the justification of the 'leading role of the Party' in any form. But ideas are the product of intellectuals, people in a particular political context. In the context of communist politics, intellectuals are in a unique position – on the one hand, subject to direct political supervision, intervention and repression, yet, on the other, offered tantalising opportunities to see their ideas realised in practice through their close relationship with the political rulers and their own dedication to serving society. Ultimately intellectuals in this situation are faced with a stark choice between the pursuit of logical consistency in their work, with the likely result of dismissal and the loss of influence over the process of change; or compromising in their intellectual work in the interest of seeing at least part of their ideas implemented, and in the hope that this will pave the way to further gradual changes. The latter course runs the risk of failure to persuade the politicians, and failure to retain intellectual credibility at the same time.

From the point of view of the regime, the problem is whether it is possible to accept some parts of the reform programme – its vital economic components – while rejecting others – the political implications. This is a practical problem of political containment – the complexity of the task centres on the ability of the regime to sustain its authority in the face of the powerful undercurrent of the democratising logic of economic reform. But logical consistency is not necessarily the hallmark of practical politics as the 'art of the possible'. The essential conditions of political containment are the provision of an environment which makes compromise on the part of intellectuals a more reasonable and attractive option than dissent, and, closely connected, the ability of the Party to adapt in a more general way to a more flexible, tolerant and responsive role *vis-à-vis* society at large.

The democratising logic of reform thought is, moreover, not absolute. The reformist debate in Czechoslovakia demonstrated at the level of ideas that economic reform made democracy possible, but it was the practical experience of the specific Czechoslovak case which impelled reformers to the conclusion that democracy was a necessary condition of the realisation of economic reform, as will be shown in Chapter 6. In Hungary, conditions were very different. The invasion of Czechoslovakia reinforced the already-existing incentives to compromise on the part of the Party, intellectuals and people as a whole. Consistent democratisation, which came on to the agenda in Czechoslovakia in 1968 was not only not 'necessary', but impossible. But sustaining the balancing act of the politics of inconsistency had repercussions for the implementation of the economic reform, as will be shown in Chapter 7.

6 Economic Reform and Political Crisis in Czechoslovakia 1963–8

The basic motive of the communist regimes of Czechoslovakia and Hungary in taking the decision to introduce economic reform in the mid-1960s was the preservation of political stability, in the face of convincing evidence that the old, centralised economic system was unable to produce the economic results on which, ultimately, the legitimacy of the regimes rested. However, the experience of actually implementing reform in Czechoslovakia was to be markedly different in political terms from that in Hungary. The basic question which is addressed in this chapter and the next, which trace developments in the respective countries, relates back to the issues originally raised in Part I, and reintroduced in Chapter 5. In Part I it was argued that in principle there is no necessary, direct functional connection between the market as a system of organisation of economic activity, and democracy, understood as the institutionalisation of pluralism and competition between autonomous individuals and group forces. As Charles Lindblom pointed out, while all democratic regimes coexist with some form of market economy, not all market economies are accompanied by democratic regimes. This raises the possibility, in the abstract at least, that a reformed socialist economy embracing significant market elements might not necessarily require the full-blown transformation of the communist political system into a pluralistic democracy. On the other hand, as intellectuals in Czechoslovakia and Hungary were aware (as we saw in Chapter 5), economic reform opened up the opportunity of very substantial change in the methods of exercising power. The question then is whether the transition from a centralised, directly planned economy to a regulated market economy can be managed politically, in the sense of effecting modifications and adjustments in the methods of exercising power, without provoking overt political crisis and the collapse of the pivot of the political system of party rule.

Indications of the likely differences to emerge in the future course of reform implementation in the two countries were apparent from its very inception, in the politics of the decision to reform, as we saw in Chapter 4. The Hungarian leadership, once persuaded by economic experts of the necessity of reform, embraced it as the centrepiece of its politics of national reconciliation after the trauma of 1956, and showed from the start adaptability and flexibility in its approach, and determination at the highest levels. This created the conditions for both the elaboration of a coherent programme, and the effective leadership vital to its successful realisation, at least in the initial phases of its implementation. As we shall see in Chapter 7, the course of reform in Hungary has by no means been free from conflict, but the political system itself survived serious threat. In the course of the 1970s, the Kádár regime in fact strengthened its authority. In Czechoslovakia, however, we see in the 1960s the escalation of political conflict to a point of systemic crisis reached in 1968, when revolutionary demands for 'democratisation', in the sense of institutionalisation of pluralistic social forces, were raised. As we have seen in Chapter 5 a substantial body of intellectual opinion became convinced of the existence of a profound inner logic of economic reform, carrying the metaphor of the market over into politics, which led to conclusions on the necessity of political change going beyond mere personnel replacements in the Party and State apparatus, to involve radical reordering of the structures of political power as a functionally necessary concomitant of the operation of the market in the economy. In the actual implementation of the reform, the abstract logic identified by reformist intellectuals appears to have worked itself out in practice. By 1968, an influential group of committed reformist economists saw the problems encountered in reform implementation as systemic in origin, and joined forces with quite different intellectual groups seeking democratic political change on non-economic grounds. From a quite different viewpoint, the explanation of the Czechoslovak political crisis given by Soviet authorities after the invasion and by the Husák regime of 'normalisation' also relates the breakdown of the political system not merely to the inadequacies of the Novotný regime, but also to the impact of introducing the market into the economic system.[1]

This chapter presents an alternative interpretation, both to that of the reformists and to that of the 'normalisers', which can be summed up as a set of propositions to be tested in the following account of the reform in Czechoslovakia, which start from the distinction made in Part I, Chapter 2, between democracy and pluralism. A *democratic* political system is defined as one in which the relative autonomy of plural social forces is institutionalised by guarantees which no one political group is able to override. The introduction of the market promotes the *pluralisation* of the underlying socioeconomic structure, since a market, even a limited one, cannot function without competition between units with a significant degree of autonomy. The transition from a centralised to a relatively decentralised economy, from detailed directive planning to a regulated market mechanism, inevitably produces intense political pressures for a one-party state of the Soviet type, both at the level of its ideological self-legitimation, and for the way in which the Party exercises its 'leading role'. But, it is argued here, the political problem of reform of the Communist Party is one of adaptation, not necessarily self-destruction. Adaptation implies change in the subjective attitudes of the occupants of leading political roles, changes in the style in which the instruments of power are wielded, and, if necessary, changes of particular personnel where they prove personally incapable of making the necessary adaptation. In certain circumstances, such adaptation may be achieved without going so far as the full institutionalisation of pluralism in a democratic revolution. In Czechoslovakia, those circumstances did not materialise, and a crisis followed.

What were the sources of the Czechoslovak political crisis of 1968? To what extend did the economic reform contribute to the crisis? On the one hand, we should start by pointing out that the degree of pluralisation actually achieved in the Czechoslovak economy between 1965 and 1968 was negligible. In fact, organisationally, the economy became more centralised after the 1965 industrial reorganisation than ever before; while the introduction of market-type instruments –decentralised investment, the use of interest-bearing credit, and, especially, the new price system – was hardly begun. The only significant change was the reduction in the number of centrally-fixed plan production targets and their replacement by gross income as the basic indicator of enterprise activity. The significance of this step itself was of course greatly reduced by the non-operation of a market in any meaningful sense. Gross income produced, rather than 'realised' or sold, was the key indicator, which looked very much like a mere financial expression of the former gross output target. Thus it could be said that it was not the introduction of the market, but the failure to introduce it, which contributed to the political crisis.

The link between economic developments and the political crisis was moreover not mainly causal at all – the two ran in parallel, rather than consecutively. The problems encountered in reform implementation were a symptom, rather than a cause of the political crisis. As we shall see in section A of this chapter, the political crisis developed largely autonomously within the political system itself, as a product of the peculiar nature and weakness of the Novotný regime, centring on its anti-intellectualism, its inability to make use of the intellectual resources available to it in a time of increasingly complex problems. The development of the economic reform, outlined in section B, reached a point of crisis at the same time as the Novotný regime, in late 1967. The link between the two crises was the reformist intellectuals. The failure of the economic reform led economic experts to advocate, as the essential condition of the reform, far-reaching changes in the political system, and thus to join forces with other, non-economic interest groups seeking such changes, as is outlined in section C. A concluding section covers economic aspects of the 1968 crisis, when, in practical terms, the economic reform was virtually stagnant, but when the open political conditions allowed discussion of the institutional changes which were necessary to the success of the reform.

A THE NOVOTNÝ REGIME

Reformist opponents of the Novotný regime in Czechoslovakia in the 1960s identified its central political problem as the 'Stalinist', dictatorial style of rule. An account of the origins of the political crisis, published in 1968, drew parallels between Novotný and Stalin, both of whom had come to power 'without an outstanding political programme and apparently without political ambitions', and yet had turned out to be ruthless personal dictators, 'unrestrained machine politicians'.[2] The consensus which emerged in the course of the late 1967 Central Committee plena which finally deprived Novotný of his Party post focused on the 'cumulation of functions', the excessive concentration of power in the hands of a single individual, as the main problem.[3] But in fact, as Galia Golan argues convincingly in a detailed study, the central feature of Novotný's whole period of rule was 'his very weakness, or perhaps more accurately, the instability of his regime'.[4] A similar interpretation was given in the mid-1960s by two acute Western observers:

> In fact, there was a gradual realisation that very little power resided anywhere in the supposedly supreme organs of Party and state. Demoralisation, disorganisation and diffusion of authority were felt

in all spheres of national life. The collapse of authority remains the decisive factor in Czechoslovakia today.[5]

Novotný appears then as both too strong and too weak. Perhaps it would be better to say that the heavy-handed and repressive characteristics so resented at the time were in fact a sign of weakness, rather than of Stalin-like strength. But what was the source of this weakness? It appears paradoxical in the face of Mlynář's comments in his memoirs. The 1963 political crisis, Mlynář suggests, brought Novotný to the height of his power, with the elimination of long-standing rivals from the 'old Gottwald–Stalinist clique', 'thus ending what must have been a long nightmare of seven years (1956–63). Now he had his own leadership, composed not of people who had brought him to power but whom he himself had appointed'.[6]

That Novotný had no clear rival for the political leadership is illustrated by the difficulty encountered by the Central Committee right up to the very end of 1967 in finding a successor to him, after years of increasingly-openly acknowledged political drift and mismanagement. Dubček was a far from obvious choice, but the only one acceptable to all the divergent groups which had come together to unseat Novotný.[7]

The basic source of weakness was the regime's inability to adapt to the new conditions of the 1960s, described by and reflected in the writings of social scientists, dealt with in Chapter 5. The Czechoslovak economy could no longer be run as if it were at a simple, underdeveloped stage. The complexity of the economy had to be recognised and allowed for in the system of management. At the same time, in the post-Stalin era, after the exposure of the 'cult of the personality', new forms of interrelation between the regime and society had to be found. A sophisticated public and well-educated labour-force had re-emerged after years of suppression by terror as forces to be reckoned with, no longer subject to the despotic paternalism of the Stalinist years. While on the one hand, dealing with the economic problem required the leadership to draw on sources of expertise hitherto excluded from power, at the same time, the expansion of educational opportunity under the socialist regime had produced a new and numerous 'socialist intelligentsia'. The ability of the regime to deal with experts, and to incorporate politically this rapidly expanded and increasingly self-confident new social force would be vital to its strength and success. As we shall see in the course of this chapter, the failure to do this was the common source both of the political crisis and the failure of the economic reform. To explain why the Novotný regime proved unable to adapt, we will assess Novotný himself as a political leader, then turn to an analysis of the nature of the Party–state apparatus over which he presided.

'There were many minor everyday incidents indicating that Novotný was not a man of penetrating intelligence', Mlynář recalls.[8] But, more than this, he suggests that Novotný was 'tormented by fears' of his own inadequacy.[9] Apparently, on his appointment to the leading Party post in 1953, he broke down in the presence of close relatives, sobbing, 'I'm not up to this job, I haven't got what it takes'.[10] However slender as a basis for psychological assessment of Novotný, acute personal insecurity provides a better explanation than the existence of immediate personal political challenges for the ultimately self-defeating way in which he wielded power. His style of rule appears to form a coherent syndrome of traits, evident in his dealings with the Party and state bodies, and with those outside.

In the post-Stalin period in communist regimes, there has been a trend towards limited 'institutionalisation' of the political system, in the sense of closer following of formal rules and attention to due procedure in decision-making, with the First/General Secretary exercising power through regular consensus-building within the Politburo, the regular convening of Central Committee plena and use of them for debate or as sounding boards for sectional or regional responses to proposed policy-measures, etc.[11] The pattern of leadership has developed from the unlimited exercise of personal power towards 'building authority'.[12] In contrast, Novotný's leadership appears as an ineffectual form of would-be Stalinism. A recurrent point of criticism of Novotný's leadership, found in both reformist and post-invasion 'normalisation' critiques, is summed up in the term *bezkoncepčnost* – lack of conceptual content. Novotný understood politics as narrow manoeuvring and manipulation. He appears to have lacked the ability to rise to the demands of redefining the tasks of politics, conveying the rather widespread perception – among the intelligentsia at least – that a new era was dawning. He singularly failed to incorporate the new ideas developing in committed communist intellectual circles into party ideology. Instead of reviving, party education and propaganda stagnated, leading to confusion and apathy at the lower levels and mounting concern at the higher levels.[13]

Instead of opening up the political system to carefully controlled discussion, as occurred in the Soviet Union under Khrushchev and Brezhnev, and promoting managed participation,[14] Novotný appears to have felt unable to trust the Party itself, let alone non-party people, as a post-invasion critique argues:

> Even after 1956 ... A. Novotný referred to the inadequate political maturity and political diversity of the membership base to justify the continuing restriction of the democratic rights of rank-and-file members and the maintenance of a situation where the decisive political force was not the elective organs, from the regional committees right up to the Central Committee itself, but their executive apparatus.[15]

Even within the apparatus, as Mlynář recalls, power was wielded very informally:

> an important criterion of influence was whether you belonged to the narrow circle of people who played cards with Novotný. The regional party secretary or minister who played cards with Novotný often had more influence and power than the Central Committee secretaries who did not.[16]

From 1965 to 1967, the Central Committee itself was prevented from discussing any of the serious issues which were emerging, as Mencl and Ouředník relate. Novotný denied the floor of the plenum to any individuals he suspected of less than complete loyalty to himself personally.[17] Decision-making was removed from the appropriate Party organs, and left to individuals, 'often not those in the highest responsible positions'.[18]

> Responsibility and any real possibility of control disappeared. Political and other questions were resolved by 'opinions', by the decision-making of individuals depending on who had most power and was able to force his 'opinions' on others by the most varied means.[19]

The Presidium itself became paralysed by the deluge of issues put before it. It was swamped by material which it was unable to deal with adequately by reason both of time, and its technical complexity.[20]

If his relations with the party organs themselves were full of mistrust and far from 'normal', in dealing with those social groups who were less dependent on him personally, and less easily brought to heel, his approach was heavy-handed in the extreme and productive of dramatic and escalating conflicts. His dealings with the Slovak minority were so insensitive as to be open to interpretation as reflecting ethnocentric neurosis. He had a long-standing reputation as an anti-Slovak bigot, which he did nothing to dispel. At a time of approaching personal political crisis, in August 1967, he chose to deliver a speech at the centenary celebrations of the Slovak cultural institution, the Matica Slovenská, which once again inflamed Slovak opposition to him: 'He behaved so grossly, delivering a speech of a Czech nationalist, he rejected the gift offered to him, and by his conduct insulted many respectable Slovak people. This did not remain a secret, reports of his behaviour quickly spread.'[21]

Young people were also mistrusted by Novotný as inherently unstable and unreliable. In fact, the proportion of the relevant age group joining the Czechoslovak Union of Youth showed a tendency to fall off consistently throughout the 1960s, from 54 per cent in 1961 to 26 per cent by 1967.[22] Party membership among the young was also declining, which was seen at the time as an undesirable trend, since the Party lost the benefits of youthful enthusiasm.[23] But Novotný himself expressed critical views on the youth of the day, with their unhealthy interest in Western life-styles, and argued that the admission of a younger generation, 'unschooled' in life and not 'ideologically steeled' in the political struggle of the early years of establishing socialism, to positions of responsibility, was a process requiring careful supervision.[24] As with the Slovaks, Novotný served to weaken himself at a crucial moment for his own survival in his dealings with youth. On 31 October 1967, a peaceful demonstration of university students from the Strahov hostel, in protest against living conditions, was met by brutal police repression, which not only politicised student opinion but aroused profound misgivings in wide social circles, and also among Central Committee members whose stormy plenary session had just closed not far away.[25]

The third major group with which Novotný came into dramatic and damaging conflict was, of course, the intellectuals, who are particularly important in this context as the link group between the political crisis and the economic reform. The history of his battles with the cultural intelligentsia is too well known to require detailed treatment here,[26] and it is sufficient only to recall the main pattern: enforced dismissals of academics, most notably in the purge of the Party High School in 1964; a succession of interventions in cultural organisations and in the editorial boards of cultural periodicals, culminating in the transfer of the Writers' Union paper, *Literární Noviny*, to the direct control of the Ministry of Culture in September 1967; the enforced expulsion of leading critical communist intellectuals from the party, or their subjection to humiliating 'party discipline'.

Novotný's dealings with economic experts showed little more subtlety. He may have intended to take a 'differentiated approach',[27] allowing economic and technical experts greater leeway as a necessity for economic reform, but this in the end was impossible, not only because of the inherent difficulty in permitting freedom to some intellectuals while crassly restricting it for others, but also because the difficulties within the economic sphere, in the implementation of reform, were themselves radicalising the perceptions of the economists and making it increasingly impossible to keep economic issues separate from wider social and especially political analysis.

As Vladimír Kusin put it, 'the history of communist rule in Czechoslovakia has ever since 1956 been a history of strife between the intelligentsia and the leadership'.[28] It is a history of astonishing failure on the part of the Novotný regime, astonishing because a large majority of the intelligentsia was, if not always enthusiastic, at least predisposed to be cooperative on the basis of a long tradition of sympathy towards the basic goal of 'socialiasm'. That Novotný came into such deep conflict with the intelligentsia reflects thus not so much the intelligentsia's own oppositional stance as Novotný's mismanagement, based, we suggest here, in significant measure on his own personal paranoia, and insecurity in dealing with those more intelligent and expert than himself. On the one hand, he treated any unsolicited opinion as an expression of intolerable 'arrogance', while on the other, his repressive actions against their leading and widely respected representatives were deeply resented and politicised their opposition to him.[29]

But anti-intellectualism was not merely a personal quirk in Novotný's character – it was also deeply embedded in the power structure, providing the essential underpinning of his rule:

> Novotný's major source of strength was a new type of Party man who, as a result of the purges, formed more than the backbone of the Party: the middle-level functionary, the *apparatchik*, who owed his position, whether it be as factory manager or state bureaucrat, to unimaginative obedience to the Party line ... [I]t is the basis of a regime founded not on ideological fervor or commitment, or solidarity born of mutual belief and experience, but on strict obedience, opportunism, and petty bureaucratism.[30]

This bureaucracy was in large part Novotný's personal creation, as a result of the most recent purges within the apparatus following Zápotocký's death in 1957, when Novotný took over as head of state. The main victims, as indicated in Chapter 4, appear to have been the more highly qualified, specialist personnel who had survived the earlier purges under the protection of Gottwald and Zápotocký, who were said to be more appreciative than Novotný of their usefulness.[31] But as the historian Karel Bartošek commented, 'The intermittent purge of 'unreliables' had not raised its [the *apparat*'s] efficiency, rather the opposite; the firings had affected for the most part clever and honest people and thus exposed a "government of dimwits".'[32]

The writer Ludvík Vaculík openly addressed the problem in a brilliant and correspondingly controversial speech delivered at the IV Congress of Writers in 1967 (which led directly to his expulsion from the Party):

> At every stage in the selection it has been the most mediocre men who showed up best while more complex creatures, people with personal charm, and above all those whose work and qualities had made them, by silent unwritten consensus, the touchstone of general decency and public conscience – these gradually disappeared from the scene ... I don't know whether you have noticed it, but all of us, Czechs and Slovaks, are inclined to believe that the men who tell us what to do are less competent than ourselves.[33]

The central problem of the regime was its own incompetence in the face of increasingly complex problems, and at the same time, its failure to draw upon the talents offered by its own intelligentsia. This can be illustrated by a certain amount of patchy and inconsistent but nevertheless interesting data on the qualification levels of leading personnel, and the underemployment of the educated.

One study of the position of the intelligentsia in Czechoslovakia revealed that only 11.9 per cent of 'leading officials' had higher education, while 60.3 per cent had only primary or junior specialised education, the remaining 27.8 per cent having secondary and senior specialised training.[34] The author could not explain this in terms of the age-structure of the personnel surveyed, since over 70 per cent were under 45 years of age, and might therefore have been expected to have benefited from the expanded educational opportunities provided by the socialist regime.

The sociologist Machonin found a high degree of discrepancy between the qualification levels of people in various responsible positions, and the officially prescribed levels of qualification for these posts, as shown in Table 6.1.

Table 6.1 Percentage of people adequately qualified for their posts

Managers and deputy managers in enterprises and factories	48
Heads of departments in enterprises and factories	48
Other technical staff in departments	57
Heads of plants	42
Foremen	38
Other technical staff	49
Other economic staff (clerical)	38

Source: P. Machonin, *Změny v sociální struktuře Československa a dynamika sociálně politického vývoje*, (Prague: Svoboda, 1967) pp. 86–7.

A poll conducted by *Rudé Právo* in 1965 found an even worse position among the managerial staff it surveyed, only 23 per cent of whom were found to possess the requisite level of qualification.[35] Little had changed by 1968, when one source gives a figure of approximately one-fifth of managerial personnel, and one half of senior management, as meeting prescribed qualifications.[36] Drahomír Kolder highlighted the problem in the automobile industry, with 180 000 workers in thirty-one enterprises, only two of which were headed by a director who met the minimum qualification requirement of two years' higher education plus ten years experience. While all had the experience, the formal educational qualification was lacking.[37]

That this situation was not caused by a shortage of educated people is indicated by the rapid growth in the numbers of specialists with higher and advanced secondary education between 1955, when they accounted for 8.6 per cent of the total labour force, and 1966, when they reached 17.4 per cent. Of these, specialists with higher education doubled their share of the labour force from 1.7 per cent to 3.4 per cent over the same period.[38] Pavel Machonin suggested in an early study that in comparison with other socialist countries – including many less economically advanced than Czechoslovakia – the proportion of the total population of specialists with higher or full secondary education was rather low,[39] but one cannot conclude from this that there was a shortage of them in the face of evidence of underemployment of graduates. Krejčí calculates on the basis of the 1961 census that 27 per cent of specialists with higher education were not in employment commensurate with their qualifications.[40] Dziedzinska's study found that of the total pool of 657 000 people with secondary or higher education in the age group 25–59 years, only 11.3 per cent held 'leading posts'.[41] *Rudé Právo* noted in 1965 that more than half of the university graduates (presumably entering the job market that year) were unable to find jobs corresponding to their qualifications.[42] The highly constrained career opportunities for the qualified finds corresponding reflection in the relationship between education level and earnings. As a major study of Czechoslovak social structure found in 1967, nearly 70 per cent of the top income earners had less than higher education (see Table 6.2).

Table 6.2 Education structure of top income earners

	%
University education	30.8
Secondary education	26.4
Lower specialist training	10.7
Skill training	16.7
Basic education	9.5
Incomplete basic education	5.9

Source: J. Večerník, 'Problémy příjmu a životní úrovně v sociální diferenciaci', in P. Machonin *et al.*, *Československá společnost* (Bratislava: Nakladatel'stvo Epocha, 1969) p. 306.

The researcher pointed out that graduates' opportunities to reach the top-paying jobs were in fact even less favourable than the figures suggest, since graduate qualifications were not usually a prerequisite for promotion, but rather followed it. Moreover, the research concluded, in financial terms the acquisition of education from the point of view of the individual was 'unprofitable'. In the course of a lifetime's earning activity:

> not only are the losses and costs of higher education not made good, but even the whole lifetime balance of people with complete secondary and higher education is as a rule on the loss side in comparison with the lifetime earnings of skilled workers.[43]

Statistics on the social composition and educational level of the Party are extremely fragmentary.[44] One party official dismissed in the late 1950s referred to anti-intellectualism affecting recruitment policy as 'the Novotný leadership's revenge for the intellectual revolt which followed the XX Congress'.[45] Party recruitment between 1958 and 1962 does indeed seem to have favoured workers, whose share of new recruits rose from 49 per cent in 1958 to a high point of 71.3 per cent in 1961.[46] As a proportion of total Party membership, the share of 'active workers' in fact began to fall thereafter, from 36.1 per cent in 1961, to 33.4 per cent in 1962, to 30.2 per cent in 1966.[47] The two groups which strengthened their representation in the Party between the XII and the XIII Congresses appear to have been 'intellectual' in terms of occupational content – engineering-technical and economic employees, and teachers, including professors and headmasters.[48] However the usefulness of these figures for the assessment of the integration and participation levels of the intelligentsia, defined in terms of educational qualification, is much diminished in the light of the evidence presented above on the low level of educational achievement of many occupying posts defined in official statistical terminology as 'intellectual'.

Table 6.3 Educational level of the Communist Party

	1957	*1962*	*1964*	*CPSU 1962*
% members with:				
University education (or equivalent)	2.9	4.3	5.0	18.2*
Complete secondary education	7.8	10.2	11.9	30.9
Incomplete secondary or basic education	89.3	85.5	83.1	50.9

*including those who did not complete their course.
Source: M. Havlíček, *Dialektika vnitrostranických vztahů* (Prague: 1968) pp. 129 and 133.

One study by a party research worker revealed the data shown in Table 6.3 on the educational level of the party membership, which show a quite rapid increase particularly in the share of those with higher education. The share of those with secondary education, however, does not show a great over-representation in comparison with their share in the total labour force, estimated by Krejčí as about 14 per cent. The researcher drew a highly unfavourable comparison with the situation in the Communist Party of the Soviet Union, as shown in the fourth column.

Rudé Právo reported in 1966 that 5.9 per cent of the membership had higher education, 13.9 per cent complete secondary education, and 80.2 per cent incomplete secondary or basic education.[49]

Barbara Wolfe Jancar suggests in her study of the Czechoslovak Communist Party that, in comparison with both the Polish United Workers' Party and the Communist Party of the Soviet Union, the educational level of the membership and of its local officials was markedly lower in the Czechoslovak Party,[50] and that it was 'far from being an educated managerial élite, such as the CPSU was becoming'.[51]

B PROGRESS AND PARALYSIS OF THE ECONOMIC REFORM

The timetable for implementation of the economic reform which emerged after the January 1965 plenum envisaged a rather slow and gradualistic approach. 1965 would see the more detailed elaboration of the reform by the specialist working group under Šik. Kohoutek, a senior official of the State Planning Commission, pointed out that so far there had been too much abstract model-building, and concentration, he felt, too much on criticism of the past which, while it had been fruitful in terms of changing the basic approach, had neglected the detailed, concrete aspects of the reform itself, and had tended to create 'unjustified illusions' about the possibility of rapid and straightforward progress in the economy as soon as the reform was adopted.[52]

Measures to be elaborated and implemented in the course of 1965–6 were seen as the first preparatory steps in a long process of change. It was not envisaged that the reform would be fully in operation until 1969, when price reform would come into effect.[53] The main practical measures taken in 1965 were to be reorganisation of the industrial system and changes in the central authorities.

The administrative reorganisation was aimed, as Prime Minister Lenárt explained, at 'creating conditions for a more extensive economic independence on the part of economic units'.[54] Contrary to what one might have expected, and to what Ota Šik held at the time,[55] these conditions were seen as lying in further concentration of production. The 236 'economic production units' (VHJ), first established in 1958, were reduced in number through mergers into 102 massive 'branch units' on the basis of both vertical and horizontal amalgamation. The average number of employees per unit was 30 000, while some, for example, in the automobile industry, iron foundries and the Ostrava–Karvina coal basin, had more than 100 000 employees.[56] Somewhat inexplicably, Lenárt envisaged that the reorganisation would lead to 'eliminating the undesirable effects of monopoly production'.[57] He suggested that competition would be promoted between 'enterprises and plants in a single field, as well as between state, cooperative and communal enterprises that produce consumer goods or perform services to the public'.[58] Eventually, with the transition towards pricing linked more closely with the world market, foreign trade could be used as a source of stimulation for competitive and technologically advanced production.

At the same time, the Western economist Holesovsky also saw some positive features in the continuation of strong elements of centralisation in the new model, as a temporary expedient in an inevitably difficult transitional period; and while he acknowledged that the new organisational structure carried the inherent danger of simply permitting the resumption of old patterns of behaviour among the former branch ministerial employees, he nevertheless felt that within the overall context of the reformed system, new behaviour patterns and hidden entrepreneurial talents might be called forth.[59] In the event, as we shall see, it was the former tendency which predominated.

From the end of 1964 and during 1965, experiments were conducted with the aim of testing individual elements of the reform, in particular, the use of gross income or profit as replacements for directive production targets. By mid-1965, 20 per cent of industrial output was being produced in enterprises operating under experimental conditions. It was soon recognised that the usefulness of these trials was quite limited. Sceptical reformists saw them as a delaying tactic, pointing out that any results were bound to be inconclusive given that the enterprises concerned were operating in a completely different environment from that anticipated under the full reform.[60] It was as if the Prague transport authority were to conduct a traffic experiment by instructing fifty cars to drive on the left.[61] Nevertheless, considerable enthusiasm was reported within the experimenting enterprises themselves, and it was quickly declared by enthusiasts that the results 'could not leave any doubts that economic management is a better framework for the solution of the most diverse questions than administrative management'.[62]

Thus, from 1966, the whole of industry was transferred onto the gross income indicator (with a small minority of enterprises using profit). Production targets set by the central planners were reduced from 1300 to sixty-seven items.[63] Control over investment was to be considerably decentralised. Branch directorates and enterprises would dispose of 25 per cent of total investment resources, as compared with the central authorities' 15 per cent. The remaining 60 per cent would be allocated by the banks as interest-bearing credit. Some transitional powers were retained by the centre to control the overall volume of branch investments – an anti-inflationary precaution no doubt strongly influenced by the memory of the 1958–60 experience. The central authorities also retained the right to set specific export targets in addition to the global export plan; to allocate research and development funds to supplement self-financed R. & D. in branch enterprises; and to give orders for defence-related production. Enterprises were however to be compensated for losses incurred in meeting such central directives. A capital charge of 6 per cent on fixed assets (net of depreciation) was to be made.[64]

Deductions from enterprise gross income would be made to both the branch association (VHJ) and the state budget. In the transitional period, it was not yet possible to fix a standard rate, given the very varied conditions of profitability among enterprises inherited from the old system; rates of reduction thus varied between 42 and 70 per cent.[65] The funds collected at the level of the branch association would be used to pay staff salaries, to fund R. & D., and also to redistribute among enterprises within the branch. After paying deductions to branch and state, the enterprise would meet credit repayment and social insurance obligations. The residual income was then to be divided into reserve, risk, renewal (including depreciation) and wage funds. The wage fund was to act as the core of the incentive system. In principle, the share of the wage fund was a matter of negotiation between management and trade union representatives. It was estimated that in the first year of operation, 30 per cent of the wage fund would be set aside for bonus payments, the proportion expected to rise thereafter. Basic wages would be set according to centrally determined scales. If an enterprise was unable to meet the basic wage requirements from its own funds, it could draw on its reserve fund, or, if necessary, turn to the branch for temporary help. In this case, greater direct control over the enterprise by the branch management would be enforced. On the other hand, however, successful enterprises were to be heavily taxed on above-average wage payments, as a temporary anti-inflation precaution – with inherent dangers for the operation of the reform as a whole, which later became clear in 1967.

A major task not tackled in 1966 was the reorganisation of the banking system in accordance with its new role. Price reform too was not scheduled for implementation in full until the beginning of 1969. Preparatory research work on this crucial and complex aspect of the reform began in 1965, and some minor adjustments to the price system were introduced in 1966, with the improvement of statistical information at the centre and simplifications of price-fixing procedures.[66] In 1966, three price categories were to be introduced, with 64 per cent of industrial output still covered by the centrally fixed category, 29 per cent 'flexibly' priced, fluctuating between centrally fixed upper and lower limits, and 7 per cent set independently by enterprises themselves. Again, fear of inflation lay behind the extremely cautious approach to decentralisation of control over prices. Eventually, a uniform rate of turnover tax, as a fixed proportion of the wholesale price, would have to be introduced in order to link wholesale and retail prices, but this problem was postponed to a later stage, and in the meanwhile, extensive subsidies and variable tax rates continued, sheltering producer enterprises from the ultimate challenge of final market demand.

Although 1965 had seen extensive work on the preparation of the conditions for the reform, the measures introduced at the beginning of 1966 were hardly more than a first step, and the original timetable envisaged a fairly protracted transitional period of stabilisation, corrections and revision of the measures introduced. In fact, at the end of 1965, ominous signs began to appear of possibly even further extension of the timetable. In September, the trade union weekly, *Práce*, announced that unanticipated problems of reform implementation had led to reconsideration of the timetable, conveying the general impression that a more gradual approach was necessary, due to 'numerous material problems, disproportions and temporary unfavourable relations which do not permit a faster realisation of the new management'.[67] There seemed to be a growing tendency, moreover, to see the reform as limited to the preparatory measures themselves, coming into effect in 1966. This appeared both from the report given at the session of the Central Council of Trade Unions in September, and at the November Central Committee plenum, which dealt with only the organisational measures (the industrial reorganisation and changes in the central bodies), and was markedly vague on any further aspects of the reform. The general impression of loss of momentum was linked to signs of increased complacency in the apparatus, now that the recovery from the recession of the early 1960s was underway, and Notovný's own public contributions to the question of reform reverted to attacks on 'destructive' critics. In October, he pronounced, 'No, comrades, we shall not allow liberalising, let alone capitalist influences in our economy.'[68]

Such symptoms of backsliding in turn evoked a new sense of urgency among reformist economic specialists at the beginning of 1966. The reform was seen as having entered a transitional phase of crucial importance. But Kohoutek's heralding of the new year as a 'year of genuinely revolutionary changes'[69] was criticised by Vladimír Škrlant in the Party's theoretical journal, *Nová Mysl*,[70] as misleadingly over-optimistic, as an assessment of the measures introduced at that time. In fact, 1966 would not see the 'complex', comprehensive implementation of the new system but only the preparation of the ground for future radical change. Without price reform, uniform enterprise deductions, economic criteria predominant in the allocation of investment resources, linkage of domestic production to foreign trade – none of which would take place in 1966 – gross income as the key enterprise indicator could not bring the full fruits expected by the reform. Gross income was, moreover, still defined on the basis of output, rather than sales, and the plan for 1966 had been drawn up in the old way.[71]

Rudolf Kocanda discussed the basic approach to reform so far taken. Gradualism and open-ended, piecemeal changes over a long period had been adopted for some admittedly sound reasons – the task of preparing everything in advance was massive and probably unmanageable, and in the existing conditions of disequilibrium, immediate full introduction of the market would lead to huge disruption.[72] But, he argued, although the approach made sense in theory, in practice reform implementation could not proceed gradually by small steps beyond a certain point. The official view of the reform as an 'improvement' of the existing system was, he suggested, an inappropriate interpretation – the old and new systems were ultimately quite different, each consisting of a core of interdependent elements. Smooth transition from one system to the other could not ultimately be made by gradual steps, which would only affect peripheral elements of the old system:

> And if after a long period, the core of the management system remains unchanged, it contains within itself sufficient strength to liquidate the partial reforms made up to now, and development will revert in essence to the old system.[73]

The measures so far introduced had only touched the outer periphery, not the core of the old system, Kocanda argued, and there was a danger that this half-way house could prove even worse than the old system itself. What was urgently needed was rapid development of the market, away from a system of 'redistribution'. This meant early introduction of wholesale price reform and the imposition of a uniform rate of turnover tax on retail sales, and the introduction of uniform enterprise deductions.[74]

Drahomír Kolder also appears to have been, by this time, convinced by the arguments for acceleration rather than delay in reform implementation:

> The period into which we have entered carries with it a grave danger: the difficulties in our economy will once again tempt us to use those directive interventions and methods which in the past had only limited effectiveness, but which still survive and whose employment in the new conditions of management can have only very limited scope. Every system of management has its own logic, which cannot be disrupted without the danger of an undesirable chain reation.[75]

In fact, the arguments of the reformists seem to have hit home. In early 1966, the notion of a coherent 'target model' (*cílový model*), gained ground among leading officials in the economic apparatus, indicating an appreciation of the systemic quality of the changes involved.[76] As a result, the Central Committee decided in May 1966 to accelerate the implementation of the reform. Work on the wholesale price reform was to be speeded up for introduction at the beginning of 1967, rather than in 1969, and at the same time, a unified deduction of 18 per cent of enterprise gross income was to be paid into the State Budget. As Josef Toman, Chairman of the State Committee for Organisation and Management, explained, the notion of a long transition period, based on the idea of restoring economic equilibrium *before* full introduction of the reform, had been abandoned as 'unrealistic', and it was recognised that to gain the full benefit of the reform, it had to be carried through 'to the end'.[77] The accelerated programme was approved formally at the XIII Party Congress in June, and was regarded by outside observers as a major political coup for reformists.[78]

In the event, the acceleration brought the whole process of reform to a point of crisis in 1967. How this occurred is an extremely complex question, involving both an assessment of the technical reasons for the failure of the price reform, and the political aspects. In the present analysis, the political aspects are the most important. The failure of the price reform was seen by economists as a reflection of the general political resistance to reform on the part of the apparatus, and of the weakness of the political leadership in overcoming this resistance. The failure of the price reform in turn led to a series of measures to put right the inflationary pressures it unleashed which amounted to abandonment of the reform. At the same time, the Novotný regime reached its nadir, and in the series of stormy Central Committee sessions in late 1968, Ota Šik, as the spokesman for economic reform, played a vital part in securing the change of leadership.

The idea of the wholesale price reform was to make the first step towards efficiency pricing, generating a set of prices which would cover production costs and provide a rate of profit reflecting the branch average efficiency with which the enterprise used its productive assets and labour.[79] The price reform was simplified by grouping individual products into 416 broad commodity categories in the hope of producing a similar rate of profit for enterprises in the same branch, and rough comparability in profit rates throughout industry. It was expected that wholesale prices would rise overall by 19 per cent, and enterprise profits by 22 per cent on average.

In the event, in 1967, wholesale prices turned out to have risen by 29–30 per cent and enterprise profits by 81 per cent.[80] The rate of deductions from enterprise gross incomes, set at 18 per cent on the assumption of a 19 per cent rise in wholesale prices, thus left the enterprises with a windfall of Kčs 6–7bn extra resources at their disposal over the planned level.[81] Moreover, a wide discrepancy in enterprise liquidity resulted, to the benefit of heavy industrial branches rather more than light industry,[82] and 'entirely random differences in profitability occurred among different groups of products'.[83] While even an inefficient enterprise might find itself in a financially buoyant position, others suffered from liquidity shortages, and 'their predicament merely served as a legitimate basis for claiming subsidies and short-term credit'.[84]

What had gone wrong? Although it has been argued that there were numerous technical shortcomings in the methods used to recompute the wholesale prices,[85] the major reason for the failure of the price reform appears to lie in the unchecked operation of vested bureaucratic interests. The basic data on costs were derived from the enterprises and branch units themselves, which of course had a powerful interest in overstating their costs – which they did with a vengeance. The skills acquired by their economic managements in the course of years of bargaining with the central authorities over plan targets were mobilised to devastating effect in negotiations over the determination of costs on which the new wholesale prices were to rely. On the other hand, the anxiety of the central authorities to cushion enterprises 'temporarily' in the interests of avoiding disruption led to little effective calculation to offset this well-known bargaining practice. It has been argued that the reform was put into practice in the wrong order – enterprise independence should have preceded the price reform.[86] In the event, the disruption which resulted led back to the familiar self-sustaining logic of recentralisation pinpointed by Komenda and Kožušník in 1964, where:

> directive management appears as the only acceptable solution to the discrepancy which it has caused, as the only guarantee which safeguards the planned nature of social production and the satisfaction of social needs against the narrow interests of the enterprise.[87]

This situation quickly put the whole reform in jeopardy, as the long-standing fears of inflation held in particular in the Ministry of Finance appeared fully justified by the scale of resources now at the disposition of enterprises, which made possible high wage payments not covered by increases in productivity, and a new surge in investment spending financed from own resources, escaping the controls which it had been hoped to exercise through central credit policy. Pressures to bring into operation the central reserve powers built into the 'transitional' measures became overwhelming. As a leading economic official put it, 'In the situation which has arisen in the course of this year, central organs have not only the right, but also the urgent duty to intervene and put matters right.'[88]

The fear of inflation focused on both wages and investments. In the first half-year, wage payments overall increased by 5 per cent, as compared with a productivity rise of 4.3 per cent.[89] But alarmist accounts in the press highlighted cases where labour productivity had fallen by 7 per cent below the 1966 level, while average monthly wages had risen by 22.3 per cent.[90] The Central Committee plena of May and September tightened controls over wage rises, limiting them first to 3.2–3.4 per cent, and then to 2.9 per cent, tying them to a rise in productivity of 4.5–5.0 per cent.[91] This move was, however, controversial. Ota Šik had consistently rejected the use of wage restrictions,[92] and now repeated his point that faster wage growth was necessary as an incentive, and to realise wage differentiation without wage cuts.[93] Rudolf Rohlíček argued that the cost of labour was still relatively lower than labour-substituting equipment, and this acted as a disincentive to modernisation.[94] Otakar Tůrek also saw the possibility of allowing wage growth to force enterprises to use resources more efficiently, and attacked the restrictive policy adopted as 'retrograde':

> [T]his leads once again to the re-emergence of the atmosphere in enterprises that someone up there is watching over wages, and thus that it is not a good thing to expose all one's reserves. The psychology of the wage ceiling arises once again instead.[95]

Cestmir Kožušník saw the restrictive measures as tending in the direction of a *de facto* 'wage ceiling', and thus the reimposition of a quasi-directive index on enterprises, and warned, 'If these methods of regulating wages were to prevail, it would practically mean the end of the new management system – a fact which must be realised, although many people do not, or do not want to, understand it.[96]

The key to restoring equilibrium was seen by both reformist economists and by the government to lie in the field of investment. There was a clear case here for central intervention in the interests of the reform. In the absence of effective market pressures to constrain enterprise demand, the only countervailing force was the centre – but, precisely because of the scale of enterprise excess liquidity, the centre was weak.[97] A first step had to be a surcharge on enterprises. This involved a plea to enterprises to hand over voluntarily their 'unearned' profits,[98] backed by the threat of a detailed central audit of the enterprise where funds were not forthcoming. This of course merely reinforced enterprises' suspicions that the centrally set deductions would not be permanent, but would change continually as before. Correspondingly, old habits of concealing their true reserves were reawakened, and enterprises prepared for a new round of bargaining with the centre as before.

A further measure, more in keeping with reform, was raising interest rates, which were increased from 4 per cent to 6 per cent on short-term credits and from 6 to 8 per cent on investment credits,[99] but even so, many enterprises found themselves in a position to finance investment without recourse to bank borrowing at all, and thus evaded the central credit policy.[100] With the difficulties in reducing investment by economic means alone, the central authorities resorted to direct measures, cutting Kčs 1bn from the plan guideline figure, and intervening directly to reallocate investment resources, without cross-branch efficiency comparisons. The favoured branches were chemicals, building materials and consumer-goods industries.[101]

By late 1967, despite some success in restoring equilibrium, the economy was clearly deeply in trouble, and displaying all the old problems. While the overall rate of growth of national income was slower than in 1966, at 6.9 per cent it was not a major cause for concern. It was in lengthening completion schedules on investment projects, the growth in stocks, and the continued corresponding faster pace of industrial output as a whole than of final production that the major problem lay. The wholesale price reform would have to be revised and repeated for 1968. It was against this background of mounting economic dislocation and a growing sense of impasse that the crisis of Novotný's leadership was to come to a head.

C THE POLITICISATION OF REFORM

The political problem which the reformers faced was devastating: a combination of massive social apathy or disaffection, entrenched vested interests, and an incompetent and vacillating leadership. Their confrontation with this array of forces against change eventually led to, or reinforced, their conviction of the necessity of far-reaching political change. The first condition of this they came to see in a change of leadership; but this would not be all – there was a need for systemic political change to revitalise the whole political framework, activating the dormant, politically excluded population, exposing the vested bureaucratic interests and weakening their covert grip both on the economy and the political leadership. What was needed above all was effective leadership based not on the monopolisation of coercive power, but on authority acquired through a process of consultation with the openly formulated pluralistic forces of society – and, especially, with intellectual and expert groups.

Economic reformers found themselves drawn inexorably into political questions at various levels. In fact, the question of the mass public attitude to reform, and the necessity of broad democratisation throughout society only became acute in the context of 1968, but well before this, reformers had become aware of the dangerous potential for manipulation of working-class anti-intellectualism by the apparatus in its own interests. But in the period 1965 to 1967, the main points at which reformers touched upon politics were in the issues of managerial competence, and the criteria for managerial appointment and promotion; the relationship of the Party to economic management; and the closely related question of the existence of interlocking and self-perpetuating bureaucratic élites, able to protect their own interest and undermine the changes introduced. All these questions led ultimately to the top – to the issue of the political leadership's role in the reform.

As we have seen in Chapter 4, the reformers quickly became aware that the apparatus would be a source of considerable resistance to reform, not so much out of ideological conviction itself, as out of concern to preserve jobs and privileges, and out of innate conservatism, rooted in its low level of intelligence, qualification and general competence, as suggested by the material presented in section A of this chapter. All this pointed towards the problem of the predominance in past recruitment policy of political criteria over technical expertise and formal qualification.

Recognition at the official level of the need to improve the standards of management is illustrated not merely by the appearance of an emphasis on 'scientific' aspects in speeches and declarations, but by some organisational measures – for example, the establishment of a State Committee for Organisation and Management, and an Institute of Management to promote specialist training. An educational drive was launched. Immediately after the January 1965 Central Committee plenum, Kolder, Šik and František Vlasák organised a series of seminars for managers, and a similar set of conferences for lower-level Party functionaries was held in the spring of 1965, all with the aim of explaining the principles of the new economic system.[102] A set of pamphlets was rapidly published to aid the educational effort, with contributions from leading specialists in the central apparatus.[103] But all these measures were in a sense cost-free in political terms and did little to change the immediate situation. When it came to the crucial question of defining the tasks of the new type of manager, thus implicitly touching upon the issue of demotion or dismissal of incompetents among the existing cadres, there were controversy and a reluctance on the part of the authorities to make radical changes.

Josef Toman, the newly appointed Chairman of the State Committee for Organisation and Management, made it clear that political criteria would remain uppermost in managerial appointments:

> A leading economic worker must above all be a man devoted to the cause of socialism, who sees correctly the aim of the socialist economy. Only under these conditions will he be able to manage with perspective to set out long-term goals for the enterprise.[104]

He rejected wide-scale replacements of existing personnel as counterproductive to the formation of 'real working collectives, allied by a principled unity of views and wholly committed to the tasks set before them'.[105] In the short term, the solution was seen in education alone. This was in a certain sense realistic, since a whole alternative cohort of new managers did not as yet exist. Nevertheless, it did not promise rapid promotion for the younger and dynamic junior managers, where they were present.

An alternative view was put forward by the sociologist, S. Vacha, who called for an end to 'the priority [given] to less able and less qualified workers solely because they are members of the Party'.[106] He put forward a broader and more sophisticated concept of 'political maturity' – in the context of the new system, this could no longer be equated with mere 'discipline' and 'passive devotion' to the Party, but implied an active and creative, independent approach to problem-solving.[107] Drahomír Kolder also within the leadership, appears to have been critical of the way in which managerial appointments had been made:

> For some comrades who take decisions on the appointment of economic cadres, often personal relations have more influence, for others again, the enumeration of functions and posts which they have passed through; and there are even cases where the decision or selection for a function has been influenced by whether the proposed comrade has performed well at a conference or meeting.[108]

Reformist economists and commentators were more sceptical than Toman of the efficacy of education alone to bring about a reversal of deeply-ingrained habits derived from years of working within a command framework, which had systematically strangled initiative, rewarding only the fulfilment of plan targets set from above.[109] Evžen Löbl warned that it was an 'illusion' to expect that the process could so easily be reversed by the promulgation of new rules of the game, 'It is relatively easy to forbid people to think and to make it impossible for them to show their ideas and abilities, but creative thinking and business acumen cannot be commanded.'[110]

It has been suggested that a major weakness of the Czechoslovak reform was that it was not the result of a political revolution, but was imposed on an inert population, and was not accompanied by willingness to effect changes in the personnel in key posts.[111] This seems to be a very powerful hypothesis, and there is evidence that the Czechoslovak reformers were also at the time aware of this problem:

> Up to now, sociological research has not taken up the subject of the forces which support and maintain workers in office who have at some time got there whether they had the required ability or not … It would probably become obvious [from such

> research] ... how important are certain personal alliances of people who give each other mutual support, how potent are the political resources for deflecting criticism directed at an individual ... what a significant factor is the 'political weight' that a worker has purposefully built up for himself, and how all these 'instruments' petrify the harmful conditions in cadre policy, how they can prolong the traditional system of cadre policy long after the duration of the traditional system of management of the economy.[112]

It was these cosy clubs which proved able to survive the reform measures by their grip over their actual practical implementation:

> to 'modify' certain rulings and principles, as they say 'with respect to special conditions', in fact, however, to suit their own image ... Certain economic managers, instead of a realistic view and concrete measures, rather adopted the terminology of the new system of management and dressed up old phrases with new words.[113]

It was this process which, as I showed in section B, was behind the ultimate failure of the price reform. Novotný himself was aware of the impact of this kind of alliance, and was critical of the conservative distortions in policy implementation which resulted.[114] But he appears to have felt powerless against them, which indeed he was, since they were the backbone of his political position.

However, Šik was becoming aware at the same time that the roots of conservatism extended beyond the apparatus into society as a whole:

> Even though it is likely that the number of those who have an inner distaste for any kind of changes in the form of management is relatively greater in the managerial and especially in the state apparatus than for example at the level of production, it would have been possible to overcome these central conservative tendencies much more quickly if they had not been able to lean on conservative and outdated attitudes of a part of our workers.[115]

In fact, 1966 saw the occasional strike as workers resisted the impact of the new measures. 'I tell you seriously', one disaffected steelworker complained to a journalist in *Život Strany*, 'that it seems to us that the new economic system was directed from the very beginning against us, the workers.'[116] At first, there had been a tendency on the part of the public to see the reform as 'just another reorganisation',[117] but as measures began to be put into practice, anxiety was stirred up over the possible threat to job security. Selucký tried to counter this by pointing to the existing labour shortage, which, he argued, would not disappear overnight. Moreover, the chronic underdevelopment of the tertiary sector meant that a reorientation of economic priorities in its favour could open up extensive new job opportunities.[118] But it had to be got across that the right to work could no longer mean the right to a particular job, to secure employment regardless of the usefulness of the product.[119]

The other major point of resistance from below was the policy of greater wage differentiation, bringing reward closer into line with effort and economic results. The State had come to be seen, according to one journalist, as a kind of benevolent uncle (*strýček*), dispensing bounty irrespective of merit or the performance of the economy: 'probably nowhere in the world has a people lived so well for so little and such poor work as we have'.[120] This kind of talk, however justified, aroused fears of a rapid deterioration in living standards – that the burden of years of mismanagement would be thrust onto the shoulders of those who bore least responsibility for it. In fact, many reformist economists, including Šik, argued against restricting the growth of wages since this would impede the development of an effective incentive system.[121] It was not envisaged that differentiation should lead to a reduction in wages for any major group. Whether this was in fact realistic is a separate question. But an all-out effort to win over the hearts of workers for the cause of reform was not undertaken until 1968, when the by now routed conservatives turned to manipulate working-class misgivings by playing on the quite deep-rooted anti-intellectualism in their attitudes.

In the meanwhile, the reformers' attention turned to the leadership itself. The hesitancy and vacillation at the top became identified as the primary problem, preventing the mobilisation of political will necessary to overcome the doubts of population and bureaucrats alike. In fact, the discussion of the qualities of a good manager already carried with it broad political overtones. Selucký's definition of what the task of management was about contained (probably not fortuitously) an implicit prescription for the exercise of leadership in general:

> A good manager should be surrounded by a staff of advisers and specialists, each of whom is better educated, more clever and better informed in his sector than the manager ... On the other hand, the

manager must be able to make the best use of all the information and advice submitted to him by his staff.[122]

As I have suggested in section A, the basic weakness of the Novotný regime itself was its inherent inability to adapt to this style of consultative rule, to see intellectuals not as a threat but as a political resource to be tapped and mobilised for the regime's own purposes. Novotný's battles with intellectuals on the cultural front in 1963 and 1964 only fuelled his suspicions of expertise as inherently a challenge to his own authority. He appears to have found it extremely difficult to accept the necessity for wide-ranging and continuous debate, which Šik saw as essential for the proper analysis of past failures and for the corresponding elaboration of appropriate solutions.[123] Instead, Novotný attacked what he identified as 'destructive' criticism, unsolicited advice from those who 'merely sat behind a table and thought they had a patent for endless, negative criticism'.[124] The reform was not merely the 'affair of a few economists', but was party policy, subject to party control and as such, limits were set to debate:

> Our socialist democracy has created broad possibilities for the exchange of opinions of all questions of social life. Of course, even this democracy has its limits, which cannot be overstepped where it is a question of the intrinsic principles of socialism, the arrangement of the State.[125]

> Only the Communist Party – and no other group which fancies itself as such – is called upon to oversee and direct the social process and to set right, as the need arises, shortcomings and mistakes which may come to light in the development of society.[126]

Thus it was the Party's definition of the aims of the reform which must prevail – which, given the way the Party itself was manipulated by Novotný, meant a very circumscribed definition. The centrality of the plan, understood in a traditional way, must remain as the core of the system, the defining feature of its 'socialist' essence: 'Our society can go forward only as … a centrally directed society.'[127]

The problem with the Novotný leadership was not merely the concept of power on which it rested, based on old centralistic and coercive assumptions and thus fundamentally at odds with the requirement of the economic reform. More important still was the real disintegration of central authority of any type, as these traditional methods proved ineffective in the management of the process of change. In fact, reformers saw determination at the centre and forceful leadership as vital to the implementation of the reform. As the journalist Kantůrek argued, the new economic system required active 'warriors' to push it through 'without excessive restrictions, retreats and compromises'.[128] In the absence of leadership, a whole range of problems of social and political disintegration was emerging, noticed even by rather orthodox commentators:

> a notable decline in labour discipline, debasement of authority at all levels of management, damaging inertia and deep-rooted routine, elevation of local and group interests over social interests, but even certain pipe-dreams, a lackadaisical attitude and sometimes downright political naivete.[129]

The pre-Congress debate within the Party in the first half of 1966 revealed the degree to which disintegration and inertia were affecting the Party itself at all levels. In West Bohemia, numerous inadequacies were reported in ideological work.[130] The West Slovak regional Party secretary complained that the basic Party units in his area seemed not to have noticed the significance of the January 1965 plenum at all. On the subject of the new economic system, there were 'rather a lot of confusion and problems' – the initial overenthusiastic expectations of immediate economic improvement had given way to disillusion as the long-term nature of the solution became apparent.[131] Activism among Party members had been falling off; there was no sense of responsibility at the grass-roots for party policy, but rather ignorance of its content and lack of confidence in it.[132] Passivity among the membership was a problem frequently raised,[133] and the dangers of it were noted:

> A passive approach to party directives and social obligations weakens the fighting power of the Party and its organisational and ideological unity. Members who have not assimilated themselves into the Party, who do not fulfil their party duties or carry them out simply inadequately or formally are not appropriate for the new exacting requirements.[134]

Various explanations were put forward for these symptoms of growing malaise in the Party. The more conservative blamed the influence of Western propaganda, particularly among young people.[135] Others saw the source of passivity in the complexity of the problems now facing the Party, and the apparent lack of immediate solutions,[136] leading to 'defeatist moods'.[137] A particular source of confusion indeed related to the economic reform, in rather widespread bewilderment about the proper role of the Party in the enterprise: some Party committees were continuing to interfere directly in management as before, while others took the January 1965 plenum as an instruction to withdraw completely from supervision of management. As one regional Party official observed, 'Functionaries do not hide their fears that the reduction in the number of party-approved functions will lead to the reduction in the influence of the Party on the management of the economy.'[138]

Little guidance on this crucial question was forthcoming from the leadership, apart from bland assertions from, for example, Lenárt, that:

> there is no contradiction when we speak of strengthening the authority and responsibility of economic executives, and simultaneously stress the necessity for furthering the leading role of the Party and the influence of Party organisations[139]

What was an enterprise Party secretary to make of the instruction 'to lead economic workers to maximal independence'?[140] Or what could it mean in practice for the local Party organs to 'defend all-social interests'? As the Prague city secretary noted, 'Apart from numerous perfectly clear-cut cases, Party organisations encounter many a complex problem, where it is difficult for them to distinguish unambiguously what is and what is not in the social interest.'[141] The 'new role', it seemed, could be defined only negatively: the Party's role was *not* to double up on or replace the function of the manager, *not* to interfere in day-to-day management, but neither was the Party to turn into a 'mere scientific research institution'[142] or to be 'reduced merely to political and ideological influence, divorced from production'.[143] It was also argued that the new system had not limited the Party's right of control', nor had it deprived the Party of the 'right to pass resolutions binding on management'.[144]

The redefinition of the Party's leading role would be difficult in any circumstances, but matters were not helped by the failure of the leadership even to begin the task. This reflected a deeper source of the growing apathy and disaffection of the membership – the lack of responsiveness of the leadership to the mounting problems, resulting from the inadequacies of inner-party life. An official of the Central Committee's Organisational–Political department pointed out that lack of commitment among the membership might be symptomatic of a basic problem: where 'full participation' of the membership was not ensured, where 'open comradely criticism' was viewed as an obstruction of Party work, where membership meetings were purely 'formal' in character, passivity could be seen as a natural response. It was a plea for more 'democracy' within the Party, as a condition of solving the pressing problems.[145]

Ota Šik played an essential part in linking the failure of the reform to the question of the lack of democracy in the Party. By 1966, his personal relationship with Novotný appears to have degenerated to a point where Novotný attempted to prevent Šik from addressing the XIII Party Congress, clearly fearing an attack on his leadership style.[146] In the event, Šik was able to speak, and although only a toned-down version of his speech has been published, he seems to have justified Novotný's fears by relating the basic problem of the reform to the way in which power in general was being exercised, citing the example of Lenin in implicit contrast to Novotný:

> Never did he make out that the Party had always only acted correctly or that things could never have turned out differently from the way they in fact did. It was by open exposure of the causes of all the difficulties which arose, and by deep theoretical analysis of them that he not only prevented the rise of pessimism and lack of faith in the Party, but on the contrary, strengthened the authority of the Party and gained greater support for its policy.[147]

In fact, the XIII Congress saw the election of a new Central Committee which, in the course of 1967, was to prove rather more responsive to the mounting problems in the economy and society, and rather less easily manipulated by Novotný. According to Hendrych's report on the election of the new Central Committee, a turnover of 43.3 per cent of the old Central Committee membership took place, with the emphasis much more obviously placed on drawing in expertise. He claimed that eighty-four of the new 166-member Central Committee had higher education, a further twenty-six had completed secondary education or had undertaken two-year or shorter courses at the Party High School.[148] As Mencl and Ouředník relate:

> In the Party and state apparatus, into which the forces of the new Party intelligentsia were entering in growing numbers, resistance to the political course of A. Novotný was strengthening. It happened more and more often that persecutory assaults did not

reach their targets, and got stuck in blind alleys of delays or various forms of 'window-dressing'.[149]

A major factor in the disintegration of Novotný's grip was the growing alienation of some of his erstwhile closest supporters, for example, Jiří Hendrych and Drahomír Kolder, both of whom were becoming concerned at the state of affairs in the Party. As Kolder commented, the debates on the Party's 'leading role' before the XIII Congress, 'did not achieve a desirable level and dealt predominantly only with subsidiary questions'.[150] The first signs of a split between Novotný and Hendrych, his right-hand man, were detected as early as January 1965, when Hendrych tried to secure more meaningful debate in the Central Committee over the political aspects of the new economic system.[151] Hendrych returned to the issue at the Central Committee plenum of February 1967, which debated the question of Party and social 'unity'. Behind this debate lay an oblique critique of Novotný's style of rule. Hendrych, in the keynote speech of the plenum, presented the problem in terms which clearly indicated his indebtedness to the ideas of the Party intellectuals with whom he was associating,[152] distancing himself from the old 'monolithic' concept with which Novotný was associated.

The unity of a socialist society was not 'one-dimensional', not a static 'ideal harmony', but should rather be conceived of as a process, an internally articulated dynamic unit, based on continual renewal and overcoming of conflicts between old and new.[153] Ideological unity in society was a goal yet to be achieved. It should be acknowledged that while a basic consensus had grown up in favour of socialism, differences of opinion still existed between social groups, since, although fundamental class antagonism had been overcome, the process of 'class *rapprochement*' was still going on, and was a complex and conflict-ridden process. Religion and other 'pre-socialist' attitudes remained, which, however, could not be dealt with by a 'sectarian and maximalist approach', but had to be acknowledged and overcome gradually by more sensitivity and differentiation in the Party's educational effort. Sources of disunity were identified in the nationality question which required an 'integrated approach' combining regional socioeconomic development and a more sensitive and 'tactful' educational effort, fostering a 'unified Czechoslovak cultural context'; and in the youth question, where Hendrych referred to the straitening of opportunities for the young, in comparison with the earlier period. He advocated a conscious policy of promoting young, better-qualified people, to work alongside their less highly-trained but experienced seniors. The economic reform was also a source of social disunity, with some showing impatience at the slow progress of reform and others doubting its wisdom, especially with respect to income differentiation, loss of security, and price rises. But Hendrych reminded his audience that the measures aimed at creating 'greater scope for strengthening the unifying elements in society' through harmonising individual and group interests with the social interest, by rewarding labour in proportion to its social usefulness. He also acknowledged the need for greater 'participation' and more effective promotion of interest-group activity, as essential concomitants of the economic reform. The need for 'specialist expertise' in decision-making was also reaffirmed, but Hendrych further argued that in order that expertise be combined effectively with the need for 'democracy', more conflict and debate among specialists should be allowed, and specialists should always provide 'democratic' decision-making organs with more than one alternative for discussion.[154]

The debate which followed Hendrych's speech at the plenum saw a quite sudden release of critical energies. Many prominent members spoke out, joined by new younger members. A wide range of complaints about passivity, drift and disorientation was expressed. Characteristically, Novotný declared in the course of a stormy Presidium meeting afterwards, that such a plenum 'must not be repeated'.[155] By his increasingly intolerable, heavy-handed repressive actions in the course of the spring and summer of 1967, he ensured that it would be.

The political crisis which came to a head at the end of 1967 drew on virtually all spheres of social and political life. A major issue was the IV Congress of Writers in June, which saw the dramatic re-emergence of open intellectual revolt against the regime's entire method of rule, but also focused on its foreign policy. Writers articulated a widespread sense of misgiving about the Czechoslovak governments' support for the Arab cause against Israel in the Middle East conflict of that year, which was seen as both anti-semitic and as a reflection of the Novotný leadership's slavish following of the Soviet line.[156] In turn, the leadership's response to the writers' criticisms was characteristically repressive. The Central Committee which met in September resolved on expulsion and party disciplinary measures against the most outspoken critics, and the Writers' Union was deprived of its newspaper, *Literární Noviny*, which was transferred to the control of the Ministry of Culture.[157] There was little evidence of dissent within the Central Committee on this, although many members later expressed doubts about the use of such severe measures. In the meanwhile, however, Novotný was clearly reverting to more overtly dictatorial methods of rule, evoking fears among some of a return to the 1950s.[158] Novotný's speech to the graduates of the Military Academy in September appeared to demonstrate an increasingly hard-line approach, emphasising 'class' conflict in contrast to the more conciliatory line embodied in the XIII Congress resolutions.[159] At a Presidium meeting on 5 September, Novotný is reported to have renewed his attack on Šik personally for raising the question of democracy.[160] But Šik was far from alone in his criticism. Regional Party secretaries expressed dissatisfaction with the excessive centralisation of power in a conference with Novotný in September. Certain areas, in particular North and South Moravia and some Slovak regions came into direct conflict with Novotný.[161]

At the October plenum, Hendrych returned to the question of the role of the Party in the new stage of development – but it was not so much the prepared material he presented which sparked off discussion, as the revelation of an incident in its preparation which, almost haphazardly, led to a sudden torrent of criticism. Alexander Dubček protested at the way in which the agreed draft of the material for discussion agreed by the Presidium, of which he was a member, had been changed overnight by Novotný and some close collaborators, without consultation. In fact, it was a very characteristic ploy of Novotný, but Dubček now used it to suggest there might be something wrong with the way the Party was run, and then went on to list in particular some Slovak grievances, relating to the way in which investment cuts had, he felt, been unfairly imposed on the less-developed Slovak area. Novotný's response was to insinuate that the old danger of 'Slovak nationalism' was behind Dubček's intervention. This in turn provoked revolt on the part of many Central Committee members, who saw in Novotný's veiled threat further evidence of a resort to 1950s-style methods of rule, and 'Finally the ominous phrase was heard: "cumulation of offices"'.[162] Novotný's leadership was now in question. But an adjournment was secured, and further discussion of the issue of leadership changes was deferred until December. In the meanwhile, however, the students of the Strahov hostel had mounted their protest and were approaching the Castle, where the Central Committee was in session. As related above, this was met on the part of the authorities by an open show of force. The plenum dispersed in an atmosphere of mounting crisis, as Novotný left for Moscow to attend the October Revolution celebrations, and to obtain Soviet support.

The Soviet leadership seems to have been indifferent to Novotný's personal survival. Novotný managed to secure a personal visit from Brezhnev in early December, but Brezhnev is reported to have refused to intervene.[163] The December plenum, which was convened only after postponement, was to tackle both economic and political problems. In the event, the political questions took over, but it was Ota Šik, who, without finding much support, brought on to the agenda not only the question of personnel changes, but broader political change. He first proposed that Novotný should relinquish his party post, but further, criticised the failure to re-examine the errors of the past in such a way as to ensure that the whole problem of excessive personal power could not recur. He proposed that the Central Committee should set up a special commission of trusted and respected colleagues, whose task would cover not only the nomination of a successor to Novotný, but also the elaboration of a set of proposals for the democratisation of party life, to overcome the apathy and stagnation, and the disaffection of the population, and in particular of the intelligentsia and youth. Such proposals, he suggested, should cover firm rules of procedure for the Central Committee, the Presidium, the Secretariat and the Party Commissions. 'The plenum must cease to be an assembly for unanimously approving cut-and-dried proposals by the Presidium', he is reported as saying.[164] Greater emphasis should be given to expertise in policy-making, by formalising the role of the Central Committee's special Commissions in place of the present role of individual officials. The simultaneous holding of the leading party post and the state Presidency or Prime Ministerial office should be stopped, and limitations on the length of service in any senior post should be imposed. Party elections should be based on the secret ballot. Cadre policy should be changed to prevent its manipulation by individuals as a means of personal political self-aggrandisment. Finally, a short-term Political and Economic Action Programme should be drawn up to deal at once with the accumulated problems of the economic reform, management and the state apparatus, culture, and other areas of crisis.

In the event, Šik's suggested procedure was adopted for the replacement of Novotný, but the final resolution issued alongside the announcement of Dubček as his successor on 5 January 1968 failed to cover the broader issues which Šik raised as of equally critical importance. The Central Committee failed at this point to face up to the broad challenge. Mlynář notes 'the inability of the Central Committee to understand what it had actually done by overthrowing

Novotný'.[165] Even its selection of Dubček, seen by many who supported it, as a compliant and inoffensive choice,[166] did not augur well for the future of reform, insofar as this needed effective and authoritative leadership. In fact, there were depressing parallels with the choice of Novotný himself in 1953. Thus the Central Committee itself contributed to providing the circumstances in which Šik's demand for democratisation within the Party would be taken up by those outside it in the course of 1968; and the political reforms which Party intellectuals had wanted took on revolutionary implications.

D ECONOMIC REFORM IN THE POLITICS OF 1968

It is not the intention of this final section of the chapter to repeat the well-known, detailed and exhaustive general accounts of the events in Czechoslovakia in 1968, which have already been written. In this regard, there remains very little new to be revealed after, for example, the monumental work by H.G. Skilling.[167] The aim is rather to highlight the main *economic* aspects of 1968, and thus to round off the general interpretation of the role of the economic reform in the political crisis which has already been presented in the preceding sections of this chapter.

The basic conclusion towards which the argument of this chapter has been moving is that the crisis of the Czechoslovak communist regime originated at the level of élite politics, rather than being a product of pluralising pressures generated by the introduction of a regulated-market-type reform – such a change in the economic system itself was not in fact realised. Economic factors of course contributed to the crisis of the Novotný regime. A decade of mounting economic difficulties provided the background against which it unfolded. The failure of the regime to implement economic reform as a means of tackling the long-standing economic problems drove economic experts into a position of political opposition.

But economic issues were by no means the only, or even the most important factor in the crisis, and economists in fact were a rather minor element in the rising current of opposition to Novotný within the Party, and in the broader social pressures for political change.[168] Regime relations with the intelligentsia as a whole, particularly with the cultural intelligentsia, the Slovak nationality issue, and long-standing personal grievances against Novotný within the Central Committee deriving from the 'unfinished business' of the 1950s political trials were more evident, potent and immediate catalysts of crisis.

This configuration of issues and forces did not essentially change in the politics of 1968. To be sure, in that year there was a dramatic broadening and deepening of the political crisis, which, after some months' continuing confinement to the political élite and its relations with the intelligentsia, did gather momentum and become a pluralising and democratising movement drawing in society at large. But the momentum was sustained largely on the initiative of the intelligentsia – that social group whose troubled relationship with the regime had been the single most important source of the élite crisis of 1967. Not until the summer of 1968 did the rest of the population, in particular, the workers begin to see events as more than an affair of the élite, and even then, evidence suggests a continuing mass scepticism about certain of the reformist intellectuals' proposals, especially in the area of economic reform.

Despite evidence of mounting economic difficulties by the end of 1967, the situation had not reached a point where either the basic plan objectives or the population's standard of living were under serious, immediate threat. This accounts in large part for the initial indifference of society at large to the political crisis. It also had the effect that economic issues remained secondary, or only sporadically assumed a central position in the politics of 1968.

The material presented in this concluding section will thus highlight the important continuities in the pattern of politics in 1968 which persisted from the previous period, despite the change of leadership and despite the turmoil at the level of the 'political superstructure'. The new leadership signalled at last a commitment to the introduction of a coherent and consistent economic reform, but it was deflected from following this through by more immediate political problems. It failed to muster the authority to assert its economic reform objectives, and crucially delayed the implementation of measures to change the institutional structure of the economic apparatus. While the political 'superstructure' disintegrated in the face of radical democratic challenges, the economic 'base' remained intact, under the predominant influence of conservative interests, as an extraordinarily tenacious 'still centre' in the moving world of the politics of 1968. The weight of conservatism was enhanced by the apathy and scepticism exhibited by the working class towards the economic component of the reformist programme. Economic reform thus remained after, as before, January 1968, only an unrealised blueprint in the minds of economists.

The Husák regime which assumed power in April 1969 nevertheless identified economic reform as a major contributory factor in the crisis, and proceeded to reverse those elements of it which had been, or were about to be put into operation. This appears to contradict the general interpretation of the political significance of the economic reform in 1968 presented here. But it can be argued that Husák's move was not so much a reflection of the real impact of economic reform, as of the importance of the vested interests against it. The success of 'normalisation' after the invasion depended on placating both the workers and the central force in the political economy of 'real socialism' – the economic apparatus. The ease with which the reversal was achieved confirms the impression that the forces for change in 1968 were far less firmly entrenched than the forces against it, despite the political turmoil.

A further point of relevance in this respect is the Soviet interpretation of the nature of the 1968 crisis. It is not clear that the reversal of the economic reform which Husák undertook was mainly a result of Soviet pressure. This is suggested by the lack of overt criticism of Czechoslovak economic reform proposals in the 'Warsaw letter' of July 1968 and in the Moscow communiqué drawn up by the Soviet and Czechoslovak Party leaderships in August immediately after the invasion. It is also noteworthy that the Hungarians, who had launched a comprehensive economic reform on 1 January 1968 were able to proceed with it after August. These points complement our argument that economic reform was not the major cause of the pluralising and democratising political crisis in Czechoslovakia. Although both the Soviets and the Hungarians were certainly not oblivious of the political risks involved in economic reform, they apparently did not conclude from the Czechoslovak crisis that fundamental democratisation was an inevitable consequence of it.

Initially, official reports on the state of the economy in early 1968 sustained the customary optimistic tone. Černík, the chairman of the State Planning Commission, reporting to the National Assembly in January, claimed that the past two years had been an 'overwhelming success' as demonstrated by an average annual rate of growth of National Income of 8 per cent.[169] Labour productivity had improved, and a more 'intensive' pattern of growth had emerged. The standard of living had risen rapidly, and although wages, in the first half of 1967, had outstripped productivity growth, the central government measures introduced had successfully checked this trend. An upward revision of the 1966–70 plan had therefore been possible. National

Income was now set to rise by 31–32 per cent over the quinquennium, as compared with the original target of 22–24 per cent. This progress had been achieved, Černík noted, despite persistent long-term problems in the economic structure, and continuing disequilibrium. Production was still inadequately adapted to demand, and stocks had grown. Investment demand had outrun the capacity and resources of the construction sector, investments were still excessively dispersed, and projects were not being completed and brought into operation on time. But there was no indication in Černík's address that the solution of these problems was seen in the immediate and rapid introduction of further measures of reform – in fact, only the vaguest and most oblique reference to reform was made.

Another State Planning Commission official, M. Kohoutek, optimistically claimed that 1967 had seen the transition to the New Economic System as an 'integrated whole', and noted that this change had been effected not only without 'undesirable fluctuations' in the economy, but with a sustained rate of growth in National Income, improved efficiency and quality, and accelerated structural change.[170] Difficulties had of course been encountered, he noted: the complexity of the task of wholesale price reform had been underestimated, and the new economic instruments (such as taxes, credit regulations, etc.) had had to be calculated on the basis of old prices, with the result that only 'crude estimates' of enterprise incomes had been possible, and the instruments themselves had not proved as effective as expected as a means of central control. Adjustments of the economic instruments would now be essential, but also, in view of the development of inflationary pressures, direct central interventions in the economy would continue to be necessary: 'unavoidably we must count on a great degree of all-social regulation'. The further development of reform, he suggested, would be a rather long and gradual process, dependent upon the prior re-establishment and maintenance of general economic stability.

The convening of a Central Committee plenum was delayed until the end of March, and in the intervening period, the Party Presidium was largely absorbed with urgent problems of a mainly political nature – setting up the framework for a thorough rehabilitation of the victims of political oppression of the Stalinist era, drawing up a comprehensive 'Action Programme' for political reforms, including the question of Slovak autonomy,[171] as well as a general move towards 'socialist democracy'. The immediate task was to contain the emerging spontaneous forces, particularly in the media, which were beginning to challenge the leadership's prerogative of initiative in demanding rapid and broad political change.

When the Central Committee finally met, its agenda reflected the primacy of purely political concerns, rather than economic issues; the resolutions passed covered rehabilitation, the rescinding of the disciplinary measures against the writers taken in September 1967, the acceptance in principle of federalisation of the Republic, and the postponement of the National Committee elections.[172] Wide-scale personnel changes figured large on the business of the plenum. Novotný's resignation from the Presidency was accepted, and Ludvík Svoboda was put forward as his replacement (and duly approved by the National Assembly). Leading Party and government officials – mainly in the fields of ideology, culture, defence, security and internal affairs – also resigned. The plenum recommended the resignation of the Lenárt government, and a new government was subsequently formed in April under Černík.

As Skilling notes, the personnel changes carried out at the plenum 'produced a substantial shift in the balance of forces, but did not represent an unambiguous transition toward a completely new and reform-oriented team'.[173] This was also true of the new economic leadership in the Černík government, where 'shifts in personnel in the central bodies were not entirely auspicious for the rapid reform of the economy or for decisive change in economic policy'.[174] Černík, and most of his senior ministers had long held leading economic posts, and were thus closely associated with the previous hesitant and half-hearted approach to economic reform. The Central Committee secretaries in charge of economic affairs – Drahomír Kolder and Štefan Sádovský – also had long careers behind them, and were not noted for vigorous commitment to reform. It was significant that Šik, who was identified most closely with commitment to consistent and immediate implementation of the economic reform, was kept rather to the side. He was not promoted to the Presidium, and although he became a deputy Prime Minister, along with four others, he was passed over for the chairmanship of the new Economic Council, which appeared to be intended as the power-house of future economic strategy, in favour of Lubomír Štrougal (we return to the Economic Council and its role below).

Despite the greater prominence of political matters at the plenum, the proceedings did in fact indicate that the new Party leadership had accepted the basic arguments of reformist economists, and was now committed to a coherent concept of reform in the way that the

Hungarian leadership had been in 1964. Alexander Dubček's address did not neglect economic issues, and he announced:

> We want to consistently introduce the new system of economic management. We must stop talking only about improving the system of management and say clearly that it is to be a profound economic reform designed to create a new system for the functioning of the socialist economy.[175]

The Action Programme approved by the plenum contained an economic section, which signified, albeit in the broadest terms, full commitment to a regulated market model of reform. The Party's aims were:

> the revival of the positive functions of the socialist market, essential changes in the economic structure, and a profound change in the role of the plan, which will no longer act as an instrument issuing commands, but will become an instrument which enables society to find the most appropriate long-range course of development in a scientific way; it will change from an instrument for the assertion of subjectively defined material proportions into a programme of economic policy, assuring effective development of the economy and growth in the standard of living.[176]

In an important respect, however, party thinking on economic reform, by the time of the March–April plenum, had advanced beyond the Hungarian official reform concept, in openly recognising the political aspects of the reform process. This was a direct product of the self-critical atmosphere following the leadership crisis, which opened the way to consideration of how the old style of politics had obstructed reform, and correspondingly, to an appreciation of the need for institutional reform as an essential prerequisite of effective functioning of the reformed planning system. The Party's daily paper *Rudé Právo* contained an important editorial statement on the economy in early March, which pointed explicitly to the impact of 'outdated political methods' on the process of reform:

> Many progressive economic measures, which gave rise to justified expectations, in those circumstances ran up against a barrier in the political sphere; the result was a feeling of a kind of impotence, vain endeavours, and ultimately, the stifling of initiative.[177]

The first condition of progress out of this situation was that the Party muster the determination to get to grips with the past, acknowledge its past mistakes and remove those responsible, the editorial noted. But this was not enough. Further reform meant not only coherent central policy measures to prepare the ground for further development of reform, it also meant looking at the roots of political resistance to reform in the organisational system: the central authorities and the branch directorates, which had remained wedded to the old concepts. This aspect of reform, the editorial pointed out, had hitherto been overlooked. The socialist enterprise must no longer be regarded as part of the state apparatus. It had to stand on its own feet, have full responsibility and bear in full the costs of risk. Supra-enterprise organisations had, therefore, to shed the administrative powers they had preserved. They should be formed, the paper advocated, on economic grounds alone, on the basis of voluntary association by their constituent enterprises. That this was not merely the line of the paper's editorial board, but reflected the new leadership's own thinking, was demonstrated at the plenum in Dubček's speech and in the Action Programme. Dubček identified institutional reform as the 'main condition for the consistent and rapid implementation of the new system of management'. This included not only providing the conditions for real enterprise autonomy, but also the introduction of 'measures designed to democratise economic management' – to create democratic bodies within the enterprise to which the management would be responsible, and to permit a more assertive role for trade unions in defending employee interests.[178] As the Action Programme explained, this was a component part of the general political process of democratisation, and a logical corollary of enterprise autonomy:

> The Party ... considers it necessary that the whole working collective which bears the consequences should also be able to influence the management of the enterprise. The need has arisen for democratic bodies in enterprises with specified rights in relation to the management of the enterprise. Managers and leading workers of the enterprises would be accountable for the overall results of their work to these bodies, which would also appoint them to their posts.[178]

These new elements in official thinking were in turn reflected in the programme of the new government, which Černík presented to the National Assembly on 24 April. Černík's report corrected the rather bland and rosy presentation he had made in January, as chairman of the State Planning Commission. 'It was clear to everybody', he now admitted, 'that despite the successes we can exhibit, the state of our economy does not correspond to the situation of an industrially advanced country more than twenty years after the war.'[180] Despite the revival of 1966–7, 'it may by no means be regarded as a turning-point'. The basic problem was to effect change in the industrial structure 'which at present is to a large extent incapable of effectively ensuring our needs in foreign trade or of satisfying our domestic market requirements'. The result had been a growing balance-of-payments problem and inefficient foreign trade; general disequilibrium in supply-and-demand throughout the economy; technological obsolescence; and the inability to satisfy the population's aspirations for a rising standard of living. This was not merely a product of a faulty economic policy, but was rooted in the system itself:

> These shortcomings were long fostered and even aggravated by the directive system of management, in that it made production for production's sake possible, divorced production from the market, operated with artificial prices, encouraged extensive development at the expense of quality, failed to insist on standards of expertise, and gave no leeway to initiative. This is why the introduction of an economic system of management is exceptionally important.[181]

The ability to break with the past depended therefore not only on policy changes, but organisational reform:

> We approached the new system of management with the old structure of a central management apparatus which was created and set up as an apparatus of directive management of the national economy and was only partially amended. There was no consistent final solution to relations between enterprise and central organs, and there remained strong elements of a superior to inferior sort of relationship. Even the changes in the organisational pattern of enterprises implemented in 1965 brought no change, because they manifested trends of their own directive administration methods of management.[182]

The introduction of the two closely-related political–organisational elements – the achievement of enterprise autonomy and the establishment of forms of workers' participation in management – into the official reform programme was a product of the unique political conditions of 1968. On the one hand, the government and Party leadership were influenced by the critical analyses of economists now appearing in the virtually uncensored press. The new leadership was overtly committed to taking greater heed of the advice of experts than the previous, discredited regime had done, and the lack of censorship allowed the full force of the economists' arguments against the administrative apparatus to make itself felt. On the other hand, both intellectual reformists and the new leadership were becoming increasingly concerned about the possibility that working-class disaffection, or at best, lack of involvement in the reform process might be mobilised by conservatives, who still held positions of some authority, against reform and against the new leadership. Workers' councils were thus not merely a natural, logical solution to the problem of managerial responsibility once enterprises became autonomous – they were also offered as a political inducement to win over working-class support.

Insofar as the major obstacles to reform before 1968 had been the lack of conviction of the Novotný leadership itself, the January plenum could be seen, as B. Šimon, head of the Party Central Committee Department of Economics, described it, as providing the definitive precondition for economic, as well as political revival. The way was now open to 'fully consummate the rationality of economic policy'.[183] What is significant, however, is that despite the overt commitment of the government and Party leadership to consistent reform, in the course of 1968 we see a continuation of the all-too-familiar paralysis in the economic field, when it came to practical action. Why?

In the first place, of course, the task of moving forward had become much more complex, as a result of the hesitancy and inconsistency of the previous approach to reform, as Karel Kouba pointed out:

> In my opinion, the main reason [for lack of change in the performance of the economy] after years of deepening difficulties is the fact that the decision-making centre in this country for a long time avoided and delayed even those decisions which were quite clear-cut and well-worked out, and might have been carried out. The problems have greatly accumulated, and many have now become so entangled that today it is much more difficult to unravel them than it was three or five years ago.[184]

The legacy of the protracted period of 'transition'[185] to the reformed system was, in particular, the deepening disequilibrium and related inflationary pressures inherited from 1967, and continuing to develop apace in 1968. In the first quarter, enterprise incomes rose by 25 per cent and personal incomes by 10.4 per cent; industrial output and productivity lagged behind, rising by 6.2 per cent and 5.3 per cent respectively, and, in April and May, showed a trend towards deceleration.[186] The major underlying source of disequilibrium was the general structure of the economy, which, it was widely recognised, could not be changed overnight. The notion hitherto widespread among the more conservative elements of the apparatus was that the economic reform could not be introduced until fundamental change in the economic structure had taken place, otherwise massive disruption and intense political conflict would result. This approach effectively meant indefinite postponement of the reform. Furthermore, conservatives were able to argue that the democratising trends which had rapidly emerged in the early months of the year were contributing to deepening the inflationary pressures – in the open political atmosphere, with the revival of interest-group activity, demands for wage rises had exploded.[187] A case could convincingly be made for a clampdown by the centre both in the economic and the political fields. If the reform movement was to survive, economists had to find an answer to these problems consistent with their general aims. This task was by no means simple. In fact, some commentators blamed the lack of action on the part of the government and the absence of a coherent strategy on the economists themselves, who were said to be failing to get to grips with the detailed, nuts-and-bolts issues of the day, continuing to dwell on the refinement of abstract models, and unable to reach agreement among themselves on a programme of action.[188]

But economists rose to the challenge, and went on the attack against 'inflationary fatalism', which was paralysing reform.[189] There was a tendency, on the one hand, as Šik argued, to exaggerate the inflationary danger, particularly in wages and in retail trade.[190] It was widely agreed that the situation must not be tackled, as in the previous year, by means of central fixing of wage ceilings, which had undermined the basic logic of reform,[191] nor by means of a price freeze. The problem was, at root, political. As a group of economists put it, 'we have only introduced those measures of the new system which did not harm anyone, but none of those measures which could have affected anybody'.[192] To put the situation right now, painful measures were inevitably called for: carrying out the price reform, to link domestic prices with the world market, and allowing some retail prices to rise; ending subsidies and, where necessary, closing down inefficient enterprises. Thus, while removing the structural roots of disequilibrium would be a long-term job, an immediate start could be made by creating a truly demanding economic environment for producers.[193] The precondition for this approach, which was, as Kouba put it, akin to 'curing the patient by shock treatment', was the formation of a 'programmatically strong centre'.[194] In contrast to the more conservative views, advocating the restoration of traditional forms of central intervention, this concept of a 'strong centre', which was widely recognised as essential to the reform,[195] involved both a plea for conceptual clarity on the part of the government, and the enhancement of its authority in new terms – not, as before, on the basis of 'subjective will', but through broad, democratic consultation with society.

In fact, as Tůrek argued, a major problem in the past had been the *weakness* of the centre, in its lack of objective information, and dependence on bureaucratic sectoral interests:

> The real strength of the centre is enhanced by its command of objective facts. Pressure does not emanate as the subjective whim of the central organs, but on the contrary as the elimination of the hitherto subjective protection of inefficiency; the replacement of state protection by the influence of realistic objective facts.[196]

The reformulation of the proper role of the central authorities led on to a comprehensive attack on 'bureaucratism' as the source of 'subjectivism' and incoherence in economic decision-making:

> The bureaucratic administration has a tendency to act by itself in laying down the scale of preferences and objectives and thus weakens democratic control over them. The set of objectives of the economic policy is then determined as the outcome of the confrontation of bureaucratic administration and monopoly groups, and does not result from a democratic confrontation of the interests of individual groups of the population ... The bureaucratic administration assigns tasks according to the objectives which it has set itself, controls the fulfilling of these tasks and imposes sanctions for non-fulfilment. It has a tendency to control everything and to remain uncontrolled.[197]

The first moves of the Černík government towards reformation of the central economic bodies, however, were inadequate and inconsistent. The new Economic Council which was set up was presumably aimed at improving coordination and devising a coherent long-term strategy. It was described as purely advisory, but in practice it dealt, in its weekly meetings, with urgent major questions facing the government. It was, *de facto*, an inner economic cabinet.[198] At the same time, the status of the Planning Commission was downgraded to the equivalent of a ministry, rather than a supreme, all-embracing body as before. However, no reduction in the number of industrial branch ministries took place – thus the vast administrative apparatus remained basically intact.

In practice, what appeared to result from the central reorganisation was a diffusion, rather than a consolidation of central economic decision-making.[199] In late May, *Literární listy's* pseudonymous commentator, 'Dalimil', warned that 'time is triumphing over our government'.[200] The Černík government had now been in power for several weeks, yet there was still no sign of a clear central programme or concept. The Economic Council seemed preoccupied with preparatory organisational matters, setting up its numerous consultative commissions to consider future measures. The 'first real economic decision' of the government was still awaited. This, in Dalimil's view, had to be the presentation of a new statute on the position of the enterprise, which must occur within 'the near future'.

The achievement of enterprise autonomy was the linchpin of the reformist strategy for dealing with both the immediate problems of disequilibrium and inflation, and the long-term evolution of consistent reform.[201] As Šik explained:

> it would be completely unrealistic to deal with these questions [inflation, etc.] by reinforcing central bureaucratic management. I am convinced that many of these difficulties can be, on the contrary, solved by giving greater freedom but also greater responsibility to the collective organs of plants.[202]

In other words, if enterprises were truly independent and financially responsible, they would be forced to limit their wage payments and investment demands to what they themselves could actually afford. Centralisation merely served to sustain inflation by maintaining the possibility of lobbying for budgetary subsidies and allocations, irrespective of economic rationality or the economic resources of the State. In turn, forcing enterprises to cover their own costs from sales would mitigate the short-term supply-and-demand disequilibrium by giving them an intense interest in producing only those goods which were in demand. The proposal of a group of economists for further development of the reform put it thus: enterprises had to be thrown into the water to force them to learn to swim, but their hands had to be untied so that they could swim, they had to be relieved of stones which might weigh them down, and, to some, life-belts should be offered for a temporary period only to help them to learn to swim.[203]

In late April, the government issued a statement on the broad principles according to which enterprises might withdraw from existing associations and new, voluntary and fully economically justified associations might be formed.[204] But a full definition of the legal rights and responsibilities of enterprises would have to await the passing of a new Enterprise Statute, on which work was underway already in the spring of 1968, but which was not in fact brought before the National Assembly until a year later – after the Soviet-led invasion.[205] The delay in introducing this measure, so vital to the whole reformist government's success, was explained by the persistence of strongly entrenched conservative forces which continued to exert a grip on central decision-making, delaying and diverting the stated intentions of the government, and obstructing the formation of a coherent reformist programme. As Šik noted:

> There can be no doubt that at present there continue to exist hidden left-wing sectarian forces which still believe in the return of the old bureaucratic centralistic socialist system. They view the present-day democratisation effort as a transitory affair, which it is necessary to live out quietly, hiding behind an inconspicuous exaggeration of the so-called anti-socialist danger and the anti-democratic character of the present political course.[206]

Dalimil argued that the central authorities – the government, the Planning Commission, the Ministry of Finance and the State Bank – were all effectively powerless against the 'real Goliaths' of the economy, the monpolistic branch production associations and the ministries, which were still acting as representatives of branch interests at the centre, rather than as agents of central policy.[207] The problem was that this apparatus, comprised of 'tens of thousands of workers whose vital interests are linked to the centralistic method of management in operation up to now',[208] had survived the January upheaval unscathed. Now, in the summer, they had become more active, latching onto the wave of democratisation itself: other groups were all making demands, so why should not they too? The lack of change – the continuing subsidies and the still only half-complete price reform – acted as a shield behind which they were able to reassert themselves. Dalimil quoted as an example the Minister of Heavy Industry, J. Krejčí, 'the real "strong man" of our economy', who had recently been able to argue, on the basis of existing prices, that heavy industry was the most 'profitable' branch and a successful exporter. It was time, Dalimil concluded, to draw back the 'veil of demagogy', which the economic apparatus was beginning to use more and more in its own self-defence:

> Ministries try to show that they are simply indispensable, that they still have to lead enterprises by the hand, that enterprises are not capable of acting as rational economic subjects, or that such action on their part would be socially harmful ... [The ministries] are trying very solicitously to 'defend' and 'protect' their enterprises, even if, in so doing they are protecting themselves. This shows up too in the fact that ministries today are outstripping each other in emphasising the long-term neglect of their branches[209]

The institutionally entrenched conservatism of the economic *aparát* was, however, only part of the explanation of the hesitancy of the government in taking rapid and decisive action in the economic field. An equally powerful force was the passivity and scepticism of the workers. The leadership was profoundly wary of deepening the political problems it already faced in containing the intellectuals' demands by provoking active working-class protest in response to unpopular economic measures.[210] But the workers could not be kept out of politics – the conservatives began to appeal to this massive latent force soon after January. In February, Novotný, while still President of the Republic, went on tour in the provinces, and met a generally sympathetic reception in the factories. He was reported as drawing a round of applause in one Prague factory when he declared, 'If to be a conservative means to oppose the lowering of the workers' standard of living, I am proud to be a conservative.'[211] Other leading conservative officials, notably the editor-in-chief of *Rudé právo*, Oldřich Švestka, began to step forward as spokesmen of the workers' interests, raising fears for the impact of the reformers' economic plans on workers' security and standard of living.[212] And indeed, when intellectuals went self-consciously into the factories to sound out working-class opinion, they met a mixed reception, and discovered widespread confusion and misgivings about the whole reform process. As one worker asked a group of representatives from *Literární listy*, even if democracy were established, what guarantee was there that things would be better than under the existing system?[213] This security of the present system, even if it was flawed, was seen as preferable to the unknown.[214] Although public opinion polls discovered that the population placed as much emphasis on the solution of economic problems as on political reform, the focus was overwhelmingly on the standard of living, which the proposed economic changes could not guarantee to protect.[215] Most people in Czechoslovakia, one *Literární listy* contributor observed, were in fact committed to 'socialism', but this meant for them security, equality, and an easy time at work.[216] The realisation of these values in the actual operation of the socialist system had been achieved at the expense of incentives to work well and to the detriment of economic efficiency. Any attempt to introduce economic reform would thus challenge the majority's conception of 'socialism': 'I fear that the resistance of this majority and not so much the resistance of the bureaucracy, will be the main obstacle to the transformation which is essential and must be accomplished.'[217]

Moreover, grass-roots activists were found to be responding to the changes taking place at the top of the political hierarchy with disillusionment and bitterness, as Ludvík Vaculík found. He quoted two typical responses from such workers:

> Today it seems as if everything we have done has been of no use! As if I ought to be ashamed in front of my own children of what I have brought them into!
>
> The intellectuals are swines because it was they who contributed towards the losses. The so-called 'new economic system' is a swindle, which is based on the assumption that the same people will stay on top, because after all, dogs don't eat dogs.[218]

The division between the intellectuals and the workers was recognised by the reformers as a major political weakness, successfully fostered and manipulated ever since 1956 by the old leadership:

> the average, uninformed worker sees the bad state of affairs in this country as the fault of the intellectual, whereas the intellectual knows that this bad state of affairs was in fact organised by professional revolutionaries in the name of the workers.[219]

The philosopher, Karel Kosík, diagnosed the problem as a form of what he termed 'corporatism' in political life.[220] Society had been organised in manipulated 'masses' rather than as independent citizens.[221] The rigid, bureaucratic two-classes-and-one-stratum scheme had tied workers to factories, peasants to villages, and intellectuals to libraries. These groups had been kept isolated from each other, could see only their own group interests, with the result that the bureaucracy had been left in the position of the 'sole bearer of the universal interest, thus the exclusive mediator of the mutual exchange of information'. The most devastating effects of this had been felt by the working class, which had been depoliticised and deprived of a political vocabulary and public voice, since its 'leading role' had been usurped by the bureaucracy.[222]

In one of his earliest public speeches as First Secretary, Dubček appealed for an end to the divide-and-rule approach:

> Nothing could be more detrimental to the healthy development of Czechoslovak society than to set the interests of one class against another. The interests of the working class today can only be defended in the development of the whole of society, in the integration of all classes and interests into society.[223]

The Action Programme correspondingly called for incorporation of the whole of society into politics through political reform:

> Socialism can only flourish if scope is given for the assertion of the various interests of the people, and on this basis the unity of all workers will be brought about democratically. This is the main source of free social activity and the development of the socialist system ... Therefore the Party will strive to activise the social life of the workers, to provide scope for making use of their political and social rights through political organisations and trade unions, and to strengthen the democratic influence of workers' collectives over the management of production.[224]

The first condition of healing the breach between intellectuals and workers was seen by reformist intellectuals in the free provision of information.[225] For too long, popularity had been courted by the leadership by painting economic achievements in a rosy hue.[226] This dishonesty had led to a corrosion of trust. Šik, in particular, took upon himself the task of exposing the 'truth' in economic life in the workers' newspaper, *Práce*,[227] and, with considerable impact, in a series of television programmes broadcast in the summer.[228] He detailed more fully than ever before for public consumption the state of affairs in the economy, drawing unfavourable comparisons with economic development in the European capitalist countries, thus forcefully presenting the case for systemic reform.

In the meanwhile, workers were beginning to shake off their lethargy, but their activism found expression mainly, at first, in demands for higher wages, of the order of 10–20 per cent.[229] Many of the demands, moreover, were aimed at restoring pay relativities and reversing the de-levelling which had occurred in the past year.[230] Managers, who were under personal political threat as a result of their identification with the old political order, felt in a weak position to resist such demands, and were anxious to curry favour with their employees. The explosion of wage demands gave ammunition to conservatives, who pounced on this trend as a sign of the dangerous 'anarchy' engendered by 'democratisation'.[231] Mlynář saw the wage demands as a threat to the reform process:

> If all demands are put forward at once in an elemental fashion – including those that are justified – the working class will itself disrupt the order of things in its socialist state and play into the hands of those who do not have socialism at heart.[232]

It was argued by reformist economists that in fact, the anxieties about wage-led inflation were to a considerable extent exaggerated, and were being used to deflect attention from the real source of inflationary pressures – the excessive incomes of enterprises resulting from continuing protection of them from economic pressures.[233] Šik repeated that there was no need for a reduction in the standard of living.[234] In fact, the economy had adequate reserves to cope with consumer demand. In 1967, a trade surplus had built up with socialist countries. As a result, it was possible to divert some export items to the domestic market, and increased imports of consumer goods were made. A substantial decline in stocks of consumer goods held by producing enterprises also took place, releasing more goods onto the domestic market.[235]

Nevertheless, the trend towards wage and personal income rises well ahead of the rates of growth of national income and productivity could not be allowed to become established, as the government and reformist economists were aware. But if they resorted to mere exhortation to self-restraint on the part of the workers, this would restrict workers' participation and confirm their scepticism about the whole purpose of the reforms as an attack on their interests. Something more had to be offered – hence the espousal of institutionalised forms of direct workers participation in management.

The place of worker participation in the politics of 1968 has already received extensive coverage in academic studies of the period;[236] the main conclusions of these studies need only be summarised here. The idea of enhanced worker participation as a necessary component of the economic reform predated 1968;[237] the questions had been raised by reformist intellectuals such as Ivan Bystřina, Michal Lakatoš and Drahomír Slejška at least as early as 1966.[238] Support for the idea was not absent either from the deliberations of official bodies prior to

1968. The State Committee for Management and Organisation had adopted the idea in a report drawn up prior to 1968, but only published in April of that year.[239] It was thus widely recognised by reformist experts both inside and outside the political apparatus that the 'one-man-management' concept of authority within the enterprise was no longer appropriate in conditions of full enterprise autonomy, where all employees would bear the costs, as well as the benefits, of economic responsibility. In 1968, the Action Programme, as noted above, finally signalled overt official Party recognition of the need for some more meaningful form of worker participation as a natural corollary of enterprise independence.

In the course of 1968, the general consensus within the reformist camp on this issue (as on many others) began to break up, in the face of the challenge of immediate introduction of practial measures. On the one hand, leading reformist economists, such as Šik, moved from their former preoccupation with enterprise autonomy and managerial authority *vis-à-vis* the administrative apparatus towards a greater concern with securing active working-class support. As a result, the concept of the 'democratic enterprise organ' broadened, in terms of the scope allowed for genuine employee influence on management. A crucial turning-point was Šik's lecture to the Czechoslovak Economics Society in May, in which he proposed that 'workers' councils' of ten to thirty members (depending on the size of the enterprise) should be set up, with workers' representatives enjoying the 'predominant' weight.[240] This was a change from his previous position, and was even seen as something of a *volte-face*: hitherto, he had appeared committed to a rather technocratic concept of a body comprising specialists from the management and from outside.[241] However, Šik's new conception of 'workers' councils' formed the basis of the government's 'Framework Principles for the Establishment of Working Peoples' Councils'.[242] The term 'working peoples' councils' signified a kind of compromise position, between the original managerialist 'enterprise councils' and the more radical school of thought emerging in 1968 which advocated a form of self-management, akin in principle to the Yugoslav model.[243] In the official government view, and in that of many committed reform economists, there persisted an underlying concern with economic rationality, and a scepticism as to the ability of workers to participate effectively in management. There was indeed room for doubts on this score, deriving not only from the practical experience of the Yugoslav model, but also from the fact that genuine enterprise autonomy had yet to be achieved. In such circumstances, workers' councils might easily become yet more powerful – because democratically legitimated – participants in the old system of bargaining for protection; and on the other, might easily be blamed for continuing economic failure, thus forfeiting the rank-and-file workers' interest in them.[244] The second school of thought originated among radical intellectuals, mainly with non-economic backgrounds, who asserted the merits of a self-management model on intrinsic, political grounds, in some cases regardless of economic considerations. A leading representative of this school was the historian, Karel Bartošek, who, in an 'Open letter to the Workers of Czechoslovakia', argued the case that 'without democracy in the enterprises, it is not possible to talk about democracy in society'.[245]

What is important from the point of view of this chapter's argument is not so much the ideas of the leadership and reformist intellectuals as the attitude of the working class. The inescapable conclusion of the studies published on this subject points to the low level of interest of the workers. There were indeed some notable developments, such as the spontaneous establishment in June 1968 of enterprise councils in ČKD Praha and Škoda Plzeň – both large enterprises of great political significance. The constitutions of these councils accorded them a much greater say in managerial decision-making than envisaged by the emergent official line.[246] The formation of these councils, on the initiative from lower-level activists, was largely responsible for prodding the government into issuing its 'Framework Principles'. However, popular opinion in 1968 did not exhibit a massive groundswell of enthusiasm for the establishment of councils throughout the economy. A poll conducted in July found that 53 per cent of respondents thought that workers' councils would be beneficial to the operation of large enterprises; but 10 per cent thought the opposite, and 33 per cent were undecided.[247] The *ad hoc* reportage of workers' opinions by *Literární listy* journalists found instead a rather deferential attitude. Some workers appeared to feel that they could not be expected to take decisions at managerial level, protesting their lack of education.[248] Enterprise Party activists reported to *Život strany* that despite a sustained popular interest in political and economic issues, there was a reluctance among the rank-and-file to participate actively, by taking on formal positions: 'After a tempestuous wave of criticism and a definite increase in the activity of the people, a clear falling-off has occurred, and many have become passive once more.'[249] As one activist admitted, 'we have fallen out of practice in drawing our own conclusions for ourselves, and making the appropriate connections between various things'.[250] The lack of a coherent central government policy did not help to clarify the situation.[251] Workers sensed the real problem in a lack of effective leadership, rather more than in their own lack of opportunity to participate. Ludvík Vaculík summed up the attitude of the workers he had encountered: 'If only the people up there would shut themselves up somewhere, come to an agreement, and tell us in a straightforward way what will be happening from tomorrow onwards, and not subject the people to all these bad jokes!'[252]

As a result of the fairly low level of interest, the actual establishment of the councils throughout the country proceeded rather slowly. People were simply not taking up the opportunity to participate in this field, as the Central Committee resolution in June noted.[253] By August, it was reported that only eighty preparatory committees for setting up councils existed.[254] It was only after the invasion that popular interest in them surged forward. They then came to be seen as a means of preserving national autonomy. By June 1969, 300 councils had been formally established, and 300 preparatory committees were in existence.[255] Even after the invasion, however, public opinion polls continued to register a significant level of apathy. Only 11 per cent of respondents in a poll conducted in March 1969 described themselves as 'well-informed', while 40 per cent were 'relatively well-informed', and 35 per cent admitted to being badly informed, and 14 per cent did not know.[256] The proportion of those who were optimistic about the effect of the councils on economic performance rose from 53 per cent in July 1968 to 59 per cent in March 1969, and opponents of workers councils fell from 10 per cent to 3 per cent. The proportion of 'don't knows', however, rose from 33 per cent to 35 per cent.[257]

In the aftermath of the invasion, the fate of the economic reform was for some time unclear. At first, the Dubček leadership was under the impression that it would be possible to continue with major elements of the reform programme as a whole, once the political situation had stabilised to the satisfaction of the Soviet leadership. But there were to emerge serious differences between the two leaderships over what constituted a satisfactorily stabilised political situation.[258] To Mlynář, the Soviet insistence at the Moscow talks immediately following the August invasion on the replacement of key reformist personalities, among them Ota Šik, signalled 'a political condemnation of the entire reform politics'.[259] Nevertheless, federalisation of the state structure, a major part of the reform programme, went ahead.[260] In fact, after August 1968, the evolution of the economic aspects of reform also proceeded at an accelerated pace, as workers turned to enterprise councils as a means of registering their objection to the external intervention and their support for reform. This occurred despite the government's instructions of 24 October that the 'experiment' in enterprise councils should not be further extended for the time being, and despite Dubček's warning at the November Central Committee plenum:

> Justified criticism of bureaucratism must not lead to simplistic and distorted attacks on the state and economic apparatus. The legitimate demand for increased worker participation in management should not take the form of a spurious democracy in production which is detrimental to the unavoidable discipline of labour.[261]

The federalisation reform in some respects furthered the cause of democratisation in the economy, since it gave the trade unions the opportunity to rewrite their statutes along federal lines, and at the same time to introduce new clauses providing for greater control by the membership over the trade unions apparatus. Preliminary congresses of the new federal organisations of the trade unions allowed personnel changes more in line with the membership's wishes.[262]

An important post-invasion development from the economic point of view was the voluntary regrouping of enterprises into new associations, which began in December. Eighteen engineering enterprises led the way, forming themselves into an 'industrial entrepreneurial group' including a foreign trade organisation. It was headed by a Board of Administrators composed of representatives of the associated enterprises.[263] These moves took place in advance of the publication of the Enterprise Statute and without the formal approval of the government. With the introduction of the new federal constitution on 1 January 1969, the cause of reform was again furthered by the simultaneous abolition of a number of industrial branch ministries (Mining, Power, Heavy Industry, Chemicals and Consumer Goods).[264] The Federal Planning Ministry continued work on a new law on planning, right through to mid-1969, which, it was later alleged, 'in reality took the form of a law abolishing unified planning, severing enterprise planning from state planning and giving the state national economic plan the character of non-binding information.[265]

It was precisely the 'spontaneous' aspect of the post-invasion developments in these fields which seems to have been most objectionable to the Soviet leadership and to their hard-line supporters inside Czechoslovakia. No doubt this contributed to their general conclusion, by April 1969, that the Dubček team could not be relied upon to 'normalise' the situation. After the installation of Husák as Party First Secretary at the April Central Committee plenum, the fate of the economic reform began to become clear stage by stage. Further discussion of the Enterprise Statute was suspended by the newly constituted Czech National Council on 29 April, and thereafter the Statute sank without trace. In May, the concept of self-managing workers' councils was formally repudiated, and in June, the federal government revoked the guidelines it had issued in 1968 for the formation of enterprise councils.[266] In June and July, it became clear that enterprise autonomy and the non-directive character of the state plan would no longer be tolerated. Executive organs of the industrial associations were required to enter into binding agreements with the government on deliveries of specified goods for export and for the domestic market. The plan targets for 1970 which emerged in July were to have an obligatory character.[267] Further measures in the second half of 1969 included the reimposition of central wage controls and a price freeze from the beginning of 1970.

To a certain extent, these measures were *ad hoc* and appeared in a piecemeal fashion. At first, they were justified in terms of an immediate response to economic chaos and inflationary pressures. In the economic field, hard-line criticism focused on personalities, such as Šik, rather than on the actual provisions of the reform model *per se*.[268] But the implications of the measures introduced added up to a clear reversal of reform, and by the end of 1969, more elaborate general justifications had begun to appear, with strongly political overtones. It was not just a question of halting inflationary pressures, but a 'definitive break with that course which profoundly damaged the interests of our people and the interests of socialism', as a document produced by the Central Committee's Economic Department explained in November 1969.[269] Economic reform had been blown off course by the activities of 'right-wing revisionists'. At the January 1970 Central Committee plenum, Husák described their aims as bringing about 'complete anarchy' through the introduction of the free market, and accused them of attempting 'to separate and create two independent spheres – the enterprise sphere and the central sphere – thus basically violating the principles of democratic centralism in national economic management.[270]

At the official XIV CPSC Congress in May 1971 (the 'Extraordinary' XIV Congress convened in a Prague factory immediately after the invasion having been disowned), Lubomír Štrougal, who took over from Černík as Prime Minister, spelled out the official position:

> In economic theory and practice the reformers were gradually preparing and implementing a transformation of the socialist economy into a system which was meant to deprive the working class and all the working people of the revolutionary attainments and of their fundamental political and economic security. The bloc of right-wing opportunist and anti-socialist forces expected the step-by-step worsening of the economic situation to create spontaneous discontent among the working people which it would then take advantage of to fight socialist power. As the most manifest expression of such endeavour, our economy ceased being controlled through a national plan. The enforcement of a market economic model gravely disrupted the proportions of the creation and distribution of resources as envisaged by the fourth five-year plan. In this way our economy found itself in a state of crisis.[271]

In the concluding chapter of his work on the events in Czechoslovakia in 1968, Skilling justifies his interpretation of their significance as an 'interrupted revolution', as opposed to the more moderate term employed by Kusin and Golan, 'reform movement'. Skilling argues that the peaceful, gradualistic and constitutional approach which was the major characteristic of the process of change was nevertheless tending towards a qualitative, fundamental break with the old order:

> Although the future was to some degree open, what seemed most likely was a continuing sequence of individual reforms, each drastic in its own sphere and reinforcing one another, the cumulative effect of which would have been a metamorphosis of the entire system. This would have been a kind of 'uninterrupted' or 'permanent' revolution ... in the sense of successive stages of radical change, each one leading on to the next over a period of years, or even decades. The ultimate result would probably have been a transformation, in Marxist terms, of both base and superstructure[272]

Speculation about the future, the writing of 'counterfactual' history, has widely recognised dangers; the justification of the exercise is analytical, as a means of formulating explanatory hypotheses about the past and present. The implication of Skilling's extrapolation of an alternative Czechoslovak future is that, although powerful internal obstacles to change existed, the Extraordinary XIV CPSC Congress would have consolidated a leadership with the power to surmount them. Had Dubček himself proved unwilling to take on the task, he would probably have been removed.[273] The main barrier to change was therefore the external intervention in August:

> The Czechoslovak program struck at the heart of the Soviet conception of socialism and offered an alternative model not only distasteful in itself but likely to infect other communist states and parties with heretical ideas, thus threatening the Soviet position in Eastern Europe and in the world communist movement, and in the long term raising the spectre of a challenge to the Soviet system at home.[274]

As an extrapolation of the logic of the reformists' programmes in 1968, Skilling's interpretation is undeniably powerful. However, the existence of a revolutionary programme itself is not enough to indicate the actual existence of a revolutionary situation.

An alternative future for the reform movement without the external constraint of foreign invasion may be put forward speculatively. There were certainly profound challenges to the legitimacy of the entire system, posed in particular in the uncensored media by radical intellectuals. But in many respects the basic system of a one-party state based on socialist ownership remained unchallenged. A large part of the reformist intelligentsia wanted change *within* this framework, and sincerely believed it was possible; and the workers certainly favoured retention of the benefits of a planned economy in terms of job security, continued price subsidies and general protection of their standard of living. While there was undoubtedly a great upsurge in spontaneous political activism in 1968, mass social mobilisation – an essential ingredient of a revolutionary situation – was largely absent until the Soviet-led invasion provoked it. The revolutionary element was a minority – the radical intelligentsia with a revolutionary programme. While workers were certainly dissatisfied with their lot, the socialist regime enjoyed a reserve of legitimacy deriving from the original mass approbation of communist power at its inception, and fostered thereafter through the protective mechanisms of the centralist economy.[275]

There were therefore also deep-rooted internal constraints on the future pace and direction of change, which entrenched conservative forces in the bureaucratic apparatus could exploit. The vigorous attacks of reform economists on the vested interests of this apparatus were effectively deflected in 1968 by the immediate situation of political instability and the Party and government's overwhelming concern with short-term measures. The introduction of economic reform in this context, as conservatives could persuasively argue, would only exacerbate this instability by threatening to provoke working-class reaction. Even had the invasion not taken place, the power of the economic apparatus in both influencing economic decisions and implementing them in practice would have remained a major obstacle to the revolutionary change Skilling sees as unfolding.

Political reforms in central institutions such as National Assembly and National Front, in the 'leading role of the Party', and in the proposed forms of 'enterprise democracy', were seen by both the political leadership and reformist intellectuals as a means of winning over working-class support and providing the authoritative leadership which could tackle the vested interests of the economic *aparát* and thus open the way for consistent economic reform. But it is not clear that the workers would in fact have seen such political reforms as adequate compensation for the anticipated negative effects on them of the economic reform. Evidence already presented in this book gives grounds for doubt. Increased 'democratism' in political institutions might even have exacerbated political instability and produced paralysis in the political leadership, by 'overloading' the government with a flood of organised and openly expressed competing demands arising from the redistribution of resources which reform would entail.[276] In this situation, the economic *aparát* could present itself as a coherent defendent of 'all-social interests', and as a key source of stability. It could thus be argued that implementation of the economic reform required not so much more democracy, as a more sophisticated and adaptable form of dictatorship.

To return from this speculative excursus into counterfactual history to actual events in 1968, it is worth noting, as Skilling does, that the Soviet leadership itself was divided or uncertain in its assessment of the situation in Czechoslovakia, 'The central theme of Soviet propaganda and the main pretext for intervention was the potential danger of counter-revolution rather than its actual existence.'[277]

Leaving aside the abstract question of whether the full realisation of the economic reform would in fact have constituted a 'revolutionary' transformation as Skilling believes, it is significant in the actual context of the Czechoslovak crisis that the Soviet leadership did not appear directly concerned with this aspect of the changes. The 'Warsaw letter' of 15 July 1968 explicitly denied a desire to 'interfere with the methods of planning and administration of Czechoslovakia's national economy or with your actions aimed at perfecting the economic structure and developing socialist democracy'.[278] The wording suggests that even the dismantling of the economic *aparát* and the introduction of workers' councils would be tolerated. Although the Soviet press did publish articles both before and immediately after August 1968 which were hostile in principle to fundamental economic reform concepts,[279] the Moscow protocol drawn up and signed by the two Party leaderships after the invasion did not contain reference to economic reform as an immediate source of 'counter-revolutionary' danger, but focused particularly on the loss of party control of the mass media.[280] After all, the Soviet Prime Minister Kosygin was still associated with the introduction of economic reform in the Soviet Union; although this was abandoned after 1968, the Hungarian leadership was allowed to continue its own reform course.

The 'necessity' of the economic reform's reversal appears therefore to have had more to do with the Husák regime's short-term search for legitimacy than with the reform's actual contribution to the political crisis. By exaggerating the real extent of the economic reform, it could transfer the blame for the economic disruption actually caused by the Soviet invasion. It could also play on the fears of the workers, and promise them the security of the *status quo ante*. It could rely on the support of the single most stable political force throughout 1968, the state economic *aparát*. Some members of the leadership who continued in office through 1968 into the period of 'normalisation' may also have felt that denunciation of a distorted exaggeration of the real reform would leave scope for a continuation of its major 'healthy' elements.[281] But this compromise proved ultimately ineffective, since the terms adopted in the hard-line critiques were too fundamental politically and too narrowly circumscribed to allow more than the most modest organisational changes in the traditional centralistic–directive economic model which re-emerged in the 1970s.

In the mid-1980s, the Husák regime – still substantially the same as that installed in 1969 – faced once again the same economic problems as first provoked systematic re-examination of the centralist model: an outdated and inflexible economic structure, declining efficiency of investment, acute tensions in supplies of raw materials and labour and inefficient use of them, an increasingly alarming technological lag, and chronic problems in foreign trade, not least with the Soviet Union. The need for systemic reform crept somewhat shamefacedly back on to the public political agenda at the end of 1985, and was cryptically hinted at in the 1986 XVII CPSC Congress. Czechoslovakia has begun to look out of step in its conservatism and rigidity not only with its neighbour Hungary (with whom relations have never been close), but also with the Soviet Union under the leadership of Mikhail Gorbachev. But the regime is trapped by the extremism of its past political rhetoric. Any meaningful reform is still closely linked in the minds of the leadership with the political crisis of 1968, and any attempts to introduce it cannot fail to run up against the understanding of 'economic reform' which its propaganda has fostered in the mind of society as a whole.

7 The Political Limits to Economic Reform in Hungary 1968–78

Political change had been a precondition of the acceptance of a comprehensive programme of economic reform by the Kádár regime in Hungary. The nature of that political change was the consolidation of Kádár's personal authority in the early 1960s, and with it, the imposition of a more flexible, pragmatic general approach to policy and the incorporation of expert advice into policy formulation. Such political change provided an adequate environment within which careful, detailed preparation of the economic reform could go ahead prior to its implementation in 1968. The question to which we turn in the present chapter is whether this degree of political change would also be adequate for the successful implementation of the economic reform in practice.

The tenth anniversary of the introduction of the reform in 1978 passed off 'without major celebrations', as István Friss, the leading Party economic expert observed. The reason for this, in his view, was that 'the reform has long become everyday practice'.[1] Other economists however, were, less sanguine in their appraisals of the experience of the past decade. Iván Berend, the prominent economic historian, suggested that the 'absence of festive balance sheets' evaluating the achievements of the reform might be due rather more to the fact that 'some of the basic principles of the reform have not, or have only partially been realised'.[2] Another leading economist, László Antal, described the 1970s as a period of 'development – with some digression'.[3] In fact, many economists were of the opinion that the reform had veered off course. Tamás Bauer, among the more critical commentators, concluded that the system operating in Hungary was 'neither plan nor market'. Despite the crucial step which had been taken – the abolition of directive plan indicators and thus of the practice of 'breaking down the plan' to the enterprise level – the operation of the market had not been successfully established, and the criterion of profit had not become the central motivating force of enterprise behaviour.[4] As the sociologist Teréz Laky put it, 'instead of the desired enterprise independence, ever more questions are decided by central organs; and direct intervention into the functioning of the economy and of enterprises has become a general practice'.[5]

The essential point is that this occurred in spite of the continued overt commitment of the political leadership to the basic goal of reform. The government's assessment of the operation of the New Economic Mechanism (NEM) in its early years had been very positive. A major point had been demonstrated, as Lajos Fehér, a Deputy Prime Minister and Politburo member claimed in late 1969:

> Experience proves not only that successful management is possible throughout the entire national economy ... without plan instructions, but also that planned development can be guaranteed – in fact, more effectively guaranteed – by economic regulators.[6]

Indeed, plan fulfilment was more successful in 1968–70 than in previous years.[7] The standard of living, production and trade continued to rise, assortment improved, structural adjustments had begun to take place, sales had increased faster than production and stockpiles were cut. The foreign trade balance with both East and West had improved (and in 1969 had been positive for the first time for many years), and in 1969 for the first time the growth of agriculture exceeded that of industry. By the time of the X Congress of the Hungarian Socialist Workers' Party in November 1970, Kádár was able to confirm that the decision to reform had been correct.[8] It was acknowledged, however, that serious problems remained in the implementation of the reform – as expected, the economic regulators (the complex set of indirect financial, fiscal, price and other instruments which replaced directive plan targets as the means of steering enterprise activity) had required adjustment. Problems with labour productivity and investment efficiency had not proved amenable to immediate solution. But the reformers were able to argue that these problems only demonstrated the necessity of pushing on with the reform, rather than retreating. Friss claimed in a lecture in November 1971 that 'in economic debates, nobody in our country suggests any more that we should revert to the old system'.[9]

But in 1971 and after, pressures began to mount, if not for the abandonment of reform, at least for the introduction of measures to dilute it, which added up to a significant recentralisation. The central political leadership found itself, despite its commitment to reform, bowing to pressures emanating from below – from more or less organised interests at the middle and lower levels of the economic and political apparatus, and, in a more diffuse way, from society as a whole. 'Hidden mechanisms' were at work 'always driving towards centralisation, independently of the economic situation or of the intention of those in control'.[10]

To be sure, the impact of the drastic changes in the external environment as a result of the world economic crisis beginning in 1973 badly affected the original assumptions of the possibility of the relatively smooth transition to a regulated market system in close contact with the world economy. But the pressures for a halt, and partial reversal of key elements of the reform had begun to build up well before 1973, and to a significant extent, the government's responses to the world economic crisis were shaped rather more by already existing domestic pressures for recentralisation than by a detached, clear perception of a rational economic strategy to cope with the changed external environment. Many economists were convinced that the modifications in the reform programme introduced in the course of the 1970s left Hungary worse placed than before to achieve its economic goals both at home and abroad.[11]

The focus of this chapter is on the domestic pressures for recentralisation. The argument starts from the point that recentralisation must be seen as a product of internal politics, rather than of an externally imposed economic necessity. The Hungarian case raises fundamental questions of the impact of the political system on economic processes. For although the regime had adopted reform, and had shown itself to be capable of a pragmatic and adaptable political style, the political system itself remained ultimately unchanged. Central bureaucratic institutions remained in place, and with them, powerful vested interests retained an organisational base from which to reassert themselves in ways which undermined the actual functioning of the reform. The Party and government leadership were also acutely sensitive to wider social responses to reform and were concerned to avoid becoming cut off from society. But the channels for articulating social interests remained bureaucratised, despite some modifications to improve their functioning as transmitters of information from society up to the leadership. The political changes which took place under the Kádár regime permitted a notable diffusion, even a limited pluralisation of power, but they did not add up to a coherent 'political reform' to match the economic reform. The central political leadership accepted that differences of interest existed, and that these could not be overridden. But it failed to grasp the nettle of institutional reform, either in the political or economic systems, and thus left itself without an adequate, legitimate framework for reintegrating the conflicting interests which surfaced, and was thus inexorably forced back on traditional centralistic means of maintaining political order, which enhanced its dependence on the unreformed bureaucratic institutional structures. The paradoxical result of the limited decentralisation, or diffusion of central control, which occurred with the introduction of the economic reform, was the ineffectiveness of the central political leadership in countering the recentralising pressures emanating from below. To the extent that these pressures did not encounter an effective means of managing conflict, evaluating openly the conflicting demands and reintegrating them, the regime's authority and ability to pursue its chosen strategy of economic reform was undermined. The impact of the economic reform on the political system in turn was to threaten the political system with a loss of cohesion, the danger of 'political decay'[12] and general social and political 'drift' – a situation in which covertly operating powerful partial interests could operate unchecked in a manner that no sociopolitical system could tolerate.

The chapter is divided into three sections. In section A, we examine the political changes which were introduced, and explain our assessment of them as ultimately shallow and limited in significance. In section B, we turn to the operation of the economy under the NEM. The major point is to explain why the crucial element of reform – enterprise autonomy – failed to be realised in practice. In section C, we examine social responses to the reform, and show how these were selectively transmitted to the leadership in such a way as to further the striving for centralisation emanating from the unreformed institutional apparatus.

A POLITICAL CHANGE UNDER THE KÁDÁR REGIME

The Kádár regime was not oblivious to the political implications of the economic reform. Rezső Nyers, the Politburo member and Party Secretary in overall charge of the reform, had addressed himself to the question of interests in socialism in the major article of 1968 discussed in Chapter 5. But the lesson of 1956 was clear, and was only reinforced by the crisis unfolding in 1968 in neighbouring Czechoslovakia: if political change was necessary, it also necessarily had to be limited and contained. The task was the 'expansion of socialist democracy', not the elaboration of a new 'political model' institutionalising 'bourgeois' pluralistic democracy. Differing interests might indeed exist in socialism, but the central ideological tenet of an ultimate 'social interest' had to be sustained, and with it, the Party's role as its guardian.

The 'expansion of socialist democracy' in the Hungarian context went hand-in-hand with the Kádárist slogan: 'He who is not against us is with us'. It signalled a greater trust in the population, more confidence on the part of the regime that the people could usefully participate in a more active way in the great endeavour which was said to be in its own interest. The economic reform was, moreover, seen as necessitating a qualitatively different degree of participation. As a leading Party economist explained, 'The Party and the government are aware that the reform can only be realised and function well with the help of society as a whole.'[13] The Kádár regime had, from the early 1960s, already accumulated a certain experience of the stabilising function of participation, as a means of securing social control: by the cooption of and consultation with economic experts, and by rewarding them with material and status advantages, the regime had both benefited from the elaboration of more effective policies and secured compliance on the part of the intelligentsia. Now the question was to extend the cooptive and consultative exercise to society as a whole. Attention turned to the revitalisation of the pseudo-parliamentary institutions of the political system. It should, incidentally, be noted that Hungary was not exceptional in this, or out of line with discussions and developments in this field elsewhere in the Soviet bloc – including Novotný's Czechoslovakia.[14]

The problem was not seen in terms of constitutional reform which would enhance the formal powers of the parliamentary institutions, but in promoting more effective use of the powers they already enjoyed.[15] Parliament was criticised for relinquishing its constitutional rights by delegating too many of its functions or leaving matters to the Presidential Council. But these practices were an inevitable product of the extreme brevity and infrequency of Parliamentary sessions, and no change was made in this respect. A somewhat more noticeable change did take place, however, in the role of the Parliamentary specialist committees, of which there were nine. In some cases, these indeed did respond to the Party's demands that deputies become more assertive and debate and scrutinise legislation more effectively.[16] County groups of deputies were enjoined to coordinate their activities in Parliament to act more convincingly as transmitters of local and regional viewpoints on forthcoming legislation.

It was obvious (if not explicitly stated) that the major reason why the elective organs had failed to fulfil their role and had fallen into apathy went beyond the personal failings of the deputies and had systemic roots in the entire mechanism of 'representation' of the people. A serious attempt to improve the situation required at the very least modification of the electoral system, and, in fact, a series of reforms was made in this area.[17] In 1966, a new electoral law introduced single-member constituencies, aiming to strengthen the link between constituents and their deputy. At the same time, the new law included a provision for a multiplicity of candidates in elections. However, the Party-dominated Patriotic People's Front retained control over the nomination process, and had the right to determine the order in which candidates' names (should more than one be approved) appeared on the ballot paper. This was an important 'loophole', since the rule was that the voter should delete all names on the ballot paper except that of the preferred candidate. If no deletions were made, the voter was deemed to have voted for the first name on the list. At the same time, the informal practice of open voting persisted. Thus the essence of the old system was preserved, since the act of marking one's ballot was in itself an indication of disagreement with the order of preference of the Patriotic People's Front as printed on the ballot.

Amendments to the Electoral Law in 1970 went some way towards rectifying the situation. Candidates' names were now to appear in alphabetical order on the ballot, and voters were required to mark their preference. Unmarked ballots were invalid. A potentially significant further innovation was introduced into the nomination procedure. The PPF monopoly of the right to put forward nominations was abolished. The right to propose candidates was granted to 'groups of workers' and individuals from the floor of the nomination meeting, as well as to the PPF, the Party and the 'mass organisations'. To secure nomination, a proposed candidate had to achieve the support of at least one third of those present at the nomination meeting. (Participants could back more than one nomination.)

However, in practice, markedly few multiple candidacies emerged from this new process, which indicated not only the level of apathy and scepticism among the participants, but also the persisting, if less blatant, control of the whole procedure by the local Party and PPF organisations, which continued informally to manipulate the conduct of the nomination meetings with virtually complete success.[18] The professed aims of the Electoral Law reforms thus ran up against the basic reality of the political system, and were diverted according to its logic. There was, and remained, an irresoluble contradiction in the representative system in the coexistence of the Party with its *a priori* claim to represent the 'social interest', and the elected institutions of the state, which seemed to be being asked to express the actual demands of society. While the reforms were geared to improving the performance of this latter function, they did nothing to alter the balance of power between the Party and the formal representative institutions.

What appears to have interested the Party in introducing such changes was not 'democracy for democracy's sake', but the improvement of information on the state of popular consciousness, helping the Party to maintain political stability. But the inherent danger of the establishment of a rival representative of the 'social interest' in the elective bodies was averted by the Party's continued manipulations of the electoral process. This in turn served to diminish the informational function of elections. Thus the Party had to find a supplementary source of accurate information on popular moods and attitudes, and it is in this connection that we should see the notable expansion of public opinion polling which took place at this time. The use of public opinion polls certainly enhanced the 'consultative' nature of rule, but of course this was very far from providing an institutional guarantee that policy-makers actually served popular opinion. The use of polls could ensure more effective presentation of policies still formulated essentially independently within the upper reaches of the Party–government hierarchy.

The activation of the trade unions was recognised as an essential accompaniment to reform, as a complement to the increased autonomy of the enterprise and authority of managers, or a 'democratic counterweight for protecting the interests of the workers' as one eminent Party economist put it.[19] The trade unions were to be the channel for increased working-class participation, through which workers would 'get closer to the actual administration of affairs, and with a better insight, gauge the possibilities and establish the reasons for results or failures'.[20] The 'collective contract' between labour and management of an enterprise would take on new significance, as the product of interest-bargaining and interest-reconciliation on matters over which, as a result of the autonomy of the enterprise, it was expected that the local participants would have real control. In addition, the new labour Code of 1966 laid down the following rights of trade unions:[21]

1. the right of *consent*, in the determination of the collective contract at the enterprise level; and, at the level of the industrial branch, over more general matters affecting living and working conditions;
2. the right of *decision*, affecting chiefly matters at enterprise level connected with the use made of the social and cultural funds;
3. the right of *control*, that is, supervision of management adherence to, and implementation of, rules, regulations and agreements;
4. the right of *veto*, which was perhaps the most significant part of the new codification of rights, to be applied where managerial action contravened the law, the collective contract, or, in more general terms, 'socialist morality'. In effect, it wrote into law a limited form of the right to strike;
5. the right of *opinion*, which the trade unions were entitled to offer on questions of the appointment, promotion, or dismissal of enterprise managers.

These rights applied at all levels of the managerial hierarchy. Thus consent of branch trade union organisations had to be acquired for decisions made at ministerial level affecting workers; consent of the top level of the trade union hierarchy, the National Council of Trade Unions (NCTU), would be required for measures taken by the ministries of health, labour or finance which affected workers' interests. The NCTU had control over the central administration of certain social security benefits (until the end of 1971), and had a right to have its opinion heard at regular meetings with the Council of Ministers, and before the government issued regulations which affected living and working conditions.[22]

However, although the new Labour Code did away with the definition of the role of trade unions as 'transmission belts' from the centre to the workers, and replaced it with the single task of 'representing the protecting the interests of the workers', discussions in the press inevitably referred to the trade unions' 'dual role', which implied that the new functions were not after all to replace the unions' co-responsibility with management for mobilising the workforce to meet production goals, but were to supplement it. This was in accord with the logic of the argument that the economy was 'socialist', that production was not an activity 'alien' to the worker, as in a capitalist economy, and that the output of workers' productive activity was 'socially', not privately appropriated. Trade unions in a socialist state were thus 'partners in power', and no conflict between their goals and that of the state and Party could be allowed.[23] As Nyers had explained:

> the workers as a class also have political interest in the development of the entire state, in the further progress of society, and these cannot always be represented by the Trade Unions with sufficient weight, since they can never completely abandon their craft interests. Therefore the Communist Party will always, and in the future too, represent the political interests of the workers best and more efficiently.[24]

Political change did not therefore affect the Party's 'leading role' *per se*, but involved measures to improve the style in which it was exercised. This also had implications for internal Party organisation:

> The Party must be able to fulfil its central function and to express the public interest effectively. If the Party fails to do this, it is not impossible in socialism either that the Party should be overtaken by events and become rigid, that it should act as a brake on development instead of furthering it.[25]

A series of measures was taken to improve the Party's own internal information system. At the IX Congress in 1966, changes to the statutes were introduced to limit the domination of leading Party officials over local Party organs. Nominating committees for internal Party elections were themselves to be elected in advance, and rank-and-file members gained the right to propose candidates. All leading Party officials were to be elected by secret ballot. In November 1969, the Central Committee issued a resolution on further improvement of the operation of the Party. The apparatus was requested henceforth to provide 'alternative variants' of proposals, in order to give more effective choice to elective Party decision-making bodies. In 1970, further modifications were adopted. In local Party elections, the nominating committees were enjoined to take into account, in their selection of candidates for election to Party offices, the results of opinion surveys not only among the rank-and-file Party membership, but among the local population at large. In Party elections, voters were also to be allowed to write in the name of any Party member as an alternative to those offered on the ballot paper, if the official candidate list was found wanting.

At the X Congress in November 1970, a new clause in the statutes was approved which required Party officials to reply on the spot to questions from the floor of Party membership meetings. A secret ballot on motions of recall of officials was instituted. Protection against reprisal for criticism of an official by a rank-and-file member was written into the Party constitution, as was the right of appeal against expulsion.[26]

All these measures could only serve to improve the functioning of the political machine. In the absence of published empirical studies of their actual impact, one can only draw impressionistic conclusions. The Hungarian Party indeed appeared to avoid the degenerative atrophy in evidence elsewhere, for example, in Poland in the 1970s. But its internal processes remained as elusive as ever. The low profile adopted by the Party was an important part of the change in its external style: Budapest is refreshingly free of the ubiquitous, obtrusive banners and slogans of banal optimism which adorn other East European capitals. But the Hungarian Party's elusiveness cannot be interpreted as more than a strategic withdrawal from a position of omnipresence which the Party itself had come to regard as counter-productive. The secrecy with which its internal affairs continued to be conducted was also a condition for the operation of the internal changes themselves. If the Party was to retain its authority *vis-à-vis* society as a whole, it could not allow the increased opportunities for internal debate and criticism to undermine its 'public face' of a united vanguard with a coherent answer to basic policy questions. Moreover, while the internal changes may well have opened up inner-Party debate, the principle of 'democratic centralism' continued to be asserted as the core disciplinary mechanism and organisational guarantee of 'action unity'.

The political changes taken as a whole were more than merely cosmetic, but amounted to less than a political reform. On the one hand, they certainly expanded the opportunities for participation, and improved the basic information flows reaching decision-makers. They represented a not wholly insignificant concession to the acknowledged diversity of interests and opinions in society. But it was basically a matter of instrumental-utilitarian concessions, not of establishing institutionalised rights and procedures within which autonomous political actors could compete for power, and by which the exercise of power itself could be checked. Ultimately, the *status quo* of power relations was preserved, with the Party retaining the initiative, and the population participating through predetermined, manipulated channels, or simply acquiescing as before.

The political changes were in a certain sense a modification of the tacit 'social contract' which had emerged since 1956, rather than a radical rewriting of its terms; economic reform had been conceived in the long term as a means of underwriting the implicit bargain whereby improved consumption was offered as an inducement to the population to restrain its demands for national independence and democratic control over decision-making.[27] But since, in the short term, the period of transition to the new economic mechanism was expected itself to threaten the basis of the 'bargain' by politically charged changes in prices, wages and job stability, increased participation was envisaged as acting as a safety valve. As it was to turn out, the changes introduced did not prove adequate to the task. Enormous social tensions rapidly developed in the early years of the reform, but were only partially and selectively channelled through the existing political institutions, as we shall see in section C.

If those changes which were introduced were in themselves rather less than radical, their significance was even further diminished in that they did not touch at all the 'hidden face' of power in the state bureaucratic apparatus. Many years ago, T. H. Rigby coined the term 'crypto-politics' to describe the peculiarities of the exercise of power in Soviet-type systems, as a form of 'government without public, institutionalised politics'.[28] The basic stuff of politics – conflict over the allocation of resources – goes on in such systems not in the formal representative institutions, in elections, Party congresses, trade-union activities and the press, but within a closed administrative machine. Of the former bodies, Rigby observes, 'Here we have "public relations" on a massive scale, but no public politics'.[29] The changes in Hungary brought conflict much more into the open than before, but did little to alter substantially the balance between the formal 'political superstructure' and the administrative machine, and nothing to alter the conduct of crypto-politics within that machine. It was this vital element of the political system which was to prove the basic obstacle to the realisation of the leadership's objective of economic reform, and which is the subject matter of this chapter.

B THE POLITICAL LIMITS TO ENTERPRISE AUTONOMY

The political problem posed by economic reform at its most general level can be described as a fundamental change in the relationship between 'politics' and 'economics'. The central feature of the Stalinist economy was its totalitarian aspiration to assert political will and political priorities in the economy, eliminating to the maximum possible degree the constraints imposed by the operation of autonomous economic laws characteristic of the market. Politics and economics became fused, or rather, politics dominated economics through a hierarchical system of organisation geared towards the realisation of tasks set by the central command plan. A pivotal role was played by the branch ministerial apparatus, which fed information from below up to the planners, and disaggregated the plan targets into detailed directives issued to enterprises, whose operations it closely supervised and checked. Economic reform aimed to break up this hierarchical fusion of politics and economics by recognising the role of enterprise self-interest as an inevitable fact of life, which could be harnessed in the general social interest if the market were allowed, albeit within circumscribed limits, to function with a significant degree of autonomy. Reform thus involved the recognition of an autonomous economic sphere, which had to be allowed to operate according to its own logic. 'Politics' was not to withdraw completely from the economy, but the political goals embodied in the national plan would be achieved without direct and constant intervention by the centre in the enterprise sphere.

Enterprises were no longer to be guided by obligatory, centrally prescribed and detailed plan targets, but by profit earned from sales of their products. The key new element in the system was the complex set of economic 'regulators', instruments in the hands of the central authorities which were to be used to manipulate the economic environment of enterprises in such a way as to reconcile their pursuit of profit with the basic objectives of central economic policy. The 'regulators' included taxation and credit policy, wage and price controls. A system of taxes, levies and charges on enterprise assets and on the components of enterprise income would guide the formation of enterprise 'funds' and thus the division of profits between investment and wage payments; credit policy would operate through the banking system, to assert central long-term development plans through the selective allocation of resources, but also to promote more rational economic calculation in the use of resources; wage controls would be introduced, to contain pressures for immediate inflationary wage payments, while also guaranteeing a social minimum; the three-tier price system of fixed, limited and free categories would also be used to contain inflationary pressures caused by structural disequilibrium and shortages in the transition period. Foreign trade and exchange controls would gradually bring about a *rapprochement* of domestic and world market prices.[30]

The regulators were thus at the heart of the new relationship between 'politics' and 'economics', between the state and the profit-seeking enterprises. They were to be the crucial means to breaking the direct dependence of enterprises on the state, forcing enterprises to use their initiative in an economically rational way and to take full responsibility for the results of their work. But the transition to the system of indirect regulation was not successfully achieved in Hungary in the 1970s. Throughout the period of operation of the reform, the system of detailed directive planning was never restored – and yet, as it turned out, enterprise behaviour did not change in the anticipated way. Enterprises' interest in profit did not become the central determinant of their activity. Instead of the anticipated focus on the satisfaction of users' or consumers' requirements, enterprises continued to 'look forward' – to bargain on non economic grounds for resources from central funds and for preferential treatment by central authorities, as they had previously bargained over plan targets. Although the continuation of these behaviour patterns at first might have been explained by 'old habits dying hard', in fact these tendencies strengthened over time, indicating that the provisions of the economic reform were not in themselves powerful enough to overcome them.

The reasons for this failure to achieve effective enterprise autonomy can be identified in three areas: first, the inherent complexity of the task of transition in itself; second, the central government's anxiety about the political consequences of economic destabilisation in the transition period, and its corresponding preparedness to permit 'temporary' compromises; and third, the pressures exerted by the unreformed system of economic institutions – the branch ministries and the large enterprises – which had strong interests in subverting the reform and exploiting the government's 'temporary' concessions to make them permanent.

On the first point, we should note that for the system of indirect control through regulators to work, it was essential for enterprises to regard them as 'objective parameters' – basic conditions which they had to accept as 'given', and over which they had no direct control. This required the regulators not only to be stable over long periods, in order for the enterprises to have confidence in them and to be able to calculate risks accurately; but also to be beyond the reach of the enterprise, so that the influence of individual enterprise interests would not penetrate into the process of defining and setting them. In order to be stable over long periods, it was of course essential that the government bodies responsible set them correctly. This in turn required that they be based on accurate, objective economic information – but it was precisely such information that was lacking *before* the reform was introduced, since only a functioning market could provide it. Thus an element of initial trial-and-error had to be allowed for in the 'transition period' of the early years of the reform. However, this immediately led into the trap of frequent adjustments of the regulators, diminishing enterprise copnfidence in them, and increasing enterprise efforts to secure changes in the regulators by showing how they were 'unjustly' penalised by 'faulty' regulators.

It is at this point that the second consideration came into play. What was required to avert the danger of simply replacing 'plan-bargaining' behaviour by 'regulator-bargaining', thus restoring the old relationship between the state and the enterprise sphere in a new guise, was a strong nerve on the part of the central authorities to ride out the pressures from below. In the early years of the reform, the central authorities did appear to be willing to act in the appropriate manner, but their ability to resist pressure from below was severely curtailed by other general and basic policy considerations and assumptions. As the economic historian Iván Berend saw it:

> the 'inherent brakes' built into the reform mechanism were not directed against phantoms but *real dangers*. The question whether without these brakes a hardly tolerable, galloping inflation and unemployment might have emerged can be answered with great certainty ... The government, when undertaking the risks of reform, certainly considered that the country, having suffered many serious shocks in the preceding decades, must not be subjected to such, not even temporarily.[31]

The regime's awareness of the profound disequilibrium of the economy which had been produced by the operation of the old system led it to hold quite legitimate fears of the immediate introduction of full-blown market pressures, and this sustained a lingering suspicion about the viability of the market system. A major problem was in the investment field, where a radical reorientation was required to effect major structural transformation in the economy. There was indeed room for doubt as to whether reliance on the enterprises' pursuit of profit was an adequate guide to the allocation of resources to meet future projected needs.[32] Similar misgivings were held about allowing the market too great a role in the determination of wages and prices. The lack of competition in a highly concentrated economy, with endemic shortages, could easily lead to 'speculative' price rises by monopolistic enterprises, and set in train an uncontrollable price-and-wage inflationary spiral. To attempt to deal with these problems, the government maintained in fact a set of highly restrictive measures, or 'brakes', whose effect was ultimately to undermine the development of enterprise autonomy and render enterprise 'profit' virtually meaningless, as Nyers and Tárdos have demonstrated:[33]

(a) The concern to ensure relative stability of producer prices to avoid inflation led to rigidity, with the result that prices failed to reflect supply-and-demand relations and world market conditions. Especially after the 1973 world price explosion, this involved increasing budgetary subsidies to enterprises, and the practical restoration of central price-fixing, with differential treatment by branch and by individual enterprise. Price revisions which took place were basically flawed by their objective – not of clearing the market but of restricting the growth of enterprise profits.

(b) The strict control of the development of incomes by relating average wages to enterprise profit drew the central authorities into granting 'special' subsidies to allow enterprises whose profit did not rise to raise their workers' wages in line with general wage trends.

(c) The enterprise development fund was kept at too low a level, following restrictive measures to counteract excess enterprise liquidity and the signs of a new cycle of investment above the planned level in 1971. The result was to increase enterprise dependence on credit from the National Bank, which was strongly influenced in its decisions to allocate credit not by considerations of the merits of individual projects in terms of profitability, but by central investment policy, centrally set branch quotas, and the backing of the enterprises' branch ministry.

A further built-in centralised 'brake' again reflecting the government's lack of faith in the market to ensure stability of supply, was the provision that 'in exceptional circumstances' enterprises could be ordered to produce a certain product,[34] or to be designated as 'responsible for supply' where the market was not believed to be an adequate stimulus to production. Such 'exceptional circumstances' would be a chronic deficit of output of the product, threatening shortages on the domestic consumer market; or foreign trade obligations, either towards CMEA partners, or, as the balance of trade with hard-currency areas worsened in the 1970s, to meet the growing need for producing saleable exports to the West. The enterprise involved would receive proper compensation for the losses involved, but this could not alter the essential effect of the provision, to undermine the criterion of profit and thus, enterprise autonomy. In fact, becoming designated as 'responsible for supply' was actually more attractive to enterprises than producing for the market, since it allowed them to evade market pressures and guarantee their security of income as effectively state-licensed and preferentially-treated monopolies.[35]

The complexity of the process of transition, and the government's very real and well-founded concern to avoid widespread disruption of the functioning of the economy both provided strong reasons for a cautious approach. But the underlying commitment to the reform as a long-term necessity remained, thus the explanation of why caution and gradualism actually led to a diversion from the basic goal has to refer to the powerful *active* pressures for recentralisation which fed upon the government's more passive, *reactive* contributions to the process. These active pressures for recentralisation came from the constellation of interests emanating from the organisational system of the economy – the branch ministries and the large enterprises – which was preserved intact in its old form under the NEM.

The reason given for the failure to carry out organisational reform at the same time as introducing the NEM was ostensibly the complexity of the task. As Csikós-Nagy put it, 'The point was not to burden the reform with the intricate problems of reorganisation. We were of the opinion that under the new conditions a clearer picture would emerge as to where and what time reorganisation is justified.'[36]

Past experience seemed to confirm the view that administrative reorganisation was only of secondary importance:

> It is a fact that the problems encountered from time to time in the Hungarian economy were thought to be solved more than once through organisation transformation instead of changing the methods of planning and economic control which virtually influence the economic process.[37]

A less openly discussed but more compelling reason was the political consideration of avoiding 'yet another' administrative upheaval. To avoid alienating politically powerful vested interests, the reform blueprint continued to maintain that there would still be a role for the ministries, albeit a different one from that exercised under the old system. But with the changed concept of the plan, the ministries effectively lost their prime reason for existence. The plan would no longer be drawn up as an aggregate of sectoral plans produced by the ministries, but was to represent an autonomous, and correspondingly more coherent concept standing above sectoral pressures; and it was no longer to be transmitted directly to enterprises in the form of disaggregated targets worked out by the ministries. The new role for the ministries was indeed only vaguely defined. They were left with residual functions of information-gathering and providing long-term forecasts on the future of their branch, with a purely 'advisory' role. This was a reduction in the scope of their activity which undermined the justification for their continued existence as specific branch-type bodies, and for the continued inflated size of their personnel. Indeed, as Friss estimated conservatively, the change would render superfluous 30 per cent of their staff.[38]

It was assumed that the 'empire-building' and 'departmentalist' tendencies frequently criticised under the old system would disappear as soon as enterprises ceased to receive obligatory plan targets from the ministries. It was assumed that this alone would be enough to cut the dependency links of enterprises on the ministries. But the reform also failed to clarify a key point arising from the issue of enterprise autonomy – the question of 'ownership' of the means of production. The rather conservative approach to this abstract but crucial question afforded scope to the ministries to maintain important powers over the enterprises in their branch.

The central factor was the designation of the ministries as guarantors of 'socialist ownership of the means of production'. This was a reflection of the ideological–theoretical insistence that enterprise *autonomy* did not mean enterprise *ownership* of their basic assets. At this point, it was held that a 'socialist' economy could only be one where basic ownership functions were exercised 'by society as a whole', and in the practice of the NEM, the ministries were accorded the right to 'represent society' in the supervision of enterprises. Although, with the acceptance of the basic principles of the NEM, it had been conceded that issuing obligatory plan targets and direct supervision of the use of the means of production could be abandoned without undermining 'socialist ownership', it was felt that this would be threatened if 'social' (i.e. state, via ministerial) control were not maintained over the establishment, liquidation and regrouping of enterprises, and over the appointment, promotion and dismissal of enterprise directors and their deputies, and the approval of managerial bonuses.[39] This gave the ministries an important hold over enterprises, through their power over managers' interests in their incomes and career prospects, as Márton Tárdos and Zsuzsa Hegedüs found in a case study of managerial behaviour, 'The freedom of the *enterprise* does not entail the freedom of the *enterprise executive*. The dependence of executives on the industrial ministry and the freedom of the enterprise contradict one another.'[40]

This dependence of managers on ministerial superiors further eroded the significance of profit as the central motivating force of the economic system, since the ministry's assessment of managerial performance, and hence its approval of bonuses and promotions, did not depend solely, or mainly, or even at all, on profit. The ministry's role, as it emerges in the study by Tárdos and Hegedüs of the Budapest stocking factory, was to transmit central requirements described as the 'social interest', which often conflicted with the enterprise's pursuit of profit, and its power to reward enterprise compliance outweighed considerations of profit for the enterprise. In the case concerned, the Budapest stocking factory was in fact the sole domestic supplier of stockings. While it may have been more profitable for the enterprise to narrow its assortment, or concentrate on production for export, the centre required it to continue to produce the full range of goods in order to ensure continuity and range of supplies to the domestic market. The enterprise was thus faced with contradictory requirements, and was forced to compromise between profit considerations and pressures from the ministry to bow to the dictates of the 'social interest'. Given that the central authorities would compensate the enterprises for losses by modifying the regulators, a situation could arise, Tárdos and Hegedüs noted, where, 'it is no longer worthwhile for the enterprise to assert its original points of view developed on the basis of profits, since bargaining with the center may yield at least as much profit'.[41]

Thus, while the system of regulators had replaced plan directives, the way the regulators were manipulated through the intermediation of the ministries preserved the hierarchical dependency relations, in a more subtle form than under the old system, but no less compelling. As one manager admitted:

> The ministry states its conditions in advance when negotiating with us, and they listen to and observe also our conditions. We ask for certain things of each other and try to fulfil requests on both sides. But the money is in their hands, thus, all that is, on their part, just a polite, proper, and cultured form of instruction. It would be illusory

– even theoretically – to oppose the ministry. Thus, if you like, we have no great independence, yet we are content with the working style of the ministry in our mutual understandings.[42]

Enterprises did not, for the most part, chafe against ministerial intervention which eroded their formal autonomy, since the ministries increasingly came to dispose of resources which were of critical importance for enterprise performance, and, most importantly, to have decisive influence over whether an enterprise obtained investment credits. Because of the importance of relations with the ministry for the enterprise managers, the latter sought in turn to enhance their bargaining power with the ministries, to increase the certainty of a favourable outcome.

There were various bargaining counters available to enterprises to enhance their importance in the ministry's eyes. A well-known phenomenon throughout the Soviet-type economies is the cultivation of good personal relationships with ministerial officials, thus obtaining useful information through informal sources in the ministry, for example, on the timing of submission and framing of a proposal for an investment project.[43] Another source of influence was being the sole supplier of a deficit product, or a successful exporter to Western markets. In fact, even being an unsuccessful enterprise, threatening failure, could be a source of favourable ministerial attention. But one of the most certain ways of ensuring priority treatment was simply being a big enterprise. A study of relations between enterprises and the Ministry of Metallurgy and Heavy Engineering showed that while large enterprises enjoyed a close relationship with their ministry, small and medium-sized firms were able to maintain only 'loose and incidental contacts', with the result that they were 'less able to influence ... decisions of the superior authorities than the large scale enterprises'.[44] Or, as one enterprise manager put it, 'Even the ministry is careful with an enterprise in which 15 000 men and two priority programmes of special importance are on their way – you must not fail here, and the ministry is well aware of it.'[45] The position of large enterprises was a further aspect of the organisational structure developed under the old system which was preserved into the NEM period. The extreme concentration of the enterprise structure of the economy was at odds with the requirements of the NEM, and, in many cases, neither technically nor economically justified. In fact, many of the trusts, in particular those based on 'horizontal integration', were highly diversified in their production profile, better characterised as conglomerations of small firms rather than large-scale concentrated production units, but enjoying nevertheless state-granted monopoly in their field.[46] Concomitantly, there was a serious deficiency of small and medium-sized firms, whose advantages in terms of technical development and innovation, small series and specialised component production, and flexibility in response to changing circumstances, was not at all widely understood or appreciated in Hungary at the time, where the basic assumption was 'big is better', disregarding the possibility that optimal enterprise size might differ from branch to branch and by type of product.

Two waves of concentration, in the late 1940s to early 1950s, and then in 1963–4 had led to 82.4 per cent of the industrial labour force being employed in enterprises of over 1000 by 1985.[47] This was the highest level of concentration in the Soviet bloc, a group of economies already characterised by high concentration. But comparisons with Western capitalist economies are even more striking.

In 1977, 49.3 per cent of Hungarian enterprises employed more than 1000 workers. In the USA, regarded as 'the country of big industrial corporations' (covert admiration of which was one important source of inspiration of the Soviet-bloc amalgamation), 69 per cent of industrial enterprises employed 1–19 people, and 88 per cent of enterprises employed less than 1000 workers in the early 1970s. Comparison with the Netherlands, closer to Hungary in geographical size and population, small enterprises (10–49 workers) and medium sized enterprises (50–900 workers) accounted for 68 per cent and 29 per cent respectively of the total of industrial enterprise. A broadly similar picture emerges with respect to Austria, where only 75 of the total 6830 enterprises employ over 1000 workers.[48]

Now the NEM required enterprises to be economically viable, independent profit-maximising units. This aim would obviously be undermined by the preservation of economically unjustified units and unchallenged monopoly producers. It can be argued that, in a small country, monopoly may be unavoidable where economies of scale demand a size of enterprise which cannot effectively be matched by domestic competition, but the reformers saw the solution to this in introducing competition from foreign imports. This opened up a further dimension to the problems – the use of imports as competition for domestic production required either increasing foreign borrowing and/or the production of exportable goods. In the short term, the Hungarian economy was not producing sufficient quantities of competitive world-standard goods. The temptation to meet the gap by central intervention to enforce export production, as provided for in the reform, whenever the balance of payments worsened, would be very strong, as became clear in the early 1970s, in the wake of the world economic crisis.

The preservation of the larger enterprises after the 1968 reform, however, was not mainly caused by this problem of maintaining economies of scale within a small economy, since a high proportion of the trusts were not in fact based on large-scale production at all, and should therefore have been disbanded from the start. To be sure, in 1968 some of the horizontal amalgamations were indeed disbanded, but nevertheless the process of amalgamation inexorably ground on thereafter. Between 1968 and 1975, ninety enterprises disappeared through mergers. A further sharp fall occurred in 1976, to bring the number of enterprises down from the 1975 total of 779 to 737. Further amalgamations took place between 1977 and 1979, especially in the engineering branches.[49] Unlike the previous phases of concentration, the process in the 1970s under the NEM was largely a movement 'from below',[50] from enterprise and ministerial pursuit of their interests, rather than as a result of a policy introduced from above.

The process of continuing concentration took place by 'extensive' forms of investment expansion, and through mergers,[51] swallowing up small firms on the pretext of assuring supply, both of material inputs and labour, which had become increasingly scarce as a by-product of the system of wage regulation by control of average wage development, which encouraged enterprises to hoard excessive average or low-paid employees in order to pay higher wages to senior staff. But the merger process also allowed large enterprises to absorb smaller competitors, and thus seriously interfered with the development of competitive market pressures.

Although size increased the bargaining power of enterprises with the ministry, it was not a threat to the ministry itself – on the contrary, the ministry was that enterprise's 'natural ally'[52] in its bidding for investment resources, since this also enhanced the power of the ministry itself in making its claims on the centre. Paradoxically, a *failing* enterprise could have the same effect for the ministry since, as long as the central authorities maintained a commitment to preserving inefficient production in the 'national interest' (e.g. as a form of import substitution) then this also gave both the enterprise, and in turn its ministry, a claim on centrally allocated resources. Thus the very existence of the ministries under the reform preserved both the relations of dependence of enterprises, and the very tendencies to 'empire building' by ministries which the reformers expected to be cut simply by the abolition of the directive system of control.

Managerial behaviour in seeking to increase enterprise size was contrary to the requirements of the reform, insofar as investment continued to be devoted to 'extensive' projects and did not enhance enterprise efficiency. A study by Teréz Laky showed that this tendency was structurally linked not only to the increased central control over investment allocation, but was directly produced by the managers' pursuit of their own interests within the organisational framework. Enterprise executives were often in a position of 'forced attachment' to the enterprise.[53] The concentration of production in Hungary often meant that there was only one enterprise in a branch, which severely curtailed the possibilities for managers to advance their careers by moving. Career changes were thus closely related to the enterprise in which a manager started his career. Enterprises could only ensure good career prospects for younger staff by expanding in size, allowing them to create new job opportunities within the firm. In turn, because of the executives' own awareness of their career dependence in the firm, they tended to display an attitude of conformity, avoiding conflicts and preferring rather to fulfill instructions. As one manager admitted, 'The higher the position, the stronger the conformism. This is because a higher position goes with a higher income level, which cannot be ensured at another place.'[54]

Thus the preservation of the organisational system sustained and enhanced a pattern of interests which ran strongly counter to the intentions and requirements of the reform. Instead of a competitive plurality of autonomous enterprises, a set of powerful vertical coalitions built up, which preserved strong links between the lowest level of the organisational hierarchy and the centre, and in fact, proved strong enough to reach up and influence central decision-making itself, which the reform had aimed to make independent of partial interests. Partial interest threatened to dominate, and in fact proved able to divert the centre from its goals. As Friss ruefully acknowledged, major policy intentions – increased technological progress, better management, more effective use of material incentives – had been deflected. 'How can such policy intentions fail which are supported by leading organs of socialist society?' he asked. The answer was to be found in the working of interests behind the scenes:

> if the direction of the actions of a great enough number of persons or groups who are also important enough does not coincide with

> economic policy concepts in practice ... In the given case, that is, in that of economic policy concepts and decisions, aimed at differentiation, a very significant, we might say, a huge group, organ or organisation must have been working in a deviating direction in order to turn all such decisions into their opposite.[55]

The problem, Teréz Laky argued, was not the existence of interests and of bargaining behaviour *per se*, but its concealed form, which meant that interests could only appear 'in a lopsided way and deviating from the desirable direction'.[56] Through their concealed operation behind the facade of the NEM, these interests had led the reform to an impasse by the end of the 1970s:

> though careful attention is paid to keeping the rules of the game of the decentralised control system, in reality a cumbersome system, translated into the language of the profitability indicators, and implemented with indirect instruments, is functioning to break down the tasks and allocate resources – but without the unambiguous hierarchy of the system of plan instructions and with an expanded cast.[57]

By the late 1970s, a broad consensus had been reached by Hungarian economists on the need for a 'reform of the reform'[58] involving a radical approach to the organisational system to ensure enterprise autonomy. As Laky noted, however, this would not come about by itself: 'the organisational system cannot be expected to propose its own reform or break up: this would be opposed to its own interests. A change can be initiated and decided only by external force, ie, by superior political power.'[59]

Thus the ball was put firmly back into the Party leadership's court. Somehow, it would have to muster the will to impose 'a very resolute and uniform principled conception', in order to reverse the trends which had emerged and become entrenched, to overthrow the logic of the old system which continued to operate, and to resist the temptation to allow the 'delicate balance of planned economy and market elements' to 'swing back more easily toward control through instructions'[60] As the late 1970s and early 1980s debate on the 'reform of the reform' progressed, the question of political reform inexorably re-emerged, as the essential condition allowing the centre to challenge these 'hidden mechanisms', by exposing them, clarifying them and thus enabling it to control them.

C SOCIAL REACTIONS TO REFORM AND THE RECENTRALISATION PROCESS

The basic underlying motivation of the Hungarian regime in undertaking economic reform was to achieve long-term legitimation and political stability on the basis of successful economic performance. But in undertaking the reform, it was acutely sensitive to the short-term political consequences of upheavals in the period of transition from the old system to the new, market-oriented system –it was fearful not only of a political backlash from the economic *apparátus*, whose powers and privileges were threatened, but even more of a social revolt on the part especially of the working class. Reform implied structural shifts in employment with the inherent threat to the job security of workers in outdated traditional branches; redistribution of incomes in favour of the more productive and efficient enterprises and the more highly skilled workers; and adjustment of consumer prices which had been fixed and stable over long periods.

Had the regime been more confident of the stability and consolidation of its power base, it would have been in a stronger position to call for popular tolerance of the short-term 'shocks' it anticipated, and would have had firmer grounds for expecting the population to believe its promises of the long-term benefits to be gained. In the absence of such a sense of its own legitimacy, the regime could have turned to increased coercion as a means of asserting its will. But since 1956 the regime had become convinced of the inappropriateness of coercive methods as the main guarantee of political stability, and this was reinforced by its appreciation that coercion would not work in the introduction of an economic reform which essentially was to rely on greater voluntary group and individual initiative. Its deep-rooted fears of working-class revolt were moreover continually reinforced by events in other East European countries – for example in Poland in 1970, where a working-class rebellion had taken place in direct response to price rises. But Biszku, at the time second only to Kádár in the Party hierarchy, drew the following, characteristically Hungarian, conclusion from the Polish events:

> The strength of the Party's power is determined by the degree to which a public opinion favourable to our system and a popular confidence in our socialist authority are integrated with the activity, persistence and consistency of the state organs ... The strength of this power cannot be increased only from the 'top' while forgetting

the activities and daily life of the working masses, who shape history.[61]

The regime thus faced a dilemma – on the one hand, it recognised the necessity of rule by a large measure of consent, and yet it was haunted by the fear that in abstaining from centralised, coercive methods, uncontrolled political liberalisation might result, in which, as in 1956, it would be swept away. Just as in the economy, the material resources to tide the regime over the transition period were deficient precisely because of the legacy of failure of the old economic system, so too in politics, the reserves of popular legitimacy needed to maintain stability would only be built up as a result of the benefits of reform, which could only come with its successful full implementation.

Thus the regime's caution, and its readiness to bow to pressures to compromise, must be understood not so much as an illustration of its *ideological* character or its lack of general political commitment to reform, but rather as a reflection of some quite practically-minded politicians' natural and reasonable perceptions of their own weakness. In such a situation, short-term considerations were almost inevitably to come to the fore. This meant, as one Party economist explained, that any aspects of the reform which did not meet with popular approval would be left out.[62] But this opened up the way to compromises which would prolong the difficult, contradictory transition period, and might even undermine the eventual implementation of a consistent reform model which the government and Party leadership had fixed as its objective.

It was an essential component of the official policy of introducing reform by popular consent that the real income of no single major stratum of the population be allowed to fall.[63] As István Huszár put it, 'Any keeping back of the level of living – in respect of any of its important elements – and particularly its reduction, will become a source of grave socioeconomic contradictions and political ills.'[64]

This attitude naturally fed in the population expectations of a general rapid rise in their standard of living as an almost immediate result of the introduction of the NEM – an expectation which the government found convenient, for political reasons, not to discourage. On the other hand, the government also had further intentions –first, to increase wage differentiation, to reward skill and responsibility more highly, and second, to maintain firm control over wage inflation – which implied from the start a highly contradictory set of policies. When to this were added the further requirements to protect the position of lower income families, and also to bring the 10 per cent of the population estimated in 1969 to fall below the poverty line[65] up to a socially acceptable standard of living, while at the same time, to allow consumer prices to develop in such a way as to reflect more closely market demand (i.e., to increase), then it is clear that the whole area of prices and incomes would become a political minefield.

The reversal of the reform in the mid-1970s has been interpreted as the product of working-class resistance, organised and articulated through the revitalised trade union movement.[66] In the discussion of working-class responses to the impact of reform on wages and prices which is covered in this section, we will demonstrate a far more complex and ambiguous picture. Indeed, the political changes which had taken place did allow social tensions to appear with increased openness. But it is not clear that workers were always or even mainly opposed to the reform *per se* – often, their resentments turn out to have been generated by the misapplication or abuse of the reform, made possible by the inconsistency of its actual implementation. The resolution of these social tensions, it can therefore be argued, might have been achieved by more consistent and resolute reform implementation, rather than by the reversal and recentralisation which actually occurred. The fact that the latter course was adopted, it will be argued, indicates the persistent political pressure of conservative forces in the political system which acted as a distorting prism through which the process of interest articulation from society to the top leadership was deflected. The recentralising measures introduced in the name of the working class were a product of selective manipulation of the interests of workers, and in some respects, even acted against their interests.

(i) Wages

By 1972, popular resentment had emerged on many aspects of the wages question – wage differentiation within the enterprises, between managerial and blue-collar grades; differentiation within the enterprises and between sectors (productive and non-productive, socialist and private, industry and agriculture). The first challenge appeared very early on, in connection with the official wage differentiation regulations, and focused on distribution of the enterprise profit-sharing fund. The total size of the fund was linked to enterprise profits. For the purposes of distribution from the fund, enterprise employees were divided into three categories – top management, middle management and technical experts, and workers. The shares of each group in the fund were related to the basic wage fund for the group – thus top managers' share was set at a maximum of 80 per cent of the top managerial wage fund; middle managers' and technical personnel's share at 50 per cent of their basic wage; while the workers' share was only 15 per cent.[67] These shares were then divided out between individual members of each category with the result that a top manager might receive ten to fifteen times as much from the sharing fund as a blue-collar worker.[68] This was bitterly resented by the rank-and-file, both as an affront to deep-rooted egalitarian assumptions, and as a form of 'class discrimination', which, it was felt, devalued the role of the worker and assigned him to third-class status. The system was abandoned in 1969.[69] Instead, the division of the sharing fund was left up to each enterprise to decide, on the basis of negotiations between management, Party and trade union bodies. The idea was to transfer antagonism from the central authorities to the local level, presumably in the hope that workers would accept differentiation when the case was argued for it enterprise by enterprise. However, ministerial approval also had to be gained for managerial bonuses, which served to enhance the dependence of enterprise executives on ministerial superiors, as noted in section B.

Pressures against differentiation of pay within the enterprise were very hard to resist, as a result of the labour shortage which became more acute with the introduction of the reform. This was caused not only by the declining reserves of labour available to be drawn off from agriculture, and the general long-term declining trend in population growth, but also by the government's wage regulation policy introduced with the economic reform. The central mechanism of wage regulation was strict control of the growth of *average* wages. This was one of the 'brakes', aimed both at restraining inflationary wage payments by enterprises now having increased autonomy over their resources, and also at avoiding unemployment by preventing enterprises from shedding excess workers in order to offer higher pay to a reduced workforce.[70] The result of the measures was that managers, striving to attract and maintain key skilled technical and managerial staff, were forced to offset the effects on the enterprise average wage of high salaries by maintaining excessive numbers of lower paid, unskilled and less productive workers on the books. The excess demand for labour thus generated strengthened the hands of workers, particularly in the more mobile, less skilled categories, to improve their incomes by changing jobs, thus further undermining the central objective of wage differentiation.

The abandonment of the attempt to enforce wage differentiation by direct regulation did not diminish workers' resentments. In November 1970, an 'anti-management' mood was reported to have emerged.[71] It is an interesting and significant point to note, however, that, although, on the one hand, basic egalitarian attitudes on the part of workers (fostered by the past rhetoric of the Party) contributed to their resentments, on the other hand, an equally significant source of grievances was the perception of managers' high rewards as 'unjustified' in the terms of the reform principles themselves – that is, that workers were prepared to see differentiation of reward for effort, expertise and responsibility, but were not convinced, in particular cases, that managers had displayed these qualities in proportion to the bonuses they received. While it is indeed possible that workers failed to appreciate managers' real contributions, it is equally appropriate to concede that the workers' point of view held some validity. The Csepel Works Party conference in November 1970 criticised the sheer lack of ability of some managers, and the Party organisation was instructed to conduct a complete overhaul of its cadre work, to replace bad managers and to put pressure on good managers to improve.[72] Not only is it entirely plausible to assume that there was a large number of incompetent managers, but also, in a context where enterprise profit was still only partially dependent on managerial performance, it was clearly both unjust and contrary to the NEM principle of reward for effort to link managers' high bonuses to that index.[73] The monopoly position of some enterprises, subsidies to the less efficient, the restricted operation of market pricing all persisted in the early years of the NEM, thus lending weight to workers' suspicions. The social and fringe benefits enjoyed by managers, cases of managerial corruption and the continuing 'connections' of managers with branch ministries, all gave managers additional opportunities in securing high incomes, and tended to support workers' perceptions of class-like, cumulative advantages,[74] unrelated to 'objective' criteria of merit.

At the same time, pressures built up from the non-productive sectors to maintain their relative position in earnings. In April 1972, substantial salary rises were granted to teachers (20 per cent); other employees in education and health (10 per cent); ancillary health workers, the armed forces (10 per cent). This was granted at an additional cost to the state budget of Ft 1520m and led to an increase in the planned budgetary deficit.[75] It was the first sign that the government would be prepared to give way to pressure, but its implementation also illustrated strong public resistance to differentiation – the allocation of the teachers' 20 per cent was directed to benefit the higher qualified and senior staff, but this led to uproar in the schools. Head teachers, instructed to implement the pay rise differentially, were reported as being 'exposed to unbearable mass pressure from those concerned'.[76]

At the end of 1971, a further group of workers, in the Budapest transport system, were granted an additional bonus, unrelated to performance.[77] By this time, the government had also conceded the necessity for an overhaul of the general basic wage system – and this aroused widespread expectations of a universal wage rise.[78] However, it was less widely understood that the revision would only affect minimum and maximum wage levels, the policy of differentiation remained, and enterprises, many of whom at the time did not dispose of adequate funds to implement the revision, were given 18 months' grace.[79]

In 1971, the question of differentiation of earnings based not only on skill, but according to individual enterprise performance aroused controversy, which was to mount into a general demand for across-the-board pay rises, irrespective of enterprise or branch profitability. The trade union chairman, Sándor Gáspár, rejected the idea that similar work should be differentially rewarded according to the profit of the enterprise or branch, in his speech to the XXII Congress of Trade Unions in 1971:

> The trade unions are of the opinion that if the wage measures of the enterprises are excessively dependent on the development of profits, this would hamper the establishment of a correct incentive and wage policy. The government must have more opportunities for seeing to it that correct wage ratios are established among enterprises and branches of industry

and further:

> We believe that the responsible state organs should formulate the concepts and methods to ensure that workers employed in manufacturing uneconomic or less economical products have a desirable level of income.[80]

There was indeed a compelling logic in Gáspár's argument. Given the government's toleration of the continued operation of uneconomical enterprises in the short-term 'national interest' (e.g. producing products as import substitutes when foreign currency funds were lacking) it was unfair to penalise the workers of such enterprises. This would not have been such a great problem if the number of such enterprises had been low, as the reformers had originally assumed in allowing the 'exceptional circumstances' clause to be inserted as a short-term expedient. But as we have seen, the tendency was for such 'exceptional' enterprises to increase in number over time. Thus the government was faced with the alternative of either enforcing genuine efficiency criteria more rigorously and closing down unprofitable enterprises, which it was reluctant to do for politicial reasons as so many enterprises and such a large number of workers were at stake, or granting 'unearned' rises to workers, irrespective of efficiency, thus undermining an essential component of reform.

(ii) Prices

Closely related to the wages issue was that of prices, which again involved the adjustment of the population's expectations to the new conditions. On the one hand, people expected a more rapid rise in wages under the NEM, while at the same time, they continued to expect virtually complete price stability as under the old system. The plan set a maximum of 2 per cent per annum increase in the consumer price level, and this was never exceeded in the period 1968–71. In 1968, the consumer price level fell by 0.3 per cent; in the following years, prices rose by 1.4 per cent, 1.3 per cent and 2.0 per cent. At the same time, real incomes and real wages rose by 2.1 per cent and 3.5 per cent on average per annum in the years 1968–74.[81] Despite this, the price rises generated resentment, as they were seen as much larger by the public. In 1969, a Budapest radio programme interviewed the chairman of the State Statistical Office, István Huszár, and the Chairman of the financial department of the Central Planning Board, in an attempt to convince the public that in fact their standard of living was rising. Workers from a Budapest factory who participated in the programme insisted however that they had not experienced a rise in their standard of living.[82] At the December 1969 session of Parliament, a lively discussion was reported,[83] and popular dissatisfaction on the standard of living and prices was conveyed. Efforts to overcome this popular 'misunderstanding' of the function of prices do not appear to have been successful.

Sándor Gáspár, the trade union leader, admitted the continuing sensitivity of the price issue at an NCTU session in October 1970, but reiterated the principle that 'the consumer in general should pay for the true value of what he is buying'.[84]

The trade unions admitted in early 1971, in the preparations for their XXII Congress that year, that 'workers have reacted more sensitively to price changes than was warranted by their actual effects'.[85] But at the Congress in May, they called for a 'better thought out' price policy, so that prices should not 'adversely affect the standard of living', thus echoing popular feeling, in contrast to their earlier recognition that popular perceptions might be inaccurate.[86] In March 1971, Nyers appeared on television to try to explain and justify price changes.[87] In fact, only about one quarter of retail trade in the early 1970s fell into the free price category, and items considered 'staple' or 'essential' continued to receive heavy budgetary subsidies. For example, the price of heating and lighting fell every year, until 1974.[88] In 1971 the fuel subsidy amounted to 53 per cent. Subsidies on food continued to be substantial – 65 per cent on beef, 46 per cent on pork, 59 per cent on milk; as were also those on public utilities, for example, 40 per cent on cinemas, 50 per cent on public laundries, 80 per cent on railway passenger transport, 84 per cent on Budapest passenger transport.[89] However, prices on some sensitive items, such as beer and tobacco, rose much faster, and prices of clothing – a significant item in family budgets – also rose more rapidly, with 80–90 per cent of turnover conducted at free prices.[90] An important item – rent on accommodation – also went up, but this was not included in the official cost-of-living index.

In 1972, moreover, the budget envisaged a more rapid rise in prices, by 3 per cent, as compared with the 1.5–2.0 per cent of preceding years. Csikós-Nagy, the Chairman of the State Price Office, acknowledged the 'sensitivity' of the problem in his announcement of the budget.[91] In the course of 1972, criticism of the development of the standard of living mounted, not without justification, as it emerged from the final report on 1972 performance in the economy. Real wages, incomes and consumption all rose at a significantly slower pace than that promised by the plan.[92]

As with the issue of wage differentiation, the popular reactions reported in the press appear to be composed not only of 'misunderstandings' of the real requirements of the reform, but also of quite valid resentments at its misapplication. In the case of prices, the sensitivity of the issue was no doubt largely caused by long-ingrained expectations of near-total price stability, and unwillingness to recognise the long-term negative economic effects of subsidies. However, it was also the case that enterprises were often in a position to make 'speculative' and 'profiteering' price rises, given their increased autonomy over price-setting, which could raise enterprise profits, and thus employee incomes, without extra effort or improvement in the product. Cases of this were regularly criticised in the press and by trade union leaders.[93] A more complex problem was the tendency of some enterprises to narrow their assortment, to concentrate on the more profitable products (usually luxuries), at the expense of less profitable, but more socially necessary basic products, thus threatening the overall government policy of ensuring stable supplies of low-priced consumer goods. Again, the solutions open to the government in this question were twofold: either it could increase the central supervision of prices as a short-term 'solution' to such 'negative phenomena'; or it could press on with the reform logic, by allowing prices to rise on less profitable products where consumer demand was unsatisfied, and by countering 'speculative' price rises by increasing competition, breaking up large firms with an over-extended product range, and allowing new firms to enter the field. The latter solution, however, threatened short-term political repercussions by further challenging the privileges of the larger firms, and their workers, who were able to extract substantial concessions for maintaining their 'responsibility for supply' of basic goods.

(iii) Workers and Peasants

A further issue which received much publicity in the early years of the reform was the change in the relative earnings between industrial workers and cooperative peasants. Since the IX HSWP Congress in 1966, it had been official policy to close the gap between the earnings of the two groups, but this of course required a more rapid rise in cooperative farm earnings than industrial earnings. Between 1966 and 1969, these rose by 42 per cent and 10 per cent respectively.[94] However, cooperative farmers' average monthly earnings were still significantly lower than industrial workers' wages, at Ft 1562 as compared with Ft 2176.[95] In 1969, 41.2 per cent of cooperative farmers earned less than Ft 1000 per month, 33 per cent earned between Ft 1000 and Ft 2000, and only 25 per cent earned over Ft 2000. Even the lowest industrial wages were above the cooperative average. In terms of social benefits, peasants continued to be disadvantaged – the retirement age for peasants was five years later than for workers; on average, peasant families received Ft 100 less per month than workers' families for child care and other family benefits; peasants' pensions, being related to their lower working incomes, were also lower than workers' pensions. However, peasants did enjoy the benefits of their private plots, but this could redress only part of their overall financial disadvantage. Average income from the plot was estimated to add Ft 300–400 per month to their earnings.

The government envisaged the expansion of the private plots under the NEM, both as a means to raising peasant incomes, and as a source of increased food supplies, especially in connection with the 'Pork Programme', launched in 1970.[96] Thus the limits on small-scale livestock holding were no longer set centrally, but were left to cooperatives to decide for themselves.[97] Tax and credit concessions were introduced, supplies of fodder in quantities small enough to be appropriate for small producers' requirements were made commercially available, and small-scale machinery and equipment was produced or imported in large quantities. In addition, a major media campaign was launched, to broadcast high-level Party pronouncements in favour of private plot cultivation.[98] A special HSWP policy committee pronounced the private plots to be in 'organic unity' with the 'socialist' cooperative,[99] and local Party organisations were called upon to help to boost private plot production.[100] The agricultural newspaper *Szabad Föld* started a special column devoted to the issues affecting private plot cultivation. This propaganda effort was necessary to overcome what was criticised in a *Szabad Föld* editorial as 'anti-plot feeling'.[101] One senior trade union official, Virizlay, pointed to working-class resentment as the major sociological component of this sentiment, resulting both from resentment of the relatively more rapid rise of peasant incomes, and dissatisfaction with the rising prices of foodstuffs, which accounted for 50 per cent of the urban worker's family expenditure.[102] The government daily, *Magyar Hírlap*, fanned any smouldering embers of working-class anti-peasant feeling by a rather provocative report on rapid improvements in living conditions in the villages, reflected in elaborate extensions to houses, including bathrooms.[103]

However, it is unclear, to say the least, that the main source of anti-peasant and 'anti-plot' feeling lay in the industrial workers, for the main reason that a large section of the working class itself still had a foothold in the countryside through close family connections – either the worker was a first-generation migrant to the town, and thus still had parents and family in the village, or he was part of a growing number of 'dual-income' families, typified by the husband commuting from his home base in the village, while the wife remained a member of the cooperative, and thus maintained the family's right to a private plot. Nearly one million industrial workers, of the total industrial labour force in 1972 of 1.74 million, were in fact commuters from rural areas, and were thus closely linked to village life.[104]

Another important means by which industrial workers' interests were tied in with small-scale agriculture was in the reverse direction, as industrial workers were encouraged, and proved extremely willing, to take on 'garden plots', as a result of a late 1968 government measure. In 1970 and 1971, a rapid increase in the numbers of garden plots, or 'auxiliary farms', took place, and factories and local council bodies quickly bought up land around towns and cities, to satisfy their employees' demand for allotments. By the spring of 1972, it was reported that there were more than 1 million people engaged in gardening 'as a hobby' – an enormous proportion of the labour force. This form of production was mainly for own consumption, but nevertheless, 20 per cent of it was brought to market. The Patriotic People's Front created a 'National Association of Garden Friends', one of the purposes of which was said to be to combat 'anti-garden views' – clearly not originating from among the worker–gardeners themselves.[105] In fact, it is clear from the widespread press coverage accompanying the 1970 promotion of the private plots and extension of the opportunities for town-dwellers to enjoy the benefits of allotment gardening, that the real core of resistance to this development came from the local Party, council and cooperative farm management officials.[106] For local political activists, the expansion of plot farming was an affront to deeply ingrained attitudes. One report revealed that many cooperative managers and council officials 'still adhere to the anti-private plot ideology of Rákosi'.[107] As the Chairman of the HSWP Central Control Commission, J. Brutyó admitted, 'we were the ones who created anti-private plot opinion; therefore it is primarily our task to change it'.[108] However, practical problems with introducing the scheme easily reinforced local level ideological misgivings – for cooperative farm managers, the main danger was seen in cooperative members diverting their energies away from collective cultivation; moreover the injunction upon them to organise and provide support for the plots was seen as an irritating additional effort, which would not be reflected fully in the overall output of the cooperative, on which managerial salaries and bonuses depended.[109] Local council officials were aware of the danger of abuses of the right to private cultivation, and could easily point to cases illustrating the validity of their broad political misgivings.

One element in increasing rural incomes which did affect industrial workers more obviously was the growth in cooperative farms' industrial auxiliary enterprises. These had been allowed to expand and increase in number as a means of providing full employment in the countryside, to overcome seasonal fluctuations in work activity, but had become so successful that they were able to offer high wages to draw in outside labour. A major field of activity was in construction, where the local cooperative firms were much better suited to building, for instance, a barn or village bus stop to meet local needs, than were the large state construction firms.[110] Construction workers' wages in the cooperative auxiliaries were, in 1971, 32 per cent higher on average than those paid by state firms,[111] although per capita productivity was lower. This was felt to be an affront to the principle of 'just reward'; also, of course, it threatened to drain off scarce manpower from the state sector. Thus, while state employees may well have resented the differential, this must have been mitigated by the opportunity offered to increase their earnings by moving to a cooperative firm. The restrictions on wage rates and the field of activity of cooperative auxiliary enterprises, introduced in June 1971, would therefore appear to serve the interests primarily of the state enterprises, ever anxious to protect their supply of labour.

(iv) Interests in the Recentralisation Process

The retreat from reform began in November 1972, when the Central Committee introduced a package of 'extraordinary measures' to put right the 'difficulties' surrounding the reform. Fifty large enterprises accounting for 50 per cent of industrial output and 60 per cent of export production,[112] were returned to direct ministerial supervision and effectively taken out of the reform; wide-ranging wage rises were granted, and increased central control of prices was also conceded. 1.3 million workers received pay rises to the total value of more than Ft 2.3 bn, most of which was to be met directly from the state budget. The policy of differentiation, however, was maintained in the allocation of the pay rises. Skilled workers' and foremens' wages in industry rose by a minimum of 8 per cent; those of semi-skilled and unskilled workers by a minimum of 4 per cent. In construction, the rises for the respective groups were 6.5 per cent and 3 per cent. Enterprises were to 'top up' these directly budget-financed rises, so that the total rise for skilled industrial workers would be a minimum of 10 per cent, for less-skilled industrial workers, 5 per cent; in construction, the final total rises would be 8 per cent and 4 per cent respectively. Enterprise administrative personnel, who had grown excessively and contrary to the government's intentions, were not included in the pay rises.[113] Further 'extraordinary' pay rises were granted in February 1974 by the Council of Ministers, to the benefit of a further 300 000 workers in trade, transport and agriculture, of a similar level to those granted in 1972; also to less-skilled auxiliary workers, who were granted 5 per cent; theatre employees, who received 8 per cent; and scientific research workers, who received 20 per cent.[114]

In 1973 and 1974, the coincidence of the world oil crisis acted as a further factor strengthening the case for halting reform: 'The first reflex of the emergency situation was definitely a cry for stronger state intervention and recentralisation.'[115] The drastic change in the terms of trade and accelerating inflation 'threatened to devastate the results of the former income and consumption policies'.[116] Increased subsidies were granted to insulate the domestic economy: 'As a result, the price system of the reform practically collapsed. It became inadequate to reflect real values and market relations.'[117] Consumer prices, held down by increasing subsidies, now fell below the level of producer prices.

With these economic developments, a political bandwaggon gathered momentum in the period 1973–5, and entrenched ideological opposition to the reform surfaced. The NEM was linked with an alleged explosion of 'petty-borgeois attitudes', a 'problem' to which the provincial press in particular devoted much attention:

> Thanks to the misinterpretation of the reform of the economic mechanism by people who cite it in their justification, individualism and egotism have regained strength and speculation and the will to make undeserved profits have gained ground.[118]

The role of the press in airing 'matters of public concern' in fact grew quite markedly in the reform years, and the freedom of discussion allowed, while a healthy development, also carried with it the danger of the press becoming dominated by the more vociferous forces and subordinated to partial interests. A characteristic result of the limited nature of the liberalisation in this sphere was that it gave voice to those middle-level and regional council and Party apparatus groups who had remained profoundly sceptical of the central leadership's commitment to reform. Imre Pozsgay, a leading Party political theorist, warned of the danger in his reflections on the November 1972 plenum:

The press, which plays an important and positive role in integrating interests by revealing the truth and by keeping the public informed and by guiding it, can do great harm if it misinterprets its role and yields to influences which attempt to divert it from the important social task, that of supporting the reform of the economic mechanism.[119]

At the same time, in 1973 and 1974, an ideological clampdown on intellectuals was enforced. The sociologist András Hegedüs and the philosophers János Kis and Mihály Vajda were subjected to investigations which led to their expulsion from the Party in May 1973. Along with Ágnes Heller and György and Mária Márkus, who had previously also been expelled from the Party, they lost their academic positions and were prevented from publishing. In 1974, Miklós Haraszti was charged with 'grave incitement' and fined, with a suspended sentence, for the publication of a book on working conditions in a factory.[120] The sociological writers György Konrád and Iván Szelényi and the poet Tamás Szentjóby were detained on charges of 'anti-socialist agitation'. Szelényi and Szentjóby left the country, as did many prominent members of the 'Budapest School' of sociological and philosophical writing.[121]

The anti-reform momentum worked its way through to the top levels of the Party, and personalities closely associated with the NEM and the cultural liberalisation of the early 1970s lost their posts. Nyers was removed from the Secretariat in November 1973 along with György Aczél, in charge of Party cultural policy. Nyers was subsequently also dropped from the Politburo at the XI HSWP Congress in 1974. At the Congress, the Prime Minister, Jenő Fock, made a self-critical speech, and in 1975, he was replaced by György Lázár.[122]

Although the economic measures and the political reaction were made in the name of the 'working class', it is clear that the process of definition of what constituted the 'workers' interests' was profoundly influenced by the role of bureaucratic interests. The campaign against 'petty-borgeois attitudes', for instance, can be seen as not so much a reflection of an issue of mass concern as a head-on attack on widespread popular expectations and aspirations, as Berend later commented:

The cries of alarm at the spread of petty bourgeois mentality filled the air of public discussions ... The monster of a consumption-oriented society had been projected by the press and in literary discussions as early as the beginning of the 1960s, the dangers of 'refrigerator socialism' had been formulated at a time when a third of the population was still struggling with the problems of subsistence and advent of the refrigerator could have been the symbol of deliverance from bread-and-butter worries rather than a wanton consumption-orientation in conflict with socialist ideals[123]

An essential point is the lack of conformity of the definition of 'workers' interests' used to justify the reform reversals with the real heterogeneity of the workers' interests. A mythical, ideological concept of the 'worker' was propounded. Workers' interests as producers were over-emphasised, at the expense of their interests as consumers; and an artificial distinction was created between 'workers', 'peasants', and 'private producers/craftsmen', when, in fact, there were significant overlaps between them in Hungary. As already noted, a substantial proportion of the industrial working class had a significant interest in peasant earnings as a component of the total household income; many workers were engaged in small allotment cultivation in their spare time, and probably the vast majority of workers derived at least part of their income from artisan-type work in the 'second economy' – to say nothing of their interests as consumers in the goods and services offered by that source. These points come through clearly when we examine the consequences of measures enforced in 1975, when, after a series of hostile pronouncements against private peasant farming at the XI Congress, the government introduced heavier taxation of peasant income, suspended the system of contract-rearing of pigs by private individuals, and reversed the increased purchase price of pigs granted in 1974. The immediate response of peasants, anticipating a clampdown, was to cut their holdings of pigs. Government figures show that the number of pigs on household plots fell by 553 000 between mid-1974 and October 1975; numbers of pigs on other smallholdings fell by 475 000.[124] Dissident sources refer to the destruction of the entire private-sector stock of sows in one week.[125] The inevitable result was a meat shortage in 1976. Vegetable and fruit production also fell, with the result that imports had to be made in the first half of 1976. As a press commentator concluded:

> Naturally, there are also calculable disadvantages and risks [in allowing the development of private production] – in influences on consciousness as well as in occasional extreme differentials in incomes ... But consciousness, the economy, and the country are

disturbed above all by shortages, by deficits, and by inflexible rigidity[126]

Probably the single most powerful political lobby behind the decisions of the November 1972 plenum was that of the large enterprises, which had become increasingly irritated by competition for materials and labour from smaller enterprises, such as the cooperative farms' industrial auxiliaries, which had sprung up with the reform. A telling indication of their direct political weight was the fact that, for the most part, those enterprises which were selected for withdrawal from operation under reform conditions, and put under direct governmental control with preferential treatment were those which had personal representatives of the Central Committee itself.[127]

The role of the trade unions in the recentralisation process was also a vital one. In many respects, the activity of the unions developed to take on the task of expressing workers' interests in an independent way. Under Gáspár, the unions did become a force to be reckoned with, but it should also be noted that their effectiveness in securing the general wage rise at the November 1972 plenum was greatly enhanced by the fact that this demand *coincided* with the pressures exerted by other groups – notably the large enterprise lobby and the ideological opponents of reform – for greater direct central intervention in the economy. In important respects, the unions failed to break out of their traditional mode of operation, remained ultimately linked with the old institutional structure, and thus failed to secure active incorporation of workers on the shop floor.

Trade unions began to provide an important mouthpiece for working-class views especially markedly in 1971 (probably spurred on by the Polish events of December 1970). The basic membership meetings in early 1971 appear to have provided an open forum for the expression of working-class discontent,[128] and this was transmitted at the branch union congresses prior to the XXII Congress of Trade Unions in May. At the branch congresses, representatives of the lower-paid branches – for example, the food and light industry unions –were reported as transmitting their memberships' grievances particularly vociferously.[129] Leading trade-union officials regularly articulated discontent on questions of prices, wages, unjustified enterprise profits, authoritarian and/or incompetent managers, pay relativities between workers and peasants, and so on.[130] The trade-union line was asserted by its leadership vigorously both in the press, at the X HSWP congress in 1970, at the XXII Congress of Trade Unions in 1971, and at regular meetings of the government and the top level of the trade-union movement.[131] At the XXII Congress of Trade Unions, Gáspár, the Trade Union Chairman, asserted that the unions no longer merely transmitted Party policy, but were active participants in the creation of policy.[132] He claimed that a 'social division of labour' had developed between the State, the Party and the trade unions, which 'institutionally serves the purpose of representing, coordinating and solving conflicts', and maintained that:

> It is in the interest of society that political decisions concerning living and working conditions, prices and wages should always be made on the basis of the coordinated opinions of the leading State and Trade Union Council bodies.[133]

A major strength of the unions in bargaining with the central authorities was the coherence of the line developed by the NCTU, which appears to have been not so much a body responsive to demands from the lower levels of the trade-union movement, as a closely-knit client group centred on the person of Sándor Gáspár.[134] Thus while crucial central policy-making bodies were hesitant, uncertain, and lacking in self-confidence, the NCTU representatives with whom they had to deal on various government and Party committees and in regular government–trade-union consultative sessions, spoke with one voice, and had that self-confidence which comes both from effective behind-the-scenes coordination of the organisation line on every issue, and from the undeniable psychological advantage of claiming to represent the workers in a 'workers' state'.

However, despite the fact that workers were able to use local trade-union meetings as a forum for expressing their grievances, the effectiveness of trade unions in the enterprise, and to some extent at branch level, appears to have been strictly limited. This was partly a question of local-level failure to assert the rights which they legally enjoyed, and partly a deeper problem of structural obstacles to their effectiveness. It was the first point which was most emphasised by the trade union leadership. A meeting of the National Council of Trade Unions in late 1970 criticised the failure of local officials to use the rights they had to defend workers more forcefully.[135] Deference and timidity seem to have characterised the attitude of a large number of trade union officials in their dealings with management. In consequence, they failed to extract adequate information from management to enable them to participate fully in enterprise wage-setting. They were too aware of their dependence on management for their own jobs, and naturally fearful of reprisals if they created 'difficulties' for management. And correspondingly, managers often carried on in their pre-reform authoritarian style, and ignored union rights. This occurred at branch level too, as one NCTU secretary expressed it in 1969:

> The main feature in this situation is the formidable trade union initiative, while the principal characteristic of ministries is reluctance... In many places the significance of the right to express an opinion is not yet clearly recognised[136]

A similar criticism was voiced in 1972, when trade unionists complained that despite their formal right to give an opinion on the performance of management and on candidates for managerial appointment, their views were not sufficiently taken into account by the state bodies, which had the final decision-making authority in these matters.[137]

Public opinion on the work of the trade unions at the enterprise level remained highly sceptical, as a survey published in the trade union paper, *Munka*, in February 1972, revealed. There was almost unanimous criticism of the trade unions.[138] The reformed labour code had in fact imposed some constraints on the shop steward's role, which was only rectified later in the 1970s.[139] Trade union secretaries remained burdened with administrative duties and obligations to attend excessively frequent meetings, which kept them inaccessible to workers. One trade union activist, commenting on the findings of the poll, noted that enterprise trade unions had remained restricted by higher-level Party and government policy decisions, which prevented them from carrying out some of their schemes. He complained, 'This made us feel that we had deceived the workers, because we had notified them in advance of our proposals and intentions.'[104]

In fact, the most important means used by the workers to defend their interests directly remained highly individualistic, and outside the scope of organised participation in trade union activity. The actual behaviour of workers shows that labour turnover and 'second' jobs were the most important means of raising incomes, rather than bargaining with management through the trade unions. Where these two strategies were unavailable or not suitable, workers continued to use informal organisation within the workshop, independent of the unions, including regulation of their work effort by slowdowns, as the most effective means of influencing their working conditions and pay rates, as was vividly illustrated by a case study of an enterprise, by the sociologists Lajos Héthy and Csaba Makó.[141] At production conferences, which were supposed to be the institution through which workers 'participated', they found that 'no matters of serious concern to labour were discussed'.[142] Although, through informal means, interest conflicts within the enterprise did find short-term solutions, 'there was a lack of lasting compromise and integration of interests'.[143] A long-term, stable enterprise wage policy could not develop, and the resolution of management-labour conflict retained the character of *ad hoc* concessions, 'revocable at any time'. The Héthy–Makó study reveals what was only partially apparent at the time – that the inadequacies of the trade unions as a means of articulating and incorporating workers' interests were the result of structural features of the situation, not merely the incompetence of individuals. The essence of these structural obstacles, Héthy and Makó demonstrated, lay in the continuing lack of autonomy of the enterprise – most importantly, in the central control over wages exerted by the restrictions on the development of the average wage level. This created in the enterprise a set of irresoluble tensions. As explained above, central controls on average wages led to managers employing excessive numbers of lower-paid workers in order to counterbalance the higher pay necessary to retain scarce skilled labour. Workers responsed to low pay either by changing jobs, or by banding together informally to defend their interests. The central point with respect to the position of the trade unions, as Héthy and Makó found, is that they were unable to back the workers' demands which contradicted the central wage regulations. Since wages were not set at the enterprise level, enterprise trade unions could not participate in wage-bargaining: 'Consequently, the Trade Union could not claim a greater say in company affairs than offered by the power concentrated at the level of the company.'[144]

The solution to the tensions generated by the central wage-control system between managers and workers was sought by the trade-union leadership not in the abolition of central wage regulation, but in fact in an even more direct form of central intervention in wage-setting, in the form of a general pay rise. The paradoxical effect of this was that while it undermined a basic element of the reform – enterprise autonomy and the role of profit – it did not enhance the role of the trade unions at the local level. In fact, although this was not widely recognised at the time,[145] the development of enterprise autonomy and the development of the trade unions as an effective interest-articulating and channelling organisation went hand in hand. In gaining the centralised wage rise in November 1972, the trade unions preserved, at the local level, their position of limited effectiveness, since wage levels continued to be determined outside the enterprise as before. Effective bargaining for higher wages for workers would take place not through local trade union pressure on management to improve the enterprise's performance or the workers' share in the profits, but through trade-union collaboration with management in seeking extra resources or preferential treatment from central authorities. This not only preserved the workers' view of the unions as an arm of management rather than 'their own' interest representative, but also served to fragment the interests both of workers and trade unionists by enterprise and by branch, pitted against each other in competition for centrally-allocated resources and favours. Thus the trade unions remained ineffective as an institution for mediating labour-management tensions within the enterprise, and workers were left to their own devices, to individual or informal group solutions to their aspirations for higher wages.

The recentralisation process therefore can be seen as a product of a coalition of forces, acting in the name of the workers, but only partially in fact serving their real interests. The demand for a general wage rise, which was a crucial component of that process, certainly benefited the workers in an important respect, but it was also closely in line with the pressures being exerted in the same centralising direction by bureaucratic interests in the ideological and economic apparatus. The general wage rise was *not* contradictory to managerial, enterprise or ministerial interest, so long as it was part of a set of concessions extracted from the government which would have the overall effect of 'softening' enterprise budget constraints, in Kornai's terminology. Managers only had an interest in holding workers' wages down as long as profit was a 'hard' category. As soon as it became possible to extract concessions, subsidies and budgetary grants from the state, managers would have a stronger interest in supporting workers' wage demands, since they were not merely 'cost-free' to the enterprise, but could also serve its interests in retaining and pacifying labour, thus allowing the enterprise to maintain its size, and consequently its bargaining power for further claims on the state. Workers' interests, in other words, turned out to be served only in those respects where they coincided with the strivings for recentralisation on the part of anti-reform bureaucratic groups entrenched in the unreformed institutional apparatus.

CONCLUSION

The aim of the preceding argument was not to demonstrate that there was no basis for working-class opposition to aspects of the reform, but rather to show how imperfectly working-class interests were in fact represented. Indeed, the government and Party leadership was acutely open to pressure and responsive to demands made on it, but the point is that the function of articulating and aggregating interests, the definition of the 'problem' and the formulation of the 'solutions' were dominated by covert groups within the élite and the State economic apparatus. 'Politics' did not develop into the open play of interest groups, but remained strongly characterised by more traditional forms of 'crypto-politics', in T. H. Rigby's term – subterranean bargaining processes within the élite. This produced a set of strongly conservative pressures, forcing a paralysis of the central bodies: on the one hand, the mass of the population remained unintegrated into the policy procress, and tended to continue inward-looking and individualised patterns of dealing with everyday life. This inhibited the development of positive legitimation for the regime, since most people remained sceptical of the benefits to be had from active participation, and fearful of openly and actively articulating their interests in case they 'rock the boat', push things 'too far', and lose the already substantial opportunities for bettering their lot which the reform had opened up, particularly in the private sector. On the other hand, organised interests acted as 'veto groups',[146] able to secure governmental concessions to their immediate demands, without taking responsibility for the impact of their demands on the 'social interest'. In fact, in this situation, the 'social interest' remained as obscure and elusive as ever, since on the one hand, sectional-interest groups couched their demands in terms of the 'social interest', while, on the other, the central decision-making authorities did not achieve the intended independence from sectional interests, and thus were not in a position to define the 'social interest' authoritatively and assert it over and against the sectional interests.

Thus, by the end of the first decade of the operation of the reform, the regime faced not only mounting unsolved economic problems, but also a crisis of political development. The failure to elaborate a comprehensive political reform to break up the institutional bases of conservatism and permit a reshaping of the pattern of interest formulation and articulation had not only contributed in large part to those economic problems, but had also become a more acute problem in itself as the regime no longer disposed of the resources to continue the pattern of concessions to powerful veto groups.

As at the inception of the reform, it was escalating difficulties in external economic relations which forced the regime to recognise the impossibility of sustaining the *status quo*. The price of the years of avoiding adjustment to the changed world economic environment was an accumulated trade deficit, and a gross hard-currency debt amounting to $7.5bn in 1978, rising to $8.5bn in 1979 and $9.1bn in 1980 (in net terms, $6.5bn, $7.3bn and $7.0bn in the respective years).[147] In late 1978, the government announced a major shift in its long term economic strategy, from the import-substitution approach adopted as a concomitant of the reform reversal in the mid-1970s, to an export orientation. This signalled the beginning of a relaunching of the reform, which began with an overhaul of the price system, to effect a 'transition from the prime cost price system to a competitive system'.[148] The final product price was to be linked to the achieved export price in non-ruble terms.[149] The aim was now to achieve vertical integration of prices, 'which should function smoothly from the world market right through to the consumer stage'.[150] Gradually, but with resolution and consistency, consumer prices were to be raised, and the burden of subsidies on the state budget to be cut back. As a result, open inflation of 10 per cent was allowed in 1979 and 1980, and continued at between 5 and 7 per cent in the following years.[151]

Institutional reform now came onto the agenda: in 1980, the branch ministries were abolished, and replaced by a single Ministry of Industry with no direct authority over enterprises, to act as a policy-formulating body. A number of large enterprises, including the massive and prestigious Csepel Engineering Works, were broken up into smaller independent units. In the early 1980s, new forms of group and individual private enterprise were legally established. A proliferation of small firms came into being, ranging from individually-run restaurants and small shops leased from the state, to forms of group subcontracting undertaken by employees of a large firm, associated in autonomous 'economic working partnerships'. Groups of independent specialists and experts in fields such as architecture, research and design, and foreign language teaching, set up private consultancies and practices.[152] In 1984, a diversification of the forms of enterprise management of state-owned enterprise began to be introduced. It is expected that about 80 per cent of enterprises will eventually be run by various forms of enterprise councils or workers' assemblies, while the rest, mainly strategically important enterprises and public utilities, will remain under state control.[153]

At the same time, the question of 'political reform' began, tentatively, to be discussed. 'Political science' was established as a recognised academic discipline in the early 1980s, and the first steps in empirical political research were made.[154] A major responsibility of the new discipline was to draw up proposals for 'political reform'. In fact, there was already broad consensus in the social sciences on the necessary changes. Economists, sociologists and political scientists were agreed that the essential task was to find a means of institutionalising and integrating autonomous, divergent interests within the framework of 'socialism' – whether they be enterprises, social groups and strata, or opinion groups. The conditions for this were suggested by a leading exponent of the new 'political science', Mihály Bihari.

Interests had to be allowed to emerge openly as clearly expressed 'political volitions', as competing ideologies. This required legal and organisational guarantees of 'democratic political equality'.[155] Only through open competition would interests become controllable. A further condition was the definition of clear areas of responsibility, which involved development of a form of separation of powers, between the 'economic basis' and the 'political system', enterprises and the state, which would ensure that 'the over-extensive policy should be forced back into its own sphere of validity, ensuring that the two social spheres, the political superstructure and the economic basis should both develop according to their own regularities'.[156] Inescapably, the issues raised first by the Czechoslovak 'spring' of 1968 re-emerge.

Conclusion

Economic reform has been the central issue on the political agenda of European communist regimes since the death of Stalin, yet it remains an item of 'unfinished business'. Accumulated evidence on the long-term unviability of the centralistic–directive economic model, manifested periodically in profound economic tensions or even crisis, has at various times driven communist leaderships to search for a way out, and economic experts have duly come forward with comprehensive proposals for a solution. Yet the problem was never merely technical–economic, but also had underlying political dimensions. Successive reform waves have been interrupted by political crises, or the fear of them. The first wave of economic reform, emerging most strongly in Hungary and Poland after Stalin's death, was strangled by the political impact of 1956; the second wave, unfolding across the Soviet bloc in the 1960s, was undermined by 1968. Economic reforms became dangerously associated with intolerable political tensions, threatening to sweep away the Party and the foundations of the political system itself. As a result, the 1970s saw the avoidance of the question of reform. In the Soviet Union under Brezhnev's increasingly torpid regime, economic problems were alleviated by windfall benefits from dramatic changes in the world prices of raw materials and fuels; in Eastern Europe, governments turned to the import of Western technology in the hope of injecting new life into their economies without undertaking radical systemic change in the methods of management. But in the 1980s, adverse economic conditions are once again forcing the issue of economic reform to the fore.

The key problems for the Soviet Union are the near-cessation of labour force growth and the vastly increased technical difficulty and economic cost of exploiting its natural resources; for Eastern Europe, the problem has become focused on external indebtedness, reflecting the failure of the strategy of modernisation through technology imports. But behind these problems and failures lie the fundamental systemic defects of the centralistic–directive model, which has been sustained, with only limited modifications, throughout the bloc: the lack of incentives to efficient use of resources, both material and human; the absence of a self-sustaining technological dynamism; the dead weight of an economic structure inherited from an earlier pattern of growth. With the unfolding of the 'third industrial revolution' of computer and electronic technology in Western capitalism, the task for the economies of the communist bloc has changed, it is argued, from merely 'catching-up' with capitalism, to keeping from falling even further behind.[1]

The problem has been described recently by a leading Soviet sociologist in explicitly systemic terms:

> it consists in the lagging of the system of production relations, and hence the mechanism of state management of the economy which is its reflection, behind the level of development of the productive forces. To put it in more concrete terms, it is expressed in the inability of this system to make provision for the full and sufficiently effective use of the labour potential and intellectual resources of society.[2]

In the Soviet Union, discussion of the state of the economy has taken on a new sense of urgency, as the political implications of long-term economic decline along present trends have become clear:

> Making the economy more dynamic, switching it to the lines of intensification, and boosting efficiency in every way are regarded as the crucial condition for the further development of Soviet society and the main line of social progress. Our country has no other alternative. The USSR's historical fortunes and the positions of socialism in the world depend directly on the successful pursuit of the envisaged line.[3]

For eastern Europe, it is not so much military power and international prestige as sheer political survival which is at stake. Since 1968, most regimes have relied on a tacit 'social compact' in order to sustain public calm and political stability, in which democratic and/or national aspirations have been traded off against personal material security and a steadily rising standard of living. The inability to satisfy domestic consumer aspirations was a major factor behind the Polish crisis of 1980–1. While that crisis was also a product of spectacular incompetence and mismanagement by the Gierek regime, the lessons drawn were general. Communist regimes were reminded of the fragility of their tenure – this includes the Soviet Union as well, where, in the course of the 1970s, consumer aspirations became a weighty political consideration for the leadership.[4]

The political imperatives of international status and domestic stability are thus beginning to generate a third wave of economic reform in the Soviet bloc. Past experience suggests that if this third attempt is to succeed, economic reform will have to be accompanied by political change. The central question upon which the present work has focused is whether the necessary political change can be contained within the framework of the communist one-party state. The political problem of economic reform involves first the possibility of reformulating the terms of legitimation in such a way as to continue to provide a justification for one-party rule in the context of the reformed economy; and second, the Party's ability to develop an alternative power base to the bureaucratic apparatus with which it has hitherto been inextricably entwined and which has been the main instrument of its rule.

(i) Economic Reform and Party Legitimation

The legitimation of the Party's monopoly of power has hitherto been derived from a pseudo-rationalistic, totalitarian concept of the 'social interest'. The Party, by virtue of its access to 'scientific' knowledge of the laws of history, claims to provide an 'objectively correct' definition of the 'social interest', which is both separate from, and superior to, the interest of individuals. This form of legitimation is intimately bound up with the centralistic–directive model of a planned economy. The Plan embodies the 'social interest'. Realisation of the 'social interest' is simply a matter of hierarchical organisation for the execution of centrally formulated 'social' objectives.

The use of the market is incompatible with the logic of this concept of socialism, since it represents an objective constraint on the assertion of the centre's political will, posing a challenge to the Party's absolute right to determine the 'social interest'. In practice, of course, the centralistic–directive model has not completely obliterated all market elements – consumers have been 'free' to exercise choice in the pattern of their expenditure, and labour has been allocated mainly through the wage system, rather than by political direction.[5] But the extent of state control over macroeconomic proportions and microeconomic decision-making has minimised the impact on central power of these restricted areas of choice. However, the extreme weakness of objective constraints on the assertion of political will in the economy led in practice to arbitrariness and irrationality. By excluding the objective constraints of economic forces, the centre also deprived itself of objective information. The poor economic performance which resulted undermines the ideological claim that this model can in fact realise the 'social interest' and thus the Party's legitimacy is ultimately under threat. A credibility gap opens up between the ideology and reality, and the danger is that the assertion of the 'social interest' in this model will come to be seen as a smokescreen behind which a self-appointed élite defends its own interests and privileged position at the expense of the general development and efficiency of the economy and the material welfare of society.

A radical alternative was presented by what we termed the 'Yugoslav model', maximising the use of the market with the joint aims of increased overall efficiency and a reduction in the power of the central bureaucracy. This model, it is claimed, can realise 'socialism' in the sense of giving the producers direct control of the means of production through the institution of self-management. But, as I argued in Part I, there are grounds for doubting whether this model of market predominance, even where the means of production are not formally in private ownership, can realise the substantive social goals which are the hallmark of a socialist system. Inflation, unemployment and cumulative inequality unrelated to actual work input seem to be inescapable problems for this model. The dominance of the private interests of the central bureaucracy, which this model aimed to eliminate, appears to be replaced by the dominance of group private interests in the self-managing enterprises. The maximalist, totalitarian concept, realised through subordination of individuals and groups, is replaced by a minimalist, pluralist concept, which consists only in the provision of a framework within which individuals and groups realise their own interests. If one-party rule has been sustained alongside an economy functioning along these lines in Yugoslavia, its justification has been in the maintenance of the independence and integrity of a deeply divided, centrifugal federation of nationalities against the external threat posed by the Soviet Union. But the legitimacy of the whole is profoundly challenged by the inability to take central decisions to rectify the dire economic problems which have accumulated – massive inflation, unemployment, regional inequalities and a huge hard-currency debt. The paralysis of the Party in the face of these problems could lead in turn to political disintegration.

Economic reform in Eastern Europe has been based on a third alternative, the combination of plan and market, which acknowledges the validity and importance of individual and group interests, while sustaining an ultimate commitment to a concept of the 'social interest'. I argued in Part I that the 'half-way' model of a planned economy with a regulated market mechanism is not an inconsistent compromise but a coherent recombination of elements in the two extremes. In Part II, chapter 5, I traced the intellectual process by which the totalitarian concept of the 'social interest' was challenged, and the regulated market model of reform put forward as an alternative, more rational and efficient means of attaining socialist objectives. The question in both Chapter 2 and Chapter 5 was whether this model has necessarily to be accompanied by democracy, understood as the political institutionalisation of competitive pluralism as the mechanism for defining the 'social interest'. This question is vital for the assessment of the possibility of economic reform in Eastern Europe, where one-party rule has to be taken as an unalterable political fact.

It is clear that democracy, as understood here, is logically incompatible with, and indeed superfluous to, the realisation of the 'social interest' in its totalitarian conception. It is hard to see how, in practice, democracy could be combined with the centralistic–directive model of a socialist economy. It was also argued in Chapter 2 that the modification of the concept of the 'social interest' embodied in the regulated-market economic model made democracy both logically and practically possible. But conclusive arguments could not be found for the functional *necessity* of democracy for a regulated-market model. The determination of the 'social interest' as a set of mutually consistent, ordered general and long-term goals appears to be feasible through either democratic processes and majority rule, or a self-appointed enlightened élite. There are advantages and disadvantages to each, as noted in Chapter 2. If democracy is to be preferred, it is on non-economic grounds as a good in itself.

The ideological problem posed by economic reform for communist one-party states is thus not that it makes the Party's position untenable, but that by opening up the prospect of democracy as an *option*, it undermines the logical basis for the Party's absolute claim to the necessity of its 'leading role' provided by the totalitarian concept of the 'social interest'. For East European regimes, the 'necessity' of the Party's 'leading role' is thus now revealed rather as contingent upon particular historical circumstances which brought the region under Soviet domination after the Second World War. The Party thus appears as merely the instrument of national subordination to a foreign power. This poses obvious, profound problems for its legitimation. The emphasis shifts from reference to the 'radiant future' of communism and the Party's infallible leadership towards that goal, to the more prosaic assertion of 'geopolitical reality' as the ultimate explanation of the Party's monopoly of power. But the bleak fatalism of this can be tempered by a supplementary 'covert mode' of legitimation,[6] in terms of the Party's practical competence as organiser of the provision of an acceptable level of mass social and consumer welfare, and its ability to act as a mediator between popular national aspirations and the dictates of Soviet domination.

Potentially, this form of legitimation of Party rule could be viable in certain circumstances. The legitimation of regimes is always a matter of both coercion and consent, of both material self-interest and moral commitment. The coercive aspect of rule – national subordination to the Soviet Union – could be significantly mitigated if this were shown to be not incompatible with the realisation of other objectives, such as material welfare and a stable, peaceful existence, which might be valued as highly as national independence. The long and traumatic historical experience of Eastern Europe, periodically devastated by war and economically underdeveloped, might serve to temper aspirations for independence, provided some hopes can be entertained of achieving these other goals. Thus economic reform could play a vital role in contributing to the reformulation of the terms of party legitimation, rather than undermining it. On one level, it is the means to achieving the promise of improved economic performance and material well-being; on another level, it represents an expression of the Party's willingness to take into account individual and group interests, and to subject its definition of the 'social interest' to the test of objective economic criteria. In this case, consent to party rule could become more than cynical resignation, insofar as the system was perceived as bringing tangible benefits to society as a whole and to individuals by relating material rewards, and hence inequalities, to economic rather than political criteria of merit. Participation need not be morally compromised 'collaboration' but responsible contribution to testing the limits of the possible.

This pattern of legitimation is not put forward either as particularly desirable in itself or as preferable to democratic legitimation. The intention is merely to elaborate its possibilities as a viable basis for sustaining political stability within the framework of a one-party state, and thus to demonstrate that on ideological grounds, economic reform is possible.

(ii) Rebuilding the Party's Power Base

The problem of reform lies not so much in the goal itself as in the process of reaching it. The difficulties were illustrated in the case studies of Czechoslovakia and Hungary in Chapters 3–7. The practical politics of transition from the centralistic–directive model to the regulated market model have yet to be successfully mastered. The nub of the problem lies in reforming both the style and institutional structures through which the Party in practice exercises its 'leading role'. The monolithic concept of the 'social interest' around which the centralistic model was constructed was realised through a unified, hierarchical bureaucratic apparatus, in which the Party and State were inextricably intertwined. The regulated market model must involve the break-up of the unified hierarchy, with the achievement of enterprise autonomy, the dismantling of the branch ministries, restriction of the role of the State, and the establishment of a new relationship between the centre and the enterprises on the basis of stable and general 'rules of the game' providing a binding definition of the competence of each level.

The change from one model to another is inevitably conflict-ridden, and the transition is a time of acute uncertainty for all the political actors involved, with the disruption of the pattern of interests, expectations and behaviour habits which grew up around the centralistic model. The danger is that in the political uncertainty surrounding the process of realignment of interests around the new model, the Party will lose control, political disintegration will ensue, and the democratising potential opened up by the economic reform will come to the fore. The Party has to steer through the reefs of the transition period, avoiding both the Scylla of recentralisation and the Charybdis of democratic revolution. The ability to refashion the basis of political stability under continued Party rule requires the evolution of a mutually reinforcing combination of strong leadership with clear-sighted commitment to economic reform, the development of participatory mechanisms in inner-Party life and in Party–society relations as an alternative to hierarchical and bureaucratic rule, and the possibility to develop and sustain an underlying consensus on the limits of the possible.

The necessity of leadership commitment to reform is an obvious precondition for change within a centralised, hierarchical political system; whether a unified leadership commitment can be sustained through the transition period will be a major determinant of the ultimate successful implementation of reform. The Czechoslovak experience was largely conditioned by the failure to form such a leadership. The prevarications of the Novotný regime over the issue of economic reform were a product of its origins in, and continued links with the Stalinist past. The failure to come to grips with the legacy of the past was reflected in the rigidity of the regime's conception of its legitimacy, derived from Stalinist totalitarian ideology. It was unable to grasp economic reform as a component of rebuilding an appropriate legitimation for the post-Stalin era. Correspondingly, the style of rule was characterised by an increasingly ineffectual coercive centralism, which served to alienate the intelligentsia, and deepened the propensity of economic experts to see political reform as an essential prerequisite of economic reform. Economic reform thus fed into the general political crisis of the Novotný regime, in which a wide range of disaffected élite and intellectual groups made increasingly radical demands. The formation of a new Party leadership in 1968 came too late to allow the political crisis to be defused and contained within the framework of Party rule.

In Hungary, the legacy of the Stalin era was dealt with by the Kádár regime which emerged after 1956. It was a new regime, and one which proved able to understand the meaning of the 1956 revolution as a product of Stalinist politics, rather than of Nagy's 'liberalism'. It thus distanced itself from Stalinism. Unlike the Novotný regime, it was able to base its legitimation on the contrast between its policies and style of rule with Stalinism. Economic reform was thus grasped as a component part of rebuilding its legitimacy, not as a disruptive or subversive intrusion.

The ability of a Party leadership to sustain its commitment to reform in the process of its implementation raises a new and different set of political problems. The major obstacle is the hierarchical bureaucratic institutional framework on which the leadership depends, but which is inextricably linked to the old ideology and the old economic system, and is the central mechanism for structuring social interests. The bureaucratic apparatus is not merely a conservative force in itself, opposed to economic reform as a fundamental threat to its own power, prestige and privilege, but can also claim to represent wider social interests affected by reform: economic reform will inevitably lead to a reallocation of resources between economic sectors and groups, away from the traditionally favoured heavy industries towards new technological branches, consumer goods and agriculture. The bureaucratic economy extended protection to a large part of the industrial working class employed in the traditional branches and in large uneconomic enterprises. In defending its own position, the bureaucratic apparatus can also claim to be defending the security of these workers. This has a powerful emotional appeal, since the workers in the traditional branches, such as metallurgy, mining and heavy engineering form the mythologised 'vanguard' of the working class which the Party has hitherto identified as the backbone of its political support.

The process of separating the Party from the bureaucracy thus also involves a reconceptualisation of the specific content of the 'social interest', in the sense that the 'social interest' can no longer be dominated by the interests of this traditional working class if economic reform is to be implemented. It must instead represent a balanced combination of diverse groups in socialist society, given at least equal status with the traditional working class: technical experts and intellectuals, 'socialist entrepreneurs' and skilled workers in modern factories, agricultural producers, workers in the tertiary sector. If the bureaucratic hierarchy is to be dismantled in the process of economic reform, then the Party must find new channels through which to relate to a pluralistic socialist society. This was the basic objective of the Czechoslovak Action Programme of 1968. The grip of the Party's own bureaucratic apparatus on inner-Party life was to be broken by the revitalisation of inner-Party debate and the correspondingly enhanced status of party elective bodies, which would represent the diverse currents of opinion and interest within the wider society. More open debate within the Party also implied resolution of differences by genuine majority rule, thus redressing the balance of emphasis in the organisational principle of 'democratic centralism' towards more democratic procedures in inner-Party life, away from the manipulated unanimity characteristic of the traditional mode of operation.

A similar revitalisation of the state representative bodies and of interest groups was put forward in the Action Programme, and has been part of Hungarian Party policy for some years. The purpose of political reform in these areas, however, can only be supplementary, or at best, complementary to the Party's leading role. For some individuals and groups this limitation may serve as a disincentive to participate, and inevitably the range of social interests and opinions represented would be restricted. But in practice, this need not completely undermine the usefulness of such bodies as a 'safety valve', as an additional mechanism for checking on the work of the state apparatus, as a means for incorporating broader segments of society and ambitious individuals into politics, and as an alternative source of information on social interests and popular morale.

The problem of political reform for the Party is to contain the limits of pluralism, to strike a fine balance between debate, conflict and the devolution of authority, and Party discipline, unity and ultimate control of the 'commanding heights' of power. The achievement of this balance will depend heavily on informal factors. Sustaining inner-Party discipline alongside freer internal debate and conflict will place extraordinary demands on the political skills of the leadership in building alliances and devising coherent compromises. It also depends on the provision of adequate incentives for the membership to comply with Party discipline in the interests of unity. This would be a function of the natural authority of the Party leadership, combined with the sanction of loss of privilege and status which exclusion from the Party would entail. Inner-Party unity in turn will be an essential condition of the Party continuing to exercise its 'leading role' *vis-à-vis* society, but this will also depend on the willingness of society, as represented in the elective organs of the State and interest groups, to accept the limits of debate as defined by the Party. This implies a strong shared perception or consensus on the limits of the possible. The Party has certain instruments at its disposal which can be used to sustain such a consensus – the use of the *nomenklatura* system, and the threat of coercion justified ultimately in terms of avoiding Soviet intervention. But national historical experience also plays a large part in the generation of social consensus on the limits of the possible.

In the circumstances of Czechoslovakia in 1968, the Party failed to establish such a consensus. This seems to be explicable by two factors: first, the accumulation of deep, unresolved tensions throughout the 1960s discredited Party authority, and produced a split within the Party itself as to the limits of desirable reform. In 1968, attempts to contain the pressures for political pluralisation appeared too easily as a return to Novotnýite coercion. Second, the fact that the Czechoslovak Communist Party achieved a convincing 38 per cent of the vote in the free elections of 1946 appears to have contributed to an illusion among some Party reformists that the Party could sustain its 'leading role' without coercion, through an open, democratic process. The quite widespread and genuine pro-Soviet sentiment after the Second World War, and the fact that the establishment of the communist monopoly of power had been achieved without overt and direct Soviet intervention seems to have fostered a certain lack of clarity on the part of some Party reformers about the nature of Soviet interests and perceptions. This was compounded by the confusing signals given by Moscow in the pre-invasion period of 1968 as to the limits of acceptable change, while the sporadic heavy-handed 'warnings' by the Soviet, East German and Polish leaderships polarised and radicalised the situation, undermining the moral viability of a compromise solution.[7]

In Hungary, by contrast, the Kádár regime began the process of reform on the basis of a society which had no illusions about the possibility of democracy. In one respect, this was an advantage from the regime's point of view, since it averted the danger of politicisation of reform as happened in Czechoslovakia. But it has also had the disadvantageous long-term effect of engendering profound scepticism, apathy and indifference in the population towards any form of positive political commitment. If Dubček's problem was one of containing a massive impetus to participate, Kádár's has become one of injecting life into the quite wide-ranging opportunities for political activity. The population participates in politics only to the extent of making demands for higher wages and the protection of its standard of living, and cannot be persuaded of the value of time spent in political activity, as compared with the more certain and tangible benefits of energy and effort expended in supplementary earning activity in the 'second economy'. Popular indifference has thus become a major obstacle to change, since further development of the economic reform in the current conditions of austerity cannot be guaranteed to produce immediate economic benefits for the population. On the one hand, the Party appears to hope that further political reforms will engender greater interest and enthusiasm for political participation, and produce a sense of shared responsibility for the state of the country and realism in popular expectations. On the other hand, the mounting social tensions in evidence in this period of economic austerity may produce conflicts which cannot be resolved through the participatory mechanisms provided, and which threaten to blow apart the carefully nurtured consensus on the limits of the possible which have sustained the reforms so far. In this situation, the strength, coherence and unity of the leadership will once again be decisive. Some uncertainty exists here too, with the imminent departure of János Kádár from the political scene. The regime has reasserted its commitment to reform, and it is unlikely that any possible successor to Kádár will either wish, or be able to effect a restoration of traditional centralistic forms of economic or political management. But there is room for doubt about the leadership's capacity to sustain a consistent course in the economic reform, while meeting at least the main social expectations. In the face of the threat of political disintegration, economic reform may well again be sacrificed.

The role of the Soviet Union in the future development of reform in Hungary, and throughout the bloc, will be vital. The Soviet response to reform in Eastern Europe has been described as conditioned by the twin objectives of viability and control.[8] The economic viability of Eastern Europe in the 1980s has become at least as urgent a problem for the Soviet Union as it was in the early 1950s. The economic problems of the region pose a serious challenge to political stability, and hence to the maintenance of Soviet control, and have become a heavy burden on the Soviet economy itself.[9] The Soviet Union must therefore have a strong interest in promoting economic reform. The formation of the new Soviet leadership under Mikhail Gorbachev presents an opportunity for reform in the Soviet Union itself. The generational change in the leadershhip, and the massive personnel turnover throughout the apparatus which has accompanied it,[10] open the way for a radical change of course, and raise the possibility of a concerted bloc-wide impetus towards reform which would greatly enhance the chances of its success in each individual case. Whether the opportunity will be grasped will depend on the outcome of the struggle for reform at present underway in the Soviet Union. At the time of writing, the outcome of that struggle is unclear.

Notes and References

Most of the works to which reference is made here are listed in full detail in the Bibliography. To avoid unnecessary duplication therefore publication details have been omitted from these notes, but readers who wish to pursue the references for themselves will find all the detail they require in the Bibliography. Publication details are given in the notes for works which are not included in the Bibliography. Please bear in mind that the Bibliography is itself in three sections – General, Czechoslovakia and Hungary.

Introduction

1. See Bauman, *Socialism: the Active Utopia*; Berki, *Socialism*.
2. Quoted by Selucký, 'Marxism and Self-management' in Vanek (ed.), *Self-management*, p. 47.

1 Economics

1. von Mises, 'Economic Calculation in the Socialist Commonwealth' in Hayek (ed), *Collectivist Economic Planning*, p. 106.
2. von Mises in Gregory and Stuart, *Soviet Economic Structure and Performance*, p. 308.
3. Ibid.
4. Hayek, 'The Price System as a Mechanism for Using Knowledge' in Bornstein (ed.), *Comparative Economic Systems*, 1st edn, p. 40.
5. Ibid, pp. 41–2.
6. Ibid, p. 44.
7. Ibid, p. 45.
8. Lange and Taylor, *On the Economic Theory of Socialism* (edited by Lippincott).
9. Ibid, p. 77 (emphasis in original omitted).
10. Ibid, p. 78.
11. Ibid, p. 82.
12. Ibid, pp. 96–7.
13. Hayek, 'Socialist Calculation: the "Competitive Solution"' in *Economica*, vol VII, p. 131.
14. Ibid, p. 136.
15. Ibid, p. 131–2.
16. Ibid, p. 141.
17. Bergson, 'Market Socialism Revisited' in Vanek (ed.), *Self-management*, p. 302.
18. Hayek, 'Socialist Calculation', p. 141.
19. Bergson, 'Market Socialism Revisited', p. 303.
20. Hayek, 'Socialist Calculation', p. 145.
21. Lange and Taylor, *On the Economic Theory of Socialism*, p. 109.
22. Horvat, 'An Institutional Model of a Self-managed Socialist Economy' in Vanek (ed.), *Self-management*, pp. 137–8.

23. See Županov, 'The Yugoslav Enterprise' in Bornstein (ed.), *Comparative Economic Systems* (3rd edn) 1974.
24. Selucký, *Marxism and Self-management*. See also Selucký, 'The Relationship Between Political and Economic Reform in Eastern Europe and in Czechoslovakia in Particular' in Kusin (ed.), *The Czechoslovak Reform Movement 1968*.
25. Horvat, 'An Institutional Model', p. 133.
26. See Neuberger and Duffy, *Comparative Economic Systems*, chapter 9.
27. Ibid, pp. 108–9.
28. Horvat, 'An Institutional Model', p. 133.
29. Ibid, p. 134.
30. See Milenkovitch, *Plan and Market in Yugoslav Economic Thought*; Shackleton, 'Is Workers' Self-management the Answer?'.
31. Horvat, 'An Institutional Model', p. 136.
32. Ibid.
33. See note 9 above.
34. See Hayek, *The Road to Serfdom*, p. 27.
35. Shackleton, 'Is Workers' Self-management the Answer?', p. 56.
36. Ibid, p. 54.
37. Horvat, 'An Institutional Model', p. 128.
38. See Neuberger and Duffy, *Comparative Economic Systems*, p. 253.
39. Ibid, p. 253.
40. See Vanek (ed.), *The General Theory of Labour-managed Market Economies* (Ithaca and London: Cornell University Press,, 1970).
41. Meade, 'The Theory of Labour-managed Firms and of Profit Sharing', p. 408.
42. Brus, *Socialist Ownership and Political Systems*.
43. Ibid, pp. 32–62.
44. Brus, *The Economics and Politics of Socialism*, p. 7.
45. Ibid, p. 50.
46. Ibid, p. 56.
47. Ibid, p. 53.
48. Brus, *Socialist Ownership*, p. 88.
49. Ibid.
50. See Neuberger and Duffy, *Comparative Economic Systems*, Chap. 9.
51. Ibid, p. 108.
52. Brus, *Economics and Politics of Socialism*, pp. 57–8.
53. Ibid, p. 58.
54. Ibid.
55. Ibid.
56. Ibid, p. 59.
57. Ibid, p. 62.
58. Brus, *Socialist Ownership*, p. 69.
59. Ibid, p. 71.
60. Ibid, pp. 68–70.

2 Politics

1. Hayek, *The Road to Serfdom*.

2. Ibid, p. 44.
3. Ibid, p. 46.
4. Ibid, p. 45.
5. See Chapter I, pp. 9–10.
6. See Hayek, 'Socialist Calculation: the Competitive "Solution"' in *Economica*, vol. VII; no 26 (May 1940) pp. 145–6.
7. Hayek, *The Road to Serfdom*, p. 45.
8. Ibid, p. 46.
9. Ibid.
10. Ibid.
11. Ibid, p. 48.
12. Ibid, p. 51.
13. Ibid.
14. See Berlin, 'Two Concepts of Liberty'.
15. Hayek, *The Road to Serfdom*, p. 53.
16. Ibid, p. 52.
17. Ibid, p. 19, footnote.
18. Carritt, 'Liberty and Equality', p. 133.
19. See Friedman, *Free to Choose*
20. Friedman, *Capitalism and Freedom*, p. 14.
21. MacPherson, *Democratic Theory*, p. 146.
22. Quoted by Carritt, 'Liberty and Equality', p. 140.
23. Ibid, p. 139.
24. MacPherson (ed.), *Property*, p. 3.
25. Ibid, p. 5.
26. See Horvat, 'An Institutional Model of a Self-managed Socialist Economy', p. 128.
27. See Chapter I, pp. 16–17.
28. See Lively, 'Pluralism and Consensus'.
29. See Hayek, *The Road to Serfdom*, p. 52.
30. Similar point is made by Lindblom, *Politics and Markets*, p. 266.
31. Hayek, *The Road to Serfdom*, p. 46.
32. This point is especially relevant to smaller European democracies – see Heisler (ed.) *Politics in Europe*; Steiner, *Politics in Austria*; Lijphart, 'Consociational democracy'.
33. MacPherson (ed.), *Property*, p. 5.
34. See Chapter I, p. 24; and Brus, *Socialist Ownership and Political Systems*, pp. 68–70.
35. Brus, *Socialist Ownership*, pp. 200–1.
36. Ibid, pp. 195–9.
37. Ibid, pp. 191–5.
38. See Woodall (ed.) *Policy and Politics in Gierek's Poland*.
39. See Lively, 'Pluralism and Consensus', p. 195.
40. Ibid, p. 198.
41. See Brunner, 'Legitimacy Doctrines and Legitimation Procedures in East European Systems'.
42. Brus, 'Political Pluralism and Markets in Communist Systems'.
43. Derived from Dahl's list in *Polyarchy*, pp. 2–3.
44. Skilling, 'Group Conflict and Political Change'.

3 The Political Preconditions of Reform

1. See Rupnik, 'The Czech Socialists and the Nation (1848–1918)'.
2. Young, *Czechoslovakia: Keystone of Peace and Democracy*, pp. 117–8.
3. Rothschild, *East Central Europe Between the Two World Wars*, p. 86.
4. See Taborsky, 'The Roots of Czechoslovak Democracy'; Taborsky, *Czechoslovak Democracy at Work*; and Seton-Watson, *History of the Czechs and Slovaks*.
5. Skilling, 'Revolution and Continuity in Czechoslovakia 1945–1948', p. 377; and Hapala, 'Political Parties in Czechoslovakia 1918–38', p. 131.
6. Skilling, 'The Formation of a Communist Party in Czechoslovakia'.
7. Skilling, 'The Comintern and Czechoslovak Communism 1921–1929'.
8. Ibid, p. 245.
9. Skilling, 'Revolution and Continuity in Czechoslovakia', p. 377.
10. See Berend and Ránki, *The European Periphery and Industrialisation 1780–1914*.
11. The plight of the peasantry was exposed by literary and social commentators of the 1930s, for example, Illyés, *The People of the Puszta*.
12. Balassa, *The Hungarian Experience in Economic Planning*, p. 25. See also Gati, 'Hungary: the Dynamics of Revolutionary Transformation'; and Berend and Ránki, *Hungary: A Century of Economic Development*.
13. Janos, *The Politics of Backwardness in Hungary 1825–1945*, p. 194.
14. Ibid, p. 199.
15. Schöpflin, 'Hungary: An Uneasy Stability', p. 133.
16. Ibid.
17. Ibid, p. 134.
18. Ibid, also Janos, *Politics of Backwardness*, p. 212.
19. On the peasant parties see Király, 'Peasant Movements in the Twentieth Century' in Held (ed.) *The Modernisation of Agriculture: Rural Transformation of Hungary 1848–1975*, and Ionescu, 'Eastern Europe'.
20. Fejtő, 'Hungarian Communism', pp. 184–7. See also Ignotus, 'Hungary 1966'.
21. Gati, 'The Democratic Interlude in Post-war Hungary', p. 100.
22. Ibid, p. 106.
23. Ibid, p. 104.
24. Suda, *Zealots and Rebels: A History of the Ruling Communist Party of Czechoslovakia*, p. 225.
25. On this period, see Skilling, 'Revolution and Continuity in Czechoslovakia'; Kusin, 'Czechoslovakia'; Eliáš and Netík, 'Czechoslovakia'; Bloomfield, *Passive Revolution*; Myant, *Socialism and Democracy in Czechoslovakia 1945–48*.
26. Schöpflin, 'Hungary' in McCauley (ed.) *Communist Power in Europe*, p. 96.

27. Ibid, p. 99.
28. Ibid.
29. See Gati, 'The Democratic Interlude'.
30. See Löbl, *Sentenced and Tried*. pp. 24–32.
31. Kusin, 'Czechoslovakia', p. 82; see also Brzezinski, *The Soviet Bloc*, pp. 58–64.
32. Tigrid, 'The Prague Coup of 1948: The Elegant Takeover'. See also Skilling, 'The Break-up of the Czechoslovak Coalition 1947–1948'.
33. See Schöpflin, 'Hungary', in McCauley (ed.) *Communist Power in Europe*; also Kovrig, *Communism in Hungary*, chapters 7–9.
34. See Schöpflin, 'Hungary'.
35. Balassa, *The Hungarian Experience*, p. 26. See also Berend and Ránki, *Hungary: A Century of Economic Development*.
36. See Löbl, *Sentenced and Tried*, pp. 20–32.
37. See Šik, 'The Economic Impact of Stalinism', pp. 2–3.
38. Spulber, *The Economics of Communist Eastern Europe*, p. 49.
39. Ibid, p. 89.
40. Ibid, chapter 7, See also Völgyes 'Dynamic Change: Rural Transformation 1945–75' in Held (ed.) *Modernisation of Agriculture*; Donáth, *Reform and Revolution, the Transformation of Hungary's Agriculture*.
41. Quoted in Spulber, *Economics of Communist Eastern Europe*, pp. 288–9.
42. Brus, 'Stalinism and the "People's Democracies"', p. 245.
43. Gadó, 'The Development of Planning and Management Methods in Hungary'.
44. Berend, 'On the Mechanism of Economic Planning' in Berend and Ránki, *Underdevelopment and Economic Growth: Studies in Hungarian Economic and Social History*, p. 259.
45. Selucký, *Economic Reforms in Eastern Europe*, pp. 81–82.
46. See Kouba, 'The Development of the Structure of the Czechoslovak Economy'.
47. Michal, *Central Planning in Czechoslovakia*, p. 198.
48. See Ulč, 'Pilsen: the Unknown Revolt'; and Duchaček, 'New Course or No Course?'.
49. Balassa, *The Hungarian Experience*, p. 32.
50. Berend, 'On the Mechanism' in Berend and Ránki, *Underdevelopment and Economic Growth*, p. 263.
51. Péter's seminal work was published in *Társadalmi Szemle*, August–September 1954.
52. Péter, 'On the Planned Central Control and Management of the Economy', p. 27.
53. Balassa, *The Hungarian Experience*, p. 33.
54. Berend and Ránki, *Hungary: A Century of Economic Development*, p. 202.
55. Quoted by Lomax, *Hungary 1956*, p. 37.
56. Nagy, *On Communism: In Defence of the 'New Course'*, p. 54.
57. Bognár, 'Economic Reform, Development and Stability in Hungary', p. 27.
58. Fejtő, *La Tragédie Hongroise*, p. 191.

59. Suda, *Zealots and Rebels*, p. 237.
60. Ibid.
61. Kaplan, 'Zamyšlení nad politickými procesy: 3', p. 1054.
62. See Brzezinski, *The Soviet Bloc*, p. 92.
63. Aczél and Meray, *The Revolt of the Mind*, p. 253; the fullest account of the trials in Hungary by a victim is Szász, *Volunteers for the Gallows*. The official Hungarian account of the Rajk trial at the time was *Lázsló Rajk and His Accomplices Before the People's Court* (Budapest: 1949).
64. Suda, *Zealots and Rebels*, p. 233.
65. Ibid.
66. See Pelikán (ed.) *The Czechoslovak Political Trials 1950–54*, pp. 75–6.
67. Suda, *Zealots and Rebels*, p. 241.
68. See Skilling, 'Stalinism and Czechoslovak Political Culture', p. 270.
69. Kusin, *Political Grouping in the Czechoslovak Reform Movement*, p. 183.
70. Pelikán (ed.) *The Czechoslovak Political Trials*, p. 249.
71. Ibid, pp. 249–77.
72. Mencl and Ouředník, 'Jak to bylo v lednu: 3', p. 19.
73. Golan, 'Antonin Novotný: the Sources and Nature of His Power', p. 435. See also Feierabend, 'The Gottwald Era in Czechoslovakia'.
74. Vaculík, 'Culture and the Party in Czechoslovakia', p. 18.
75. Taborsky, *Communism in Czechoslovakia*, p. 130. See also Skilling, 'Czechoslovakia'.
76. See Bloomfield, *Passive Revolution*.
77. Medvedev, *Khrushchev: the Years in Power*, pp. 2–3.
78. Mlynář, *Nightfrost in Prague*, p. 65.
79. Ibid, pp. 65–6.
80. Mencl and Ouředník, 'Jak to bylo v lednu: 2', p. 13.
81. Golan, 'Antonin Novotný', pp. 245–6.
82. Mlynář, *Nightfrost in Prague*, p. 66.
83. Taborsky, *Communism in Czechoslovakia*, p. 116.
84. Mencl and Ouředník, 'Jak to bylo v lednu: 3', p. 18.
85. Ibid.
86. Mencl and Ouředník, 'Jak to bylo v lednu: 2', p. 13.
87. Skilling, *Czechoslovakia's Interrupted Revolution*, p. 30.
88. See Pelikán (ed.) *The Czechoslovak Political Trials*, p. 149.
89. Ibid, pp. 218–9.
90. See Eliáš and Netík, 'Czechoslovakia', pp. 243–5.
91. Pelikán (ed.) *The Czechoslovak Political Trials*, p. 150.
92. Mencl and Ouředník, 'Jak to bylo v lednu: 3', pp. 19–20.
93. Skilling, *Czechoslovakia's Interrupted Revolution*, p. 33.
94. Ibid, p. 34.
95. Ibid.
96. Mlynář, *Nightfrost in Prague*, pp. 41–2.
97. *Rudé právo*, 8 December 1956, translated in *East Europe*, 1957:1, p. 44.
98. Michal, *Central Planning*, p. 142. See also G. L., 'New Policy in Czechoslovakia'.

99. Duckaček, 'New Course or No Course', p. 15.
100. Skilling, *Czechoslovakia's Interrupted Revolution*, p. 31.
101. Michal, *Central Planning*, p. 142.
102. Ibid, p. 201.
103. Ibid, pp. 200–1.
104. Mlynář, *Nightfrost in Prague*, p. 49.
105. Taborsky, *Communism in Czechoslovakia*, pp. 446–9.
106. Mlynář, *Nightfrost in Prague*, p. 50.
107. *Rudé právo*, 29 January 1957.
108. Reported in *East Europe*, 1957:7, p. 41.
109. *East Europe*, 1957:9, p. 41.
110. Ibid (1958:1) p. 5.
111. See Breslauer, *Khrushchev and Brezhnev as Leaders*, Chap. 5.
112. Feiwel, *New Economic Patterns in Czechoslovakia*, p. 104.
113. Taborsky, *Communism in Czechoslovakia*, p. 107.
114. *Rudé právo*, 23 October 1957, translated in *East Europe*, 1957:12, p. 45.
115. Zauberman, *Industrial Progress in Poland, Czechoslovakia and East Germany 1937–62*, p. 8.
116. *Rudé právo*, 1 March 1958, translated in *East Europe*, 1958:4, p. 49.
117. Zauberman, *Industrial Progress*, pp. 8–10.
118. Šik, *Plan and Market Under Socialism*, p. 92.
119. Ibid, p. 93.
120. Zauberman, *Industrial Progress*, p. 10.
121. Breslauer, *Khrushchev and Brezhnev*, p. 74.
122. *Rudé právo*, 21 May 1958, translated in *East Europe*, 1958:7, p. 45.
123. *Rudé právo*, 14 August 1962, translated in *East Europe*, 1962:10.
124. Nagy, *On Communism*, p. 85.
125. Ibid, p. 66; and Fejtő, *History of the People's Democracies*, p. 38.
126. 'Imre Nagy's Secret Speech', translated with an introduction by B. Lomax, *Labour Focus on Eastern Europe*, vol. 8, no 1 (Summer 1985).
127. See Kecskemeti, *The Unexpected Revolution*; Vali, *Rift and Revolt in Hungary*; Lomax, *Hungary 1956*.
128. Fejtő, *History of the People's Democracies*, p. 193.
129. See Lewin, *Political Undercurrents in Soviet Economic Debates*; Cohen, *Bukharin and the Bolshevik Revolution*.
130. On the Soviet industrialisation debate, see Erlich, *The Soviet Industrialisation Debate 1924–28*.
131. Excerpts translated in Fejtő, *History of the People's Democracies*, pp. 193–201.
132. Balassa, *The Hungarian Experience*, p.36.
133. In Fejtő, *History of the People's Democracies*, p. 193.
134. Nagy, *On Communism*, especially chapter 9, 'Socialist Expanded Secondary Production'.
135. Lomax, *Hungary 1956*, p. 67.
136. Ibid.
137. Berend, in Berend and Ránki, *Underdevelopment and Economic Growth*, p. 265.

138. This refers to the perceptions of the general run of Party and state functionaries – the systemic nature of the defects was not obscured for certain economists at the time, notably György Péter.
139. Berend, in Berend and Ránki, *Underdevelopment and Economic Growth*, p. 266.
140. See Balassa, *The Hungarian Experience*, pp. 38–42; and Fejtő, *History of the People's Democracies*, pp. 206–10.
141. The most notable example of the research conducted in the period is Kornai, *Overcentralisation in Economic Administration*, researched in 1955 and the first half of 1956, published in Hungary in 1957, and in English translation in 1959.
142. Robinson, *The Pattern of Reform in Hungary*, p. 17.
143. Vass (Director of the Institute for Hungarian Party History) in 1966. Quoted by Robinson, *The Pattern of Reform*, p. 18.
144. Berend, in Berend and Ránki, *Underdevelopment and Economic Growth*, p. 267.
145. Kovrig, *Communism in Hungary*, p. 329.
146. See Robinson, *The Pattern of Reform*, pp. 18–21.
147. This interpretation is strongly argued by Berend, *Gazdasági Útkeresés 1956–1965*.
148. Kovrig, *Communism in Hungary*, p. 340.
149. Vali, 'Hungary since 1956'.
150. Zala, '1958–67: The Economic Trends of a decade', p. 139.
151. Kovrig, *Communism in Hungary*, p. 240–1. Further sources on recollectivisation are Donáth, and Völgyes, (see note 40).
152. Robinson, *The Pattern of Reform*, p. 50 (footnote).
153. Kovrig, *Communism in Hungary*, p. 343.
154. Vali, 'Hungary since 1956'.
155. Kovrig, *Communism in Hungary*, p. 344.
156. Gadó, 'The Development of Planning and Management Methods'.
157. Hetényi, 'Salient Features in the Development of National Economic Planning in Hungary'.
158. See Robinson, *The Pattern of Reform*, p. 22.
159. Vajda, 'Economic Science in Hungary and the "Acta Oeconomica"', p. 3.
160. Kornai, 'Economic Systems Theory and General Equilibrium Theory', p. 299.
161. Berend, 'Thirty Years of Hungarian Socialist Economic Policy', p. 171.
162. Berend, 'Ten Years After: Instead of a Balance Sheet', p. 49.
163. Berend, 'Thirty Years', p. 174.

4 The Decision to Reform

1. Tucker, 'Stalinism as Revolution from Above' in Tucker (ed.) *Stalinism: Essays in Historical Interpretation*, p. 102.
2. A similar argument is presented convincingly on the basis of a comparison of the Soviet, Chinese and Yugoslav cases by Azrael, 'Varieties of Destalinisation' in Johnson (ed.) *Change in Communist*

Systems, pp. 135–52, esp. p. 141.

3. See Montias, 'A Plan for All Seasons', in *Survey*, no 51, April 1962, p. 68. A useful discussion on the nature of economic development from the late 1950s is provided by Rendl and Kubík, 'K vývoji naší ekonomiky v posledních letech', pp. 1–12.
4. See 'Current Developments: Czechoslovakia', *East Europe*, vol. IX; no 8 (August 1960) p. 35.
5. See 'Zákon o třetím pětiletém plánu rozvoje národního hospodářství ČSSR' in *Plánované hospodářství*, vol. XIII, no 12 (December 1960).
6. United Nations/Secretariat of the Economic Commission for Europe *The European Economy in 1961*, Chapter 2, Table 8, p. 6. (This publication is produced annually; references below to further editions will be abbreviated to UN/ECE and the year covered in the survey).
7. *Statistická ročenka ČSSR 1969* (Prague: Federální Statistický Úřad ČSSR/Nakladatelství technické literatury 1969) p. 31.
8. UN/ECE 1961, Chapter 2, Table 8, p. 6.
9. Ibid, p. 21.
10. *Statistická ročenka ČSSR 1969*, p. 412.
11. UN/ECE 1962, Chapter 1, p. 14.
12. *Statistická ročenka ČSSR 1969*, p. 409.
13. See Montias, 'A Plan for All Seasons', p. 66.
14. UN/ECE 1962, Chapter 1, Table 2, p. 4. (NB: *Statistická ročenka ČSSR 1969* indicates 6 per cent and 4.2 per cent growth of industrial labour productivity in 1961 and 1962 respectively.)
15. Ibid, p. 22.
16. Montias, 'A Plan for All Seasons', p. 67.
17. *Statistická ročenka ČSSR 1969*, p. 31.
18. Ibid; see also UN/ECE 1964, Chapter 1, p. 16.
19. UN/ECE 1963, Chapter 1, p. 10.
20. Bernášek, 'The Czechoslovak Economic Recession 1962–65'.
21. Montias, 'A Plan for All Seasons', p. 70.
22. UN/ECE 1964, Chapter 1, p. 14.
23. 'O výhledech dalšího rozvoje naší socialistické společnosti', special supplement, *Rudé právo*, 14 August 1962. See also Mlynář, 'Socialistická demokracie a problémy řízení', p. 1048.
24. *Rudé právo*, 7 December 1962; see also interview with Novotný, 'President Novotný Denies Differences with Russia on De-Stalinisation', *The Times*, 12 June 1963, p. 10.
25. UN/ECE 1965, Chapter 1, p. 3; see also Ignotus, 'Hungary: Existence and Coexistence'.
26. Montias, 'A Plan for All Seasons', p. 68.
27. UN/ECE 1963, Chapter 1, pp. 53 and 55; see also Müller and Singer, 'Hungary: Can the New Course Survive?', p. 34.
28. UN/ECE 1961, Chapter 2, p. 10.
29. UN/ECE 1962, Chapter 1, p. 7.
30. Ibid.
31. Zala, '1958–1967: The Economic Trends of a Decade', p. 135.
32. Berend and Ránki, *The Hungarian Economy in the Twentieth*

Century, p. 235.
33. UN/ECE 1962, Chapter 1, p. 21.
34. Ibid, p. 4.
35. UN/ECE 1963, Chapter 1, p. 13.
36. See Berend, 'On the Mechanism of Economic Planning' in Berend and Ránki, *Underdevelopment and Economic Growth*, p. 269.
37. UN/ECE 1963, Chapter 1, p. 3.
38. Fekete and Varga, 'Household Plot Farming of Cooperative Peasants in Hungary', pp. 353–4.
39. Berend and Ránki, *The Hungarian Economy*, Table 8:7, p. 270.
40. UN/ECE 1963, Chapter 1, p. 28.
41. Berend and Ránki, *The Hungarian Economy*, p. 271. See also Donáth, *Reform and Revolution: Transformation of Hungary's Agriculture*, pp. 302–13 and 317–33.
42. On peasant morale after recollectivisation, see Donáth, *Reform and Revolution*, pp. 333–40.
43. On Czechoslovak agricultural policy see the proceedings of the Central Committee plenum devoted to this subject in February 1961, *Rudé právo*, 12 February 1961; and 'Current Developments: Czechoslovakia' in *East Europe* vol X; no 8 (August 1961) p. 38.
44. Berend and Ránki, *The Hungarian Economy*, p. 232.
45. Donáth, *Reform and Revolution*, p. 341.
46. Berend and Ránki, *The Hungarian Economy*, p. 232.
47. UN/ECE 1963, Chapter 1, p. 13.
48. Fekete and Varga, 'Household Plot Farming'.
49. UN/ECE 1965, Chapter 1, p. 2.
50. *Statistical Pocketbook of Hungary 1967*, p. 35.
51. UN/ECE 1961, Chapter 2, p. 32, Table 20.
52. Zala, '1958–1967: Economic Trends', p. 136.
53. UN/ECE 1961, Chapter 2, p. 33.
54. Ibid, p. 32.
55. UN/ECE 1962, Chapter 1, p. 14; and Zala, '1958–1967: Economic Trends'.
56. Berend and Ránki, *The Hungarian Economy*, p. 240.
57. Zala, '1958–1967: Economic Trends'.
58. Berend and Ránki, *The Hungarian Economy*, p. 240.
59. See Medvedev, *Khrushchev: the Years in Power*, pp. 146–7.
60. See Taborsky, 'Political Developments in Czechoslovakia Since 1953', pp. 89–113; and Taborsky, 'Czechoslovakia's March to Communism', p. 40.
61. See Eliáš and Netík, 'Czechoslovakia', p. 243.
62. Pelikán (ed.) *Czechoslovak Political Trials 1949–1954*, pp. 218–19.
63. The source of this suggestion is the Albanian press comment on Barák's arrest. See Taborsky, 'Czechoslovakia: Out of Stalinism?', p. 7, footnote 13.
64. Golan, *The Czechoslovak Reform Movement*, p. 19.
65. See Eliáš and Netík, 'Czechoslovakia', p. 244.
66. Ibid, p. 245; and Golan, Czechoslovak Reform Movement, p. 19.

67. Reported by Duchaček 'Czechoslovakia: The Past Reburied', pp. 22–3.
68. Ibid. Quoted on p. 26.
69. See Golan, 'The Road to Reform', p. 13.
70. Eliáš and Netík, 'Czechoslovakia', p. 258.
71. See Steiner, *The Slovak Dilemma*, p. 113.
72. See Riveles, 'Slovakia: Catalyst of Crisis'; and Steiner, *The Slovak Dilemma*, Chapter 12.
73. Taborsky, 'Czechoslovakia: Out of Stalinism?'.
74. *Rudé právo*, 14 May 1963; see Golan, *The Czechoslovak Reform Movement*, p. 32; and Skilling, *Czechoslovakia's Interupted Revolution*, p. 46.
75. *Kultúrny život*, 5 April 1963; translated excerpts in *East Europe* vol. XII; part 7 (July 1963) pp. 27–9; see also Taborsky, 'Czechoslovakia: Out of Stalinism'.
76. 'Prague's Political Crisis', *East Europe*, vol. XII, no 7 (July 1963) p. 24.
77. Published in *Pravda* (Bratislava) 3 June 1963; translated excerpts, accompanied by the Party's official reply, published in *Rudé právo*, 15 June 1963, are to be found in *East Europe*, vol. XII; no 8 (August 1963) pp. 22–5.
78. See Steiner, *The Slovak Dilemma*, p. 117.
79. *Rudé právo*, 22 August 1963; see Golan, *Czechoslovak Reform Movement*, p. 47.
80. *Rudé právo*, 23 September 1963.
81. Golan, *Czechoslovak Reform Movement*, pp. 22–3.
82. The term was used by Rutland 'Ideology and Power in the Czechoslovak Political System'. See also, Hejzlar, 'Changes in the Czechoslovak Communist Party' in Kusin (ed.) *The Czechoslovak Reform Movement 1968*, p. 125.
83. Eliáš and Netík, 'Czechoslovakia', p. 269.
84. Golan, 'Antonin Novotoný: the Sources and Nature of his Power', pp. 421–41.
85. Mencl and Ouředník, 'Jak to bylo v lednu: 3', p. 13.
86. Mlynář, *Nightfrost in Prague*, p. 111.
87. Eliáš and Netík, 'Czechoslovakia', p. 269.
88. *Rudé právo*, 26 September 1963.
89. Mlynář, *Nightfrost in Prague*, pp. 124–5.
90. Ibid, p. 111.
91. 'Usnesení plenárního zasedání ÚV KSČ', *Rudé právo* 22 September 1963, pp. 1–2; see also Kolder, 'Komplexně řešit rozvoj naší ekonomiky'; Průsa, 'Řídící činnost státního aparátu'.
92. This group published a preliminary report on its findings in *Sociologický căsopis*, vol. II (1966) no 2, and its full report was published in Prague in 1966 – Richta *et al., Civilizace na rozcestí*. An English translation is *Civilisation at the Crossroads*.
93. Its report was published as Machonin *et al.*, *Změny v sociální struktuře Československa a dynamika sociálně politického vývoje*.

94. Mlynář, *Nightfrost in Prague*, p. 57.
95. Ibid, p. 62.
96. Ibid, p. 60.
97. See 'Proti dogmatismu za tvořivý rozvoj ekonomické vědy', parts I and II, *Hospodářské Noviny*, 8 and 15 November 1963; 'K otázkam řízení národního hospodářství, *Politická ekonomie*, vol. XII, no 3 (March 1964) and 'Politická organizace a právo při řízení národního hospodárství', *Pravník*, vol. CIII, nos 6 and 7, June and July 1964.
98. Klofáč, 'Jak je to s naší sociologie?' *Rudé právo*, 2 November 1963, p. 3.
99. Machonin and Večeřa, 'Z jednání stranických orgánů UV KSČ o sociologie v ČSSR'.
100. *Rudé právo*, 6 March 1964.
101. Mlynář, *Nightfrost in Prague*, p. 70.
102. Editorial, *East Europe*, vol. XIII, no 12 (December 1964).
103. J.F.N. Brown, *The New Eastern Europe*, p. 32. A similar view is held by Meier, 'Czechoslovakia: The Struggle for Reform', p. 26.
104. Novotný, 'Za rozkvět našich národů and další upěvnování jednoty lidu'; see Steiner, *The Slovak Dilemma*, p. 120.
105. On Hendrych, see Taborsky, *Communism in Czechoslovakia 1948–1960*, p. 114; on Koucký, see Eliáš and Netík, 'Czechoslovakia', p. 270.
106. On Císař, see Mlynář, *Nightfrost in Prague*, pp. 106–7.
107. Mlynář, *Nightfrost in Prague*, pp. 57 and 64.
108. Ibid, p. 70. A similar impression is given by Šik, 'The Economic Impact of Stalinism', in *Problems of Communism*, vol. XX, no 4 (September–October 1971) p. 9.
109. See Berend, 'Változások es folytonosságok; a gazdaságpolitika útja Magyarországon 1956–57 fordulója után', in Vass (ed.) *Válság es megújulás*, pp. 51–79.
110. Kovrig, *Communism in Hungary*, p. 320.
111. Meray, 'Genealogical Troubles', in *Survey*, no 40, January 1962, p. 110 (Speical issue: 'Hungary Five Years After').
112. Kovrig, *Communism in Hungary*, p. 333.
113. Ibid; see also Fejtő, 'Hungarian Communism', in Griffith (ed.) *Communism in Europe*, vol. I, pp. 211–19; Meray, 'The Sources of Power: The Origin and Development of the Party', in Aczél (ed.) *Ten Years After*; Vali, 'Hungary Since 1956: The Hungarian Road to Communism', in György (ed.) *Issues of World Communism* (Princeton, New Jersey: Van Nostrand, 1966); Sándor, 'Pártunk szervezeti fejlődésének nehány kérdése', pp. 37–47.
114. Kovrig, *Communism in Hungary*, p. 331.
115. Ibid, pp. 331–3. See also Robinson, *The Pattern of Reform in Hungary*, p. 31.
116. See Kovrig, *Communism in Hungary*, pp. 329–34.
117. See Fejtő, 'Hungarian Communism', pp. 197–8.
118. Ibid, p. 252
119. On Hungarian–Yugoslav relations in 1956, see, in addition to Fejtő,

'Hungarian Communism in Griffith (ed.) *Communism in Europe*, Brzezinski, *The Soviet Bloc*, pp. 233–8.

120. See Griffith, 'European Communism and the Sino–Soviet Rift' in Griffith (ed.) *Communism in Europe*, vol I, pp. 1–18; and Brzezinski, *The Soviet Bloc*, chapters 12 and 16; and Fejtő, *A History of the Peoples' Democracies*, p. 83.
121. Fejtő, (1974), p. 113.
122. Kovrig, *Communism in Hungary*, pp. 338–9.
123. Ibid, p. 353.
124. Ibid, Appendix 2, p. 335 and p. 448.
125. See Landy, 'Hungary: Pressures from Above', p. 31.
126. Fejtő, 'Hungarian Communism' in Griffith (ed.), *Communism in Europe*, p. 215, note 66; quoting Szántó, *Népszabadság*, 4 December 1962.
127. Landy, 'Hungary: Pressure from Above', p. 29.
128. Schreiber, 'Changes in the Leadership', pp. 120–1.
129. Ibid.
130. See Kovrig, *Communism in Hungary*, p. 350.
131. Ibid, p. 351.
132. Ibid, p. 352.
133. Ibid, p. 353.
134. Ibid, pp. 352–5.
135. Robinson, *Pattern of Reform*, p. 79.
136. On Kádár's personal political style see Savarius, 'Janos Kádár – Man and Politician'; Fehér, 'Kádárism as the Model State of Khrushchevism'; and Selucký, *Economic Reforms in Eastern Europe*.
137. *Pravda* (Moscow), 9 September 1962. For a discussion of the impact of this article, see Gamarnikow, *Economic Reforms in Eastern Europe*, pp. 45–6; and UN/ECE 1962, chapter 1:5, 'Reforms of Planning and Management', pp. 45–50.
138. Golan, 'The Road to Reform', p. 13.
139. See Selucký, *Economic Reforms*, p. 85.
140. Selucký, 'Lidé a plán', *Kulturní Tvorba*, 7 February 1963, p. 1.
141. Mišár, 'Frázemí naše plánování nezlepšíme', *Rudé právo*, 23 February 1963.
142. *British Embassy (Prague) Press Review*, no 47, 7 March 1963.
143. Golan, *Czechoslovak Reform Movement*, p. 27, note 1.
144. Novotný, 'Jednotně, celá strana, všichni pracující, za uskutečnění sjezdem stanovených cilů', p. 4.
145. Golan, *Czechoslovak Reform Movement*, p. 27; Stregel, 'Jde o soulad slov a činů'.
146. Šik, 'Překonat pozůstatky dogmatismu v politické ekonomie', p. 1030.
147. Šik, 'Problémy zdokonalení soustavy plánovitého řízení', p. 3.
148. Ibid.
149. Contribution to discussion at the Central Committee plenum, December 1963, *Rudé právo*, 22 December 1963, p. 4.
150. Ibid.
151. Ibid.

152. Ibid.
153. Ibid
154. Ibid.
155. See Kosta, 'The Main Features of the Czechoslovak Economic Reform', in Kusin (ed.) *The Czechoslovak Reform Movement 1968*, p. 180.
156. Šik, 'Nezastavit se v půli cesty o využívání socialistických zbožních vztahů', p. 3.
157. Kadlec, 'Kybernetické modelování v řízení národního hospodářství', p. 48.
158. Hájek, *Mýtus a realita ledna 1968*, p. 17; see also Šik, 'Economic impact of Stalinism' p. 9; and Mlynář, *Nightfrost in Prague*, p. 70.
159. Mlynář, *Nightfrost in Prague*, p. 105, suggests reasons of personal rivalry behind Kolder's and Černík's refusal to have Šik on the Party Presidium in 1968.
160. Mlynář makes some interesting observations on Kolder as a poorly educated, loyal and sincere party apparatchik, well-meaning but limited in understanding (*Nightfrost*, p. 127).
161. See *Rudé právo*, 6 April 1964, pp. 1–2.
162. Ibid, 29 May 1964, pp. 1–5.
163. Ibid.
164. Ibid, p. 3.
165. Ibid, 6 April 1964, p. 2.
166. Ibid.
167. Šik, 'O pravdě v ekonomice a politice a skutečních zajmech pracujících', pp. 4–5.
168. 'O návrhu zásad zdokonalení plánovitého řízení národního hospodářství', *Rudé právo*, 17 October 1964, pp. 3–4.
169. See Holesovsky, 'Czechoslovakia's Economic Debate', p. 14; Plachky, 'Lze vědecky plánovat?', especially p. 8.
170. Montias, 'Economic Reform in Perspective', p. 55.
171. See Staller, 'Czechoslovakia: The New Model of Planning and Management', p. 565; also Holesovsky, 'Prague's Economic Model', p. 16.
172. See Michal, 'The New Economic Model, pp. 66–67.
173. See Selucký, 'Ekonomické názory se vyjasňuje', pp. 150–3; and Korda 'O ekonomické vědě a vyuce'. Later post-invasion self-criticism on this was published by Korda and Moravčik, 'Reflections on the 1965–68 Czechoslovak Economic Reform', and Kýn, 'The Rise and Fall of Economic Reform in Czechoslovakia'.
174. See Bernášek, 'The Czechoslovak Economic Recession', p. 457.
175. See for example Šik, 'Pozůstatky dogmatismu'.
176. Proceedings published as 'Proti dogmatismu za tvořivý rozvoj ekonomické vědy', *Hospodářské noviny*, 8 and 11 November 1963.
177. Holesovsky, 'Czechoslovakia's Economic Debate'. This complaint was also made at the time by a senior Planning Commission official, Kohoutek, 'From General Discussion to Concrete Preparation for Improving the System of Planned Management', p. 32.
178. Novotný in *Rudé právo*, 29 May 1964, p. 1.

179. *Rudé právo*, 13 November 1964.
180. *Rudé právo*, 22 December 1964, p. 1.
181. Sokol, 'Uplatnění zbožních vztahů při řízení', p. 31.
182. Ibid, p. 36.
183. Komenda, 'Podminky fungování tržního mechanismu v socialistickém hospodářství', *Plánované hospodářství* vol XVII (1964); no 7.
184. See Kouba, 'The Development of the Structure of the Czechoslovak Economy', pp. 20–33; also Goldmann, 'Tempo růstu a opakující se výkyvy v ekonomice některých socialistických zemí', *Plánované hospodářství*, vol. XVII (1964) no 9, and 'Tempo růstu některých socialistických zemích a model řízení národního hospodářství' in the same journal, no 11. A translated summary of these two articles is Goldmann, 'Fluctuations and Trend in the Rate of Economic Growth in Some Socialist Countries', pp. 13–19.
185. See Selucký, *Economic Reforms in Eastern Europe*, p. 85.
186. See for example, Šik, 'Czechoslovakia's New System of Economic Planning and Management', pp. 15–21; Šik, 'Příspěvek k analýze hospodářského vývoje'. This criticism of Šik is also made by Korda and Moravčik, 'Reflections', pp. 45–6.
187. Šik, 'Budouci vyžáduje kritiku minulého', p. 3.
188. Novotný, *Rudé právo*, 3 January 1965, p. 1.
189. Lenárt, *Rudé právo*, 10 January 1965, translated as 'Improvement of the Organisation and Planned Management of the Economy', pp. 42–60. (The quotation is from page 45 of this translation). On Lenárt's views, see interview in *The Times*, 9 February 1965, p. 10.
190. See, for example, Šik in *Kulturní tvorba*. The point will be elaborated on at greater length in Chapter 5.
191. *Rudé právo*, 3 January 1965, p. 1.
192. Ibid.
193. Ibid; see also *Rudé právo*, 28 April 1964.
194. Šik in *Hospodářské noviny*, 14 February 1964, p. 3.
195. See, for example, Sokol 'Postavení plánu v nové soustavě'; and Krejčar and Tesar 'K úloze ceny v soustave plánovitého řízení'.
196. Orban, 'Plán – nebo zbožně-penežní vztahy?'.
197. Feiwel, *New Economic Patterns in Czechoslovakia*, p. 131.
198. See Kýn, 'O úloze plánu', pp. 23–31.
199. See Berend, *Gazdasági útkeresés 1956–65*, p. 452.
200. Ibid.
201. Reprinted in Nyers, *Gazdaságpolitikánk és a gazdasági mechanizmus reformja*.
202. Berend, *Gazdasági útkeresés 1956–65*, p. 453 (quoting Party archives).
203. Ibid.
204. Nyers, 'Az ötéves terv derekán', p. 19.
205. Reproduced in Nyers, *Gazdaságpolitikánk*.
206. See Gy. Ránki, *Magyarország gazdasága az első 3 éves terv időszakában*, (Budapest: Közgasdasági es Jogi Könyvkiadó, 1963); and I. Berend, *Gazdasági politika az első ötéves terv*

meginditásakor, (Budapest: Közgazdasági es Jogi Könyvkiadó, 1964). A brief outline of the content of these two works is provided by Robinson, *Pattern of Reform*, pp. 73–6.

207. See Robinson, *Pattern of Reform*, p. 76. On the literary revival in 1964, see Tikos, 'Hungary; Literary Renaissance'.
208. See Robinson, *Pattern of Reform*, p. 76.
209. *Népszabadság* 21 March 1964 – translated in Robinson, *Pattern of Reform*, p. 84. Also interestingly reproduced in the Slovak cultural weekly, *Kultúrny život*, 18 April 1964.
210. Népszabadság, 21 July 1964 – translated in Müller and Singer, 'Hungary: Can the New Course Survive?', p. 34.
211. Reports of lower-level dissent are given in Müller and Singer, 'Hungary', p. 37, and Landy, 'Hungary: Pressures', p. 28; and Meray, 'Sources of Power' p. 135.
212. Liberman, 'Terv, nyereség, prémium', *Társadalmi szemle*, vol. XIX (1964) no 12, pp. 107–8.
213. Berend, *Gazdasági Útkeresés*, p. 456.
214. See interview with Nyers, *Népszabadság*, 25 April 1965, translated in *New Hungarian Quarterly*, vol. VI, no 20 (1965) pp. 11–12.
215. See Robinson, *Pattern of Reform*, p. 86.
216. UN/ECE 1965, Chapter 1, p. 53, Table 28, and p. 55.
217. UN/ECE 1966, Chapter 2, p. 14, Table 5.
218. UN/ECE 1965, Chapter 1, p. 48.
219. See 'Current Developments: Hungary' in *East Europe*, vol. XIV, no 4 (April 1965) p. 46 and no 8 (August 1965) p. 21.
220. See 'Current Developments; Hungary' in *East Europe*, vol. XV, no 2 (February 1966) p. 48; and 'Hungary: Politics and Prices' in *East Europe*, no 3 (March 1966) pp. 29–30.
221. See Robinson, *Pattern of Reform*, pp. 88–9; also Kovács, 'The Establishment in Hungary' p. 2.
222. 'Current Developments: Hungary', *East Europe*, vol. XV, no 3 (March 1966) pp. 48–9; and *East Europe*, no 4 (April 1966) pp. 41–2.
223. *East Europe*, no 2 (February 1966) p. 49.
224. See *East Europe*, vol. XIV, no 3 (March 1965) pp 44–5; and no 4 (April 1965) p. 42.
225. Excerpts translated from *Kortárs*, December 1964, as Veres 'Alienation: A Hungarian View, in *East Europe*. The quotation here is from p. 26.
226. Quoted in 'Current Developments: Hungary', *East Europe*, vol. XIV, no 5 (May 1965) p. 45.
227. Kiss, 'Hungary's Economic Situation', p. 21.
228. See Robinson, *Pattern of Reform*, p. 85.
229. Kovrig, *Communism in Hungary*, p. 364.
230. This point is especially emphasises by Berend, *Gazdasági Útkeresés*, pp. 457–9 *passim*.
231. *A Magyar Szocialista Munkáspárt határozatai és dokumentumai 1963–66* (Budapest: Kossuth Kiadó, 1978) 2nd edn, pp. 234–9.

232. Ibid.
233. Berend, *Gazdasági Útkeresés*, p. 458.
234. *A Magyar Szocialista*, p. 239.
235. Bognár, 'Overall Direction and Operation of the Economy', p. 31.
236. Péter, 'On the Planned Central Control and Management of the Economy', p. 42.
237. Péter, 'Az egyszemelyi felelős vezetésről' pp. 109–24.

5 The Logic of Reform Thought – from Economics to Politics

1. Szamuely, 'The First Wave of the Mechanism Debate in Hungary (1954–57)'.
2. Ibid, p. 5.
3. Ibid.
4. Ibid, pp. 7–9.
5. Ibid.
6. Péter, 'A gazdaságosság jelentőségéről és szerepéről a népgazdaság tervszerű irányításában'. See discussion in Szamuely, 'The First Wave', pp. 11–14: and in Robinson, *The Pattern of Reform in Hungary*, pp. 8–9.
7. Published in English as *Overcentralisation in Economic Administration* (Oxford: Oxford University Press, 1959).
8. Szamuely, 'The First Wave', p. 15. 'Sociography' is a Hungarian term describing a school of proto-sociological descriptive writing by ethnographers, journalists and novelists in the inter-war period, focusing on social problems, particularly in rural life.
9. Szamuely, 'The First Wave', p. 15.
10. Kornai, *Overcentralisation in Economic Administration*, p. 204.
11. Ibid.
12. Ibid, p. 206.
13. Ibid, p. 207.
14. Ibid, p. 212.
15. Szamuely, 'The First Wave', p. 17.
16. Szamuely, 'The Second Wave of the Economic Mechanism Debate and the 1968 Reform in Hungary', p. 53.
17. Nyers, 'Megnyitó beszed a Kommunista Közgazdász-aktiván (1963 december 13.)'. in Nyers, *Gazdaságpolitikánk és a gazdasági mechanizmus reformja*, pp. 18–19.
18. See Selucký, 'Ekonomické názory se vyjasňuje'; Korda, 'O ekonomické věde a vyuce'.
19. Komenda and Kožušník, 'Některé základní otázky zdokonalení soustavy řízení socialistické národního hospodářství'.
20. Ibid, p. 220.
21. Ibid, p. 222.
22. Ibid, p. 223.
23. Ibid, p. 224.
24. Friss, 'Ideas on the Improvement of National Economic Planning', p. 12.

25. Ibid, pp. 13–14.
26. Bognár, 'Towards a New System of Guidance of the Socialist Economy', p. 7.
27. On the Czechoslovak model see 'Draft Principles of a System to Improve Planned Management of the Economy' *Rudé právo* 17 October 1964, translated in *East European Economics* vol III; no 4 (Summer 1965); Šik, 'Czechoslovakia's New System of Planning and Management'; Šik, *Economic Planning and Management in Czechoslovakia*. On the Hungarian model, see Friss (ed.) *Reform of the Economic Mechanism in Hungary*; Nyers, *Economic Reform in Hungary: 25 Questions and 25 Answers*.
28. Csapó, 'Central Planning in a Guided Market Model'.
29. *The Times* 9 February 1965, p. 10.
30. Friss, 'Ideas on the improvement of national economic planning' p. 12.
31. Friss, 'Principal Features of the New System of Planning, Economic Control and Management in Hungary' in Friss (ed.) *Reform*, p. 12. See also Kemenes, 'Three Years of the Hungarian Economic Reform', p. 204.
32. Tůrek, 'Úloha centrálního plánu a impulsy zdravého vývoje hospodářství'.
33. See Szamuely, 'The Second Wave', p. 47.
34. Liska's work still provokes debate in Hungary – see Barsony, 'Tibor Liska's Concept, the Socialist Entrepreneurship'; Kornai, 'Comments on Tibor Liska's Concept of Entrepreneurship'; and Varga, 'The Experiment of Szentes'. Also Siklaky (ed.) *Koncepció és kritika*.
35. Löbl, 'Plán a trh; rovnica s dvoma neznámými', p. 3.
36. Ibid.
37. Ibid.
38. Selucký and Selucká, *Člověk a hospodářství*, p. 101.
39. Ibid, p. 104.
40. Ibid, pp. 105–6.
41. See Kosta, 'Czechoslovak Economists Discuss Ways of Improving the System of Planned Management'; and Kodousek, 'Czechoslovak Theory and Practice as Reflected by Economic Journals'.
42. Tůrek, *O plánu, trhu a hospodářské politice*, p. 13.
43. Szamuely, 'The First Wave', p. 18.
44. See, for example, 'Z jednání stranických orgánů Ústredního Výboru Komunistické Strany Československa o sociologii v ČSSR', *Sociologický časopis*, vol. I (1965), no 4, pp. 357–69.
45. Richta *et al.*, *Civilizace na rozcestí: společenské a lidské souvislosti vědeckotechnické revoluce* (Prague: Svoboda 1966), or in English, *Civilisation at the Crossroads: Social and Human Implications of the Scientific and Technological Revolution*.
46. See Šik, *Plan and Market under Socialism*; and Richta *et al.*, pp. 37ff.
47. Richta, 'Povaha a souvislosti vědeckotechnické revoluce', p. 149.
48. Ibid, p. 150.
49. Ibid, p. 149.
50. See Löbl, *Úvahy o duševnej práci a bohatstve národa*.

51. Löbl, 'Ekonómia a politika', p. 76.
52. Tondl and Někola, 'Nové rysy v úloze vědy' *Sociologický časopis*, p. 311.
53. Löbl, 'Ekonómia a politika'.
54. Richta, *Civilisation at the Crossroads*, p. 37.
55. Machonin *et al.*, *Změny v sociální struktuře Československa a dynamika sociálně politického vývoje*.
56. Ibid, p. 16.
57. Ibid, p. 91.
58. Ibid, p. 81.
59. For an interesting discussion of the adoption of the structural–functionalist framework in Soviet sociology, see Gouldner, *The Coming Crisis of Western Sociology*, Chapter XII.
60. Jodl, 'K pojetí sociologického výzkumu'.
61. Ibid.
62. Machonin *et al.*, *Změny v sociální*, p. 14.
63. Urbanek, *Sociologický časopis*, vol. II (1966), no 2, p. 455.
64. Lakatoš, 'Niektoré problémy socialistickej demokracie z hl'adiska postavenia občana v našej společnosti', pp. 214 and 217.
65. See Lakatoš, 'K niektorým problémom štruktury našej politickej soustavy', 'Dvadsať rokov budovania socialistickej demokracie', and *Občan, Právo a Demokracie*.
66. Hegedüs, 'Optimizálás es humanizálás' pp. 17–32; English translation 'Optimisation and Humanisation'.
67. Hegedüs, 'Historical Antecedents of the Fight against Bureaucracy' *Kozgazdasági szemle* no 7–8, 1966, translated in his *Socialism and Bureaucracy*.
68. Hegedüs, 'Optimisation and Humanisation', p. 24.
69. Ibid, p. 22.
70. Ibid, p. 46.
71. See Hegedüs, 'Towards a Sociological Analysis of Property Relations' *Maygar Filozófiai Szemle* no 6, 1969, translated in his *Socialism and Bureaucracy*.
72. See Hadja, 'The Role of the Intelligentsia in the Development of Czechoslovak Society' in Rechcigl (ed.) *The Czechoslovak Contribution to World Culture*; also Hruby, *Fools and Heroes: the Changing Role of Communist Intellectuals in Czechoslovakia*.
73. Machonin *et al.*, *Změny v sociální*, p. 92.
74. Slejška, contributing to discussion as reported in 'I. celostátní porada československých sociologů', *Sociologický časopis*, vol III (1967) no 3, p. 350.
75. Ibid.
76. Hegedüs, 'L' "autocritique" de la société socialiste en tant que realité et necessité' in Hegedüs (ed.) *Etudes sociologiques*; see also Hegedüs, 'The intelligentsia and socialism' in his *Socialism and Bureaucracy*.
77. Quoted in Robinson, *The Pattern of Reform in Hungary*, p. 258.
78. See Robinson, 'Hegedüs, his Views and his Critics'.
79. See *Programme of the CPSU-Adopted at XXII congress 1961* (supple-

ment to *New Times*, no 48, 1961) Moscow; Trud, 1961. Also Breslauer, 'Khrushchev Reconsidered'.

80. Kusin, *Intellectual Origins of the Prague Spring*.
81. Ort, Hád, Kratký, 'Politická věda-ano či ne?'
82. Loukotka, 'Rozvoj vědecké teorie politiky'.
83. Kučera, 'Vědecká politika a politická věda'.
84. Kratochvil, 'Obsah a funkce politické vědy', p. 13.
85. Soukup, 'Ke koncepci a úkolům politické vědy', p. 13.
86. Kratochvil, 'Obsah a funkce', p. 12.
87. See Kratochvil and Soukup (notes 84 and 85); and Láb, 'Stranická práce v nových podminkách'.
88. Mlynář, *Stát a člověk*, pp. 113ff; Lakatoš, 'Aby právo ne překáželo ekonomice', p. 5.
89. Mlynář, 'Úloha práva v řízení hospodářství'.
90. Ibid, p. 42.
91. Ibid, p. 43.
92. Ibid, p. 40; see also Mlynář, 'Nová soustava řízení, právo a demokracie', pp. 1 and 6.
93. Selucký, 'The Relationship between Political and Economic Reform in Eastern Europe and in Czechoslovakia in Particular' in Kusin (ed.) *The Czechoslovak Reform Movement 1968*, p. 4.
94. Ibid; cf. Szamuely, 'The Second Wave', p. 63.
95. Selucký and Selucká, *Člověk á Hospodářství*, p. 147.
96. See for example, Crick, *In Defence of Politics*.
97. Mlynář and Pavlíček, 'Politická organizace ve vztahu k vývoji sociální struktury socialistické společnosti' in Machonin (ed.) *Sociální struktura socialistické společnosti*, p. 656.
98. Mlynář, 'Problems of Political Leadership and the New Economic System', p. 58.
99. Ibid, pp. 58–9.
100. Hendrych, contribution to debate at the Central Committee plenum, January 1965, *Rudé právo*, 3 February 1965, p. 3.
101. Mlynář, 'Problems of Political Leadership', p. 59.
102. Nyers, 'Social and Political Effects of the New Economic Mechanism', p. 6.
103. Ibid, p. 9; see also Nyers, 'Az új gazdasági mechanismus várható társadalmi és politikai kihatásai' (March 1968) reproduced in his *Gazdaságpolitikánk*, pp. 348–67.
104. Nyers, 'Social and Political Effects', p. 16.
105. Mlynář, *Nightfrost in Prague*, p. 62.
106. Ibid, pp. 82–3.
107. See ibid, 'Zdeněk Mlynář's Contribution to the Action Programme', pp. 267–81; and Mlynář, 'K demokratické politické organizaci společnosti'.
108. Komunistická Strana Československa, *Akční program*, p. 15.
109. For more extended discussion, see Pravda, 'Reform and Change in the Czechoslovak Political System', *January–August 1968*; and Skilling, *Czechoslovakia's Interrupted Revolution*, chapter XII.
110. *Akční Program*, pp. 8–10.

111. Reproduced in Mlynář, *Nightfrost*, pp. 282–6.
112. See for example, 'What Otto Šik preached' translated from *Sovietskaya Rossiya*, 21 September 1968 in *Current Digest of the Soviet Press* vol XX; no 38 (9 October 1968) p. 8; and Mrachkovskaya, *From Revisionism to Betrayal: A Criticism of Ota Šik's Economic Views*; CPCS Department of Economics document 'Záměry a skutečnost ekonomické reformy', *Nová mysl*, vol XXIII (1969) no 11.
113. Gy Aczél, 'The Guiding Principles of Hungarian Science Policy', p. 12.
114. Ibid.
115. Ibid, p. 10.
116. Ibid.
117. Ibid, p. 13.
118. Gy Aczél, 'The People and the Intellectuals', p. 7.
119. See Robinson, *The Pattern of Reform*, p. 261. A redefinition of the proper role of sociology was given by Hegedüs's replacement as head of the Sociological Research Group, Kalmán Kulcsár, 'Sociology in Hungary'.
120. Aczél, 'The People and the Intellectuals', p. 6.
121. Aczél, 'Guiding Principles of Hungarian Science Policy', p. 19.
122. Nyers, 'Social and Political Effects', p. 6.
123. Pozsgay, 'A pártdemokrácia erősítése a szocialista demokrácia kulcskérdése', p. 20.
124. Ibid, p. 21.
125. Pozsgay, 'Gazdaságirányítási rendszerünk és a pártszervezetek erkölcsi-politikai munkája', p. 54.
126. Ibid, p. 51.
127. Ibid, p. 55.
128. Ibid, p. 54.
129. Pozsgay, 'A párt és az össztársadalmi érdek', translated by Radio Free Europe Research, 14 February 1972.
130. Ibid.
131. Pozsgay, 'Gazdaságirányítási', p. 56.

6 Economic Reform and Political Crisis in Czechoslovakia, 1963–8

1. See the post-invasion report by the CPCS Central Committee Economic Department, 'Záměry a skutečnost ekonomické reformy', *Nová mysl*, vol. XXIII, no 11 (November 1969); Čermák and Kysilka, *Vývoj Československé Ekonomické Reformy*; and Mrachkovskaya *From Revisionism To Betrayal: A Criticism of Ota Šik's Economic Views*.
2. Mencl and Ouředník, 'Jak to bylo v lednu: II', p. 13.
3. See Tigrid, 'Czechoslovakia: a Post-mortem', for a detailed account of the proceedings of the late 1967 plenary sessions.
4. Golan, 'Antonín Novotný: The Sources and Nature of His Power', p. 422.

5. Eliáš and Netík, 'Czechoslovakia', in Griffith (ed.), *Communism in Europe*, vol. II, p. 269.
6. Mlynář, *Nightfrost in Prague*, p. 69.
7. See Tigrid, 'Czechoslovakia'.
8. Mlynář, *Nightfrost*, p. 65.
9. Ibid, p. 66.
10. Ibid.
11. On Soviet politics see Hough, 'Petrification or Pluralism?', in *The Soviet Union and Social Science Theory*.
12. See Breslauer, *Khrushchev and Brezhnev as Leaders*.
13. See below, section C.
14. See Hough, 'Political Participation in the Soviet Union'; and Friedgut, *Political Participation in the USSR*.
15. Hájek, *Mýtus a realita ledna 1968*, p. 12.
16. Mlynář, *Nightfrost*, p. 54.
17. Mencl and Ouředník, 'Jak to bylo v lednu: IV', p. 34.
18. Ibid.
19. Ibid.
20. See, for example, Šik, 'O pravdě v ekonomice a politice a skutečných zajmech pracujících', p. 5; also Wightman, 'The Changing Role of Central Party Institutions in Czechoslovakia 1962–67'.
21. Bartošek, 'Revoluce proti byrokratismu?: IV', p. 3. See also the account given by Steiner, *The Slovak Dilemma*, pp. 151–3.
22. See Kusin, *Political Grouping in the Czechoslovak Reform Movement*, p. 125.
23. Kumeš, 'Nejlepší lidí do strany', *Život strany*, no. 16, 1966, pp. 1–4.
24. Novotný, 'Aktuální problémy rozvoje socialistické společnosti', *Život strany*, no 21, 1966, p. 4.
25. See Kusin, *Political Grouping*, pp. 136–7; and Golan, *The Czechoslovak Reform Movement*, pp. 262–5.
26. In addition to the works cited in note 25, see Hamšik, *Writers Against Rulers* and Skilling, *Czechoslovakia's Interrupted Revolution*, chap. 3.
27. As suggested by Mencl and Ouředník, 'Jak to bylo ... III', p. 21.
28. Kusin, *Political Grouping*, p. 55.
29. See Mencl and Ouředník, 'Jak to bylo ... III', p. 21.
30. Golan, *Antonin Novotný*, pp. 425–6.
31. See Taborsky, *Communism in Czechoslovakia 1948–1960*, p. 107.
32. Bartošek, 'Revoluce proti byrokratismu: II', p. 5.
33. Translated in Hamšik, *Writers against Rulers*, pp. 186–7.
34. L. Dziedzinska, *Inteligence a Dnešek* (Prague: Melantřich, 1968), quoted in Kusin, *Political Grouping*, p. 63.
35. Stejškal, 'Současné úkoly kladou vysoké nároky', *Rudé právo*, 13 May 1965, p. 2.
36. Jirásek, 'Co a hlavně jak', *Hospodářské noviny* 11 October 1968, p. 6.
37. Kolder, 'Stranické řízení národního hospodářství', p. 6.

38. See Krejčí, *Social Change and Stratification in Post-war Czechoslovakia*, p. 59.
39. Machonin, 'K celkové charakteristice sociální struktury socialistické společnosti' in Machonin (ed.) *Sociální struktura socialistické společnosti*, p. 115.
40. Krejčí, *Social Change*, p. 57.
41. Dziedzinska, *Intelligence* quoted by Kusin, *Political Grouping*, p. 63.
42. Stejškal, 'Současné úkoly ... nároky'.
43. Večernik, 'Problémy příjmu a životní úrovně v sociální diferenciaci' in Machonin *et al.*, *Československá Společnost*, p. 309.
44. Brown and Wightman note that they are considerably less full and systematic, and more scattered, than data for the Communist Party of the Soviet Union. See Brown and Wightman, 'Changes in the Levels of Membership and Social Composition of the Communist Party of Czechoslovakia 1945–73', p. 408, note 64.
45. Quoted in ibid, p. 410.
46. See Jancar, *Czechoslovakia and the Absolute Monopoly of Power*, pp. 108–9, footnote.
47. Brown and Wightman, 'Changes', p. 406 and p. 410, Table I.
48. Ibid.
49. 'Složení a počet členů KSČ', *Rudé právo*, 21 June 1966, p. 3.
50. Jancar, *Czechoslovakia*, pp. 129–30, notes 12 and 13.
51. Ibid, p. 113.
52. Kohoutek, 'From General Discussion to Concrete Preparation for Improving the System of Planned Management', p. 32. See also Holesovsky, 'Planning and the Market in the Czechoslovak Reform', p. 315.
53. A useful summary of the reform programme can be found in United Nations/Secretariat of the Economic Commission for Europe, *Economic Survey of Europe in 1965*. (This publication will be cited hereafter as UN/ECE and the year covered in the survey.)
54. Lenárt, 'Improvement of the Organisation and Planned Management of the National Economy', p. 54.
55. See his 1968 interview in *Práce*, 5 March 1968, pp. 4–5.
56. See UN/ECE 1965, p. 63.
57. Lenárt, 'Improvement ... Economy', p. 54.
58. Ibid.
59. Holesovskly 'Problems and Prospects'.
60. Kohoutek, 'Ekonomický experiment a nová soustava', *Hospodářské noviny*, no 6, 1965 (12 February 1965) pp. 1–10.
61. Kotrbaty, 'Neexperimentovat s experimenty'.
62. Stěfek, 'Rok velkých zámerů', *Rudé právo*, 22 November 1964, p. 1.
63. 'Jak a kdy nová soustava řízení' *Práce*, 10 September 1965.
64. See UN/ECE 1965, p. 63.

65. Ibid, p. 64.
66. Ibid, p. 65.
67. 'Jak a kdy nová soustava řízení', *Práce*, 10 September 1965 and *Práce* 25 September 1965. This was critically commented upon by Škrlant, 'Na prahu velkého experimentu', p. 27.
68. Novotný, 'Iniciativa lidí – hnací sila dalšího rozvoje socialistické společnosti', *Rudé právo* 29 October 1965, p. 2.
69. See 'Příprava zdokonalené soustavy plánovitého řízení', *Plánované hospodářství*, vol. XVIII (1965) no 7–8, p. 2.
70. Škrlant, 'Na prahu ... experimentu', p. 28.
71. Ibid.
72. Kocanda, 'Důsledně ke komplexní soustave', p. 21.
73. Ibid, p. 22.
74. Ibid, p. 23.
75. Kolder, 'Pětiletka a nová soustava', *Hospodářské noviny* 14 October 1966, pp. 1 and 5.
76. This was viewed by a 'normalisation' critique as the first indication of the reform's 'subversion' by rightist forces and the abandonment of planning. See Čermák and Kysilka, *Vývoj Československé Ekonomické Reformy*, p. 20.
77. Toman, 'O urychleném zavádění nové soustavy', pp. 6–10.
78. See Holesovsky, 'Planning Reforms in Czechoslovakia', p. 545.
79. For such an analysis, see Holesovsky, 'Planning and the Market', in Bornstein (ed.) *Plan and Market*, p. 319.
80. Taborsky, 'Czechoslovakia's Economic Reform: a Balance Sheet of the First Year'.
81. UN/ECE 1967, chap. 2, p. 64.
82. Feiwel, *New Economic Patterns in Czechoslovakia*, p. 327.
83. Ibid, p. 325.
84. Holesovsky, 'Planning and the Market', p. 322.
85. Ibid, p. 319.
86. Ibid, pp. 325–7.
87. Komenda and Kožušník, 'Některé základní problémy soustavy řízení socialistického národního hospodářství', p. 220.
88. Quoted in Penkava and Zeměk, 'Starosti před koncem roku', *Život strany*, no 22, 1967, pp. 3 and 5.
89. UN/ECE 1967, p. 65.
90. See Penkava and Zeměk, 'Starosti ... roku'.
91. UN/ECE 1967, p. 65.
92. See, for example, Šik, 'Cesta k novej sústave nie je l'ahká', p. 1.
93. Šik, 'Overcoming disequilibrium in the economy', p. 29.
94. Rohlíček, 'Economic Development and the New System of Management', p. 3.
95. Tůrek, 'O plánu, trhu a hospodářské politice', p. 9.
96. Quoted in Feiwel, *New Economic Patterns*, p. 345.
97. See Tůrek, 'Národohospodářská rovnovaha – klíčový úkol hospodářské politiky', pp. 13–21.
98. See Taborsky, 'Czechoslovakia's Economic Reform'.
99. Golan, *Czechoslovak Reform Movement*, p. 227.
100. Taborsky, 'Czechoslovakia's Economic Reform'.

101. UN/ECE 1967, p. 65.
102. See 'Current Developments: Czechoslovakia', *East Europe*, vol. XIV (1965) no 4, p. 39.
103. See 'Nová soustava rízení ve stranické výchove', *Hospodářské noviny*, 29 January 1965, pp. 8–9.
104. Toman, *Úvod do zásad nové soustavy plánovitého řízení*, p. 51.
105. Ibid, p. 52.
106. Vacha, 'Budou řídit a jaci budou?', pp. 1 and 4.
107. Ibid.
108. Kolder, 'Stranické řízení národního hospodářství', p. 7.
109. See for example Selucký, translated from *Mladá fronta*, 2 November 1964 in *East Europe*, vol. XIV (1965) no 2.
110. Löbl, 'Nielen chlebom'.
111. Holesovsky, 'Planning Reforms in Czechoslovakia', p. 547.
112. Vacha, 'Budou řidit'.
113. Kotrbaty, 'Neexperimentovat s experimenty'; also, by the same author, 'Reálně bez iluzí'.
114. See, for example, his speech to the XIII CPCS Congress, in *XIII Sjezd Komunistické Strany Československa* (Prague: Svoboda, 1966) pp. 73–4; and in *Život strany*.
115. Šik, 'Problémy přechodu na novou soustavu', p. 3.
116. Kolisko, 'Nová soustava a příběhy ze života'.
117. Kantůrek, 'Nová soustava a staré myšlenky'.
118. Selucký, 'Is there a danger of unemployment in our country?'.
119. Šulc, 'Jsme všude dost připravení?', *Rudé právo*, 30 June 1966, p. 2.
120. Kantůrek, 'Nová soustava ... života'.
121. See notes 92 and 93.
122. See Selucký, *East Europe*, vol. XIV (1965) no 2.
123. See Šik's speech at the XIII CPCS Congress, in Komunistická Strana Československa *XIII. sjezd* , p. 303.
124. Novotný, 'Naše budoucnost závisí na vysledcích společné práce', p. 2.
125. 'Z projevu soudruha Antonína Novotného', *Rudé právo*, 1 February 1967, p. 3.
126. Novotný, 'Budujeme armadu v duchu zásad naší Komunistické strany', *Rudé právo*, 2 September 1967, p. 2.
127. Novotný, 'Aktuální problémy rozvoje socialistické společnosti', *Život strany*, no 21, 1966.
128. Kantůrek, 'Nová soustava ... myšlenky'.
129. Valenta, 'Čeho je nam zapotřebí', *Život strany*, no 1, 1966.
130. Kohout, 'Zvýšit ideovou připravenost komunistů', *Život strany*, no 17, 1966.
131. Dvorský, 'Rok po lednovému plénu', *Život strany*, no 3, 1966.
132. 'O návrhu změn ve stanovách strany', *Život strany*, no 6, 1966, pp. 3–5.
133. See ibid; also report of the Party Control and Auditing Commission, *Život strany*, no 14, 1966, p. 3; and K. Ondřis, 'Další vývoj socialistické demokracie', *Život strany*, no 2, 1967.

134. Uhlíř and Kumeš, 'Otázky členství ve strane', *Život strany*, no 7, 1966, pp. 24–5.
135. For example, 'Znepokojující tendence', *Život strany*, no 1, 1966.
136. Nemec, 'První seznámení nestačí', *Život strany*, no 14, 1966.
137. Horák, 'Všichni ještě nepochopili', *Život strany*, no 7, 1966.
138. Kohout, 'Hospodářské vedení a stranická organizace', *Hospodářské noviny*, 27 January 1967, p. 1.
139. Lenárt, 'Improvement of the Organisation', pp. 56–7.
140. Dvorský, 'Rok po lednovému plénu'.
141. Vaculík, 'V práci strany podle podmínek'.
142. Rohan, 'Strana a společnost'.
143. See Central Committee resolution, *Rudé právo*, 30 January 1965, pp. 1, 3. and 4.
144. Šedivý, 'Strana a hospodářství'.
145. Komarnyckij 'Revoluční strana'.
146. See Mencl and Ouředník, 'Jak to bylo ... 4', p. 34.
147. Šik, in *XIII. Sjezd ...*, p. 303.
148. 'Zpráva volební komise přednesená soudruhem Jiřím Hendrychem' in *XIII. sjezd ...*, p. 371.
149. Mencl and Ouředník, 'Jak to bylo ... 3', p. 20.
150. Kolder, 'Stranicke rizeni'.
151. See Mencl and Ouředník, 'Jak to bylo ... 3', pp. 20–1.
152. See Mlynář's account, *Nightfrost*, pp. 72–3.
153. Hendrych, 'O upevňování jednoty naší socialistické společnosti se zvláštním zřetelem k mladé generaci', pp. 3–5.
154. Ibid.
155. Mencl and Ouředník, 'Jak to bylo ... 4', p. 35.
156. See Hamšik, *Writers Against Rulers*.
157. Ibid.
158. Mencl and Ouředník, 'Jak to bylo ... 4', p.35.
159. Ibid, p. 36.
160. Ibid, pp. 35–6.
161. Ibid, p. 36.
162. See Tigrid, 'Czechoslovakia: A Post-mortem', pp. 133–4.
163. Ibid; and Mlynář, *Nightfrost*, p. 71.
164. Šik's speech is reported in Tigrid, 'Czechoslovakia', pp. 137–9.
165. Mlynář, *Nightfrost*, p. 95.
166. Tigrid, 'Czechoslovakia', p. 148.
167. Skilling, *Czechoslovakia's Interrupted Revolution*; see also Golan, *Reform Rule in Czechoslovakia*; Kusin, *Political Grouping*; Pravda, *Reform and Change in the Czechoslovak Political System January–August 1968*.
168. See Paul, 'The Repluralisation of Czechoslovak Politics in the 1960s'; by the same author, *The Cultural Limits of Revolutionary Politics*; and Brown, 'Pluralistic Trends in Czechoslovakia'.
169. O. Černík, report to the National Assembly, *Rudé právo* 11 January 1968, p. 3; see also Černík, 'Československe hospodářství a

jeho výhledy', pp. 1 and 6.
170. Kohoutek, 'Další kroky v ekonomickém řízení', pp. 1 and 6.
171. See Skilling, *Czechoslovakia's Interrupted Revolution*, pp. 183–95.
172. Ibid, pp. 211–14.
173. Ibid, p. 215.
174. Ibid, p. 419.
175. *Rudé právo* 6 April 1968, translated in Ello (ed.), *Czechoslovakia's Blueprint for 'Freedom'*, p. 69.
176. Komunistická Strana Československa, *Akční Program*, p. 34.
177. 'Hospodářství a systém jeho řízení', *Rudé právo*, 1 March 1968, pp. 1–2.
178. In Ello (ed.), *Czechoslovakia's Blueprint*, p. 70.
179. *Akční Program*, p. 36.
180. 'Programme Declaration of the CSSR Government, 24 April 1968', *Rudé právo* 25 April 1968, translated in Remington (ed.), *Winter in Prague: Documents on Czechoslovak Communism in Crisis*, p. 148.
181. Ibid, p. 150.
182. Ibid, p. 152.
183. Šimon and Říha, 'Rozvoj ekonomické reformy v ČSSR'.
184. Kouba, 'Ekonomové a hospodářská politika', speech to the Czechoslovak Economics Society 20 May 1968, reproduced in Kouba, *Ekonomický růst a soustava řízení*, p. 415.
185. The concept of a 'transitional' phase of reform was elaborated by Tůrek, *O plánu, trhu a hospodářské politice*.
186. See Komarek, 'The Situation in the National Economy Does Not Permit Temporising', *Rudé právo* 3 July 1968, translated in *New Trends in Czechoslovak Economics*, no 6, 1968, p. 32.
187. Ibid.
188. See, for example, Kadlec, 'Ekonomicky Zajistit Socialismus', p. 3; Dalimil, 'Naš Komentář', p. 4; and Daneček, 'Some Notes on the Development of the System of Management', *Plánované hospodářství*, no 3, 1968, translated in *New Trends in Czechoslovak Economics*, no 3, 1968, p. 39.
189. The phrase was coined by Horálek, Sokol, Kožušník and Tůrek, 'Nástin koncepce dalšího rozvíjení ekonomické soustavy řízení', p. II.
190. Šik, 'Whither Economic Policy?', speech to Czechoslovak Economics Society (May 1968).
191. See Tůrek, 'Jak dál v nové soustavě řízení', p. 1; and Vergner, 'Jak na tom skutečně jsme v hospodářství?', *Rudé právo* 28 March 1968, p. 5; Šimon and Říha, 'Nová soustava dnes a jak dál?'.
192. Horálek *et al.*, 'Nástin koncepce ... řízení', p. L.
193. See Šik, 'Whither Economic Policy' (speech to CSES); and Horálek *et al.*, 'Nástin koncepce ... řízení'.
194. Kouba, 'Ekonomové ... politika', p. 425.
195. For example, Dalimil, 'Přechodný stav', p. 4.
196. Tůrek, 'Jak dál v nové soustavě řízení'.
197. Horálek *et al*, 'Nástin koncepce ... řízení', p. II.

198. See Skilling, *Czechoslovakia's Interrupted Revolution*, p. 420; and V. Komarek, 'O úkolech Hospodářské Rady', *Hospodářské noviny*, 26 April 1968, p. 3; and Vosecky, 'Nová vlada před starými problémy', *Hospodářské noviny*, 26 April 1968, p. 1.
199. Skilling, *Czechoslovakia's Interrupted Revolution*, p. 420.
200. Dalimil, 'Čas vítězí nad naší vladou', p. 4.
201. For example, see Kožušník 'Rozhodující krok dalšího rozvoje ekonomické reformy'; Šimon and Říha, 'Podnik v nové soustavě'; Suchan, 'Podnik a centrum'; Suchan, 'Podnik a integrační seskupení', *Nová mysl*, vol. XXII (1968) no 6.
202. Šik, 'Whither Economic Policy', p. 5.
203. Horálek *et al.*, 'Nástin koncepce ... řízení', p. 11.
204. 'Zásady pro postup při změnách v organizačním začlenění podniků', *Rudé právo*, 24 April 1968, pp. 1 and 3.
205. See Skilling, *Czechoslovakia's Interrupted Revolution*, pp. 425–7; Kusin, *From Dubček to Charter 77*, p. 124; excerpts of the draft bill are reproduced in Fisera (ed.), *Workers' Councils in Czechoslovakia: Documents and Essays 1968–69*, pp. 76–93.
206. Šik, 'Whither Economic Policy', p. 5.
207. Dalimil, 'Přechodný Stav'.
208. Dalimil, 'Naš Komentář'; see also Kožušník, 'Rozhodující křok ... reformy'.
209. Dalimil, 'Naš Komentář'.
210. See Mlynář, *Československý pokus o reformu 1968, analyza jeho teorie a praxe*, pp. 186ff.
211. Quoted by Pravda, 'Some aspects of the Czechoslovak economic reform and the working class in 1968', p. 104.
212. Švestka, 'Otázky dělnické politiky', *Rudé právo*, 14 July 1968, pp. 1–2.
213. Contribution by Vörös to discussion, 'Hledání společné řeče', *Literární listy*, 30 May 1968.
214. Ibid.
215. See Piekalkiewicz, *Public Opinion Polling in Czechoslovakia 1968–9*, Chap 10.
216. Müller, 'Co je to socialismus?', *Literární listy*, 23 May 1968, pp. 1 and 3.
217. Ibid, p. 3.
218. Vaculík, 'And What About the Workers?', *Literární lísty*, 4 April 1968, translated in Oxley, Pravda and Ritchie (eds), *Czechoslovakia: The Party and the People*, pp. 168 and 170.
219. Ibid, p. 166.
220. Kosík, 'Naše nynější krize:3. Krize tříd a společností', p. 3.
221. Kosík, 'Naše nynější krize:1. Krize politické soustavy – strana a nestranické', p. 3.
222. Kosík, 'Naše nynější krize:3.'
223. Dubček, speech at the Allied Steel Works in Kladno, *Rudé právo* 5 March 1968, translated in Oxley, Pravda and Ritchie (eds), *Czechoslovakia: The Party and the People*, p. 163.
224. *Akční Program*, pp. 10–11.

225. Kosík, 'Naše nynější krize:3'; Kouba, 'Ekonomové ... politika'.
226. Vergner, 'Jak na tom ... hospodářství?'.
227. Šík, 'O pravdě v ekonomice a politice a skutečných zajmech pracujících', pp. 4–5.
228. Reproduced as Šik, *Czechoslovakia: the Bureaucratic Economy* (White Plains, NY: International Arts and Sciences Press, 1972).
229. See Pravda, 'Some Aspects of Czechoslovak Economic Reform', p. 112.
230. Ibid, pp. 111–12.
231. Ibid, p. 114.
232. *Rudé právo*, 20 April 1968, p. 3; quoted in Kusin, *Political Grouping* p. 17; a similar 'alarmist' view was expressed by Schmidt, 'Mzdy jako třaskavina', *Literární listy*, 23 May 1968, p. 3.
233. See Horálek *et al.*, 'Nástin koncepce ... řízení'; and Vergner, 'Jak na tom ... hospodářství?'
234. Šik, 'Whither Economic Policy?'
235. See Stevens, *Czechoslovakia at the Crossroads*, p. 140.
236. See Pravda, 'Some Aspects of Czechoslovak Economic Reform'; Fisera (ed.), *Workers' Councils*; Viták 'Workers' control in Czechoslovakia' in Vanek (ed.), *Self-management* (Harmondsworth: Penguin, 1975); Kosta, 'Workers' Councils in the Czechoslovak Reform of 1968', in Heathfield (ed.), *The Economics of Co-determination* (London Macmillan, 1977); Kovanda, 'Czechoslovak Workers' Councils 1968–69'.
237. A group of proponents of Yugoslav-style self-management was suppressed in the early 1960s – see Kusin, *Intellectual Origins of the Prague Spring*, p. 115, footnote.
238. Bystřina, 'Nová soustava a demokracie', p. 3; Lakatoš, 'Společenske organizace a zajmy pracujících', *Hospodářské noviny* 26 March 1965, p. 1; Slejška, *Sociologický časopis*, vol. III (1967) no 3, p. 350.
239. See Rezníček and Toman, 'Demokratizace hospodářství a postavení podniku'.
240. Šik, 'Whither Economic Policy?', p. 7.
241. See Pravda, 'Some Aspects of Czechoslovak Economic Reform', p. 116.
242. *Rudé právo* 30 June 1968, pp. 1, 3; reproduced in Fisera, *Workers' Councils*, pp. 22–8.
243. Pravda, 'Some Aspects of Czechoslovak Economic Reform', p. 119.
244. This point was made particularly by Šilhán in a round-table discussion of workers' councils, 'O demokracie v oblasti výroby', *Nová mysl*, vol. XXII (1968) no 8, pp. 948–9.
245. Bartošek, 'Open Letter to the Workers of Czechoslovakia', *Reporter*, 8 May 1968, translated in Oxley, Pravda and Ritchie (eds) *Czechoslovakia: Party and People*, p. 195.
246. See Fisera (ed), *Workers' Councils*, pp. 36–47.
247. Piekalkiewicz, *Public Opinion Polling*, p. 281, Table 10.6. A further 4 per cent of respondents were entered as holding 'another viewpoint' on the question.

248. For example, the worker Vörös, in *Literární listy*, 30 May 1968 (see note 213).
249. 'Beseda: O politice strany', *Život strany*, no 14, 1968, pp. 16–19.
250. Ibid.
251. See Pravda, 'Some Aspects of Czechoslovak Economic Reform', pp. 110–11.
252. Vaculík, 'And What about the Workers?', p. 171.
253. See Fisera (ed.), *Workers' Councils*, p. 13.
254. Pravda, 'Some Aspects of Czechoslovak Economic Reform', p. 123, note 66.
255. Kusin, *Political Grouping*, p. 41.
256. Piekalkewicz, *Public Opinion Polling*, p. 280, Table 10.5.
257. Ibid, p. 281, Table 10.6.
258. Skilling, *Czechoslovakia's Interrupted Revolution*, pp. 813–20.
259. Mlynář, *Nightfrost*, p. 215.
260. See Kusin, *From Dubček to Charter 77*, pp. 119–23.
261. Quoted by Fisera (ed.), *Workers' Councils*, p. 16, note 14.
262. Holesovsky, 'Planning and the Market in the Czechoslovak Reform', in Bornstein (ed.) *Plan and Market*, pp. 336–7.
263. Ibid, pp. 332–4.
264. Ibid.
265. 'Záměry a skutečnost ekonomické reformy', *Nová mysl*, vol. XXIII (1969) no 11, p. 1371.
266. See Kusin, *From Dubček to Charter 77*, p. 125.
267. Holesovsky, 'Planning and the Market', p. 339.
268. Ibid, p. 338.
269. 'Záměry ...', (note 265).
270. Quoted in Stevens, *Czechoslovakia at the Crossroads*, p. 190.
271. Quoted in Kusin, *From Dubček to Charter 77*, p. 125.
272. Skilling, *Czechoslovakia's Interrupted Revolution*, pp. 835–6.
273. Ibid, pp. 841–2.
274. Ibid, p. 842.
275. A similar argument is presented by Zdeněk Mlynář in *Československý pokus o reformu 1968: analýza jeho teorie a praxe*, especially chap. II.3.
276. Mlynář (in ibid, p. 182) argues that the leadership's fear of unleashing such a wave of demands which could not be met was a major factor in limiting the development of the political reform in 1968. Such a political reform, he argues, could have been successfully managed and contained had it been introduced in time, early in 1968.
277. Skilling, *Czechoslovakia's Interrupted Revolution*, p. 837.
278. Translation in Remington (ed.), *Winter in Prague*, p. 226.
279. See Valenta, *Soviet Intervention in Czechoslovakia 1968: Anatomy of a Decision*, p. 22.
280. Reproduced in Mlynář, *Nightfrost*, pp. 282–6.
281. Muffled debate of the methods of managing the economy continued for some years after the invasion. See Holesovsky, 'Planning and the Market', pp. 340–4.

7 The Political Limits to Economic Reform in Hungary 1968–78

1. Friss, 'Ten Years of Economic Reform in Hungary', p. 1.
2. Berend, 'Ten Years After – Instead of a Balance Sheet', p. 45.
3. Antal 'Development – With Some Digression'.
4. Bauer 'The Hungarian Alternative to Soviet-type Planning'.
5. Laky, 'Hidden Mechanisms of Recentralisation', p. 95.
6. Quoted in Robinson, *The Pattern of Reform in Hungary*, p. 101.
7. See Kemenes 'Three Years of the Hungarian Economic Reform'.
8. See Robinson, *The Pattern of Reform*, pp. 100–2.
9. Friss, 'Practical Experiences of the Economic Reform in Hungary', p. 6.
10. Laky, 'Hidden Mechanisms', p. 97.
11. See for example Berend and Ránki, *The Hungarian Economy in the Twentieth Century*, chs 7 and 8.
12. Huntington, *Political Order in Changing Societies*.
13. Kemenes, 'Three Years', p. 215.
14. On Czechoslovak political changes in this area under Novotný, see Golan, *The Czechoslovak Reform Movement*, ch 13; and Brown, 'Pluralistic trends in Czechoslovakia'.
15. See Bihari 'The Development of Socialist Democracy in Hungarian Political Institutions'.
16. See Robinson, *The Pattern of Reform*, p. 217; also Ortutay, 'A Standing Parliamentary Committee'.
17. See Bihari, 'Development of Socialist Democracy, and Robinson, *The Pattern of Reform*, pp. 206–9.
18. Robinson, *The Pattern of Reform*, p. 207.
19. Bognár, 'Economic reform, development and stability in Hungary', p. 34.
20. Nyers,, 'The Comprehensive Reform of Managing the National Economy in Hungary, p. 34.
21. See Robinson, *The Pattern of Reform*, pp. 238–40.
22. Ibid.
23. See Gáspár, *The Hungarian Trade Unions in the Building of Developed Socialism*.
24. Nyers, 'Social and Political Effects of the New Economic Mechanism', p. 9.
25. Ibid, p. 6; see also Pozsgay, 'A pártdemokrácia erősítése a szocialista demokrácia kulcskérdése'.
26. See Robinson, *The Pattern of Reform*, pp. 202–13.
27. See Fehér and Heller, *Hungary 1956 Revisited*, ch 2 (vi) 'Kádárist Hungary: The Product of a Crushed Revolution'.
28. Rigby, 'Crypto-politics', p. 144.
29. Ibid.
30. See Sulyok, 'Major Financial Regulators in the New System of Economic Control and Management', in Friss (ed.) *Reform of the Economic Mechanism in Hungary*.
31. Berend, 'Ten Years After', p. 51.

32. Schweitzer, 'Some Interrelations Between the Enterprise Organisation and the Economic Mechanism in Hungary', p. 297.
33. Nyers and Tárdos, 'Enterprises in Hungary before and after the Economic Reform', pp. 35–6.
34. See Friss, 'Principal Features of the New System of Planning Economic Control and Management in Hungary in Friss (ed.) *Reform of The Economic Mechanism*, p. 18.
35. See Schweitzer, 'Some Interrelations'.
36. Csikós-Nagy, 'First Experiences Gained in the Implementation of the Economic Reform in Hungary', p. 8.
37. Varga, 'Enterprise Size Pattern in Hungarian Industry', p. 237.
38. Friss, in Friss (ed.), *Reform of the Economic Mechanism*, p. 17.
39. Ibid.
40. Tárdos and Hegedüs, 'Some Problems Concerning the Role and Motivations of Enterprise Executives', p. 105.
41. Ibid, p. 94 (emphasis in the original omitted).
42. Quoted by Laky, 'Enterprises in Bargaining Position', p. 237.
43. Ibid, p. 235.
44. Quoted in ibid, p. 232, footnote.
45. Quoted in ibid, p. 232.
46. See Wilcsek, 'Modern Small and Medium-sized Enterprises in Hungarian Industry'; and Szikra-Falus, 'On Competition'.
47. Wilcsek, 'Modern Small and Medium-sized Enterprises', p. 321, Table I.
48. Varga, 'Enterprise Size Pattern', p. 232.
49. Révész, 'Enterprise and plant size structure of the Hungarian industry', p. 62.
50. Laky, 'Enterprises in Bargaining Position', p. 233.
51. See Hare 'The Investment System in Hungary', in Hare, Swain and Radice (eds), *Hungary: A Decade of Economic Reform*; Kertesi 'Two Types of Development of Small-scale Industry in Hungary'.
52. Laky, 'Enterprises in Bargaining Position', p. 244.
53. Laky, 'Attachment to the Enterprise in Hungary'.
54. Quoted in ibid, p. 280.
55. Friss, *Ten Years of Economic Reform*, p. 17.
56. Laky, 'Enterprises in Bargaining Position', p. 244.
57. Antal, 'Development', pp. 271–2.
58. Bauer, 'A második gazdasági reform és a tulajdonviszonyok'.
59. Laky, 'Hidden Mechanisms', p. 108.
60. Ibid.
61. Reported in *Radio Free Europe Research: Situation Report/Hungary* 12 January 1971 (This publication will henceforth be referred to in an abbreviated form as RFER).
62. Kemenes, 'Three Years of the Hungarian Reform', p. 215.
63. Friss, 'Practical Experiences', p. 14.
64. Huszár, 'On Living Standard Policy in Hungary', p. 41.
65. RFER, 3 November 1970.
66. See for example Robinson, 'Hungary's Industrial Workers: Increasing Success as a Pressure Group'.

67. Nyers, *Economic Reform in Hungary: 25 questions and 25 answers*, pp. 27–8.
68. Robinson, *The Pattern of Reform*, p. 149.
69. Ibid.
70. See Berend and Ránki, *The Hungarian Economy*, p. 243.
71. RFER, 17 November 1970.
72. Ibid.
73. A point made by Sándor Gáspár at the X HSWP Congress in 1970. See RFER, 20 October 1970.
74. See RFER, 12 September 1972.
75. RFER, 21 April, 1971.
76. RFER, 3 June 1971.
77. RFER, 18 October 1971.
78. RFER, 5 October 1971 and 12 October 1971.
79. RFER, 29 October 1971.
80. RFER, 11 May 1971.
81. Márton, 'Trends of Consumer Prices in Hungary 1968–75'.
82. RFER, 18 November 1969.
83. RFER, 22 December 1969.
84. RFER, 20 October 1970.
85. RFER, 26 January 1971.
86. RFER, 11 May 1971.
87. RFER, 9 March 1971.
88. Márton, 'Trends'.
89. Friss, 'Practical Experiences', p. 14.
90. Márton, 'Trends'.
91. RFER, 18 January 1972.
92. RFER, 6 February 1973, See also Rácz, 'Incomes of the Population and Their Proportion in Hungary'.
93. For example, see RFER, 2 October 1969 and 2 March 1971.
94. RFER, 20 October 1970.
95. RFER, 28 April 1970.
96. RFER, 24 March 1970 and 14 April 1970.
97. RFER, 10 February 1970.
98. RFER, 16 June 1970 and 26 June 1970; also Robinson, *The Pattern of Reform*, p. 115.
99. RFER, 9 June 1970.
100. RFER, 10 February 1970.
101. RFER, 16 June 1970.
102. RFER, 20 October 1970.
103. Ibid.
104. See Völgyes, 'Hungary: The Lumpenproletarianisation of the Working Class'; also Böhm and Pál, 'Political attitudes of commuting workers', in Szoboszlai (ed.), *Politics and Political Science in Hungary*; and Timar, 'About Commuting'.
105. RFER, 13 June 1972.
106. RFER, 14 April 1970, 19 May 1970, and 18 August 1970.
107. RFER, 18 August 1970.
108. RFER, 30 June 1970.

109. See Swain 'The Evolution of Hungary's Agricultural System', in Hare, Swain and Radice (eds), *Hungary: A Decade*, p. 245.
110. Enyedi, 'Industrial Activities on Larger-scale Farms', p. 371.
111. Robinson, 'Hungary's Industrial Workers', p. 4.
112. See Heinrich, *Hungary: Politics, Economics and Society*, p. 147.
113. RFER, 21 November 1972, 20 December 1972, 30 January 1973.
114. RFER, 5 March 1974.
115. Berend and Ránki, *The Hungarian Economy*, p. 246.
116. Ibid.
117. Ibid.
118. RFER, 30 November 1971.
119. Pozsgay, 'The Party and the Social Interest', *Társadalmi Szemle* January 1973, translated in full in *RFER Hungarian Press Survey*, no. 2253, 15 January 1973.
120. Haraszti's book has been published in English as *A Worker in a Workers' State*.
121. On the ideological counter-offensive, see Kovrig, *Communism in Hungary*, pp. 403–7.
122. Ibid, pp. 371–2.
123. Berend, 'Ten Years After', p. 53.
124. Swain, 'The Evolution of Hungary's Agricultural System', p. 246.
125. Ibid.
126. Tábori, 'Small businesses in socialist Hungary', p. 65.
127. Heinrich, *Hungary: Politics, Economics and Society*, p. 147, quoting research by Szalai, 'A reform folyamat új szakasza és a nagy-vállalatok', *Valóság*, no. 5, 1982.
128. RFER, 26 January 1971.
129. RFER, 2 February 1971, 23 February 1971 and 4 May 1971.
130. RFER, 2 October 1969, 20 October 1970, 3 October 1970, 2 March 1971.
131. RFER, 2 October 1970, 20 October 1970, 11 May 1971.
132. RFER, 11 May 1971.
133. Ibid.
134. This insight was derived from the sociologist Tamás Kolosi in an interview at the HSWP Institute for Social Sciences, Budapest, April 1984.
135. RFER, 6 November 1970.
136. RFER, 2 October 1969.
137. RFER, 11 July 1972.
138. RFER, 14 March 1972.
139. See Bálogh, 'The trade unions and interest transmission in the political system of socialism' in Szoboszlai (ed.) *Studies in the field of Political Science in Hungary*.
140. RFER, 14 March 1972.
141. Héthy and Makó, 'Work Performance, Interests, Powers and the Environment'. See also by the same authors 'Labour Turnover and the Economic Organisation: Sociological Data on an Approach to the Question'.
142. Héthy and Makó, 'Work Performance', p. 146.

143. Ibid, p. 147.
144. Ibid, p. 148.
145. A hint of this was, however, raised at a reported NCTU discussion; see RFER, 6 November 1970.
146. A term used by T. Kolosi in an interview with the author. See note 115.
147. See A. Gaworzewska, 'Soviet and East European Hard Currency Debt and Trade with the West' in The Economist Intelligence Unit *Regional Review of Eastern Europe and the USSR 1985* (London: Economist Pulbications, 1985).
148. Csikós-Nagy, quoted in Vajna, 'Problems and Trends in the Development of the Hungarian New Economic Mechanism' p. 208.
149. Ibid.
150. Ibid.
151. Berend and Ránki, *The Hungarian Economy*, p. 247.
152. Laky, 'Small Enterprises in Hungary – Myth and Reality'; also Tárdos 'The increasing role and ambivalent reception of small enterprises in Hungary'.
153. See Economist Intelligence Unit, *Quarterly Review of Hungary* no. 2, 1985, p. 4.
154. See the two publications edited by Szoboszlai, cited above.
155. Bihari, 'Political relations of interest in socialism' in Szoboszlai (ed.) *Studies*, p. 54.
156. Ibid, p. 55. See also Bihari, 'Political Mechanism and Socialist Democracy'.

Conclusion

1. See Bialer and Afferica, 'The Genesis of Gorbachev's world', p. 607.
2. Zaslavskaya, 'The Novosibirsk Report', p. 88.
3. Aganbegyan, 'Socio-economic Development: A Strategy of Acceleration', p. 19.
4. See Hanson, 'Mikhail Gorbachev and the Economic Destiny of the USSR'.
5. See Brus, 'Political Pluralism and Markets in Communist Systems', pp. 115–7.
6. See Márkus, 'Overt and Covert Modes of Legitimation in East European Societies'.
7. See Valenta, *Soviet Intervention in Czechoslovakia 1968: Anatomy of a Decision*; and Dawisha, *The Kremlin and the Prague Spring*.
8. See Korbonski, 'Eastern Europe' in Byrnes (ed.), *After Brezhnev: Sources of Soviet Conduct in the 1980s*.
9. See Hanson, 'Soviet trade with Eastern Europe' in Dawisha and Hanson (eds) *Soviet-East European Dilemmas: Coercion, Competition and Consent*.
10. See Brown, 'Change in the Soviet Union'.

Bibliography

(i) General, Theoretical and Comparative Works

AGANBEGYAN, A., 'Socio-economic Development: A Strategy of Acceleration' *World Marxist Review* vol. XXVIII; no 9 (September 1985).

BAUER, T. and SZAMUELY, L., 'The Structure of Industrial Administration in the European CMEA Countries: change and continuity' *Acta Oeconomica*, vol. XX (1978) no 4.

BAUMAN, Z., *Socialism: The Active Utopia* (London: Allen & Unwin, 1976).

BERGSON, A., 'Market Socialism Revisited' in J. Vanek (ed.) *Self-Management* (Harmondsworth: Penguin, 1975).

BERKI, R., *Socialism* (London: Dent, 1975).

BERLIN, I., 'Two Concepts of Liberty' in A Quinton (ed.) *Political Philosophy* (Oxford: Oxford University Press, 1967).

BIALER, S. and AFFERICA, J., 'The Genesis of Gorbachev's World' *Foreign Affairs*, vol. 64 (1986) no 3.

BIRNBAUM, P. *et al* (eds) *Democracy, Consensus and Social Contract* (London and Beverly Hills: Sage Publications, 1978).

BORNSTEIN, M. (ed.) *Comparative Economic Systems* (Homewood, Illinois: Irwin, 1965).

BORNSTEIN, M. (ed.) *Plan and Market* (New Haven and London: Yale University Press, 1973).

BORNSTEIN, M. (ed.) *Comparative Economic Systems* (Homewood Illinois: Irwin, 1974) 3rd edn.

BRESLAUER, G., 'Khrushchev Reconsidered' in S. Cohen, A. Rabinowitch and R. Sharlet (eds) *The Soviet Union Since Stalin* (London: Macmillan, in association with Indiana University Press, 1980).

BRESLAUER, G., *Khrushchev and Brezhnev as Leaders* (London: Allen & Unwin, 1982).

BROMKE, A. (ed.) *The Communist States at the Crossroads* (New York: Praeger, 1965).

BROWN, A. and GRAY, J. (eds) *Political Culture and Political Change in Communist States* (London: Macmillan, 1979) 2nd edn.

BROWN, A., 'Change in the Soviet Union', *Foreign Affairs*, vol. 64 (1986) no 5.

BROWN, J., *The New Eastern Europe* (London: Pall Mall, 1966).

BRUNNER, G., 'Legitimacy Doctrines and Legitimation Procedures in East European Systems' in T. Rigby and F. Fehér (eds) *Political Legitimation in Communist States* (London: Macmillan, 1982).

BRUS, W., *The Market in a Socialist Economy* (London: Routledge & Kegan Paul, 1972).

BRUS, W., *The Economics and Politics of Socialism* (London and Boston: Routledge & Kegan Paul, 1973).

BRUS, W., *Socialist Ownership and Political Systems* (London and Boston: Routledge & Kegan Paul, 1976).

BRUS, W., 'Stalinism and the "Peoples' Democracies"' in R. C. Tucker (ed.) *Stalinism: Essays in Historical Interpretation* (New York: Norton, 1977).

BRUS, W., 'Political Pluralism and Markets in Communist Systems' in S. G. Solomon (ed.) *Pluralism in the Soviet Union* (London: Macmillan, 1983).

BRZEZINSKI, Z., *The Soviet Bloc* (Cambridge, Massachusetts, and London: Harvard University Press, 1967) revised edn.

BYRNES, R. (ed.) *After Brezhnev: Sources of Soviet Conduct in the 1980s* (London: Francis Pinter, in association with the Center for International Studies, Georgetown University, 1983).

CAHM, E. and FISERA, V-C. (eds) *Socialism and Nationalism*, vol. I, (Nottingham: Spokesman, 1979).

CARRITT, E. F., 'Liberty and Equality' in A. Quinton (ed.) *Political Philosophy* (Oxford: Oxford University Press, 1967).

COHEN, S., *Bukharin and the Bolshevik Revolution* (London: Wildwood House, 1974).

CRICK, B., *In Defence of Politics* (London: Weidenfeld & Nicolson, 1964) revised edn.

DAHL, R., *Polyarchy* (New Haven and London: Yale University Press, 1971).

DAHL, R., *Dilemmas of Pluralist Democracy: Autonomy vs Control* (New Haven and London: Yale University Press, 1982).

DAWISHA, K. and HANSON, P. (eds) *Soviet–East European Dilemmas: Coercion, Competition and Consent* (London: Heinemann, in association with the Royal Institute for International Affairs, 1981).

ECONOMIST INTELLIGENCE UNIT, *Regional Review of Eastern Europe and the USSR 1985* (London: Economist Publications, 1985).

ERLICH, A., *The Soviet Industrialisation Debate 1924–1928* (Cambridge, Massachusetts: Harvard University Press, 1960).

FEJTŐ, F., *A History of the People's Democracies* (Harmondsworth: Penguin 1974).

FRIEDGUT, T., *Political Participation in the USSR* (Princeton, New Jersey: Princeton University Press, 1979).

FRIEDMAN, M., *Capitalism and Freedom* (Chicago: University of Chicago Press, 1962).

FRIEDMAN, M. and R., *Free to Choose* (Harmondsworth: Penguin Books, 1980).

GAMARNIKOW, M., *Economic Reforms in Eastern Europe* (Detroit: Wayne State University Press, 1968).

GATI, C. (ed.) *The Politics of Modernisation in Eastern Europe* (New York: Praeger, 1974).

GYÖRGY, A. (ed.) *Issues of World Communism* (Princeton, New Jersey: Van Nostrand, 1966).

GOULDNER, A., *The Coming Crisis of Western Sociology* (New York: Basic Books/London: Heinemann, 1970).

GRANICK, D., *Enterprise Guidance in Eastern Europe* (Princeton, New Jersey: Princeton University Press, 1975).

GREGORY, P. and STUART, R., *Soviet Economic Structure and Performance* (New York and London: Harper & Row, 1974).

GRIFFITH, W. E. (ed.) *Communism in Europe* vols I and II, (Cambridge, Massachusetts: MIT Press, 1964 and 1966).
GROSSMAN, G., 'The Solidarity Society: A Philosophical Issue in Communist Economic Reforms' in G. Grossman (ed.) *Essays in Socialism and Planning in Honour of Carl Landauer* (Englewood Cliffs, New Jersey: Prentice-Hall, 1970).
GROSSMAN, G., 'Economic Reforms – A Balance Sheet' *Problems of Communism*, vol. XV; no 6 (November–December 1966).
HANSON, P., 'Mikhail Gorbachev and the Economic Destiny of the USSR' in M. McCauley (ed.) *The Soviet Union under Gorbachev* (London: Macmillan, forthcoming).
HAYEK, F. A. (ed.) *Collectivist Economic Planning* (London: Routledge, 1935).
HAYEK, F. A., 'Socialist Calculation: The "Competitive Solution"', *Economica*, vol. VIII; no 26 (May 1940).
HAYEK, F. A., *The Road to Serfdom* (London: Routledge & Kegan Paul, 1944).
HAYEK, F.A., 'The Price System as a Mechanism for Using Knowledge' in M. Bornstein (ed.) *Comparative Economic Systems* (Homewood, Illinois: Irwin, 1965).
HEISLER, M. (ed.) *Politics in Europe* (New York: Pared Mackay, 1974).
HORVAT, B., 'An Institutional Model of a Self-managed Socialist Economy' in J. Vanek (ed.) *Self-Management* (Harmondsworth: Penguin, 1975).
HOUGH, J., 'Political Participation in the Soviet Union', *Soviet Studies*, vol. XXVIII; no 1 (January 1976).
HOUGH, J., *The Soviet Union and Social Science Theory* (Cambridge, Massachusetts, and London: Harvard University Press, 1977).
HUNTINGTON, S., *Political Order in Changing Societies* (New Haven, Connecticut: Yale University Press, 1968).
IONESCU, G., 'Eastern Europe' in G. Ionescu and E. Gellner (eds) *Populism* (London: Weidenfeld & Nicolson, 1969).
JOHNSON, C. (ed.) *Change in Communist Systems* (Stanford California: Stanford University Press, 1970).
KOMMUNISTICHESKAYA PARTIYA SOVETSKOGO SOYUZA, *The Programme of the Communist Party of the Soviet Union adopted at the XXII Congress* (Moscow: Trud, 1961).
KUCZYNSKI, W., 'The State Enterprise under Socialism', *Soviet Studies*, vol. XXX; no 3 (July 1978).
LANGE, O. and TAYLOR, F., *On the Economic Theory of Socialism* (edited by B. Lippincott) (Minneapolis: University of Minnesota Press, 1938).
LEWIN, M., *Political Undercurrents in Soviet Economic Debates* (London: Pluto Press, 1975).
LIJPHART, A., 'Consociational Democracy', *World Politics*, vol. XXI; no 2 (January 1969).
LINDBLOM, C., *Politics and Markets* (New York: Basic Books, 1977).
LINDEN, C., *Khrushchev and the Soviet Leadership* (Baltimore and London: Johns Hopkins University Press, 1966).

LIVELY, J., 'Pluralism and Consensus' in P. Birnbaum *et al.* (eds) *Democracy, Consensus and Social Contract* (London and Beverly Hills: Sage Publications, 1978).

MCCAULEY, M. (ed.) *Communist Power in Europe 1944–49* (London: Macmillan, 1977).

MACPHERSON, C. B., *Democratic Theory* (Oxford: Oxford University Press, 1973).

MACPHERSON, C. B. (ed.) *Property* (Oxford: Basil Blackwell, 1978).

MÁRKUS, M., 'Overt and Covert Modes of Legitimation in East European Societies' in T. Rigby and F. Fehér (eds) *Political Legitimation in Communist States* (London: Macmillan, 1982).

MEADE, J., 'The Theory of Labour-managed Firms and of Profit-sharing' in J. Vanek (ed.) *Self-management* (Harmondsworth: Penguin, 1975).

MEDVEDEV, R. and Zh., *Khrushchev: The Years in Power* (London, Oxford and Melbourne: Oxford University Press, 1977).

MEDVEDEV, R., *Khrushchev* (Oxford: Blackwell, 1982).

MILENKOVITCH, D., *Plan and Market in Yugoslav Economic Thought* (New Haven and London: Yale University Press, 1971).

MISES, L. VON., 'Economic Calculation in the Socialist Commonwealth' in F. A. Hayek (ed.) *Collectivist Economic Planning* (London: Routledge, 1935).

NEUBERGER, E. and DUFFY, W., *Comparative Economic Systems* (Boston, Massachusetts: Allyn & Bacon, 1976).

NOVE, A., *The Soviet Economic System* (London: Allen & Unwin, 1977).

NOVE, A., *Political Economy and Soviet Socialism* (London: Allen & Unwin, 1979).

NOVE, A., *The Economics of Feasible Socialism* (London: Allen & Unwin, 1983).

RIGBY, T., 'Crypto-politics' in W. Laqueur and L. Labedz (eds) *The State of Soviet Studies* (Cambridge, Massachusetts: MIT Press, 1965).

ROTHSCHILD, J., *East–Central Europe between the Two World Wars* (Seattle and London: University of Washington Press, 1974).

SCHUMPETER, J., *Capitalism, Socialism and Democracy* (London: Allen & Unwin, 1976), 5th edn with new introduction.

SELUCKÝ, R., *Economic Reforms in Eastern Europe* (New York, Washington and London: Praeger, 1972).

SELUCKY, 'Marxism and Self-management' in J. Vanek (ed.) *Self-management* (Harmondsworth: Penguin, 1975).

SELUCKÝ, R., *Marxism, Socialism and Freedom* (London: Macmillan, 1979).

SHACKLETON, J., 'Is Workers' Self-management the Answer?' *National Westminster Bank Quarterly Review*, February 1976.

SOLOMON, S. G. (ed.) *Pluralism and the Soviet Union* (London: Macmillan, 1983).

SPULBER, N., *The Economics of Communist Eastern Europe* (Westport, Connecticut: Greenwood Press, 1976) reprint of original published in 1957.

SPULBER, N. (ed.) *Organisational Alternatives in Soviet-type Economies* (Cambridge: Cambridge University Press, 1979).

STEINER, K., *Politics in Austria* (Boston, Massachusetts: Little, Brown, 1972).

TUCKER, R. C. (ed.) *Stalinism: Essays in Historical Interpretation* (New York: Norton, 1977).
UNITED NATIONS SECRETARIAT OF THE ECONOMIC COMMISSION FOR EUROPE, *Economic Survey of Europe* (New York: United Nations, various years).
VANEK, J. (ed.) *Self-management* (Harmondsworth: Penguin, 1975).
WOODALL,, J. (ed.) *Policy and Politics in Gierek's Poland* (London: Francis Pinter, 1982).
ZASLAVSKAYA, T., 'The Novosibirsk Report' *Survey*, vol. XXVIII; no 1 (Spring 1984).
ZAUBERMAN, A., *Industrial Progress in Poland, Czechoslovakia and East Germany 1937–62* (London, New York and Toronto: Oxford University Press in association with the Royal Institute for International Affairs, 1964).
ŽUPANOV, J., 'The Yugoslav Enterprise', in M. Bornstein (ed.) *Comparative Economic Systems* (Homewood, Illinois: Irwin, 1974) 3rd edn.

(ii) Works on Czechoslovakia

BARTOŠEK, K., 'Revoluce proti Byrokratismu?', parts 1–4, *Rudé právo*, 18, 24, 26, and 30 July 1968.
BERNÁŠEK, M., 'The Czechoslovak Economic Recession 1962–65' *Soviet Studies*, vol. XX; no 4 (April 1969).
BLOOMFIELD, J., *Passive Revolution* (London: Allison & Busby, 1979).
BROWN, A., 'Pluralistic Trends in Czechoslovakia', *Soviet Studies*, vol. XVII; no 4 (April 1966).
BROWN, A. and WIGHTMAN, G., 'Changes in the Levels of Membership and Social Composition of the Communist Party of Czechoslovakia 1945–73', *Soviet Studies*, vol. XXVII; no 3 (July 1975).
BYSTŘINA, I., 'Nová soustava a demokracie', *Literární Noviny*, 7 December 1966.
ČERMÁK, V. and KYSILKA, H., *Vývoj Československé Ekonomické Reformy* (Prague: 1970).
ČERNÍK, O., 'Hospodářská politika v nejbližším období', *Rudé Právo*, 25 July 1967.
ČERNÍK, O., 'Československé hospodářství a jeho výhledy', *Hospodářské Noviny* 5 January 1968.
'DALIMIL', 'Přechodný Stav', *Literární Listy*, 2 May 1968.
'DALIMIL', 'Čas vítězí nad naší Vladou', *Literární Listy*, 30 May 1968.
'DALIMIL', 'Naš Komentář', *Literární Listy* 11 July 1968.
DAWISHA, K., *The Kremlin and the Prague Spring* (Berkeley, Los Angeles and London: University of California Press, 1984).
DUCHAČEK, I., 'Czechoslovakia: the Past Reburied?' *Problems of Communism*, vol. XI; no 3 (May–June 1962).
DUCHAČEK, I., 'New Course or No Course?' *Problems of Communism*, vol. IV; no 1 (January–February 1965).

ELIÁŠ, Z. and NETÍK, J., 'Czechoslovakia' in W. E. Griffith (ed.) *Communism in Europe*, vol. II (Cambridge, Massachusetts and London: MIT Press, 1966).

ELLO, P. (ed.) *Czechoslovakia's Blueprint for 'freedom'* (Washington, DC: Acropolis, 1968).

FEIERABEND, F., 'The Gottwald Era in Czechoslovakia', *Journal of Central European Affairs* vol. XIII; no 3 (October 1953).

FEIWEL, G., *New Economic Patterns in Czechoslovakia* (New York, Washington and London: Praeger, 1968).

FISERA, V. (ed.) *Workers' Councils in Czechoslovakia: Documents and Essays 1968–9* (London: Allison & Busby, 1978).

GOLAN, G., *The Czechoslovak Reform Movement: Communism in Crisis 1962–1968* (Cambridge: Cambridge University Press, 1971).

GOLAN, G., 'The Road to Reform', *Problems of Communism*, vol. XX; no 3 (May–June 1971).

GOLAN, G., *Reform Rule in Czechoslovakia* (Cambridge: Cambridge University Press, 1973).

GOLAN, G., 'Antonin Novotný: The Sources and the Nature of His Power', *Canadian Slavonic Papers*, vol. XIV (Autumn 1972).

GOLDMANN, J., 'Fluctuations and Trend in the Rate of Economic Growth in some Socialist Countries', *East European Economics*, vol. IV; no 1 (Autumn 1965).

GOLDMANN, J. and KOUBA, K., *Economic Growth in Czechoslovakia* (White Plains, New York: International Arts and Sciences Press/Prague: Akademia, 1969).

HÁJEK, J., *Mýtus a realita ledna 1968* (Prague: Svoboda, 1970).

HAMŠIK, D., *Writers against Rulers* (London: Hutchinson, 1971).

HAPALA, M., 'Political Parties in Czechoslovakia 1918–38', in M. Rechcigl (ed.) *Czechoslovakia Past and Present* (Paris and The Hague: Mouton, 1968) vol. I.

HENDRYCH, J., 'O upevňování jednoty naší socialistické společnosti se zvláštním zřetelem k mladé generaci', *Rudé Právo*, 10 February 1967.

HOLESOVSKY, V., 'Czechoslovakia's Economic Debate', *East Europe*, vol. XVIII, no 12 (December 1964).

HOLESOVSKY, V., 'Prague's Economic Model', *East Europe*, vol. XVI; no 2 (February 1967).

HOLESOVSKY, V., 'Problems and Prospects', *Problems of Communism*, vol. XIV; no 5 (September–October, 1965).

HOLESOVSKY, V., 'Planning reforms in Czechoslovakia', *Soviet Studies*, vol. XIX; no 4 (April 1968).

HOLESOVSKY, V., 'Planning and the Market in the Czechoslovak Reform' in M. Bornstein (ed.) *Plan and Market* (New Haven, Connecticut and London: Yale University Press, 1973).

HORÁLEK, M., SOKOL, M., KOŽUŠNIK, Č., and TŮREK, O., 'Nástin koncepce dalšího rozvíjení ekonomické soustavy řízení' *Hospodářské Noviny*, 5 April 1968, special supplement.

HRUBY, P., *Fools and Heroes: The Changing Role of Communist Intellectuals in Czechoslovakia* (Oxford: Pergamon, 1980).

'I. Celostátní Porada Československých Sociologů', *Sociologický Časopis*, vol. III (1967) no 3.
JANCAR, B. W., *Czechoslovakia and the Absolute Monopoly of Power* (New York, Washington and London: Praeger, 1971).
JODL, M., 'K pojetí sociologického výzkumu', *Literární noviny*, 2 November 1963.
KADLEC, V., 'Kybernetické modelování v řízení národního hospodářství, *Plánované Hospodářství*, vol. XVII (1964) no 3.
KADLEC, V., 'Ekonomicky zajistit socialismus' *Literární Listy*, 1 August 1968.
KANTŮREK, J., 'Nová soustava a staré myšlenky', *Kulturní Tvorba*, no 21, 1966.
KAPLAN, K., 'Zamyšlení nad politickými procesy' parts 1–3, *Nová Mysl*, vol. XXII (1968) nos 6, 7, and 8.
KOCANDA, R., 'Důsledně ke komplexní soustave', *Nová Mysl*, vol. XX (1966) no 8.
KODOUŠEK, K., 'Czechoslovak Theory and Practice as Reflected by the Economic Journals', *Czechoslovak Economic Papers*, no 9, 1967.
KOHOUTEK, M., 'From General Discussion to Concrete Preparation for Improving the System of Planned Management', translated from *Plánované Hospodářství*, no 2, 1965, in *East European Economics*, vol. III; no 4 (Summer 1965).
KOHOUTEK, M., 'Příprava zdokonalené soustavy plánovitého řízení', *Plánované hospodářství*, vol. XVIII (1965) nos 7–8.
KOHOUTEK, M., 'Ekonomický experiment a nová soustava' *Hospodářské Noviny*, 12 February 1965.
KOHOUTEK, M., 'Další kroky v ekonomickém řízení', *Hospodářské Noviny*, 12 January 1968.
KOLDER, D., 'Komplexně řešit rozvoj naší ekonomiky', *Život Strany*, no 21, 1963.
KOLDER, D., 'Stranické řízení národního hospodářství', *Nová Mysl*, vol. XX (1966) no 11.
KOLDER, D., 'Pětiletka a nová soustava', *Hospodářské Noviny*, 14 October 1966.
KOLISKO, M., 'Nová soustava a příběhy ze života', *Život Strany*, no 13, 1966.
KOMARNICKIJ, M., 'Revoluční Strana', *Život Strany*, no 14, 1966.
KOMENDA, B. and KOŽUŠNÍK, Č., 'Některé základní otázky zdokonalení soustavy řízení socialistického národního hospodářství', *Politická Ekonomie*, vol. XII (1964), no 3.
KOMENDA, B., 'Podminky fungování tržního mechanismu v socialistickém hospodářství' *Plánované Hospodářství* vol. XVII (1964) no 7.
KOMUNISTICKÁ STRANA ČESKOSLOVENSKA, 'Draft principles of a system to improve planned management of the economy', translated from *Rudé Právo* 17 October 1964 in *East European Economics*, vol. III, no 4 (Summer 1965).
KOMUNISTICKÁ STRANA ČESKOSLOVENSKA, *XIII. Sjezd* (Prague: Svoboda, 1966).

KOMUNISTICKÁ STRANA ČESKOSLOVENSKA, *Akční Program* (Prague: Svoboda, 1968).

KORDA, B., 'O ekonomické vĕde a vyuce', *Plánované hospodářství*, vol. XXVII (1964) no 4.

KORDA, B. and MORAVČIK, I., 'Reflections on the 1965–68 Czechoslovak Economic Reform', *Canadian Slavonic Papers*, vol. XIII (Spring 1971).

KOSÍK, K., 'Naše nynĕjší krize', parts 1–3, *Literární Listy*, 11, 18 and 25 April 1968.

KOSTA, J., 'Czechoslovak Economists Discuss Ways of Improving the System of Planned Management', *Czechoslovak Economic Papers*, no 4, 1964.

KOSTA, J., 'Workers' Councils in the Czechoslovak Reform of 1968', in D. Heathfield, *The Economics of Co-Determination* (London: Macmillan, 1977).

KOTRBATY, J., 'Neexperimentovat s experimenty', *Kulturní Tvorba*, no 14, 1966.

KOTRBATY, J., 'Reálnĕ bez iluzí', *Kulturní Tvorba*, no 14, 1966.

KOUBA, K., 'The Development of the Structure of the Czechoslovak Economy', *East European Economics*, vol. IV; no 1 (Autumn 1965).

KOUBA, K. *et al.*, *Úvahy o Socialistické Ekonomice* (Prague: Svoboda, 1968).

KOUBA, K., *Ekonomicky Růst a Soustava Řízení* (Prague: ČSAV Ekonomický Ústav, 1969).

KOVANDA, K., 'Czechoslovak Workers' Councils 1968–9' *Telos*, no 28 (Summer 1976).

KOŽUŠNÍK, C., 'Rozhodující krok dalšího rozvoje ekonomické reformy', *Nová Mysl*, vol. XXII (1968) no 5.

KRATOCHVIL, F., 'Obsah a funkce politické vĕdy', *Nová Mysl*, vol. XX (1966) no 8.

KREJČÁR, B. and TESAR, K., 'K úloze ceny v soustave plánovitého řízení', *Plánované Hospodářství*, vol. XVII (1964), no 11.

KREJČÍ, J., *Social Change and Stratification in Post-war Czechoslovakia* (London: Macmillan, 1972).

KUČERA, S., 'Vĕdecká politika a politická vĕda', *Nová Mysl*, vol. XX (1966) no 25.

KUSIN, V., *The Intellectual Origins of the Prague Spring* (Cambridge: Cambridge University Press, 1971).

KUSIN, V., *Political Grouping in the Czechoslovak Reform Movement* (London: Macmillan, 1972).

KUSIN, V. (ed.) *The Czechoslovak Reform Movement 1968* (Proceedings of a conference held at Reading University, July 1971 (Santa Barbara, California, and Oxford: ABC-CLIO, 1973).

KUSIN, V., 'Czechoslovakia' in M. McCauley (ed.) *Communist Power in Europe 1944–49* (London: Macmillan, 1977).

KUSIN, V., *From Dubček to Charter 77* (Edinburgh: Q Press, 1978).

KÝN, O., 'O úloze plánu', *Plánované Hospodářství*, vol. XVII (1964) no 12.

KÝN, O., 'The Rise and Fall of Economic Reform in Czechoslovakia', *American Economic Review*, vol. LX (1970) no 2.

KÝN, O., 'Czechoslovakia' in K. Höhmann, M. Kaser and H. Thalheim (eds) *The New Economic Systems of Eastern Europe* (London: Hurst, 1975).

L., G., 'New Policy in Czechoslovakia', *The World Today*, vol. IX; no 10 (October 1953).

LÁB, M., 'Stranická práce v nových podmínkách', *Nová Mysl*, vol. XX (1966) no 18.

LAKATOŠ, M., 'Aby právo ne překáželo ekonomice', *Hospodářské Noviny*, no 2, 1965.

LAKATOŠ, M., 'K niektorým problémom štruktury našej politickej soustavy', *Právny Obzor*, vol. 48 (1965) no 1.

LAKATOŠ, M., 'Dvadsať rokov budovania socialistickej demokracie', *Právny Obzor*, vol. 48 (1965) no 5.

LAKATOŠ, M., 'Společenské organizace a zajmy pracujících', *Hospodarske Noviny*, 26 March 1965.

LAKATOŠ, M., 'Niektoré problémy socialistické demokracie z hľadiska postavenia občana v našej společnosti', *Právny Obzor*, vol. 49 (1966) no 3.

LAKATOŠ, M., *Občan, Právo a Demokracie* (Prague: Svobodné Slovo, 1966).

LENÁRT, J., 'Improvement of the organisation and planned management of the national economy', translated from *Rudé Právo* 10 January 1965 in *East European Economics*, vol. III, no 4 (Summer 1965).

LÖBL, E., 'Nielen Chlebom', *Kultúrny Život*, 16 January 1965.

LÖBL, E., 'Ekonómia a politika', *Plánované Hospodářství*, vol. XVII (1965) no 10.

LÖBL, E., 'Plán a trh: rovnica s dvoma neznámými', *Hospodářské Noviny*, 8 December 1967.

LÖBL, E., *Úvahy o duševnej práci a bohatstve národa* (Bratislava: Vydavateľstvo Slovenskej Akademie Vied, 1967).

LÖBL, E., *Sentenced and Tried* (London: Elek Books, 1969).

LOUKOTKA, J., 'Rozvoj vedecké teorie politiky', *Nová Mysl*, vol. XX (1966) no 25.

MACHONIN, P. and VEČERA, J., 'Z jednání stranických orgánů ÚV KSČ o sociologie v ČSSR', *Sociologický Časopis*, vol. I (1965) no 1.

MACHONIN, P. (ed.) *Sociální Struktura Socialistické Společnosti* (Prague: Svoboda, 1967).

MACHONIN, P. *et al.*, *Změny v. sociální structuře Československa a dynamika sociálně politického vývoje* (Prague: Svoboda, 1967).

MACHONIN, P. *et al.*, *Československá Společnost* (Bratislava: Nakladateľstvo Epocha, 1969).

MEIER, V., 'Czechoslovakia: the Struggle for Reform', *East Europe*, vol. XIV, no 8 (August 1965).

MENCL, V. and OUŘEDNÍK, F., 'Jak to bylo v lednu', parts I–IV, *Život Strany*, nos 14–17, 1968.

MICHAL, J., *Central Planning in Czechoslovakia* (Stanford, California: Stanford University Press, 1960).

MICHAL, J., 'The New Economic Model', *Survey*, no 59 (April 1966).

MLYNÁŘ, Z., 'Socialistická demokracie a problémy řízení', *Nová Mysl*, vol. XVI (1962) no 9.

MLYNÁŘ, Z., 'Nová soustava řízení, právo a demokracie', *Kulturní Tvorba*, no 48, 1964.

MLYNÁŘ, Z., *Stát a Člověk* (Prague: Svobodné Slovo, 1964).

MLYNÁŘ, Z., 'Úloha práva v řízení hospodářství, *Plánované Hospodářství*, vol. XVII (1964) no 10.

MLYNÁŘ, Z., 'Problems of Political Leadership and the New Economic system', *World Marxist Review*, vol. VII (1965) no 12.

MLYNÁŘ, Z., 'K demokratické politické organizací společnosti', *Nová Mysl*, vol. XXII (1968) no 5.

MLYNÁŘ, Z., *Československy Pokus o Reformu 1968: Analýza jeho Teorie a Praxe* (Cologne: Index, 1975).

MLYNÁŘ, Z., *Nightfrost in Prague* (London: Hurst, 1980).

MONTIAS, J. M., 'A Plan for all Seasons', *Survey*, no 51 (April 1962).

MONTIAS, J. M., 'Economic Reform in Perspective' *Survey*, no 59 (April 1966).

MRACHKOVSKAYA, O., *From Revisionism to Betrayal: a Criticism of Ota Sik's Economic Views* (Moscow: Progress, 1972).

MYANT, M., *Socialism and Democracy in Czechoslovakia 1945–48* (Cambridge: Cambridge University Press, 1981).

NOVOTNÝ, A., 'Jednotně, celá strana, všichni pracující za uskutečnění sjezdem stanovených cílů', *Rudé Právo*, 24 March 1963.

NOVOTNÝ, A., 'Za rozkvět našich národů a další upevňování jednoty lidu', *Rudé Právo*, 13 June 1963.

NOVOTNÝ, A., 'Projev Soudruha Antonína Novotného', *Rudé Právo*, 13 November 1964.

NOVOTNÝ, A., 'Naše Budoucnost závisí na vysledcích společné práce', *Rudé právo*, 17 May 1965.

NOVOTNÝ, A., 'Iniciativa lidí – hnací sila dalšího rozvoje socialistické společnosti', *Rudé Právo*, 29 October 1965.

ORBAN, P., 'Plán – nebo zbožně-penežní vztahy?', *Nová Mysl*, vol. XIX (1965) no 4.

ORT, A., HAD, M. and KRATKÝ, K., 'Politická věda – ano či ne?', *Nová Mysl*, vol. XIX (1965) no 5.

OXLEY, A., PRAVDA, A. and RITCHIE, A. (eds) *Czechoslovakia: the Party and the People* (London: Allen Lane/The Penguin Press 1973).

PAUL, D., 'The Repluralisation of Czechoslovak Politics in the 1960s', *Slavic Review*, vol. XXXIII; no 4 (December 1974).

PAUL, D., *The Cultural Limits of Revolutionary Politics* (Boulder, Colorado: East European Monographs, 1979).

PELIKAN, J. (ed.) *The Czechoslovak Political Trials 1950–54* (London: MacDonald, 1971).

PELIKAN, J. (ed.) *The Secret Vysočany Congress: Proceedings and Documents of the Extraordinary XIV Congress of the Communist Party of Czechoslovakia, 22 August 1968* (London: Allen Lane/The Penguin Press, 1971).

PIEKALKIEWICZ, J., *Public Opinion Polling in Czechoslovakia 1968–9* (New York, Washington and London: Praeger, 1972).

PLACHKY, M., 'Lze vědecky plánovat?', *Hospodářské Noviny*, 24 May 1963.

'Politická organizace a právo při řízení národniho hospodářství', *Právník*, vol. CIII (1964) nos 6 and 7.

'Prague's Political Crisis', *East Europe*, vol. XII; no 7 (July 1963).

PRAVDA, A., 'Some Aspects of the Czechoslovak Economic Reform and the Working Class in 1968', *Soviet Studies*, vol. XXV; no 1 (July 1973).

PRAVDA, A., *Reform and Change in the Czechoslovak Political System January–August 1968* (Beverly Hills and London: Sage Research Papers in the Social Sciences 1975) vol. 3, no 90–020.

'Proti dogmatismu za tvořivý rozvoj ekonomické vědy', parts 1 and 2, *Hospodářské noviny*, 8 and 15 November 1963.

PRŮSA, O., 'Řídící činnost Státního Aparátu', *Nová Mysl*, vol. XVII (1963) no 11.

RECHCIGL, M. (ed.) *The Czechoslovak Contribution to World Culture* (The Hague: Mouton, 1964).

RECHCIGL, M. (ed.) *Czechoslovakia Past and Present* (Paris and the Hague: Mouton, 1968) vol. I.

REMINGTON, R. (ed.) *Winter in Prague: Documents on Czechoslovak Communism in Crisis* (Cambridge, Massachusetts and London: MIT Press, 1969).

RENDL, V. and KUBIK, J., 'K vývoji naší ekonomiky v posledních letech', *Plánované Hospodářství*, vol. XIX (1966) no 4.

REZNÍČEK, J. and TOMAN, J., 'Demokratizace hospodářství a postavení podniku', *Hospodářské Noviny*, 19 April 1968, special supplement.

RICHTA, R., 'Povaha a souvislosti Vědeckotechnické Revoluce', *Sociologický Časopis*, vol. II (1966) no 2.

RICHTA, R. *et al., Civilisation at the Crossroads: Social and Human Implications of the Scientific and Technological Revolution* (Prague: Akademia/New York: International Arts and Sciences Press, 1969).

RIVELES, S., 'Slovakia: Catalyst of Crisis', *Problems of Communism*, vol. XVII, no 3 (May–June 1968).

ROHAN, R., 'Strana a Společnost', *Nová Mysl*, vol. XX (1966) no 11.

ROHLÍČEK, R., 'Economic Development and the New System of Management', *New Trends in Czechoslovak Economics*, no 6, 1967.

RUPNIK, J., 'The Czech Socialists and the Nation (1848–1918)', in E. Cahm and V. Fisera (eds) *Socialism and Nationalism*, vol. I (Nottingham: Spokesman, 1979).

RUTLAND, P., 'Ideology and Power in the Czechoslovak Political System', paper presented to the Conference on Legitimation in Eastern Europe, held at Westfield College, University of London, September 1982.

ŠEDIVÝ, I., 'Strana a Hospodářství', *Život Strany*, no 15, 1966.

SELUCKÝ, R., 'Ekonomické názory se vyjasňuje', *Věda a Život*, no 3, 1964.

SELUCKÝ, R., 'Lide a Plán', *Kulturní Tvorba*, 7 February 1963.

SELUCKÝ, R., 'Is There a Danger of Unemployment in our Country?' translated from *Přiroda a společnost*, no 11, 1967, in *East Europe*, vol. XVI, no 9 (September 1967).

SELUCKÝ, R. and SELUCKÁ, M., *Člověk a Hospodářství* (Prague: Svobodné Slovo, 1967).

SELUCKÝ, R., *Czechoslovakia: The Plan that Failed* (London: Nelson, 1970).

SELUCKÝ, R., *Economic Reforms in Eastern Europe* (New York, Washington and London: Praeger, 1972).

SELUCKÝ, R., 'Marxism and Self-management', in J. Vanek (ed.) *Self-management* (Harmondsworth: Penguin, 1975).

SELUCKÝ, R., *Marxism, Socialism and Freedom* (London: Macmillan, 1979).

SETON-WATSON, R. W., *A History of the Czechs and Slovaks* (London: Hutchinson, 1943).

ŠIK, O., 'Překonat pozůstatky dogmatismu v politické ekonomii', *Nová Mysl*, vol. XVII (1963) no 9.

ŠIK, O., 'Problémy zdokonalení soustavy plánovitého řízení', *Rudé Právo*, 22 November 1963.

ŠIK, O., 'Nezastavit se v půli cesty o využívání socialistických zbožních vztahů', *Hospodářské Noviny*, 14 February 1964.

ŠIK, O., 'Budouci vyžáduje kritiku minulého', *Kulturní Tvorba*, 19 November 1964.

ŠIK, O., 'Czechoslovakia's New System of Planning and Management', *World Marxist Review*, vol. VIII, no 3 (March 1965).

ŠIK, O., 'Příspěvek k analýze našeho hospodářského vývoje', *Politická Ekonomie*, vol. XIV (1966) no 1.

ŠIK, O., 'Problémy přechodu na novou soustavu', parts 1–3, *Rudé Právo*, 18, 22, and 23 February 1966.

ŠIK, O., 'Cesta k novej sústave nie je l'ahká', *Práca*, 4 June 1966.

ŠIK, O., *Plan and Market under Socialism* (White Plains, New York: International Arts and Sciences Press/Prague: Akademia 1967).

ŠIK, O., 'Overcoming Disequilibrium in the Economy', *New Trends In Czechoslovak Economics*, no 5, 1967.

ŠIK, O., 'O pravdě v ekonomice a politice a skutečných zajmech pracujících', *Práce*, 5 March 1968.

ŠIK, O., 'Whither Economic Policy?', *New Trends in Czechoslovak Economics*, no 5, 1968.

ŠIK, O., *Economic Planning and Management in Czechoslovakia* (Prague: Orbis, 1968).

ŠIK, O., 'The Economic Impact of Stalinism', *Problems of Communism* vol. XX; no 3 (May–June 1971).

ŠIK, O., *Czechoslovakia: The Bureaucratic Economy* (White Plains, New York: International Arts and Sciences Press, 1972).

ŠIMON, B. and ŘÍHA, L., 'Rozvoj ekonomické reformy v ČSSR', *Život Strany*, no 10, 1968.

ŠIMON, B. and ŘÍHA, L., 'Nová soustava dnes a jak dál?', *Život Strany*, no 11, 1968.

ŠIMON, B. and ŘÍHA, L., 'Podnik v nové soustavě', *Život Strany*, no 14, 1968.

SKILLING, H. G., 'The Formation of a Communist Party in Czechoslovakia', *American Slavic and East European Review*, vol. XIV; no 3 (October 1955).

SKILLING, H. G., 'The Comintern and Czechoslovak Communism 1921–1919', *American Slavic and East European Review*, vol. XIX; no 2 (April 1960).
SKILLING, H. G., 'The Break-up of the Czechoslovak Coalition 1947–1948', *Canadian Journal of Economics and Political Science*, vol. XXVI; no 3 (August 1960).
SKILLING, H. G., 'Revolution and Continuity in Czechoslovakia 1945–48', *Journal of Central European Affairs*, vol. XX; no 4 (January 1961).
SKILLING, H. G., 'Czechoslovakia', in A. Bromke (ed.) *The Communist States at the Crossroads* (New York: Praeger, 1965).
SKILLING, H. G., 'Group Conflict and Political Change', in C. Johnson (ed.) *Change in Communist Systems* (Stanford, California: Stanford University Press, 1970).
SKILLING, H. G., *Czechoslovakia's Interrupted Revolution* (Princeton, New Jersey, and Guildford, Surrey: Princeton University Press, 1976).
SKILLING, H. G., 'Stalinism and Czechoslovak Political Culture' in R. C. Tucker (ed.) *Stalinism: Essays in Historical Interpretation* (New York: Norton, 1977).
ŠKRLANT, V., 'Na prahu velkého experimentu', *Nová Mysl*, vol. XX (1966) no 2.
SOKOL, M., 'Uplatňení zbožních vztahů při řízení' *Plánované Hospodářství*, vol. XVII (1964) no 5.
SOKOL, M., 'Postavení plánu v nové soustavě', *Nová Mysl*, vol. XIX (1965) no 2.
SOUKUP, M., 'Ke koncepci a úkolům politické vědy', *Nová Mysl*, vol. XX (1966) no 18.
STALLER, H. G., 'Czechoslovakia: The New Model of Planning and Management', *American Economic Review*, vol. LVIII; no 2 (May 1968).
Statistická Ročenka ČSSR (Prague: Federální Statisticky Úřad/Nakladatelství Technicke Literatury, various years).
STEINER, E., *The Slovak Dilemma* (Cambridge: Cambridge University Press, 1973).
STEVENS, J., *Czechoslovakia at the Crossroads* (Boulder, Colorado: East European Monographs, 1985).
STREGEL, K., 'Jde o soulad slov a činů', *Hospodářské Noviny*, 15 March 1963.
SUCHAN, K., 'Podnik a centrum', *Politická Ekonomie*, vol. XVI (1968) no 2.
SUCHAN, K., 'Podnik a Integrační Seskupení', *Nová Mysl*, vol. XXII (1968) no 6.
SUDA, Z., *Zealots and Rebels: A History of the Ruling Communist Party of Czechoslovakia* (Stanford, California: Hoover Institution Press, 1980).
TABORSKY, E., *Czechoslovak Democracy at Work* (London: Allen & Unwin, 1945).
TABORSKY, E., 'Political Developments in Czechoslovakia since 1953', *Journal of Politics*, vol. XX, no 1 (February 1958).
TABORSKY, E., 'Czechoslovakia's March to Communism', *Problems of Communism*, vol. X, no 2 (March–April 1961).

TABORSKY, E., *Communism in Czechoslovakia 1948–1960* (Princeton, New Jersey: Princeton University Press, 1961).

TABORSKY, E., Czechoslovakia: Out of Stalinism?', *Problems of Communism*, vol. XIII, no 3 (May–June 1964).

TABORSKY, E., 'Czechoslovakia's Economic Reform: A Balance Sheet of the First Year', *East Europe*, vol. XVII, no 4 (April 1968).

TABORSKY, E., 'The Roots of Czechoslovak Democracy', in M. Rechcigl (ed.) *Czechoslovakia Past and Present* (Paris and The Hague: Mouton, 1968).

TIGRID, P., 'Czechoslovakia: A Post-mortem', *Survey*, no 73 (Autumn 1969).

TIGRID, P., 'The Prague Coup of 1948: The Elegant Takeover', in T. Hammond (ed.) *The Anatomy of Communist Takeovers* (New Haven and London: Yale University Press, 1975).

TOMAN, J., 'O urychleném zavádění nové soustavy', *Život Strany*, no 15, 1966.

TOMAN, J., *Úvod do Zásad Nové Soustavy Plánovitého Řízení* (Za vyšší úroveň plánovitého řízení, no 1) (Prague: Nakladatelství Politické Literatury, 1965).

TONDL, L. and NEKOLA, J., 'Nově rysy v úloze védy', *Sociologický Časopis*, vol. II (1966) no 2.

TŮREK, O., 'Úloha centrálního plánu a impulsy zdravého vývoje hospodářství', *Plánované Hospodářství*, vol. XVII (1964) no 12.

TŮREK, O., *O Plánu, Trhu a Hospodářské Politice* (Prague: Svoboda, 1967).

TŮREK, O., 'Národohospodářská rovnovaha – kličový úkol', *Plánované Hospodářství*, vol. XX (1967) no 5.

TŮREK, O., 'O plánu, trhu a hospodářské politice', *Hospodářské Noviny*, 27 October 1967.

TŮREK, O., 'Jak dál v nové soustavé řízení?', *Hospodářské Noviny*, 26 January 1968.

ULČ, O., 'Pilsen: The Unknown Revolt', *Problems of Communism*, vol. XIV, no 3 (May–June 1965).

ULČ, O., *Politics in Czechoslovakia* (San Francisco: Freeman, 1974).

VACHA, S., 'Budou řídit a jaci budou?', *Hospodářské Noviny*, no 17, 1965.

VACULÍK, L., 'Culture and the Party in Czechoslovakia', translated in *East Europe*, vol. XVI, no 9 (September 1967).

VACULÍK, M., 'V práci strany podle podmínek', *Život Strany*, no 21, 1966.

VALENTA, J., *Soviet Intervention in Czechoslovakia 1968: Anatomy of a Decision* (Baltimore and London: Johns Hopkins University Press, 1979).

VITAK, R., 'Workers' control in Czechoslovakia', in J. Vanek (ed.), *Self-management* (Harmondsworth: Penguin, 1975).

WHEELER, G. S., *The Human Face of Socialism: The Political Economy of Change in Czechoslovakia* (New York: Lawrence Hill, 1973).

WIGHTMAN, G., 'The Changing Role of Central Party Institutions in Czechoslovakia 1962–67', *Soviet Studies*, vol. XXXIII, no 3 (July 1981).

YOUNG, E., *Czechoslovakia: Keystone of Peace and Democracy* (London: Gollancz, 1938).
'Záměry a skutečnost ekonomické reformy', *Nová Mysl*, vol. XXII (1969) no 11.
'Zákono třetím pětiletém plánu rozvoje narodního hospodářství ČSSR', *Plánované Hospodářství*, vol. XIII; no 12 (December 1960).

(iii) Works on Hungary

ACZÉL, GY., 'The People and the Intellectuals', *New Hungarian Quarterly*, vol. X (1969); no 35.
ACZÉL, GY., 'The Guiding Principles of Hungarian Science Policy', *New Hungarian Quarterly*, vol. X (1969) no 36.
ACZÉL, T. and MERAY, T., *The Revolt of the Mind* (New York: Praeger, 1960).
ACZÉL, T. (ed.) *Ten Years After* (London: MacGibbon & Kee, 1966).
ANTAL, L., 'Development – With Some Digression', *Acta Oeconomica*, vol. XXIII (1979) nos 3–4.
BALASSA, B., *The Hungarian Experience in Economic Planning* (New Haven: Yale University Press, 1959).
BÁRSONY, J., 'Tibor Liska's Concept, the Socialist Entrepreneurship', *Acta Oeconomica*, vol. XXVIII (1982) nos 3–4.
BAUER, T., 'The Contradictory Position of the Enterprise under the New Hungarian Economic Mechanism', *Coexistence*, vol. XIII (1976) pp. 65–80.
BAUER, T., 'Investment Cycles in Planned Economies', *Acta Oeconomica*, vol. XXI (1978) no 3.
BAUER, T., 'The Hungarian Alternative to Soviet-type Planning', paper presented to the Round Table on the Hungarian Economy and East–West Relations, Bloomington, Indiana, 21–4 March 1982.
BAUER, T., 'A második gazdasági reform és a tulajdonviszonyok', *Mozgó Világ*, no 11, 1983.
BEREND, I., 'The Historical Background of the Recent Economic Reforms in Eastern Europe (the Hungarian Experiences)', *East European Quarterly*, vol. XI (1968) no 1.
BEREND, I. and RÁNKI, Gy., *Hungary: A Century of Economic Development* (Newton Abbott: David & Charles, 1974).
BEREND, I., 'Thirty Years of Hungarian Socialist Economic Policy', *Acta Oeconomica*, vol. XIV (1975) nos 2–3.
BEREND, I., 'Current Hungarian Economic Policy in Historical Perspective', *Acta Oeconomica*, vol. XVIII (1977) no 2.
BEREND, I., 'Ten Years After: Instead of a Balance Sheet', *Acta Oeconomica*, vol. XX (1978) nos 1–2.
BEREND, I. and RÁNKI, Gy., *Underdevelopment and Economic Growth: Studies in Hungarian Economic and Social History* (Budapest: Akadémiai Kiadó, 1979).

BEREND, I., 'Hungary's Road to the Seventies', *Acta Oeconomica*, vol. XXV (1980) nos 1–2.

BEREND, I. and RÁNKI, Gy., *The European Periphery and Industrialisation 1780–1914* (Budapest: Akadémiai Kiadó, 1982).

BEREND, I., *Gazdasági Útkeresés 1956–1965* (Budapest: Magvető Könyvkiadó, 1983).

BEREND, I. and RÁNKI, Gy., *The Hungarian Economy in the Twentieth Century* (London and Sydney: Croom Helm, 1985).

BIHARI, M., 'Political Mechanism and Socialist Democracy', *New Hungarian Quarterly*, vol. XXIII (1982) no 88.

BIHARI, O., 'The Development of Socialist Democracy in Hungarian Political Institutions', *New Hungarian Quarterly*, vol. XII (1971) no 42.

BOGNÁR, J., 'Towards a New System of Guidance of the Socialist Economy', *New Hungarian Quarterly*, vol. VI (1965) no 20.

BOGNÁR, J., 'Overall Direction and Operation of the Economy', *New Hungarian Quarterly*, vol. VII (1966) no 1.

BOGNÁR, J., 'Economic Reform, Development and Stability in Hungary', *Acta Oeconomica*, vol. VIII (1972) no 1.

CSAPÓ, L., 'Central Planning in a Guided Market Model', *Acta Oeconomica*, vol. I (1966) no 2.

CSIKÓS-NAGY, B., 'First Experiences Gained in the Implementation of the Economic Reform in Hungary', *Acta Oeconomica*, vol. IV (1969) no 1.

DONÁTH, F., *Reform and Revolution: the Transformation of Hungary's Agriculture* (Budapest: Corvina Kiado, 1980).

ENYEDI, Gy., 'industrial Activities on Larger-Scale Farms', *Acta Oeconomica*, vol. XXV (1980) nos 3–4.

FEHÉR, F., 'Kádárism as the Model State of Khrushchevism', *Telos*, no 40 (Summer 1979).

FEHÉR, F. and HELLER, A., *Hungary 1956 Revisited* (London: Allen & Unwin, 1983).

FEJTŐ, F., *La Tragédie Hongroise* (Paris: Editions Pierre Horay, 1956).

FEJTŐ, F., 'Hungarian Communism', in W. E. Griffiths (ed.) *Communism in Europe* (Cambridge, Massachusetts: MIT Press, 1964) vol. I.

FEKETE, F. and VARGA, GY., 'Household Plot Farming of Cooperative Peasants in Hungary', *Acta Oeconomica*, vol. II (1967) no 4.

FRISS, I., 'Ideas on the Improvement of National Economic Planning', *Acta Oeconomica*, vol. I (1966) no 1.

FRISS, I. (ed.) *Reform of the Economic Mechanism in Hungary* (Budapest: Akadémiai Kiado, 1969).

FRISS, I., 'Practical Experiences of the Economic Reform in Hungary', *East European Economics*, vol. XI, no 3 (Spring 1973).

FRISS, I., 'Ten Years of Economic Reform in Hungary', *Acta Oeconomica*, vol. XX (1978) nos 1–2.

GADÓ, O., 'The Development of Planning and Management Methods in Hungary', *Acta Oeconomica*, vol. IX (1972) nos 3–4.

GADÓ, O. (ed.) *Reform of the Economic Mechanism in Hungary: Development 1968–1971* (Budapest: Akadémiai Kiado, 1972).

GÁSPÁR, S., *The Hungarian Trade Unions in the Building of Developed Socialism* (Budapest: Tancsis Publishing House, 1978).

GATI, C., 'The Democratic Interlude in Post-War Hungary', *Survey*, vol. XXVIII, no 2 (Summer 1984).
GATI, C., 'Hungary: The Dynamics of Revolutionary Transformation', in C. Gati (ed.) *The Politics of Modernisation in Eastern Europe* (New York: Praeger, 1974).
HARASZTI, M., *A Worker in a Workers' State* (Harmondsworth: Penguin, in association with New Left Review, 1977).
HARE, P., SWAIN, N. and RADICE, H. (eds) *Hungary: A Decade of Economic Reform* (London: Allen & Unwin, 1981).
HEGEDÜS, A., 'Optimizalás es Humanizalás', *Valóság*, no 3, 1965.
HEGEDÜS, A., 'Optimisation and Humanisation' (Budapest: Hungarian Academy of Sciences, 1965) mimeo.
HEGEDÜS, A. (ed.) *Etudes Sociologiques* (Budapest: Corvina Kiadó, 1969).
HEGEDÜS, A., *Socialism and Bureaucracy* (London: Allison & Busby, 1976).
HEINRICH, H. G., *Hungary: Politics, Economics and Society* (London: Francis Pinter, 1986).
HELD, J. (ed.) *The Modernisation of Agriculture: Rural Transformation in Hungary 1848–1975* (Boulder, Colorado: East European Monographs, 1980).
HETÉNYI, I., 'Salient Features in the Development of National Economic Planning in Hungary', *Acta Oeconomica*, vol. XV (1975) no 1.
HÉTHY, L. and MAKÓ, Cs., 'Work Performance, Interests, Powers and the Environment (The Case of Cyclical Slowdowns in a Hungarian Factory)', in P. Halmos (ed.) *Hungarian Sociological Studies*, Sociological Review Monograph no 17 (University of Keele, February 1972).
HÉTHY, L. and MAKÓ, Cs., 'Labour Turnover and the Economic Organisation: Sociological Data on an Approach to the Question', *Sociological Review*, vol. XXIII (1975) no 2.
'Hungary Five Years After', special issue of *Survey*, no 40 (January 1962).
'Hungary: Politics and Prices', *East Europe*, vol. XV, no 3 (March 1966).
HUSZÁR, I., 'On Living Standard Policy in Hungary', *Acta Oeconomica*, vol. IV (1969) no 1.
HUSZÁR, T., KULCSÁR, K. and SZALAI, S. (eds) *Hungarian Society and Marxist Sociology in the 1970s* (Budapest: Corvina Kiadó, 1978).
IGNOTUS, P., 'Hungary: Existence and Coexistence', *Problems of Communism*, vol. X, no 2 (March–April 1961).
IGNOTUS, P., 'Hungary 1966', in T. Aczél (ed.) *Ten Years After* (London: MacGibbon & Kee, 1966).
ILLYÉS, Gy., *The People of the Puszta* (Budapest: Corvina Kiadó, 1967).
JANOS, A., *The Politics of Backwardness in Hungary 1825–1945* (Princeton, New Jersey: Princeton University Press, 1982).
KECSKEMETI, P., *The Unexpected Revolution* (Stanford, California: Stanford University Press, 1961).
KEMENES, E., 'Three Years of the Hungarian Economic Reform', *New Hungarian Quarterly*, vol. XII (1971) no 42.
KERTESI, Gy., 'two Types of Development of Small-Scale Industry in Hungary', *Acta Oeconomica*, vol. XXVIII (1982) nos 1–2.

KISS, S., 'Hungary's Economic Situation', *East Europe*, vol. XIV, no 5 (May 1965).

KORNAI, J., *Overcentralisation in Economic Administration* (Oxford: Oxford University Press, 1959).

KORNAI, J., 'Economic Systems Theory and General Equilibrium Theory', *Acta Oeconomica*, vol. VI (1971) no 4.

KORNAI, J., *The Dilemmas of a Socialist Economy: The Hungarian Experience* (Twelfth Geary Lecture) (Dublin: The Economic and Social Research Institute, 1979).

KORNAI, J., 'Comments on Tibor Liska's Concept of Entrepreneurship', *Acta Oeconomica*, vol. XXVIII (1982) nos 3–4.

KOVÁCS, I., 'The Establishment in Hungary', *East Europe*, vol. XIV, no 5 (May 1965).

KOVRIG, B., *Communism in Hungary* (Stanford, California: Hoover Institution Press, 1979).

KULCSÁR. K., 'Sociology in Hungary', *New Hungarian Quarterly*, vol. XII (1971) no 41.

LAKY, T., 'Attachment to the Enterprise in Hungary', *Acta Oeconomica*, vol. XVII (1976) nos 3–4.

LAKY, T., 'Enterprises in Bargaining Position', *Acta Oeconomica*, vol. XXII (1979) nos 3–4.

LAKY, T., 'Hidden Mechanisms of Recentralisation', *Acta Oeconomica*, vol. XXIV (1980) nos 1–2.

LAKY, T., 'Small Enterprises in Hungary – Myth and Reality', *Acta Oeconomica*, vol. XXXII (1984) nos 1–2.

LANDY, P., 'Hungary: Pressures from Above', *Problems of Communism*, vol. XI, no 3 (May–June 1962).

LOMAX, B., *Hungary 1956* (London: Allison & Busby, 1976).

MAGYAR SZOCIALISTA MUNKÁSPÁRT, *A Magyar Szocialista Munkáspárt Határozatai és Dokumentumai 1963–66* (Budapest; Kossuth Kiadó, 1978) 2nd edn.

MÁRTON, A., 'Trends of Consumer Prices in Hungary 1968–75', *Acta Oeconomica*, vol. XIV (1975) no 4.

MERAY, T., 'Genealogical Troubles', *Survey*, no 40 (January 1962).

MERAY, T., 'The Sources of Power: The Origin and Development of the Party', in T. Aczél (ed.) *Ten Years After* (London: MacGibbon & Kee, 1966).

MÜLLER, G. and SINGER, H., 'Hungary: Can the New Course Survive?', *Problems of Communism*, vol. XIV, no 1 (January–February 1965).

NAGY, I., *On Communism: In Defence of the New Course* (London: Thames & Hudson, 1957).

NYERS, R., 'Az ötéves terv derekán', *Társadalmi Szemle*, vol. XIX, no 2 (February 1964).

NYERS, R., 'Interview with Rezső Nyers', *New Hungarian Quarterly*, vol. VI (1965) no 20.

NYERS, R., 'The Comprehensive Reform of Managing the National Economy of Hungary', *Acta Oeconomica*, vol. I (1966) no 1.

NYERS, R., *Gazdaságpolitikánk és a Gazdasági Mechanizmus Reformja* (Budapest: Kossuth Kiadó, 1968).

NYERS, R., 'Social and Political Effects of the New Economic Mechanism', *New Hungarian Quarterly*, vol. X (1969) no 34.

NYERS, R., *Economic Reform in Hungary: 25 Questions and 25 Answers* (Budapest: Pannonia Press, 1969).

NYERS, R. and TÁRDOS, M., 'Enterprises in Hungary before and after the Economic Reform', *Acta Oeconomica*, vol. XX (1978) nos 1–2.

ORTUTAY, Gy., 'A Standing Parliamentary Committee', *New Hungarian Quarterly*, vol. XVI (1975) no 59.

PÉTER, G., 'Az egyszemelyi felelős vezetésről', *Társadalmi Szemle*, vol. IX (1954) nos 8–9.

PÉTER, G., 'A gazdaságosság jelentőségéről és szerepéről a népgazdaság tervszerű irányításában', *Közgazdasági Szemle*, vol. I; no 3 (December 1954).

PÉTER, G., 'On the Planned Central Control and Management of the Economy', *Acta Oeconomica*, vol. II (1967) no 1.

POZSGAY, I., 'A Pártdemokrácia erősítése a szocialista demokrácia kulcskérdése', *Pártélet*, vol. XIV; no 6 (June 1969).

POZSGAY, I., 'Gazdaságirányítási rendszerünk és a pártszervezetek erkölcsi-politikai munkája', *Társadalmi Szemle*, vol. XXV; no 11 (November 1970).

POZSGAY, I., 'A Párt és az össztársadalmi érdek', *Társadalmi Szemle*, vol. XXVII; no 1 (January 1973).

POZSGAY, I., 'The Party and the Social Interest', translated in full from *Társadalmi Szemle* (January 1973) in *Radio Free Europe Research/Hungarian Press Survey* no 2253 (15 January 1973).

RÁCZ, A., 'Incomes of the Population and their Proportion in Hungary', *Acta Oeconomica*, vol. XIX (1977) no 2.

RADICE, H., 'The Hungarian Economic Reforms: an Assessment', discussion Paper no 72, University of Leeds School of Economic Studies, January 1979.

RADICE, H., 'The State Enterprise in Hungary: Economic Reform and Socialist Entrepreneurship', in I. Jeffries (ed.) *The Industrial Enterprise in Eastern Europe* (New York, Washington and London: Praeger, 1981).

RÉVÉSZ, Gy., 'Enterprise and Plant Size Structure of the Hungarian Industry', *Acta Oeconomica*, vol. XXII (1979) nos 1–2.

ROBINSON, W. F., 'Hegedüs, His Views and His Critics', *Studies in Comparative Communism*, vol. II, no 2 (April 1969).

ROBINSON, W. F., *The Pattern of Reform in Hungary* (New York, Washington and London: Praeger, 1973).

ROBINSON, W. F., 'Hungary's Industrial Workers: Increasing Success as a Pressure Group', *Radio Free Europe Research*, 8 March 1973.

SÁNDOR, J., 'Pártunk szervezeti fejlődésének nehány kérdése', *Társadalmi Szemle*, vol. XVI no 6 (June 1961).

SAVARIUS, V., 'János Kádár – Man and Politician', *East Europe*, vol. XV, no 10 (October 1966).

SCHÖPFLIN, G., 'Hungary: An Uneasy Stability', in A. Brown and J. Gray (eds) *Political Culture and Political Change in Communist States* (London: Macmillan, 1979) 2nd edn.

SCHREIBER, T., 'Changes in the Leadership', *Survey*, no 40 (January 1962).

SCHWEITZER, I., 'Some Interrelations between the Enterprise Organisation and the Economic Mechanism in Hungary', *Acta Oeconomica*, vol. XXVII (1981) nos 3–4.

SÍKLAKY, I. (ed.) *Koncepció és Kritika* (Budapest: Magvető Könyvkiadó, 1985).

Statistical Pocketbook of Hungary (Budapest: Hungarian Central Statistical Office/Jogi és Közgazdasági Könyvkiadó, various years).

SZAMUELY, L., 'The First Wave of the Mechanism Debate in Hungary', *Acta Oeconomica*, vol. XXIX (1982) nos 1–2.

SZAMUELY, L., 'The Second Wave of the Economic Mechanism Debate in Hungary', *Acta Oeconomica*, vol. XXXII (1984) nos 1–2.

SZASZ, B., *Volunteers for the Gallows* (London: Chatto & Windus, 1971).

SZIKRA-FALUS, K., 'On Competition', *Acta Oeconomica*, vol. XIII (1974) no 1.

SZOBOSZLAI, GY. (ed.) *Politics and Political Science in Hungary* (Budapest: HSWP Institute for Social Sciences, 1982).

SZOBOSZLAI, GY. (ed.) *Studies in the Field of Political Science in Hungary* (Budapest: Hungarian Political Science Association, 1982).

TÁBORI, A., 'Small Businesses in Socialist Hungary', *New Hungarian Quarterly*, vol. XXIII (1982) no 86.

TÁRDOS, M. and HEGEDÜS, ZS., 'Some Problems Concerning the Role and Motivation of Enterprise Executives', *East European Economics*, vol. XXIII, no 2 (Winter 1974–5).

TÁRDOS, M., 'Impacts of World Economic Changes on the Hungarian Economy', *Acta Oeconomica*, vol. XV (1975) nos 3–4.

TÁRDOS, M., 'Enterprise Independence and Central Control', *East European Economics*, vol. XV, no 1 (Fall 1976).

TÁRDOS, M., 'The Increasing Role and Ambivalent Reception of Small Enterprises in Hungary', *Journal of Comparative Economics*, vol. VII, no 3 (September 1983).

TOMA, P. and VÖLGYES, I., *Politics in Hungary* (San Francisco: Freeman, 1977).

TIKOS, L., 'Hungary: Literary Renaissance', *Problems of Communism,* vol. XII, no 3 (May–June 1964).

TIMÁR, J., 'About Commuting', *Acta Oeconomica*, Vol. XXV (1980) nos 1–2.

VAJDA, I., 'Economic Science in Hungary and the *Acta Oeconomica*', *Acta Oeconomica*, vol. I (1966) no 1.

VAJNA, T., 'Problems and Trends in the Development of the Hungarian New Economic Mechanism: A Balance Sheet of the 1970s', in A. Nove *et al.* (eds) *East European Economies in the 1970s* (London: Butterworths, 1982).

VALI, F., *Rift and Revolt in Hungary* (London: Oxford University Press, 1961).

VALI, F., 'Hungary since 1956: the Hungarian Road to Communism', in A. György (ed.) *Issues of World Communism* (Princeton, New Jersey: Van Nostrand, 1966).

VARGA, GY., 'Enterprise Size Pattern in Hungarian Industry', *Acta Oeconomica*, vol. XX (1978) no 3.

VARGA, GY., 'The Experiment at Szentes', *Acta Oeconomica*, vol. XXVIII (1982) nos 3–4.
VASS, H. (ed.) *Válság és Megújulás* (Budapest: Kossuth Kiadó, 1982).
VERES, P., 'Alienation: A Hungarian View', translated excerpts from *Kortárs*, December 1964, in *East Europe*, vol. XIV, no 3 (March 1965).
VÖLGYES, I., 'Hungary: The Lumpenproletarianisation of the Working Class', in J. Triska and C. Gati (eds) *Blue-Collar Workers in Eastern Europe* (London: Allen & Unwin, 1981).
WILCSEK, J., 'Modern Small and Medium-sized Enterprises in Hungarian Industry', *Acta Oeconomica*, vol. VI (1971) no 4.
ZALA, J., '1958–67: The Economic Trends of a Decade' in *Acta Oeconomica*, vol. III (1968) no 2.

Index